AFRICAN RIGHTS

GW00371144

FACING GENOCIDE:

THE NUBA OF SUDAN

July 1995

A Publication of African Rights

11 Marshalsea Road
London SE1 1EP

Tel: 0171 717 1224
Fax: 0171 717 1240

Published by African Rights, July 1995

Copyright © African Rights

ISBN 1 899 477 04 7

Printed in the U.K.
Cover photograph by Alex de Waal

AFRICAN RIGHTS

African Rights is an organisation dedicated to working on issues of grave human rights abuses, conflict, famine and civil reconstruction in Africa. The urgent motivation for setting up African Rights is that we have become acutely aware of the limitations upon existing human rights, humanitarian and conflict resolution approaches to Africa's most pressing problems.

Any solution to Africa's problems—the emergency humanitarian needs as much as the long-term demands for political reconstruction and accountability—must be sought primarily among Africans. International organisations should see their principal role as primarily facilitating and supporting efforts by Africans to address their own problems. It is Africa's tragedy that the existing institutions for addressing these problems have not looked to the African people for answers. African Rights tries to give a voice to Africans concerned with these pressing issues, and to press for more accountability from the international community.

Rakiya Omaar   Alex de Waal

African Rights:

11 Marshalsea Road, London SE1 1EP
Tel: 0171 717 1224, Fax: 0171 717 1240

TABLE OF CONTENTS

i

African Rights

Payment received with thanks

With Compliments

11 Marshalsea Road London SE1 1EP
Tel: 0171 717 1224 Fax 0171 717 1240

PREFACE

This book examines the war waged by the Sudan Government against the Nuba people of South Kordofan. After ten years of war, it is the first exposure of the crimes being committed there by the Sudan Government: all-out assault on the rural Nuba, and the nightmare of life in what the government calls "peace camps".

Do the crimes against the Nuba warrant the term "genocide"? They certainly fit the legal definition contained in the 1948 Genocide Convention (see the Conclusion), and if the Sudan Government is able to pursue its programme unhindered for one or two more years, many thousands of Nuba people will have been killed, the majority of women and girls raped, and children separated from their parents and subjected to a forcible change of identity. In addition to the tens of thousands who will have perished, the Nuba people will no longer exist in a recognisable state. They will be politically subjugated and socially dismembered, with their distinctive cultures obliterated.

There is an international responsibility to prevent genocide, for the countries of the region and the western donors. Many Nuba suspect that they are being sacrificed as the acceptable price of an internationally-brokered peace agreement between the government and the SPLA—an agreement that may involve "self-determination" for the South, but will deliver the Nuba to the North without any safeguards. If the Nuba are eradicated in secret, then there will be no embarrassment to those who resolve on this "compromise".

The Nuba are excluded from humanitarian programmes. Those in the SPLA-controlled areas receive absolutely nothing at all, while those in the government "peace camps" receive assistance—often very meagre—on the condition of total submission. Exceptionally severe famine raged in the Nuba Mountains from 1990 to 1993, and utter destitution is the norm today. The failure of the humanitarian international in the Nuba Mountains has facilitated the government's war against the Nuba people.

The obligation to prevent genocide also falls upon Sudanese opposition forces, including the northern parties and the SPLA, which have so far conspicuously failed to make a clear commitment to the rights of the Nuba people. In fact, it is important to remember that it was "democratic" politicians, now in opposition, who were the first architects of the war against the Nuba in the 1980s.

The one group who are not passive in the face of this genocide are the Nuba people themselves. They have been forced into self-reliance. There was no self-pity, no pleading for an international rescue. During nearly two months of travelling, we were never begged for charity. The people in the non-government controlled areas have come to rely only on no-one but themselves.

Nuba cultures are vibrant in a way that we had never expected. We spent scarcely a night in the Nuba Mountains without hearing music. Every evening and night there was drumming, singing and dancing, in an astonishing variety of musical styles. We were presented with locally-woven clothes, with elaborately-decorated gourds, with beads and cowrie shells. We were treated to displays of wrestling. Certainly the cultures are changing under the strain of the war, and cultural traditions are being distorted or irretrievably lost, but in the heat of war, facing the abyss of eradication, the Nuba peoples are finding immense strength in their cultures. It is striking that many Nuba people who, ten or fifteen years ago, would have used solely their Arabic names, are proudly using their Nuba names today.

The cultures of the Nuba have been celebrated, and rightly so. But much more profound is the rediscovery of Nuba political identity in the midst of war. In 1992, a remarkable conference was convened in the centre of the non-government controlled area, in which two hundred delegates from all parts of the Nuba Mountains, most of them civilians, openly debated whether the SPLA should be given a popular mandate to continue the war. It was not a propaganda exercise (it has never been reported outside the Nuba Mountains before this book)—it was a genuine debate, with prominent civilians and SPLA commanders arguing on both sides.

This conference ushered in a Nuba political renaissance, in which villagers have pressed the SPLM leadership to institute a full range of civil institutions and social services. With no outside assistance whatsoever, medical clinics, schools, law courts, district administration and relief programmes have been set up. A "General Assembly" and "Consultative Council" meet regularly. A large conference on religious tolerance has been held. The clinics use medicines bought on the black market or locally fabricated; the courts function with a single printed copy of the penal code, laboriously copied out by hand. There is not a single typewriter in the SPLA-held areas, nor a single wheeled vehicle, and scarcely a school textbook. But the Nuba are determined to succeed.

The active political participation of large sections of the Nuba dramatically shows up the shallowness of the debate on "self-determination." For most Sudanese politicians and international diplomats, "self-determination" is just an event, such as a referendum, which decides who is to rule which area. For the Nuba who are practising self-determination, it is a political process of self-enfranchisement. The Nuba certainly have a long way to go: but they have started.

However, the Nuba are desperately isolated. The intellectual starvation of lack of news, lack of education and lack of books is more keenly felt than the material deprivation. The few requests that we received were never for food, and only occasionally for medicines (by people who mistook us for doctors)—they were for books, for batteries for radios, or for pens and paper. The isolation has engendered a sense of absolute solitude, the feeling that the Nuba Mountains are completely cut off from the rest of the world. The very fact that the suffering of the people was worthy of being recorded came as a pleasant shock. They had not regarded themselves and their struggles as part of history.

This book is the product of African Rights' investigations into human rights abuses in the Nuba Mountains of Sudan. We have made two visits to the non-government controlled areas of the Nuba Mountains in 1995. The first visit, following up on preparations made in 1994, was to establish a human rights monitoring programme that covers each of the seven districts of the region. This programme uses Nuba citizens as monitors; to date it is the only formal human rights monitoring programme in Sudan. The second visit was to see how the monitoring programme was progressing, to debrief the monitors, and to undertake further investigations ourselves.

African Rights is the only human rights organisation to have undertaken such a programme of monitoring and investigation in the Nuba Mountains since the war began there exactly ten years ago. Indeed, we are the first outsiders to have travelled so extensively in this region, which has been effectively sealed off from the rest of Sudan, and the rest of the world, for the best part of a decade. This enforced isolation is partly a testament to the high stakes in the war in South Kordofan, and the determination of the Sudan Government to commit its crimes in secrecy. It also attests to the lack of interest by the international community, which has been ready to make only minimal gestures of concern.

One purpose of this book is to draw international attention to the plight of the Nuba people. We hope that international public opinion can shame the Sudan Government into halting and reversing its policy of genocide against the Nuba people. But equally importantly, we hope that this book can stimulate the Nuba people themselves to reflect upon their remarkable capacities and their recent history of facing and resisting genocide, relying on no-one but themselves.

Acknowledgements

We were privileged in that many Nuba people were prepared to tell to us the horrific, humiliating and often distressingly intimate details of the abuses they had suffered. Many of our informants have been acknowledged and named. Others, notably the victims of rape, have had their identities concealed. We hope that this book can go some way to repaying the debt that we owe them, and the faith that they have entrusted in us.

African Rights' human rights monitors have taken to their arduous task with enthusiasm and commitment, despite their meagre rewards—modest incentives rather than payments. We would like to thank them all: Daud Siddig, Hassan Osman Tutu, Ahmed Sayed Nur, el Amin Omer Gardud, Nira Suleiman Bashir, Simon Noah, Mahjoub Ismail, Joseph Aloka Jardi, Arno Karkon Kuwa, Ibrahim

Yunan Angelo and Giorgis Kori. Staff members of the Nuba Relief, Rehabilitation and Development Society deserve praise and gratitude for their assistance to our work. We would like to thank especially Suleiman Jabona and his team, Jubara Hussein, and the staff in Nairobi, Yunis Domi Kallo and Mary James Kuku.

Members of the SPLA/SPLM facilitated our travels inside the Nuba Mountains, providing security, porters, and the freedom to interview whomever we wanted in conditions of privacy. SPLA soldiers and commanders alike were remarkably frank about their experiences and their own shortcomings.

In London, our work has been facilitated by the contribution of Nuba Mountains Solidarity Abroad, especially Suleiman Musa Rahhal.

For reasons of security, we are unable to thank by name those individuals who worked extremely hard and took considerable risks to make our visit possible. At the appropriate time, we hope they will receive the recognition that they deserve.

Alex de Waal
Yoanes Ajawin

London, June 1995.

GLOSSARY AND LIST OF ACRONYMS

Anyanya	Term popularly used for the SPLA
Dar el Salaam	Peace camp or peace village
GUN	General Union of the Nuba Mountains
Jebel	Mountain
Khalwa	Koranic school
Kujur	Traditional priest
LS	Sudanese Pound (LS600=US$ 1.00)
Malwa	Measure of one bowl (usually sorghum)
MFC	Mechanised Farming Corporation
Nafir el Sha'abi	"Popular Mobilisation"
NIF	National Islamic Front
PDF	People's Defence Force
RCC	Revolutionary Command Council
Salaam min al Dakhal	"Peace from Within"
SNP	Sudan National Party
SPLA	Sudan People's Liberation Army
SPLM	Sudan People's Liberation Movement

SUMMARY

The Nuba people of central Sudan are faced with oblivion. The Government of Sudan is actively engaged in a campaign against the Nuba people, that, if followed through to its conclusion, will mean that there is no society recognisable as Nuba remaining in existence. The government campaign in the Nuba Mountains does not involve armed confrontation with the SPLA—the army avoids military engagements with the guerrillas, and concentrates its efforts on attacking defenceless villages and kidnapping and killing unarmed civilians. It is a war against the people. It is genocide.

The Nuba Mountains has been completely sealed off for more than six years, so that the government can pursue its programme undisturbed by international attention. African Rights' report is the first detailed investigation into the genocide in the Nuba Mountains. The report is based on more than 130 first-hand testimonies of victims and witnesses of human rights abuse, twenty detailed reports by African Rights human rights' monitors, and previously-secret military documents from the Sudanese army.

Components of Genocide in the Nuba Mountains

The bulk of this report is concerned with current human rights violations in the Nuba Mountains. Chapter III documents the range of abuses

Under the name "combing", the army and militias engage in wholesale destruction or removal of everything in the rural Nuba Mountains. Villages are burned. Furniture, clothes and household goods are destroyed or taken off. Food stocks are burned or looted. Livestock are raided. African Rights visited several burned villages, two of them that were still smouldering after army attacks, and

1

talked to dozens of people who had witnessed the destruction of everything they owned. Details of the "combing" operations undertaken in 1994-5 are presented for each of the different districts of the Nuba Mountains.

The destruction of the rural Nuba serves two main purposes: it creates hunger, destitution and demoralisation, thus encouraging villagers to come to government-controlled centres to obtain relief and thereby submit to the government; and it enables soldiers and officers to enrich themselves. For the rural population, the result is often famine.

Many people have been killed or injured in "combing" operations. The army kills with complete impunity. Old or disabled people who cannot run away are often killed, by shooting or burning to death inside houses. Others are killed in the shelling of villages, mountainsides and caves, shot down while running away, or executed after capture

The Sudan Government is forcibly abducting rural Nuba people. In the attack on one village, Toror, on 24 February 1995, 250 people were abducted and taken to a government garrison. Over half were children. Groups of soldiers also ambush villagers as they come to collect water or mangoes, herd their animals, or walk to market. Those who have taken refuge in caves are attacked there, sometimes using tear gas to force them out into the open so they can be captured. It is a strategy designed to depopulate the rural areas and provide a captive civilian population for the garrisons and attached "peace camps." African Rights interviewed many villagers who had been abducted and later succeeded in escaping, who detailed their experiences.

The Sudan Government has a systematic programme of eliminating educated Nuba and community leaders. Since this programme began in 1988, hundreds of chiefs, teachers, merchants, civil servants, priests, lawyers, health workers—in fact anyone with an education who might be a spokesman for the people—have been killed. Those who remain in the government-held areas have been terrorised into silence or acquiescence, and the death squads are currently focusing their efforts on the rural areas. The report documents cases of government assassination.

2

A central component of the genocide is the Sudan Government's policy of rape. Women are raped as they are abducted, raped on arrival in garrisons, repeatedly raped in peace camps or labour camps, or forcibly "married" to soldiers for the duration of the soldiers' tours of duty. Some women have been raped dozens, even hundreds of times. Every woman who has been in a peace camp has either been raped or threatened with rape. Girls as young as nine years old have been raped. Six testimonies of rape victims are presented in the report, together with numerous other accounts that testify to the ubiquity of sexual violence. The aim of the policy is to destroy the social fabric of Nuba society by raping every single woman.

The innocuously-named "peace camps" are concentration camps in the true sense of the word. They are where the rural population is forcibly concentrated so they can be controlled and their political and cultural identity can be changed. Peace camps are the location of mass and systematic rape of women. They are where children are separated from their parents and "educated" to become extremist Moslems in the mould of the ruling National Islamic Front, in a process of forced acculturation. All able-bodied men are forcibly conscripted to join the "Popular Defence Force" militia, to become accomplices in the destruction of their own communities. Others, particularly women and boys, are used for forced labour, both in the garrisons and in specialised labour camps close to mechanised farms. Captives are treated harshly and often tortured; control over relief aid is used to force the internees to submit to the demands of their captors, which include conversion to Islam, forced labour, conscription, or sex. Evidence from peace camp escapees is presented, detailing aspects of life and death in the camps.

The peace camps are part of a wider strategy of "Popular Mobilisation" whereby the Sudan Government is using bribery and coercion to obtain the support, or at least the acquiescence, of selected Nuba chiefs in their programme. (Chiefs are government appointees, paid a salary like civil servants.) The rationale of this strategy is discussed and some of the leaders of the programme are named in Chapter III.

The government tries to entice rural people into the peace camps by providing basic relief, such as food rations and clothes. For people who are absolutely destitute, even the offer of one meal can sometimes be enough to coerce them into forfeiting their freedom. In order to maintain this strategy of emptying the rural areas, the government enforces a strict blockade of the SPLA-held areas. No trade is permitted. No relief agencies have operated there since the war began; the only assistance programmes are on the government side. United Nations agencies and other humanitarian organisations have failed to challenge this exclusion.

Attack on Christianity; Attack on Islam

The genocide is committed in the name of Islam. Beneath the smokescreen of confusion put up by the Sudan Government, it is clear that an extremist Islamic agenda is at work, dedicated to the social, cultural and political transformation of the Nuba peoples. Such a policy is of course deeply offensive to most Moslems, in Sudan and around the world.

The Christian church has been a focus of the government campaign since the war began. Priests and catechists have been killed and churches are regularly burned. Christian captives in the peace camps are often forced or pressured into converting to Islam. Chapter IV deals with the issue of religion in the Nuba Mountains, including a discussion of religion in Nuba history and tradition, and the two conferences on religious dialogue in 1994, one held in Khartoum and the other in an SPLA-held village in the Nuba Mountains.

Among the victims of government abuses, there are Moslems as well as Christians and traditional believers. In the *Fatwa* of April 1993 which underpins the Nuba Mountains *Jihad*, the Sudan Government tried to legitimise this:

> An insurgent who was previously a Moslem is now an apostate; and a non-Moslem is a non-believer standing as a bulwark against the spread of Islam, and Islam has granted the freedom of killing both of them.

4

The result is perhaps the darkest secret of the Sudan Government. For more than three years, the government has officially held that Moslems in the rebel-held areas are not "true Moslems", and their mosques are not "real mosques", and therefore they have a licence to kill and destroy them. Government propaganda—on the radio, told to captives, or scrawled as graffiti in desecrated mosques—says that there is no Islam in the non-government held areas, only in the garrisons and peace camps. Imams and Moslem scholars in the villages dispute this extraordinary interpretation of Islam: "Allah is everywhere," they say. The report presents testimonies of Imams, who detail the widespread burning and desecration of their mosques and the destruction of Holy Books.

Background: A Struggle for Identity

The war in the Nuba Mountains arises from a long history of discrimination against the Nuba peoples and their political, economic and social marginalisation. The term "Nuba" carries two very different sets of connotations: to the people themselves, it refers to the myriad cultures and traditions of the more than fifty different tribal groups in the Nuba Mountains. The music, dance, body art and wrestling of the Nuba peoples have been made rightly famous by some western photographers and anthropologists, and most Nuba people are proud of their distinctive traditions. But, for the dominant class in Sudan, and in particular the ruling National Islamic Front, "Nuba" refers to second class citizens—"primitive" black people, servants and labourers. The Nuba, along with Southerners, are the victims of a racism that pervades life in Northern Sudan. In an important sense, the war is a struggle for who has the right to define Nuba identity.

Discrimination has been a constant in the Nuba experience. In education, Nuba students were consistently disadvantaged—and many volunteers for the SPLA are frustrated students. Due to lack of economic opportunities at home, many Nuba men were forced to become labour migrants, where they were exposed to discrimination and exploitation. In local government, the Nuba were usually not awarded their fair share of jobs.

There is also an intense struggle for natural resources in the Nuba Mountains. The region is rich in fertile land, and is the main area where mechanised farming—a favoured investment of the ruling elite—can be expanded. Successive governments have supported the aggressive expansion of mechanised farms, enacting ever-more-sweeping land legislation to enable land confiscation to proceed. The issue of land ownership was the most explosive question in the pre-war Nuba Mountains, as merchant farmers, under the aegis of the government's Mechanised Farming Corporation, expropriated smallholders' land. For many farmers, the fight for land eventually turned into a guerrilla war against the government.

The struggle over land sharpened the other areas of dispute in the Nuba Mountains. The Baggara Arab herders who share the plains with the Nuba also lost grasslands to the big farms, and were pushed to pasture their animals on Nuba farms. Farmer-nomad relations always have the potential for friction, and by the 1980s acrimonious and bloody disputes were becoming common. Increasingly, the Nuba would not get a fair hearing in the courts or the inter-tribal conferences convened by the government. One of the tragedies of the Nuba Mountains is the way that the Baggara, themselves a poor and deprived group, were manipulated by politicians to be the vanguard of the attack on the Nuba.

Since independence, the Nuba have struggled to achieve political representation in Khartoum. Despite winning seats in general elections, and forming coalitions with parties representing other marginalised areas of Sudan, the Nuba political agenda has consistently been blocked. This is due not only to the northern elites' stranglehold on power, but also due to infighting within the Nuba political parties. From the late 1970s, a more radical Nuba youth movement, Komolo, became influential. Headed by Yousif Kuwa Mekki, now SPLA commander in the Nuba Mountains, Komolo aimed to recreate Nuba identity, and made it clear that it was prepared to resort to armed struggle to achieve its aims.

The background to the war and a brief overview of the history, geography and culture of the Nuba are presented in Chapter I.

Civil War in the Nuba Mountains

The war in the Nuba Mountains began in July 1985. There were two events: an isolated raid by an SPLA unit on a cattle camp for Baggara Arab nomads close to the north-south internal boundary, and the government decision to arm the Baggara as a militia to fight the SPLA and the civilian population thought to be sympathetic to it. While the SPLA was not present in force until 1989, militia attacks became routine and an army crackdown became intense. A history of the war from 1985 to 1993 is presented in Chapter II.

The first stage of the war was marked by militia raids, to loot cattle, kill and occasionally to burn villages. In areas where SPLA units penetrated, the army also undertook mass reprisals, always targeted at villages and civilians. Military intelligence also began a crackdown on chiefs it suspected of sympathising with the SPLA. The testimony of one sheikh, left for dead in a mass execution, is presented. This campaign culminated in 1988 with mass arrests in the towns of the members of a "subversive" organisation called "Nihna Kadugli". African Rights' investigations show that this organisation did not in fact exist, and was invented by military intelligence as a pretext for the arrests and killings.

This stage of the war, and in particular the militia strategy, was designed by elected politicians, mainly from the Umma Party. These politicians, most of whom are now in opposition and who speak grandly of "democracy" and "human rights", are among those who bear most guilt for the crimes committed against the Nuba.

The war intensified with the arrival of the SPLA New Kush Division in 1989. It quickly overran large areas of the Nuba Mountains, and unleashed a ferocious response from the militia and army. Between 1989 and 1991 scores of villages were burned and thousands of villagers killed in joint army and militia assaults. The crackdown on educated Nuba intensified, culminating in wholesale arrests, executions and "disappearances" in 1991. In its initial entry into the mountains, the SPLA was also abusive; many soldiers went on the rampage and killed and looted. However, while the government policy was to encourage its forces to violate rights, the

SPLA command took firm action and reduced the excesses of its troops.

By 1991, repeated raids and the destruction of villages, and the economic disruption due to lack of trade and the collapse of employment caused the beginning of a severe man-made famine in the Nuba Mountains. Over the subsequent years, famine has been an intrinsic part of the government strategy to force the Nuba to submit.

Government assaults on the Nuba reached a new peak with the *Jihad* (Holy War), declared in 1992. This involved a military offensive of an unprecedented scale and nature, and the start of a massive programme of forced relocation that was designed to depopulate the Nuba Mountains. This period witnessed exceptionally severe human suffering and human rights abuses. But the assault failed: despite overwhelming numerical superiority, the army failed to capture its main target, the Tullishi mountain, and the programme of "ethnic cleansing" proved both embarrassing and expensive, and had to be modified. But even as the military strategies changed, the *Jihad* was re-affirmed by the issuing of a *Fatwa* in 1993.

The current government strategy of *Nafir el Sha'abi* ("Popular Mobilisation"), *Salaam min al Dakhal* ("Peace from Within"— encouraging SPLA commanders to defect and promoting co-operative local big men) and "combing" dates from the end of 1993. It is a more subtle but equally destructive *Jihad*.

The SPLA Record

The SPLA human rights record is examined in Chapter V. There are abuses associated with the poverty of the soldiers and lapses in discipline, and also a disturbing practice of killing many prisoners of war. However, the SPLA command has taken measures to enforce its disciplinary code, and has also sought to address some of the underlying reasons for abuses, such as lack of food and the high costs of marriage. Some specific allegations of SPLA abuses, such as assassinations of chiefs, were investigated and found to be untrue. However, the SPLA appears to tolerate a low level of harassment and stealing by some of its troops, without enforcing disciplinary measures.

Prospects for the Nuba

One of the most remarkable aspects to the contemporary history of the Nuba people is the way in which, at the height of the *Jihad*, the population removal and the policy of famine, in 1992, people in the SPLM-administered areas began an open debate about their future. An "Advisory Council" to the SPLM was convened, which, in its first session, debated a single issue: whether to continue the war or sue for peace. The decision was to continue. But, equally importantly, the two hundred members of the Council, most of them civilians, strongly influenced the SPLA leadership in the Nuba Mountains to establish a full array of civil institutions. The civil administration has been expanded, the judiciary improved, schools and clinics opened, a relief organisation created (based entirely on self-help) customary laws reformed, and a religious dialogue conference convened. This is an unprecedented political renaissance, begun and developed without any external input whatsoever. There is a new pride in Nuba identity, and a renewed determination to resist domination and influence political leaders, which augurs well.

But it may be too late. There are probably only 200,000 people remaining in the SPLM-administered areas of the Nuba Mountains. The Sudan Government's policies add up to genocide by attrition. One or two more seasons of "combing" and the food production in the non-government held areas will be shattered. More peace camps are established every month, and thousands more villagers abducted by force. Nuba children are being inculcated with values wholly alien to their traditions, Nuba women and girls are being raped. There is a moral imperative to halt the crime against humanity being perpetrated by the Government of Sudan against the Nuba people.

I

THE NUBA IN SUDAN:

A PEOPLE PUSHED TO THE MARGINS

The war in the Nuba Mountains raises the most profounds question about the identity and destiny of the Sudanese nation. Whereas the war in the South is increasingly concerned with the issue of whether the South should be part of a single state, or separate, the war in the Nuba Mountains raises the question of the basic premise on which the state exists in the North itself.

The current government in Khartoum has an ambitious project for remoulding Sudan as a homogenous, Arabised, extremist Islamic state. According to all democratic principles, the Nuba should be entitled to exercise their rights to freedom of expression, religion and choosing their own political representation. But, for the Nuba to obtain recognition as a legitimate, indigenous group of peoples with their own identities and religions (including tolerant Islam) would be a challenge to the very foundations of the present government's project.

WHO ARE THE NUBA?

The Nuba Mountains lie in the geographical centre of Sudan, covering an area of about 30,000 square miles in South Kordofan. This area lies north of the internal North-South frontier. Although the SPLA has recently spoken of the possibility of the Nuba Mountains joining the South as a separate state, this is not countenanced by any Northern political parties, and is a highly controversial proposal among the Nuba themselves. The Nuba have become integrated into the Sudanese state—socially, economically and politically. That integration has been on very adverse terms, which is the reason for the war.

The Nuba as a people have had their identity defined by outsiders. They are themselves a cluster of more than fifty different ethnic groups, thrown together by a common experience of oppression and discrimination by outsiders, notably the ruling elite of Sudan. The Nuba share South Kordofan with Sudanese Arabs, cattle herders such as the Misiriya Zurug and Hawazma (collectively known as "Baggara"—which means simply "cattle people"), and some camel herders such as the Hamar and Shanabla. Some Nuba groups historically developed close relations with the Baggara while others were isolated from them, but the relationship was always one of underlying suspicion. The advent of the Baggara was one main factor in driving the Nuba to the mountains. A second category of Arabs includes Jellaba traders from Khartoum and the Northern Nile valley, and Arab soldiers and administrators. These urban Arabs represent the power of the Sudanese state, and the basic reason for their presence in the Nuba Mountains was—and is—to bring the area and its peoples under the writ of central government.

The central theme of Nuba history is the tension between political incorporation into the state of Sudan and the maintenance of local identity. There is an irony here. Local, tribal identities are strong. But, until recently, many Nuba villagers had no conception of the wider community of the Nuba as a whole. They had little reason to travel to other Nuba areas; if they left their villages, it was to travel to towns, or outside the region altogether. Only in towns would a sense of Nuba identity as such emerge, when the Nuba saw how they were treated by the urban elites. It is this common experience of discrimination and repression that has created a unified Nuba identity.

The very word "Nuba" itself is not indigenous in any Nuba language. Essentially, "Nuba" was used by Egyptians and Northern Sudanese from the Nile to refer to black people to their south, whom they considered enslaveable. The names given to the Nuba tribes are often themselves the work of Arab outsiders—and reflect racist attitudes. The indigenous name for one tribe, Legalege, was replaced with the Arabic *Kawalib*—literally, "dogs." The name *Ghulfan* means "uncircumcised." *Mesakin* translates as "poor," "harmless" or "miserable" and it groups together two unrelated tribes, the Mesakin Tuwal ("Tall Mesakin") and Mesakin Qisar ("Short Mesakin"). Some place names are also offensive or degrading. Among intellectuals in the SPLA, there is now an attempt to return to traditional Nuba names for places and tribes.

Geography and Population

The geography of the region is central to its history. The Nuba hills themselves rise sharply from the plains, sometimes in long ranges, sometimes as isolated massifs or single crags. They rise some 500-1000 metres from the surrounding plains. The mountains are rocky, with cultivable hillslopes and valleys. Though they dominate the landscape, the area covered by the hills themselves is less than a third of the total area of the Nuba Mountains; the remainder of the land is extensive clay plains, some forested, some farmed. It is some of the most fertile land in Sudan—a fact that is both a blessing and a curse to the Nuba. While drought-induced famine is almost unknown in the Nuba Mountains, the fertile soils have also attracted the attention of outsiders.

The total number of Nuba is not known. The 1955/6 census was the only systematic attempt to enumerate Sudan's different ethnic groups, and found 572,935 Nuba, 61% of the population of South Kordofan. But by that stage there was already large-scale labour migration, so at least another five per cent must be added to the figure. On the basis of subsequent censuses and population growth statistics, it can be estimated that by the time the war intensified in 1989, the Nuba population was more than 1.3 million, plus migrants. Since then, the number in the Nuba Mountains has probably decreased, due to deaths, fewer births, and mass outmigration to Khartoum. There has also been massive population movement within the Nuba Mountains, with hundreds of thousands forcibly displaced to government towns and "peace camps", and a large number living as internal refugees in the areas secured by the SPLA. Currently, the best estimate for the population under the administration of the

SPLA is about 200,000 people; those under government control number about one million.

Most of the people in the Nuba Mountains belong to the myriad Nuba tribes. But the presence of other groups indigenous to the area must not be overlooked. Perhaps one quarter of the inhabitants of the the region are Arabs, mainly pastoralists, traders and civil servants. There are also non-Arab groups, principally the Daju (an offshoot of a Darfur tribe, living south of Lagowa) and Fellata communities spread throughout the area. The Fellata are descendants of West African immigrants to Sudan, and are farmers, herders and traders.

A "Bewildering Complexity" of Cultures

The Nuba peoples possess extraordinarily rich and varied cultures and traditions. Sometimes it is said that they live on "ninety-nine hills". A measure of the variety of Nuba cultures can be obtained by looking at the linguistic variety, as summarised by an early anthropologist of the Nuba, Siegfried Nadel:

> It has been said that there are as many Nuba languages as there are hills. This is but a slight exaggeration. Students of the Nuba languages have reduced this bewildering complexity to certain comprehensive categories...[1]

More recently, the noted linguist of the Nuba, Roland Stevenson, classified more than fifty Nuba languages and dialect clusters into ten separate groups.[2] There is thus more linguistic diversity within the Nuba Mountains than the entire rest of Sudan, and indeed as much diversity as the whole of Africa south of the Equator. To give one illustration: the Katla language is linguistically closer to Shona and Ndebele than it is to the Nyima[3] language, whose speakers live on the next range of hills. (Nyima belongs to the Nilo-Saharan

---

[1] S. F. Nadel, *The Nuba: An Anthropological Study of the Hill Tribes of Kordofan*, Oxford University Press, 1947, p. 2.

[2] R. C. Stevenson, *The Nuba People of Kordofan Province*, Khartoum, University of Khartoum Graduate College Publications, 1984.

[3] Also known as Nyimang.

language group, along with Dinka, Acholi and others, whereas Katla, like the majority of Nuba languages, is in the Niger-Kordofanian group, which includes Bantu languages.)

Cultural diversity is equally marked. The common elements in traditional Nuba culture essentially reflect the way in which dissimilar groups have adjusted to living in similar conditions. One of these common elements is the farming system. The Nuba are largely farmers, cultivating fields in the hills, at the foot of the hills, and in the plains. The hill farms (sometimes called "near farms") can be elaborately terraced, or gardens divided into small plots by lines of stones, and sometimes they are irrigated. Farms in the clay plains (sometimes called "far farms") are generally larger and more productive. The main crops are sorghum, beans and sesame, grown during a single rainy season that lasts from May-June until September. The harvest is gathered during November-January. All smallholder cultivation is by hand.

Dependence on the rain has contributed to many rituals around rainfall in many Nuba tribes, with ceremonies to encourage the rain.

The need for social and political relations between different Nuba tribes has also contributed to the emergence of similar political and judicial institutions in many groups. Tribes may share the institutions of "ambassadors" and judicial methods for resolving disputes. Over the last century, with an administration in common, and the use of Arabic as a *lingua franca*, much more of a common culture has developed.

In all other respects, one Nuba tribe can differ hugely from another in its music or dance, or its forms of social organization, or the corpus of beliefs in its traditional religion. Some tribes, mainly in the south-eastern jebels, are well-known for their body art, specialising in body painting and elaborate scarification. Some are famous for wrestling, or other sports such as stick fighting or bracelet fighting (the latter have long been discouraged because of the serious physical injuries that often occur). The photographer George Rodgers, the film-maker Leni Riefenstahl, and the ethnographer James Faris have made these aspects of Nuba culture well-known to western audiences. (It is precisely these same qualities that attracted the embarrassment and displeasure of the

14

A traditional household in the Achiron Mountains. *Photo: Julie Flint.*

A Nuba woman in the Tira Limon Mountains. *Photo: Julie Flint.*

Sudanese authorities.) Universal among the Nuba is a love of music and dancing, though the styles are again extremely varied. The musicologist Gerd Baumann describes the role of music and dancing among the Miri:[4]

> Music and dance are not the preserve of specialists or even professionals, but a normal part of every individual's life experience.... In a village of upwards of 450 people, such as Miri Bara, there is no person, whether hard of hearing, crippled, or insane, that does not engage in music or dance on a number of occasions each month, and there is not a day when music or dance are not performed in one compound or another, in a field that is being cultivated, or in the village square. Far from being an occasional diversion, music and dance form an intrinsic part of social life.

The Nuba have adapted and incorporated other musical styles. The Northern Sudanese love-song genre *daluka* has been widely adopted (and sometimes adapted) by Nuba singers, who have developed their own expertise in performance. Nuba tribes have also adopted some of the dances of their Arab neighbours, notably the Baggara, which are performed for entertainment and variety.

A Brief History

Recorded history refers to only a handful of Nuba groups, but it is possible to reconstruct the general historical processes that moulded the Nuba peoples. Most probably, the Nuba represent the remnants of indigenous populations that once lived far more widely across Sudan. Over the centuries, powerful states raided the black populations of Sudan for slaves. From the treaty of Baqt in AD 652 for six hundred years, Christian Nubia (along the Nile) had to pay a tribute of 360 slaves, which came from Fazughli and the Nuba Mountains. Later, powerful states developed in the Funj (on the Nile) and Dar Fur (to the west), which continued to raid for slaves in

---

[4] Gerd Baumann, *National Integration and Local Integrity: The Miri of the Nuba Mountains in the Sudan*, Oxford, Clarendon Press, 1987, pp. 28-9.

Kordofan. The groups that were attacked and raided retreated to places of refuge, where they would be hard to find and could defend themselves.

In the sixteenth century, Arab pastoralists began to penetrate South Kordofan from both east and west. They moved with their livestock on the plains, also taking slaves, both on their own behalf and for sale to commercial interests in Khartoum and further north.

A recent Nuba arrival is the Shatt, a group whose history is almost certainly characteristic of many other Nuba tribes. The Shatt migrated from the west, probably in the eighteenth and early nineteenth century. They were driven from South Darfur by the attacks of the Dar Fur slavers and the encroachment of the Rizeigat Arab cattle-herders, and moved to a cluster of hills south of what is now Kadugli. Like others before them, they became Nuba, while retaining their own language and many of their customs.

Most Nuba groups were small, numbering (at the turn of the century) anything from a few hundred to twenty thousand in each tribe. Almost all tribes had no chiefs or chiefly institutions, but governed themselves on the basis of custom and consent. Only one or two Nuba states existed. The Kingdom of Tegali, in the far north-eastern part of the Nuba Mountains, was the most prominent Nuba state for over three centuries. From its foundation in 1530 to its demise at the time of the Mahdi in the 1880s, Tegali was a Moslem state, itself involved as an intermediary in the slave trade—a compromise between the demands of the powers to the north and east, and the requirements of its Nuba inhabitants.

As with much of Northern Sudan, the Mahdist period (1883-98) was a time of massive upheaval and turmoil. The Nuba suffered doubly. In the early stages of his campaign, the Mahdi himself resided for a while in the northern mountains, and fought campaigns there, resisting the attacks of the Turko-Egyptian armies. Later, some Nuba tribes refused to submit to the Mahdist state and provide the tribute that was demanded. The Mahdi's successor, the Khalifa Abdullahi (a Baggara Arab from Darfur) sent several military expeditions against different Nuba tribes. Though resistance was not crushed, there was widespread bloodshed and destruction in the Nuba Mountains.

The Nuba resisted the British vigorously. Between 1900 and 1945 there were over thirty uprisings and rebellions in the Nuba Mountains, including a major revolt in Nyimang in 1908, a revolt involving the Miri and their neighbours (including some Misiriya Arabs) in 1915, a widespread revolt in the western jebels in 1926, and prolonged resistance in Jebel Tullishi during the Second World War.[5] A legacy of the Mahdist period, the Nuba were estimated to possess some twenty thousand rifles in 1930, and in the 1926 rebellion the Julud and Tima forces fielded one thousand soldiers with four hundred rifles. As well as having the advantage of familiar and rugged terrain, an older generation of Nuba soldiers had received professional training as slave soldiers in the armies of the Turco-Egyptian regime and the Mahdist forces.

INTEGRATION—ON WHOSE TERMS?

The British never resolved the dilemma of whether the Nuba as a whole should be "preserved" and isolated from Arab influence, or assimilated (on unequal terms) with the North. A policy of isolation was enforced, for a while.

The Closed Districts Ordinance of 1922 imposed a state of isolation on the Nuba, at the same time as creating a Nuba Mountains district separate from Kordofan. Arab traders, preachers and others needed special permits to enter the district. The principle enunciated by the most enlightened British administrators was that this was a temporary measure, which would enable the Nuba to "discover" themselves and decide on what terms they should be integrated into the rest of Sudan. In a much-quoted memorandum in 1931, the then-Governor of Kordofan, J. A. Gillan asked:

Can we evolve a structure or series of structures, to fit all these different cultures and stages of civilisation? Can we at the same

---

[5] Ahmed Uthman Muhammed Ibrahim, *The Dilemma of British Rule in the Nuba Mountains, 1898-1947*, Khartoum, University of Khartoum Graduate College Publications, 1985.

time preserve all that is best in the Nuba side by side with an Arab civilisation?[6]

To protect the Nuba "while they learn to stand on their feet" (in Gillan's patronising language) would have required a programme of social and economic development. In reality, this was restricted to encouraging small-scale cotton cultivation, and a handful of mission schools. Lack of economic opportunities meant that many Nuba men began to migrate to the Northern towns and the Gezira scheme to look for work, as agricultural labourers, casual workers, servants and soldiers—the Closed Districts Ordnance did not prevent migration *out*, and colonial labour policies actually encouraged it.[7] This had the ironic effect of promoting Arabic and Islam among the Nuba far more effectively than if the Mountains had been open to Northern Sudanese. But in the North, Nuba migrants always had an inferior status.

In 1937, the Nuba Mountains District was abolished and the area was absorbed back into Kordofan. Ten years later, a long-running debate about what language of instruction should be used in Nuba schools was resolved in favour of Arabic. By default, the Nuba were integrated into the Northern social and political system. But, because of lack of education, economic development and political access, the Nuba were no better prepared for playing an active role in Sudanese politics in 1947 than in 1922.

Since then, the "mainstream" culture of Northern Sudan has been actively promoted in the Nuba Mountains. Partly this has been done by government fiat. In the early 1970s, the government tried to enforce wearing clothes, by forbidding traders to sell goods to anyone who was not "properly" clothed and banning naked and semi-naked people from entering towns. There were also campaigns against pigs. Among the Nuba Moslems, pressure to conform more closely to Northern culture was especially strong. The agents of this pressure were more likely to be Nuba Moslems who had lived in

---

[6] J. A. Gillan, "Some aspects of Nuba administration," Khartoum, Sudan Government Memorandum No. 1, 1931, pp. 6-7.
[7] African Rights, *Sudan's Invisible Citizens: The Policy of Abuse against Displaced People in the North*, February 1995, pp. 7-9.

towns, rather than traders or preachers from the Nile Valley. The same process, sometimes called "Sudanisation", has been described among non-Arab Moslem peoples in neighbouring Darfur:

> Over a period of five years, the author has witnessed the virtual disappearance of tribal dancing and a growing polarisation within communities. This polarisation is concerned with opinions as to the proper way to live as a Muslim. The different ethnic groups in the area have lost a great deal of their original cultural identity over recent decades. This change represents the conversion from what is considered an increasingly irrelevant, narrow ethnic ethos and worldview to a new, prestigious and powerful ideology and praxis. While splitting some local communities, 'Sudanisation' simultaneously strengthens certain class and national identifications.[8]

Many aspects of Northern Sudanese culture have now become so deeply entrenched in Nuba society that they can never be reversed. The prime case of this is clothing: two generations ago, public nudity or semi-nudity was the norm for many Nuba. Clothing was adopted through social pressures, but today all Nuba have accepted that being fully clothed is an absolute requirement of modernity, and almost all people feel ashamed to appear in public without "proper" clothing. This was well-expressed by an elderly Achiron lady, Kaka Zubri.[9]

> In the past when I was younger we had a lot of beads and no clothes. We didn't feel ashamed when we came down the mountain. But then clothes came and people said, 'You have to wear clothes to be a civilised woman.' When the Arabs were here, we had clothes, salt, sugar, everything. But when the SPLA came and liberated the area, the Arabs left with all the things they had brought. The clothes stopped. But now we feel ashamed to go back to traditional dress.

The current dire shortage of clothes in SPLA-controlled parts of the Nuba Mountains has become a major hindrance on people's

---

[8] Paul Doornbos, "On becoming Sudanese," in T. Barnett and A. Abdelkarim (eds.) *Sudan: State, Capital and Transformation*, London, Croom Helm, 1988, p. 99.
[9] Interviewed by the BBC in Achiron, 13 May 1995.

participation in social events. Some women were reluctant to meet with African Rights' representatives because they did not consider themselves to have adequate clothes. One forty-year-old woman, Amal, said, "We have many problems. My children are completely naked. We cannot go to occasions like the dances that are celebrating SPLA day because we have no clothes, so we just stay at home."[10]

For a while, and for some Nuba peoples, it appeared that "Sudanisation" could be achieved without losing what was valuable in traditional cultures. During the hopeful decade of the 1970s, this was the case for the Miri, as argued by the anthropologist Gerd Baumann: "To the first observer of these processes, it may often appear that Miri villagers are determined to cast off their heritage as Nuba and to see themselves as primarily Sudanese. Yet Miri villagers do not recognise such a conflict of identities."[11]

This was optimistic. Baumann also noted that, "What is common to virtually all Nuba groups, is a history of enmity and strife with precisely those populations to whom 'integration' is now expected to tie them."[12] The reality was that national integration could only be achieved on highly unequal terms—another subjugation, this time losing local integrity in the process. The realities of exploitation, expropriation and discrimination became so harsh that many Nuba ultimately resorted to arms.

Integration into the Sudanese state came through four main means: (1) political administration, especially the imposition of chieftancy; (2) education; (3) labour migration and (4) Islam. The first three are discussed here; the religious question is left for Chapter IV.

DIVIDE AND RULE

The Nuba presented many problems to the British administration, which responded with force, guile and patience. Certain groups (Tira el Akhdar, Tullishi) were compelled to move down from the

---

[10] Interviewed in Um Dulu, 17 May 1995. SPLA day is 16 May.
[11] Baumann, 1987, p. 63.
[12] Baumann, 1987, p. 9.

mountains to settle in the plains, where they could be policed more easily. Punitive expeditions were mounted, including the first use of aerial bombardment (Tima and Julud were bombed on 4 February 1926). Most significant, however, was the British decision to institute "indirect rule", which began to be implemented in the 1920s. The theory was that the colonial authorities would rule through a "native administration" of chiefs, who would combine local legitimacy with responsiveness to the demands of "modern" government.

Nuba Chiefs

However, with just a handful of exceptions, there were no chiefs in the Nuba Mountains. One exception was the Dilling tribe, who had been ruled by a Sultan for as long as oral history could recall. Another was Tegali, where the ruler had historically traced his ancestry to an Arab stranger. But, the big men (sometimes calling themselves "chief" or "sultan") who existed in other places were at best temporary, opportunistic war leaders—often the very people who led resistance against the British.

Communal cohesion among Nuba groups was traditionally not provided by chiefs, but by a variety of means, including traditional priests ("kujurs") and age sets (organisations of age-mates). Many Nuba groups were "stateless societies", ruling by custom, consent and consultation. But the British needed chiefs, and so they set about both creating the institutions of chieftanship, and appointing the chiefs (or vetting the candidates for popular election). This *imposition* of chieftanship is a fact of fundamental importance, and its impact is felt today.

Sometimes, the chieftanship was created simply from scratch, for example among the Nyima or Tullishi. In Otoro and Kawalib, an indigenous chieftanship was beginning to emerge in the early twentieth century, but the government chiefs bore little resemblance to those who had emerged. Nadel observed the process: "To study [Otoro chieftanship] is to watch it emerge from a chiefless society. Heiban still represents this chiefless state, save for the superstructure

21

of modern Government chieftanship."[13] In Korongo Angolo and Mesakin, there were offices of "ambassadors" who negotiated between different tribes, but held little or no power within them, and the titles for chiefs and sometimes the individuals themselves were grafted onto government chieftanship. In Moro and Tira, the institution of "big men" or (in Nadel's words) "pseudo-chiefs" served as a model.

The Nuba peoples had been subjugated, often violently. The people they preferred for chiefs were not the real loci of authority—the rain-makers, traditional priests and others—but people who had been migrants, soldiers or civil servants, who knew the ways of the government. Often, the spheres of traditional authority and government liaison were kept deliberately separate, so that one man was prevented from holding the two different kinds of position. Nadel describes the process of selection:

In electing their modern chiefs or sub-chiefs, the people look for qualifications of a new kind: knowledge of Arabic, acquaintance with the ways of the *Hakuma* [government], an energetic temperament, and suitable age for undertaking the new tasks of office, like tax-collection, recruiting labour for road work, &c.[14]

The government provided a salary, status, authority in a court and control over a few local policemen, and perks such as education for the chief's sons. In return they demanded absolute loyalty and obedience. A chief could be summarily dismissed for failing to collect the taxes or subdue the people, and many were. The Nuba chief was not a representative of his people (though some of them evolved to be close to that over the decades), but a civil servant. Old habits die hard: today, a chief's first, almost instinctive loyalty, is to his superiors. After the experience of some of the early rebellions, which were led by chiefs appointed or approved by the government, the British were also keen to restrict the powers of the chiefs.

The British introduced a three tier system, of chieftancy. The lowest level were sheikhs, one for each village (or ward of a large

---

[13] Nadel, 1947, p. 146.
[14] Nadel, 1947, pp. 164-5.

village). Several sheikhs were put under one omda (a word and institution imported from Egypt). The highest level was the mek (a version of the Arabic *melik*, "king").

In the later colonial period, the administration was relatively benign, and the institution of chieftancy became more widely accepted. Some sheikhs, omdas and meks even became popular with their people, and were respected by both villagers and government. This situation persisted unevenly after independence in 1956, notably in Sudan's "development decade" of the 1970s, that false dawn of economic progress and social integration. But, even when the institution of chieftancy was at its most popular, it was kept at a distance from the true loyalties of the people. In the 1970s, among the Miri, the separation of traditional priestly offices and chieftancy was strictly enforced.[15]

The "native administration" system was abolished in 1971 and replaced with a system of "people's councils." This was less of a disruption than it might have appeared, because of the real status of chiefs as government servants. In reality, moreover, the chiefs continued to exercise their influence, often by taking senior positions in the people's councils. As the new system of local government ground to a halt, due in part to lack of finance, the provincial authorities *de facto* reinstated the chiefs and used them for their familiar purposes. After the 1989 coup, chiefs were formally reinstated, and the current government is following a policy that in many respects closely resembles their British predecessors.

Nuba-Arab Relations

One of the deepest tragedies of the Nuba Mountains is that the Baggara Arabs who have implemented so much of the government's policies against the Nuba, are themselves an impoverished and marginalised group in Sudan. The Baggara are mostly poor, and despite close links to powerful political forces such as the Umma Party of Sadiq el Mahdi, there has been little economic development or provision of social services in the Baggara areas. However, for

---

[15] Baumann, 1987, p. 81.

historical reasons, the Baggara Arabs have been unwilling to make common political cause with their Nuba neighbours.

In the western jebels, in Lagowa area, colonial and independent governments faced the most acute manifestation of the widespread problem of how Nuba-Baggara Arab relations should be managed. In this area, the geographical separation between the Arabs, the seven Nuba tribes and the Daju was simply an impossibility, and the population was split in such a way that no group formed a natural majority. But the British insisted on creating a tribally-based administration nonetheless. They experimented with a system of political federation, and also toyed with separating the district from the remainder of the Nuba Mountains and allowing it to become "Arabised." But the colonial authorities failed to resolve on any one strategy. This left the best-organised group, the Misiriya Zurug, in the dominant position. The Nazir[16] of the Misiriya Zurug had authority over the Nuba tribes and the Daju, who were represented only by wakils (deputies). It was only in the 1980s, after prolonged complaints by the Nuba tribes and the Daju, that the Kordofan Regional Government agreed to appoint senior chiefs from the Nuba and Daju.

Another point of contention was the question of who owned the town of Lagowa itself. Historically it is a Kamda area, but when it became a district headquarters, it came to be dominated by the Misiriya Zurug.

By default rather than design, British policies ended up favouring the Arabs, by giving them better education, more economic opportunities, and better representation in the centres of power. This relentlessly fed through into systematic discrimination in favour of the Arabs in post-independence local government. Hassan Osman Kuku is a teacher from the western jebels. He described some of the components of institutional discrimination in favour of the Arabs in the area.[17]

---

[16] The paramount chief of an Arab tribe.
[17] Interviewed in Tira Limon, 23 May 1995.

Before the war, the relation with the Arabs was generally one of brotherhood. But there were some disagreements, for example over bringing cattle onto farms, and discrimination and segregation.

A second problem was education. If the Tima took their children to school, they were not encouraged to go ahead.... [see below for more discussion of this issue].

A third problem concerned the co-operative shop and the distribution of essential commodities. The distribution was not done properly. Even though the Tima area had a larger population than the Misiriya area, the treatment was not equal. We were given two bags of sugar for distribution per month, so that one family would get only one quarter of a pound. The other Misiriya places, even though they were less in number, would get a bigger quantity.

It was in response to this unequal treatment that the Nuba began to agitate for stronger representation in the administration. They did meet with some success, in the early 1980s.

Another big problem was farming schemes. Sometimes the government created agricultural schemes for the people. They would call the people together and demarcate the area. But we would find that when the allocation of schemes is made, all the leaseholders are Arabs. In Subakha in the 1970s, Fadallah Hamad, who is a big Misiriya politician, controlled the distribution of land in the scheme. At least Subakha was on virgin land. The same thing happened with Um Dorota in the 1980s, and that scheme took land away from the Tima farmers. There was no compensation, and the farmers who had lost [land] were forced to find new land. The farmers protested and even took the case to court, but the judge refused to accept the case.

One dispute was at Khor al Far, especially at Rimti. The Misiriya went to the government to try to get gardens in that place. They even went as far as Khartoum, and the scheme was given a name: the Rimti scheme. The Khartoum government people discussed the matter and said, 'Okay, if the people of the area agree.' Then the government people came and found that only Misiriya were planning it, and stopped the scheme.

At a village level, relations between Nuba farmers and Baggara herders were usually cordial. When there was no political dispute, and no reason such as drought for violent competition for water or grazing, the two groups were very amicable. As the Nuba colonised the plains from the 1920s onwards, they began to become cattle owners, and by the 1950s and '60s, many Nuba were large cattle herders in their own right. Meanwhile, many Baggara also started farms. Relations varied from village to village: in some places they were very good. Ahmed Sayed Nur, a nurse from Delami, said:[18]

> In the past, we were living with our Arab neighbours, the Ayatigha and Awlad Ghabbush. The relationship was good, though there was no intermarriage. There was trade. We grazed our cattle together. Sometimes a Nuba would entrust his cattle to an Arab to take them to pastures for the dry season, and sometimes an Arab would settle with us for farming. We would have just minor clashes over grazing.

At the time there was considerable interest among scholars in the "Baggarisation" of the Nuba and the "sedenterisation" of the nomads: it was expected that the two groups would become gradually integrated.

In the 1980s, friendly relations broke down. In the western jebels, the local balance of power shifted decisively in favour of the Misiriya. This was due to the policy of the Transitional Military Council, that took power in April 1985 during the Popular Uprising against President Nimeiri, to arm the two sections of the Misiriya—Humr and Zurug—as a militia to fight the SPLA. This is discussed in Chapter II.

Bias in Dispute Resolution

One major type of dispute occurs in the Nuba Mountains with predictable regularity: pastoralists bringing their animals onto farms before harvesting is complete. The colonial records are filled with such cases. Until the early 1980s, such disputes were generally settled equitably. But then the balance tilted decisively in favour of the Arabs, and Nuba litigants lost any confidence that they would

---

[18] Interviewed in Tira Limon, 20 May 1995.

obtain a fair hearing in courts. Many Nuba police officers, magistrates and administrative officers were transferred out of the Nuba Mountains in the 1980s. Nuba communities discovered that the government would almost always support the Arab cause in the case of an inter-tribal dispute.

A characteristic incident is reported by one farmer from Korongo Abdalla:

> Before the war we had problems over farmland. The nomadic Arabs brought their cattle onto our farms. In our area they were Misiriya Zurug—Jubrat and Salamat. The army armed the Baggara, who then caused trouble. Whenever we wrote a petition they would say, 'These are nomadic routes.' These problems began in 1983-84.
>
> There was one incident in June 1984. Some Baggara took our cows, and when we pursued them to the police post at Juheilat, the police came out, armed, and sent us back. The Arabs then wrote a petition accusing us of taking their cows. Our own chief, Omda Anja Tutu, was bribed to give witness against us. So, in February [1985], the police arrested and tied up four of our boys—they tied them up in trees and lit fires under them to torture them with heat and smoke. We have two of the names: Saraf Tiya and Hassan Ab Shok. Then a Nuba soldier with the government army cocked his rifle and threatened to shoot unless the men were released. They were. But the Arabs kept pursuing the affair, until the SPLA arrived and they dropped it.[19]

There were innumerable such cases. One obstacle that the Nuba side consistently faced was the perfidy of their own chiefs: as government servants, accustomed to handsome payment for their work, they were frequently ready to accept bribes to support the Arab side in a dispute. A farmer from Kufa village in the Miri jebels described some of the problems they faced:

> Our Arab neighbours used to be Misiriya Zurug, Humr, and Awlad Muman. At one time we had peaceful settlement of disputes. I recall one case in 1978 when the Awlad Muman killed one Miri

---

[19] Jaafar al Fadl, interviewed in Um Dulu, 17 May 1995.

man, Zeidan Ibrahim Kafi. *Diya* [bloodmoney] was negotiated but they refused to pay. Then the government made a conference and the matter was settled. They paid.

From about 1980 we had more problems resolving our cases. There was one community health worker, Abdel Gadir Tiya, who was seriously wounded in 1981, speared by an Arab. Despite our attempts, the case was never settled. The Arabs were paying the Miri negotiators to stop the case going ahead.

Another case was in 1985. The Arabs came to the village of el Akhwal, they attacked it and occupied it. They didn't kill anyone. The people just ran away. One man, Taj el Sir—he later died in the SPLA—complained to the mek, Mohamed el Zaki, who took the case to Kadugli. Ten days passed before anyone responsible came to visit the place. We saw no sign of any police for ten days. The case was settled by the police and the mek, but we weren't happy. The accused were let go free because there was no-one to witness against them. Mek Mohamed el Zaki was responsible for this.[20]

Frustration with the betrayal by their chiefs was an important reason why many Nuba youths and farmers turned to the SPLA.

A particularly important dispute occurred in early 1987, in the Shatt area south of Kadugli. It started with a minor incident, but rapidly developed into a national political issue, that reveals many components of the unfolding crisis. An issue of particular sensitivity that was raised was the value, in terms of *diya*, of a Nuba life *vis-à-vis* an Arab life.

Kuku Idris al Izerig Kafi is now an SPLA officer. In 1987, he was one of the educated members of the Shatt Damam community who was asked to represent the Shatt side in negotiations. He recounted the background to the incident:[21]

Our neighbours at Shatt Damam are Misiriya Zurug and Fellata Hausa (mostly merchants), as well as the Kadugli people. Before the war, we would see the Misiriya after the rains, when they would come from the north and make their *farigs* [nomadic camps]

---

[20] Musa Kuwa Jabir Tiya, interviewed in Um Dulu, 17 May 1995.
[21] Interviewed in Tira Limon, 20 May 1995.

outside our villages. They would share our water and come to seek boys to work with them as cowherds. Our contact was limited.

On 2 February 1987 a serious problem started. The Misiriya came as usual the previous November and December, and found that our people had gathered the harvest, which remains in the farms in heaps until March. But on that day some of them released their cows onto the stored sorghum in the farms. Two farmers were present, guarding their crops. They came to chase the cattle away. The Arab was armed and shot at them. One was injured and his brother who came after him was killed.

There are several different versions of what happened next. Some witnesses claim that the Misiriya attacked the following day, with three lorry-loads of gunmen, and killed between four and six Shatt farmers, for the loss of one or two lives among the Arabs. However, Kuku Idris is even-handed in his allocation of responsibility for the fighting that followed.

People ran and told their relatives. The Arabs at that moment were encamped between Shatt Damam and Shatt Safiya. We made a *fasha* [war cry]. Both groups of Shatt people mobilised and attacked the Arab camps. Two Arabs were killed that night. The Shatt people took 435 Arab cows, and the Arabs ran with their children. The cattle were too many to eat, but the people slaughtered them all, anyway.

For five days there was fighting. At that time I had just come from Khartoum. I met with the police commander, Abdel Gadir Darjol (a Ghulfan [Nuba]) and the military commander, Major al Sir Khalifa, and I tried to see about stopping the fighting. We went to Shatt Safiya, and found the fighting continuing. We were accompanied by the riot police, and we succeeded in stopping the fighting and forming a reconciliation committee. The committee had fifteen members: five Misiriya, five Nuba and five from the government.

The committee agreed that before any final settlement is reached, during an interim period, any aggressive Nuba or Arab will be punished with a fine of LS [Sudanese pounds] 5 thousand million [a huge and symbolic sum]. This was signed by all groups on 25 February.

The day after the ceasefire, the Misiriya Arabs mobilised and attacked Genaya. They came with their lorries. They looted crops, both sorghum and sesame, and burned. They didn't raid any cattle, but they loaded their lorries with looted crops. They killed one man and wounded four.

Hamad Tutu Dabah is a farmer from Shatt Safiya who was nearby when the incident occurred. He told African Rights:[22]

> The Arabs returned to Genaya and shot randomly. But there was no-one there—all the people had run to Jebel Kuwa the day before. The Arabs looked for cows to steal but they found none. So they burned 77 houses.
> The administrators of the area went to Kadugli to report to the government there. The Government sent a delegation and evaluated the amount of losses, and we formed a committee. We demanded *diya* for the people killed on our side, who were eight.

Kuku Idris was one of those who went to Kadugli to report on the incident.

> We went to the garrison and reported what had happened. The army came to Shatt Safiya and decided to call for a big conference in Kadugli, *Muatimir al Ajawid* [Conference of Mediation]. This conference opened on 6 March.
> The conference was enlarged to include twelve from each side and twelve from the government—who were going to be members of the political parties. But those who were represented were the northern political parties, Umma and DUP, six—six. The Sudan National Party [which is Nuba-dominated] was not represented. We protested, arguing that all the five political parties in Kadugli should be represented.[23] We objected. The government refused. The conference went ahead. It was chaired by the Governor of Kordofan, Mohamed Ali el Mardi. We repeated our objection, and the government refused again.
> The conference made no resolutions. It was derailed by the comments of the Governor himself. He himself said, 'The Nuba are

---

[22] Interviewed in Um Dulu, 17 May 1995.
[23] The other two were the Baath Party and the Sudan Communist Party.

mistaken. They have cultivated on land which is supposed to be a cattle route for the Arabs.' We disagreed: 'We don't have any nomadic routes in Shatt.' Our evidence was first that sugar is given by the Ministry of Supply to nomads in areas where they have registered livestock routes, and we had never received any such sugar for the nomads. Secondly, in the Council itself there was a map with the nomadic routes marked on it, and none were marked at Shatt.

The Governor also said that the Shatt people had got drunk on *merissa* [sorghum beer] and attacked the Arabs. We argued that even if people were drinking *merissa*, who is mistaken, the person who drinks *merissa* in his house or the person who invades another person's farm?

At last the conference was adjourned. The Governor said, 'I will communicate with the Prime Minister [Sadiq el Mahdi] and decide, and fix another date.'

The delegation then began to raise another issue: compensation, and ran into another layer of delays and obstructions.

We asked for assistance for the people whose houses were destroyed. We were called to el Obeid. I went with a delegation. The Governor asked us to come to Khartoum, so we went to Khartoum. We were four: Mohamed Mojo Shelali, Musa Kafi, el Amin Kuwa, and me. We met the Governor in the presence of the Prime Minister. They said, 'Let's meet again in el Obeid.' We continued arguing, 'It's not necessary to return to el Obeid. When the SPLA attacked el Azraq Murahaliin camp in 1985, you immediately provided relief, and took the Murahaliin to Kadugli and created a residential area for them called Salamat. Why are we different?' They insisted. The Governor went by aeroplane to el Obeid and we followed by road.

We met the Governor again in el Obeid. There was still no date fixed for the conference. We insisted on assistance, citing el Azraq again. We said, 'After that incident, Fadallah Burma went, saw and provided arms to the Arabs. Why are we not assisted and why are we not armed?' We felt he was deceiving us.

We returned to Khartoum and made our protest public through the newspapers. We made it clear that if there was no government protection or assistance, we would protect ourselves. After seeing this in the newspaper, Sadiq's government began accusing us of following the methods of Yousif Kuwa against the Governor of Kordofan.

By the end of March, we saw that things were getting too difficult. Security had been following us from the start, with the intention of framing charges. Mojo and I left to join the SPLA, and the other two left for Saudi Arabia.

The departure of the Shatt delegation handed the advantage to the Misiriya and their allies in the government: there were now no educated people to represent the Shatt case or to campaign publicly. Kuku Idris said, "After we left, pressure was put on our people." Hamad Tutu Dabah was one of those who now had to deal with the negotiations:

The Arabs demanded 435 head of cows taken by the Nuba during the fighting, and 36 sheep. They also demanded *diya* for one man killed. We demanded *diya* for eight dead and compensation for the houses burned and property destroyed. The Arabs then demanded a *diya* of sixty cows for each Arab, but said they could pay only 31 for each Nuba dead.[24] We went to the Commissioner to complain and say that the *diya* should be equal for Arabs and Nuba. The Commissioner agreed but he was secretly supporting the Arab side.

Each side wanted the other side to pay first. The Commissioner was leaning on us. We paid the 435 cows, including healthy cows and young cows. The Arabs divided the cows. They owed us 248 for *diya*; they chose the old and sick cows and gave them. We refused: we wanted a proper mixture of cows.

The estimate for the loss of the burning in Shatt Safiya was LS 138,000. We demanded this; they refused. While we paid all what we owed, they stalled. We went to the Commissioner's office. He went round and obtained some voluntary contributions from the Arabs in the town and added to it from the Government's own funds. They gave us LS 52,000. We gathered the people who had lost properties and gave them what we could, and said, 'Wait, we will try to get you the remainder.' But when we returned to the Commissioner, we were refused.

---

[24] In colonial days, the British decreed that the *diya* for an Arab was twice as high as for a Nuba.

This continued for some months. In June, we held a conference with the Deputy Commissioner in Shatt Safiya to discuss the same case. The Arabs and the Government were still refusing to pay what was due.

Before that time, the Government was arming the Arabs. They continued to arm them. When we returned, the Commissioner said, 'We have made peace between the Nuba and the Arabs, but you are demanding more and also continuing to fight. If you want, go and fight with them. But you know they are armed and you are not.'

So we left it at that, saying that God will help.

The Shatt case was not helped by the fact that the mek showed more loyalty to the government than his people. The Shatt people expected little else from a government chief, but it was a betrayal nonetheless. Kuku Idris explained what he heard about the subsequent progress of the negotiations:

The same committee took over implementing the payment of *diya* and compensation. The Nuba were to pay 435 cows: this was enforced. They insisted that the *diya* for an Arab should be twice as much as for a Nuba. If the *diya* for a Nuba was fifteen cows, for an Arab it was to be 31. If it was thirty for a Nuba, for an Arab it should be 61. Our Mek, Kafi Tayara el Bedin, was part of this. A formal agreement was reached that made the *diya* equal, but practically the government and Arabs made sure that we paid double. Some of the *diya* was collected and paid by October 1988, but they were still collecting the second part when the SPLA entered on 24 March 1989. There was a fierce battle at Fama. Then the whole committee ran from Shatt Damam and abandoned the plan. From then on, no-one has talked about payment.

The strategy of formally agreeing to equal treatment for both sides, but in practice working towards enforcing terms advantageous to one side, was something the Nuba had become familiar with. Meanwhile, further disputes erupted in Shatt Damam; at the end of 1987, Arab militiamen killed five villagers after the burning of the house of Fellata merchant who was suspected of selling the area's sugar ration for personal profit. The authorities in Kadugli called for

33

another conference to settle the issue, to which the Shatt responded with scepticism. The time for negotiation had passed.

Favoured Tribes

The British policy of divide and rule had another important component: dividing the Nuba tribes against each other. One tribe, the Nyima, who live at the northern extremity of the Nuba Mountains west of Dilling, came to play a prominent role in this strategy. They still do.

In the colonial days, the Nyima were the Nuba tribe most exposed to the influence of the new government. At first, the Nyima chiefs and kujurs resisted the British, with a major uprising in 1908. After this, the British imposed chiefs on the Nyima, most of whom were former soldiers or civil servants. They recognised the value of education for their children, and when Anglican missionaries chose a Nyima village, Salara, to be the site of one of its first mission stations and schools in the Nuba Mountains, they eagerly embraced education. Since then, the Nyima have provided a disproportionately high number of educated Nuba. They are both Moslems and Christians: many migrated for work in Dilling or the cities of the North, and became Moslem, and many others were educated in Salara mission school.

The colonial government played a game of divide and rule within the Nuba Mountains. It encouraged the Nyima to play a role as the elite, and then co-opted them as a "Nuba" leadership that could represent, and control, the other Nuba tribes. Educational and employment opportunities were never extended to other Nuba areas to a comparable extent. The tendency of the Nyima elite to co-operate with the government remains strong to this day.

A SECOND-CLASS EDUCATION

Another legacy of British rule was education. Throughout the colonial period, educational policy was marked by ambiguity. Mission stations were opened in Heiban, Abri, Tabanya, Kauda,

Salara and Katcha, and Nuba children were given an opportunity of an education in all these places. Several of the Nuba languages were written down (in Roman script) for the first time. There were also government schools, in Kadugli, Talodi and Dilling, but for a long while Nuba children were excluded. This was because the education was in Arabic, and at the time colonial policy was to isolate the Nuba from Arab influence. The colonial authorities wrung their hands over whether the Nuba should have a separate educational policy (as in the South), or whether it should be integrated into the Northern, Arabic system.

In 1947, the decision was made to use Arabic as the medium of instruction in the Nuba Mountains. From the outset, the Nuba were at a disadvantage—they had fewer teachers and fewer schools. They were merely inserted into a national educational system as a minority without the linguistic skills or political weight to obtain fair treatment. They have suffered accordingly.

From their earliest days at school, Nuba boys and girls were—and are—made to feel that their futures lie as servants and labourers, not as professionals or leaders. Teachers passed on such attitudes with striking success and consistency. Even the Nuba teachers have often transmitted these attitudes to their pupils, consciously or unconsciously. Frustration at discrimination in education was a major factor why many youths joined the SPLA.

Hassan Osman, a teacher, described some of the elements that discouraged Tima children from proceeding with their education:

> If the Tima took their children to school, they were not encouraged to go ahead. Some were even chased from the schools—they were told by the teachers and their Arab schoolmates just to go and look after animals. The headmaster of the intermediate school in Lagowa, Gadim Jabar, a Misiriya who was born in the Tima area, was particularly aggressive in this respect. After the exam to graduate from primary to intermediate school, the boys who pass should be admitted. But then the problem is how to stay. The Arab children were given all the boarding places, or they had relatives in town and could put up with them. But the Nuba children had no

place to stay in town, and so they found it difficult to stay in school.[25]

Kokani Musa Mudir, from Tura village in Tira el Akhdar, joined the SPLA in 1988 at age twelve. Like many Nuba, the petty discrimination that appeared to be destroying his chance of a future drove him into rebellion. After seven years in the SPLA, six of them as a soldier, the yearning for education is still strong.

I spent four years at Kauda primary school. Six months after I left, the school was closed because all the teachers left, fearing the SPLA.

The school was not functioning well at the time. We were not getting a good education. We were being frustrated. For example, there used to be a Tilly lamp so we could study after sunset; we used to contribute money for the gas. We paid the money. But the teachers refused to teach us in the daytime, and then at night they took the Tilly lamp so that they could play cards. Most of the teachers were Shanabla Arabs.

The food at the school was also not good. So we organised a strike. We wanted better food, and we refused to pay for the gas for the Tilly lamp unless we were able to use it in the evenings.

In the morning assembly and inspection on the day of our strike, the teachers told us, 'Teaching you is a waste of time. We are hearing that the SPLA is here. It is useless to teach you as you will just go and join the rebels.'

So most of the students decided to join the SPLA, and lose their education. We thought we may get a better education if 'the land is out' [i.e. liberated], instead of paying for education that was not being provided anyway. We were paying school fees of LS 6 per year for each student, and what for?

That was in 1988. So I decided to join the SPLA. There were 36 of us from Kauda who went together. I was the youngest, I was twelve years old. We assembled in Karkar. Our commander was Juma Kabbi, and when we reached a total of four hundred, we all went together to Ethiopia...

Education is still a vital concern for Kokani:

---

[25] Interviewed in Tira Limon, 23 May 1995.

I have a little spare time, and I try to read. But I really need to study in a class. I want to go back to school, even before freedom is achieved. I don't mind what subject. I am still ignorant. Education will make me more aware of my environment, so I can make others more aware too. If I can't get these things, then we will have achieved nothing. My plan is to write to the Governor [Yousif Kuwa] and propose that there should be schools for those of us who are in the army.[26]

Elyas Ismail Gorab, a Moro student from Um Dulu, joined the SPLA at the age of seventeen. Changes in educational policies were a key factor that drove him to take up arms.

I joined the SPLA in 1987. I was at school in Um Sirdiba, in second year intermediate (grade eight). The school was still open, it had just closed for the normal school holidays. But it wasn't functioning properly. There were many rumours at that time about the SPLA entering the Nuba Mountains. Because of those rumours, the teachers began to suspect the students, that they were Anyanya [i.e. SPLA].

Our school was eighty students, with just three teachers. The head teacher and one other were Nuba, and the administrator was an Arab. The Nuba teachers were sympathetic, but the policy was dictated from above.

The teachers implemented a new policy, that if you fail two subjects, you are not allowed to repeat—you have to leave the school. We saw this as a strategy for denying us. They also made Islam a compulsory subject. An Islamic teacher was brought for the first time. His name was Farah and he came from North Kordofan, from Bara. He came to the class and when the Christians asked permission to leave, he said that no-one should leave, and we must study Islam. We complained but no-one listened. In our class, the majority were Christians.

Also, in May 1987 a militia centre was set up in Aggab that started attacking the Moro people. That month, they burned Um Dulu. Only when the SPLA reached Achiron was the militia camp withdrawn. We saw that the Arab policy was to wipe out the Moro.

---

[26] Interviewed in Tira Limon, 20 May 1995.

Lupa was the first village to be burned, in April, also by the militia. Um Dulu was the second. But the Moro had been assembling guns, and resisted.

We left for the SPLA in a group of seven.[27]

As the war intensified, it set in motion a vicious spiral of denying educational opportunities to those suspected of sympathising with the SPLA—i.e. almost all Nuba youths. The schools, though officially open, were no longer centres of learning. It was this that drove another schoolboy, William Samuel Musa, from Kanbara village in Otoro, to join the SPLA in 1989. He was fifteen at the time.

I completed up to grade four in school, in Heiban. We felt the teachers were not teaching us properly. We saw this in the exam results—the Arab boys are always given better marks by the teachers. Simply because they had the money and we didn't. The SPLA was in our area at that time, and there were a lot of arrests in Heiban. The teachers were frightened and they were not teaching. Some pupils left the school to join the SPLA. This created fear. That also persuaded me to go to Khartoum. Even though the school was open, I felt that it was unofficially closed—it was closed but we had not been told that it was closed. Some of the parents who had means were taking their children away. We who remained became few. My parents were poor. So I opted for Khartoum.

I decided to join the SPLA when I was in Khartoum. While I was there I felt that I had nothing—no clothes, no education, sometimes even no job. The basic problem was that I had no freedom. When I learned about the struggle, I volunteered. Many colleagues from my school and my village went to the SPLA.[28]

The importance of discrimination in education cannot be underestimated, not least because a large proportion of the recruits to the SPLA are frustrated students. An earlier generation of disappointed students had simply opted to become migrant labourers in Khartoum or other Northern cities; the generation that was in

---

[27] Interviewed in Tira Limon, 21 May 1995.
[28] Interviewed in Tira Limon, 21 May 1995.

school when the war broke out had more direct ways of channelling their anger at a system that appeared set up to deny them.

WHO OWNS THE NUBA MOUNTAINS?

The single biggest issue of contention in the Nuba Mountains on the outbreak of war was land ownership. The issue of land reform remains one of the biggest unspoken questions in Sudan, protected by a conspiracy of silence that can be attributed to the fact that all the leading Northern families, whatever their political colour, are major landowners, and the failure of the SPLA to develop a policy on land reform.

Since the "pacification" of the Nuba Mountains by the British, Nuba farmers were encouraged (and sometimes forced) to leave their mountains and live and farm in the plains. Smallholdings spread out from the slopes of the hills, so that large areas of the plains were cultivated. According to customary law, unoccupied land is available to whoever cuts the trees and bushes and plants his crops. Though not formally registered, these farms were not a primitive or reckless "slash and burn" form of agriculture. Farmers often developed systems of rotational cropping, alternating sorghum with groundnuts or sesame, and long fallow periods to enable the soil to regain its fertility.

The growth of mechanised farming shattered the viability of Nuba smallholder farming. It also destroyed amicable relations with the Arab pastoralists. This took a while to become evident. The encouragement of semi-mechanised cotton production (reaching a total of 63 small schemes in the 1970s) brought extra income to wealthier smallholders, at the cost of hardly any loss of land. But government high-handedness, and manipulation of the system by Arab traders and government officials were clear from the start. One Miri villager reported:

> From 1973, mechanised farms started in the Miri area. They were all for cultivating cotton: Lima, Mashisha, Kanga, Abu Sunun, Kufa, Kadi and Keiga. We were told in advance that the Government had plans for schemes, and we had to go and clear the

land in advance. First we were told that we would cultivate, and that we could grow any crops we liked. Later, when the schemes were surveyed, they told us we would have to plant cotton. Their plan involved rotating the cultivation—some land was left fallow. So we tried to plant sorghum on the fallow land. This led to problems with the government. At the end, we were forced to accept cotton, and look for land to plant sorghum elsewhere.

These schemes were all on new land. No-one lost land to them. But the new owners included people from outside, including Fellata and Arabs from Kadugli. We were not happy with this. Some lands were reserved for the Arabs before the schemes were started. For example, Mubarak Zaroug [first foreign minister of Sudan, 1956]. He was granted the area from Gallab village to Keiga, and used tractors to grow cotton. This was in fact the first scheme in our area. After Mubarak died in the 1960s, the area was re-surveyed and was supposed to be granted to the local people, but most of it was taken by the Jellaba.[29]

The collapse of cotton prices in the 1970s meant that many of the schemes were not profitable, and they began to close in the late 1970s.

It was the introduction of large-scale mechanised sorghum farms that brought disaster. The Mechanised Farming Corporation was established in 1968. Its first and largest scheme in the Nuba Mountains was at Habila, between Dilling and Delami. In the 1970s it established nine more schemes. Equally importantly, the MFC demarcated areas and gave 25-year leases on schemes of one thousand or 1500 *feddans*[30] to private merchant farmers. In theory, farming experience was a requirement for obtaining a lease; in practice any wealthy or well-connected merchant, civil servant or army officer could obtain a lease. Contrary to the MFC's stated policy, very few leaseholders were local "small farmers." According to a 1975 agreement, half the finance for the expansion of private mechanised farming was provided by the World Bank.

The MFC legally based its operations on the Land Registration Act of 1925, amended in 1961. This amendment awarded

---

[29] Musa Kuwa Jabir Tiya, interviewed in Um Dulu, 17 May 1995.
[30] One feddan equals 1.038 acres or 0.42 hectares.

unregistered land to the government, subject to the approval of the Registrar of Lands, who recognised limited customary title to land. But the key legal instrument is the remarkable Section 380 of the Sudan Penal Code of 1974, which concerned trespassing:

> Whoever enters into or upon property in the possession of another with intention to commit an offence or intimidate, insult or annoy any person in possession of such property, or, having lawfully entered into or upon such property, unlawfully remains there, with the intent thereby to intimidate, insult or annoy such a person, or with the intent to commit an offence, is said to commit criminal trespass.

The second part of this section means that any farmer whose land, owned in accordance with customary law, was expropriated, was guilty of criminal trespass if he or she should remain there with the intentention of so much as "annoying" the new owner. The MFC was aggressive in using the law to intimidate such smallholders. This section was retained in the subsequent 1983 and 1990 acts.

Habila had two hundred schemes. Four were leased to local co-operatives, one was leased to a consortium of local merchants, and four individually to local merchants. The remaining 191 were leased to absentee landlords, mainly merchants, government officials and retired army officers from the north.[31] This was typical of the land ownership pattern that became established. From a registered area of two million hectares in 1968, mechanised farms expanded to cover over eight million hectares in 1986. One quarter of this area was in South Kordofan.[32] The worst-affected areas were the most northerly jebels (from east to west: the Rahad area, Kawalib, Kaduru, Ghulfan, Nyimang and Abu Januq) and the eastern side (Tira el Akhdar), but the MFC had plans to develop a belt of mechanised farms right

---

[31] Mohamed Suleiman, "Tanks and Tractors Against the Nuba," London, Institute for African Alternatives, 1995.

[32] M. A. Mohamed Salih, "Political Coercion and the Limits of State Intervention," in Anders Hjort af Ornäs and M. A. Mohamed Sahih (eds.), *Ecology and Politics: Environmental Stress and Security in Africa*, Uppsala, Scandanavian Institute for African Affairs, 1989, p. 107.

across the southern jebels as well. The land problem became acute in many localities in the early 1980s. A community leader from Korongo Abdalla told African Rights:[33]

Land is a big problem. In 1984 the government began to talk about a scheme at Abu Shanab. The land there was already prepared by the local people, but the government brought its tractor and began to prepare cultivation. We asked them to go to another side. They refused. We went to our kujur, who made a spell, and the tractor got stuck. It did not move again.

The government demarcated the area, for one hundred farms. They told us that any civilian can take a lease in the scheme, but a certain proportion of the harvest will go to the government. But in fact only merchants from Kadugli and other people from outside were involved. We only found this out when they started cultivating the scheme. The government people then said to us, 'Your land is in the hills. This land is free.' They were wanting our lands.

In May 1986, the Arabs bribed our omda, Anja Tutu, to petition against fifteen men, including two teachers, who they said were anti-government and were preventing the agricultural schemes of the government from going ahead. They were arrested and taken to Kadugli and fined.

The Government was telling us, 'We can benefit from the Arabs but not from you.'

The disaster of mechanised farming was in fact evident to agricultural experts and economists by the time this scheme was planned. A well-known Sudanese economist published a critique of the whole policy in 1980. He found that mechanised farms were costly and unproductive, and questioned the rationale for supporting them:

[First], the production efficiency of agricultural mechanisation is questionable in comparison with the traditional agriculture practised in the region, second, the pattern of income distribution has worsened and income inequalities among different groups have widened as a result of the commercialisation of agriculture, and third, the conventional idea of replacing labour by machine is

---

[33] Jaafar al Fadl, interviewed in the Nuba Mountains, 17 May 1995.

irrelevant in the savannah situation since it suits only some operations, i.e., labour remains the main factor in production.[34]

This soon became accepted wisdom. As the Ministry of Finance began to prepare its recovery programme after the famine of 1984-5, it strongly recommended that mechanised farming should play no part:

> Plans for further extension [of] large mechanised farming should be rejected as such projects are detrimental to long term use of the soil for agricultural purposes and create little opportunities for migrants who wish to establish themselves as independent cultivators or livestock herders.[35]

But there were powerful forces behind mechanised farming: it was returning huge profits for the merchants who were investing, especially during a period of high grain prices. The Islamic banks that were behind the merchants also saw a good return on their investment. While the brake was put on the MFC, a massive expansion took place in privately-owned mechanised farming. It has become extremely difficult to keep track of the amount of land under cultivation in such schemes, because often the true areas of land are under-registered. By 1984, perhaps half of the total area of mechanised farmland in Southern Kordofan was in such private schemes. Two residents of Delami described how mechanised farms continued to spread during the 1980s:

> There are a lot of mechanised farms in Delami county. There is a big part of the Habila scheme, including Amara and Ginei in our area. Other schemes include Abrini, Fayo, Gardud el Basham and Sinarla. All of them involved taking land from the natives. Most people tried to protest. They complained to the government. In

---

[34] M. H. Saeed, "Economic effects of agricultural mechanisation in rural Sudan: The case of Habila, Southern Kordofan," in G. Haaland, *Problems of Savanna Development: The Sudan Case*, University of Bergen, Department of Social Anthropology, Occasional Paper No. 19. 1980, pp. 182-3.
[35] Ministry of Finance and Economic Planning, "Project Rehabilitation Kordofan and Darfur", 1985, p. 3.

1987, this issue was discussed in the Kadugli conference hall between the government, the merchants and the people. The issue was not resolved. I remember one remark, from an Arab, 'The Nuba have no land. They should only throw a stone from the mountain—where the stone falls, that is the limit of their land.'[36] Another one said, 'As for the cows, we will continue taking [stealing] them. The Nuba should drink pig's milk.'

Some people who were active in protesting against the farms were arrested, but I can't think of anyone who was killed. One of the things that people did was they burned the barrels of diesel belonging to the merchants on the schemes. The merchants came with tractors and ploughed right on top of people's cultivation. They could do this because anyone who objected would be arrested. Jeli al Amin is one prominent scheme owner. Adam Kurmiti is another. Musa Osman is one Nuba merchant who was very big—he is with the SPLA now. Others are Fadl Hamad, Hamad Abu Sudur, Jurham Kodi, Merkazu Kuku, Mohamed Merkazu. Many of them have now joined in the *Nafir el Sha'abi* ["Popular Mobilisation"— see Chapter III].[37]

The presence of a number of local Nuba men among the scheme leaseholders demands comment. Some were part of a small but prominent local business elite. Others were richer smallholders. Under its conditions for obtaining finance from the World Bank, the MFC ran what was misleadingly called a "small farmer" project, which meant providing leases of smaller areas—fifty, a hundred or two hundred *feddans*—to the wealthiest among the local farmers. In practice, the allocation of these leases was simply a form of bribery. The influential men of the village were persuaded to support the scheme by being given a small stake in it. Today, the Sudan Government uses the allocation of land leases as one of its major forms of political patronage.

A Sudanese scholar conducted research in four of the villages of this area, Fayo, Kortala, Delami and el Faid (the latter is an Arab

---

[36] This remark was often made, by both local Arabs and government officials.

[37] Ahmed Sayed Nur and El Amin Omer Gardud, interviewed in the Nuba Mountains, 20 May 1995.

village). He found that socio-economic polarisation was most advanced in Fayo.

> In Fayo... in 1981 the entire village was encircled by the establishment of a large-scale scheme, and all the villagers—about 500 families—were reported to have lost their initial [former] plots. In the early 1970s, some of the households started to migrate, while the majority put up a struggle against the MFC plan, and took the matter to the central government offices at Khartoum. Later, the authorities of the MFC allocated nine schemes to the villagers in Fayo. Six of these, with an area of 1000 feddans each, were allocated to the whole village, distributed on the basis of household size and number of dependants. The remaining three schemes, with an area of 1500 feddans each, were allotted to some [45] prominent rich peasants, referred to officially as 'small farmers.' The most obvious and immediate effect of this encroachment is to limit the land available to the peasant households, disrupting their farming system. The households lost access to their previous rotational areas. All the village land has been affected. Indeed it has been taken away as a result of these changes. Although the peasants have been compensated with new plots within the planned area, their overall position has deteriorated because: (i) the land which was taken away was clean and clear of trees and bushes, whereas the compensation plots were not cleared and incurred clearance costs for which no compensation was given; (ii) the bulk of the peasants lost land due to its reallocation to capitalist farmers. The newly granted plots are far smaller than those which were previously cultivated.[38]

He also detailed some of the other losses to the people. They were forced to abandon their rotational system and hence over-exploited the land; they could no longer obtain forest products such as honey, leaves for baskets and mats, building wood and firewood; and they could no longer graze their animals freely.

---

[38] Abdalla Mohammed Elhassan "The encroachment of large-scale mechanised agriculture: Elements of differentiation among the peasantry," in T. Barnett and A. Abdelkarim (eds.) *Sudan: State, Capital and Transformation*, London, Croom Helm, 1988, pp. 163-4.

Not all influential local men were bought off. One was Mek Hussein Karbus el Ehemier, of Sabat.[39]

I was elected mek in 1977. My father was mek before me. I am responsible for the whole of the southern part of Delami. Under the Sudan Government my tasks included collecting taxes, administration and holding the courts. I also participated in inter-tribal conferences. For example in 1986 there was a conflict between the Nuba and the Arabs of Dar Faid. This was related to one Nuba man who was killed by the Arabs while collecting gum Arabic. This became a big issue, and we had a major reconciliation and payment of *diya* [bloodmoney] of LS 33,000. The spirit of the inter-tribal meetings was not good. It was not fair to the Nuba side. What matters is finance, how much you can pay. The Nuba are poor, and the Arabs consider us to be inferior. The administration always supported the Arabs, who were obstinate and had money.

Most Nuba judicial officers used to deny their roots and behave like the Arabs. I felt they were not helpful. Only in rare cases did they assist us. For example there was Deldum el Khatim Asghar, a lawyer in el Obeid. Most of the educated Nuba in our area were inclined to the Arabs.

Land is the big question. The government decided to make agricultural schemes. I felt that the people of Delami were not given their fair share. But when we complained, our boys in the administration sided with the Arabs. Their names were on the list to receive agricultural schemes.

For that reason I spent 65 days in prison. I was arrested in May 1978.

There was an agricultural scheme being made at Hadaba Sinnar, in our area. Each farm in the scheme was 1,500 feddans, as usual. There were five Nuba men from Delami who were taking land in that scheme. We were not consulted. The Government came and said it would distribute the leases. Our Nuba boys agreed with the Jellaba over the cultivation plan. The five who were taking leases were Hamad Abu Sudur, al Hadi Sayed, Nasir Salim, Jurham Omer and Merkazu Kuku. They went and agreed with the director of the MFC. They agreed that it was all undemarcated land. But we

---

[39] Interviewed in Um Dulu, 16 May 1995.

villagers had been using the land for cultivation. So when they came to start their scheme they were evicting us.

I went and complained to the manager of the MFC in Habila. They sent me to Dilling. I went and met the manager of the MFC in Dilling. There I was arrested. I was not charged, but I was told to sign a bond that I would not interfere with the agricultural scheme. I refused. I only accepted to sign that bond after 65 days in prison.

After I signed and came out, a merchant came with his tractor to the scheme to begin cultivation. He was Ali Haroun, a Fellata. He was attacked by villagers and his tractor was destroyed. Another merchant, Izz el Din Suraj, had the same experience. Our people were arrested, so [that] the merchants could continue their farming. They continued until the SPLA came, when the schemes were closed. That was in September 1987. The SPLA arrested Izz el Din and others, including his brother Kamil and another merchant.

At that time the villagers also felt insecure so they left the place. It is abandoned up to now.[40]

Mek Hussein went on to detail another aspect of the land question: disputes with Baggara herders.

We also had problems with the local Arabs. They are Ayatigha and Toghiya. They were always creating problems, especially concerning water. When they came with cows, we would assign them wells so that the cows could drink. But once they had been assigned a well they would capture it for themselves and refuse the villagers access to come and drink.

Another problem was that the Arabs would always enter the farms with their cattle. When the crops were still growing they would come and let their cows graze. If someone complains, the Arab will say, 'What is your farm? Let the cows eat.' And when the people are harvesting they will come and destroy the heaps of crops.

As mek, I would hear the complaints, convene a court and pass judgement. I could impose fines and send people to prison. When I discovered that the Arabs were ready to pay any fine without being worried, I began to send them to prison in Delami. Many were released when they appealed to Dilling, so they never spent the

---

[40] He was released from captivity in Ethiopia after negotiations between the SPLA and the National Alliance in 1988.

terms of their sentence inside. I would sentence up to my maximum power of six months but they never spent longer than two or at most three months in prison.

There were several reasons for the increase in the number and violence of farmer-nomad disputes in the early and mid-1980s: one of them was the spread of mechanised farming itself. The mechanised farms were a disaster for the nomads, who lost their pastures and their migration routes, losses that became particularly disastrous during times of drought, such as 1983-4, 1987 and 1990. One Sudanese scholar who has studied the Nuba Mountains writes:[41]

> The same awkward situation applies to the nomads who lost their traditional grazing lands, water points and animal routes to the schemes. It is estimated that 80 per cent of the 350,000 pastoralists and agro-pastoralists of Southern Kordofan province are seriously affected by the expansion of large-scale mechanized schemes. This is mainly because the owners of the schemes do not abide by the agricultural practices devised by the Mechanised Farming Corporation. They have in many cases cultivated even the animal tracks (width two kilometres) specified by the Corporation. [There is] continuous conflict between the owners of the large-scale mechanized schemes and the pastoralists... pastoral nomads are driven out of the best areas of their traditional pasture to places which are not favourable to their herd growth, and agropastoralists are being subjected to various socio-economic pressures to abandon one of the two activities and change over to agricultural labourers with lower standards of living.

For nomads, mechanised farming also spelled major disruption to the entire cycle of pastoralism. Freedom of the range is essential to livestock rearing in dry climes. In South Kordofan, cattle-herders normally move north in June and south in September-October. They used to follow the routes with the greenest pasture and most plentiful

---

[41] M. A. Mohamed Salih, "The tractor and the plough: The sociological dimension," in M. A. Mohamed Salih (ed.) *Agrarian Change in the Central Rangelands: Sudan, A Socio-economic Analysis*, Uppsala, Scandanavian Institute of African Studies, 1987, pp. 112-13.

water. Now, the nomadic herds must move rapidly and under tight control down narrow corridors—a labour-intensive operation. In the hot, dry season of February-May, every acre of grassland becomes precious, and the survival of an entire herd—the livelihood of many families—can depend upon finding grass or fodder on the right day. In the dry season of a dry year, Baggara herders were under acute stress.

Mechanised farms are well-defended: the penalties for intrusion are severe. Smallholdings are not. Pastoralists and their cattle increasingly pushed onto smallholdings. This was no small factor in the explosion of disputes over land that began in the 1980s.

Nuba farmers resisted the merchant farmers and their tractors. Many burned the barrels of diesel, others threatened the labourers. Ultimately, many turned to the SPLA. Yagoub Osman Kaloka described the confrontation in Tira el Akhdar:[42]

In the Tira area, our big problem in the late 1970s and early '80s was the Government of Sudan policy of taking fertile land for mechanised farms. They drove the local people off. This happened at Karandel, el Azraq and Um Lubiya, a total of three projects. The government people came and said, 'Go back to your mountains.' The leaseholders of the schemes were all Arabs and Nuba from the north. People lost their farms and were driven to go to the mountains. But they also had a big problem of where to graze their animals. The policy on the schemes was very strict. If a single cow passes into the farm, the fine can be one sack of sorghum or the equivalent in money—or even the cow itself.

When our youth in Khartoum and the northern towns saw these things, they began to know that the Sudan Government is not our government. The people became hostile. Even Moslem elders abandoned Islam for Christianity or traditional religion. They said, 'If all Moslems are brothers, then we are not their brothers. We are not Arabs, and not even brother Moslems. It is better not to be slave Moslems.'

So we began to organise. Some youth contacted Anyanya II in Ethiopia during 1980-82. Some Anyanya II groups came to the mechanised farms, pretending to be workers, to recruit people

---

[42] Interviewed in Tira Limon, 23 May 1995.

there. This was before the SPLA. The Anyanya II cadres even came into the village at night and recruited youth. The youth in our area took a position against the government. But there were also some government spies, and the administration in Heiban focused its attention on Tira el Akhdar.

In 1983, I came on holiday to Lubi [my village]. At that time the Governor of Kadugli visited Lubi. The people raised their problems with him. They said, 'We are Nuba Tira. We only want the government to leave our land, and leave us to cultivate and graze our animals in peace. If the government does not solve our problem, we Tira will solve the problem by ourselves.' So the Governor became worried. He said he would send a committee to solve our problems. But nothing happened.

The mechanised farms were not keen on hiring local workers. They brought their labourers from Dilling and Rahad by lorry. This made the Tira people unhappy. So they came *en masse* with their spears, carbines and knives and so on and threatened the workers. That was in June 1983. The workers took the threat and left. Then—it was the beginning of the rainy season—the locals came with their seeds and began to plant their sorghum and sesame. There was no problem that season. We cultivated and harvested.

The government did not let this challenge pass without reprisals. The fate of the Tira people was to bear the brunt of one of the government's first big offensives in the Nuba Mountains, which is described in Chapter II.

During the brief multi-party period of 1985-9, a few politicians began to take up the issue of land, and try to defend the interests of smallholders. This was one of the concerns of the General Union of the Nuba Mountains, whose political charter stated its intention "to implement a land reform policy for the benefit of the indigenous farmers of the Nuba Mountains and to eradicate the feudalistic land policies and relations of production [and] all forms of exploitation."[43] Unfortunately, this debate did not progress far, and was completely silenced by the 1989 coup.

The present military government has been far more draconian in its land policies than any of its predecessors. The expropriation of

---

[43] Quoted in M. A. Mohamed Salih, 1989, p. 109.

land for mechanised farming has accelerated, based upon legislation that gives the government almost unlimited power over land allocation. The 1990 amendment to the Civil Transactions Act has swept away *all* customary title to land. The first provision of the amendment states that "All non-registered land should be considered as if registered in the name of the State." It also decreed that all land cases before the courts were to be struck off, and prohibited judicial recourse against land allocation decisions made by the government. In a single legal act, the Sudan Government took legal hold of all smallholders' land, not only in the Nuba Mountains, but throughout Sudan. Combined with the law against "criminal trespass," this is the legal foundation for the dispossession of the Nuba.

SERVANTS AND LABOURERS

One of the commonest experiences of Nuba men is working as a migrant labourer in Khartoum, the Northern towns, or on the big agricultural schemes of central and eastern Sudan. By the 1970s, as many as half of the adult men of some Nuba tribes were migrant labourers. It was in these towns that much Nuba political consciousness was moulded. Nuba migrants experienced discrimination at first hand. In the North, "Nuba" does not refer to the rich variety of proud cultures to be found in the Nuba Mountains, but to the second-class citizens who sweep the streets and clean the latrines.

The formative role of labour migration is made clear in the following account, provided by an SPLA soldier, explaining his reasons for taking up arms. Tom Suleiman Umbele is 33. He is from Eri, in Otoro, and joined the SPLA at the age of 25—older than most of his comrades. He first left the Nuba Mountains in the 1970s:[44]

> I was a student in primary school in Kauda. I was in third form when I left to Khartoum to stay with my uncle. That was during the school holidays. I was hoping to get a better education in Khartoum. I found that my uncle had no resources to put me

---

[44] Interviewed in Tira Limon, 21 May 1995.

through school, but I decided it was better to continue in Khartoum. Even I had no money for transport back to Kauda.

I immediately worked as a casual labourer in Wad Medani. While we were working, we had many disputes with our employers, mostly because of the deductions from our pay for daily allowances. It was a textile company, and we felt it ought to have regulations, rather than being run in that way. So I went to Gedaref and worked as an agricultural labourer. In Gedaref, I cut sesame. But the same situation came up again. At the end of the contract, when we had finished, again they gave us less money than we had agreed. When we complained, they said, 'You do not have the right to complain as you are rebels.' Being in the bush, those merchants had the means to eliminate us without trace.[45] So we submitted. We moved to the Kenana sugar factory to cut sugar cane. But the same situation continued in the sugar plantations. Also they told us, 'We have to reduce your pay from what we agreed because we have to give a portion to the Sudan army to fight against the rebels, because you black people have rebelled. This will be your contribution to the army.'

This made me and the others decide that the best thing to do is to go and join the SPLA and get freedom, so at least our children can have a brighter future than us. A group of four of us, all Nuba, left Kenana in June 1987. We moved from Chukur in August 1987, and met up with a group of 480 at Achiron. We were students, farmers, workers, teachers. Our commander was Telefon Kuku [Abu Jelha]. From there we went for training at Bilfam in Ethiopia. We returned here in 1989.

Innumerable Nuba migrant workers have had similar experiences. Racism pervades their lives in the North. Osman Nyatembe Jarad, an Otoro from Kauda aged 27, had been subjected to the same pattern of humiliation and hopelessness. He spent seven years as a migrant worker in Khartoum:[46]

I was always approached to become a servant, though I am a grown-up person. Sometimes you are just walking on the street, and

---

[45] Killing of Nuba and Southern labourers in Gedaref was not uncommon in the late 1980s.

[46] Interviewed in Tira Limon, 21 May 1995.

you are arrested for no reason. This happened to me many times. I worked as a casual labourer. I also worked two years as a servant, employed by an Arab family, washing clothes, ironing, going on errands to the market.

Discrimination has affected Nuba in all positions. Najib Musa Berdo, aged 38 is now a judge in the central court of Lagowa, having been demobilised by the SPLA and asked to train as a lawyer.[47]

I joined the SPLA in 1990. Before that I was in the military HQ in Khartoum. Our people in Khartoum were always being tortured. I used to see them being tortured; even I was asked to come and participate. Even for us, who continued to work with them, we were not given a fair chance for training or promotion. In short we were doing the dirty jobs.

I have my brother who was a soldier in the [government] army and who was killed in the South. He left a wife and two children. One of the sad incidents was in the rains [floods] of 1988. Sahafa was affected and their house, just one room, was destroyed. The woman went to the local authorities for assistance. She was refused. She went to the army as the wife of a martyr. Also she was not assisted. Then she came home and decided to make *merissa* [sorghum beer] to get some money to rebuild her house. She was arrested and taken to prison. At that time she had a very small child who died in prison. She continued in prison, while her other children stayed alone in the house. I was moving between the prison and the house. I was very unhappy.

Because I was bitter I went to the General HQ and complained. I was militarily disciplined and accused of being a fifth columnist [SPLA sympathiser]. I was due to go to the military college—a big chance for NCOs—but my name was cancelled and I was put under surveillance. When the surveillance became tight and I felt they were going to harm me, I left my family and my brother's family behind and came to the SPLA.

I reported to the SPLA at Julud, in Dilling county.

---

[47] Interviewed in Achiron, 7 May 1995. See Chapter V for a discussion of the administration of justice under the SPLA.

Such discrimination was intensified during the war, caused by the government's suspicion that Nuba people had sympathies with the SPLA. But it was built upon a longer, deeper history of systematic denial of opportunities to Nuba. It was only when the first generation of educated Nuba began to obtain jobs that the realities of discrimination became clear, and resistance began to be organised. Commander Ismail Khamis Jellab explained part of the background to his own reasons for joining the SPLA:[48]

Historically, there were relations between some Nuba tribes and some Misiriya clans. For example, we the Tima had good relations with the Duhreymat, Awlad Salim, Eyeinat and Awlad Serer; the Tullishi had good relations with the Awlad Kudu. My name Ismail was given to me because we had an Arab who was a good friend of the family who had that name.

There were many incidents of difference or dispute but we always succeeded to settle them peacefully. The main incidents were farm issues, such as nomads bringing cattle on to farms. Sometimes there were cases of homicide. By the 1980s we didn't feel serious political differences with them, but that was because of a lack of political awareness. We had few educated people.

Our generation is the first group of educated people in the area. We realised there was oppression and exploitation. We found that education was dominated by the Misiriya and Jellaba. Even the lower jobs, the Nuba never got them. We felt this deeply, that there was a policy for the Nuba tribes in our area, to stop their education at the level of intermediate school.

Even the few educated people, when they come back to the area, they are harassed and not given any opportunities in the area. The lucky ones who have a position, the moment they have any differences with the Misiriya or Jellaba, they are alleged to be agitators and are immediately transferred away.

---

[48] Interviewed in Um Dulu, 19 May 1995.

POLITICAL MOBILIZATION

Nuba politicians were active as members of various different political parties during the 1950s but the first Nuba political party was organised in 1963, under the name General Union of the Nuba Mountains (GUN). Father Philip Abbas Ghabboush was one of the founding members, and has continued to play an influential role in both Nuba and national politics ever since. In the 1965 general elections which followed the October 1964 popular uprising against the military government, GUN won eight seats in South Kordofan. Fr. Philip was the leader of the party. He was active in the parliament, and tried to build a coalition with MPs from other marginal areas of Sudan including Darfur and the Beja Hills.

But the promise of democracy was betrayed. During the 1965-9 parliamentary period, there was no resolution to the war in the South and no political enfranchisement of the marginal areas of the North. Politics remained dominated by a cartel of Northern families. There was discontent among Nuba army officers, some of whom spoke with Southerners about the possibilities of joint military action.

In Sudan, plans for military take-over instigated by Nuba and Southerners are invariably referred to as "racist coup plots". Fr. Philip himself was involved in a coup plot, scheduled for 28 May 1969. This was forestalled by Colonel Jaafar Nimeiri by a matter of days, and Fr. Philip and other leading Nuba politicians either went into exile or became politically inactive. There was another attempted coup, centred among Nuba and Southerners in the garrison in Juba, in 1976, which was betrayed to the government just hours before it was planned to go ahead.[49]

Fr Philip and other former GUN politicians returned to Sudan with the policy of "national reconciliation" in 1978. Fr Philip became a member of the National Assembly. He was arrested in 1983 for

---

[49] One of the leading plotters, Yousif Karra Haroun, is now an SPLA commander in the Nuba Mountains. Another, Yunis Domi Kallo, is now a civilian, and Secretary General of the Nuba Relief, Rehabilitation and Development Society (NRRDS).

allegedly a "racial coup", along with some Southern and Nuba military officers including Yunis Abu Sudur.[50] They were amnestied in 1984.

For two decades, Yousif Kuwa Mekki has had a profound influence on the politics of the Nuba Mountains. In 1977, he was among a group of Nuba at the University of Khartoum who took the lead in rejecting what they saw as the bankrupt politics of the older generation of Nuba politicians, and instead founded a Nuba political movement upon the new generation. They felt that the GUN and its leaders had failed them, while the Sudan Socialist Union (the sole legal party at the time) was dominated by Baggara and Jellaba. A basic principle of the movement was a return to the cultural roots of the Nuba. Clandestine from the outset, the organization was given the name "Komolo", a word that in the Miri and Kadugli languages means "youth".

Yousif Kuwa was the first president of Komolo. Other important members included Telefon Kuku Abu Jelha[51], Daniel Kodi,[52] and Abdel Aziz al Hilu[53] all of whom later joined the SPLA. In the elections to the National Assembly, Daniel Kodi won a seat. Komolo made approaches to Southern political organisations, but was rebuffed. In 1980, Yousif Kuwa returned to Kadugli as a schoolteacher. He took the opportunity to begin organising Komolo in the town.

In 1981, President Nimeiri embarked upon a policy of regionalisation, which involved creating a Regional Government for Kordofan in el Obeid. Elections to the Regional Assembly were held, and despite his lack of resources to finance a campaign, Yousif Kuwa won a seat.

---

[50] Yunis Abu Sudur later joined the SPLA, and died in 1994 in suspicious circumstances (see Chapter V). Ismail Khamis Jellab was also briefly detained in connection with this alleged coup.

[51] An SPLA commander in the Nuba Mountains, currently under detention and charged with mutiny.

[52] Currently SPLM Minister of Tourism, resident in Cairo.

[53] An SPLA commander, currently head of logistics at SPLA headquarters. His ancestors originally came from Dar Masalit, in Darfur, but he has fully assimilated to the Nuba.

Regionalisation should have been an opportunity for marginal groups such as the Nuba. In fact, it became another obstacle to their political advancement. The Kordofan Regional Government was dominated from the outset by powerful Arab interests—a coalition of North Kordofan interests with South Kordofan Baggara and Jellaba—who were ruthless in distributing largesse to their local supporters. Perhaps most importantly, the Regional Ministry of Agriculture distributed land leases on its own behalf, putting more distance between the leaseholders and the regulations theoretically enforced by the MFC—and increasing the leeway for abuse. Bias in the allocation of rationed commodities such as sugar and wheat became more marked.

The Nuba members in the Regional Parliament also felt that the entire electoral process was also against them. From a total 55 seats in the Regional Assembly, only four were won by the Nuba. They argued that this represented a deliberate bias in the allocation of seats—North Kordofan had more than South Kordofan. This in fact can be explained by the higher population of North Kordofan. The scarcity of Nuba members of the assembly was more closely related to their problems in organising a political front within a single-party system and the lack of finance for campaigning costs. Another complaint from the Nuba members was the appointment to positions in the Regional Government, by the Governor, Fatih Bushara. Members from North Kordofan took most of the senior positions, and the highest given to a Nuba member was deputy. Yousif Kuwa was appointed Deputy Speaker in the assembly, and repeatedly clashed with the Governor on this and other issues.

Komolo and its leaders also had a problem of rivalry with the former GUN politicians such Fr. Philip Ghabboush. The question arose of whether it should be a regional or a racial movement. Fr. Philip preferred to form a regional movement, with a significant Baggara representation. Komolo, on the other hand, was fiercely Nuba in its identity. Splits in the Nuba movement were becoming more evident by 1984. Yousif Kuwa opted to join the SPLA.

After the 1985 Popular Uprising, Fr Philip formed the Sudan National Party (SNP). It was a feverish and hopeful time, with the Transitional Military Council of General Abdel Rahman Suwar el

Dahab and Prime Minister Gizouli Dafallah promising democracy. But the commitment to pluralistic democracy did not run deep. In October 1985, Prime Minister Gizouli claimed to have uncovered a "racial coup" led by Philip Abbas Ghabboush and some Southerners to overthrow the government. Fr Philip was arrested along with many Nuba soldiers and civilians. Three months later the civilian detainees were released without charge, but the soldiers remained in prison for up to four years after conviction in a court martial that was a mockery of justice—no witnesses nor documentary evidence were produced.

The SNP quickly emerged as the principal Nuba party. The high status of Fr Philip Ghabboush ensured that it would garner most of the Nuba votes. It organised not only in the Nuba Mountains, but also among Nuba communities in Khartoum, Gedaref and Port Sudan. Even before the elections, scheduled for April 1986, the Nuba began to show their electoral muscle. In Port Sudan, the Nuba formed part of an electoral coalition against the National Islamic Front, which was strongly represented by the Beni Amer. In a violent riot in February 1986, the Nuba played the leading role in expelling the Beni Amer from a ward of Port Sudan. A number of lives were lost on the Beni Amer side.

A second Nuba party was also formed, that used the name General Union of the Nuba Mountains (GUN). Led by Professor el Amin Hamoda, it represented younger Nuba intellectuals. Although it failed to make headway amongst ordinary voters, it exercised influence through the trade union movement. While GUN shared with Komolo the agenda of forging a specifically Nuba identity, the SNP had aspirations to be a national party. But this did not prevent co-operation. In July 1985, both SNP and GUN were instrumental in creating a coalition known as Rural Solidarity, that embraced political organisations from all the marginalised areas of Sudan, including the South, Darfur, Southern Blue Nile and the Beja Hills. Meanwhile, Komolo continued its underground activities in Khartoum and Kadugli.

Strong Nuba representation in Khartoum and active campaigning by the Rural Solidarity coalition made two seats in the capital virtually safe for the SNP: Umbadda South and Haj Yousif. But internal politics within the SNP undermined the chances for success. Fr Philip was chairman of the SNP when the decision was taken of how to distribute the constituencies. The party had decided that Mohamed Hamad Kuwa should contest the Nuba-dominated Umbadda South while Fr Philip's deputy, Hassan al Mahi, who is a Misiriya, should contest a safe seat in Kordofan. But Fr Philip decided unilaterally to nominate Hassan al Mahi for Umbadda South, at a stroke making it a marginal seat. Mohamed Hamad Kuwa was transferred to Mayo, a seat dominated by the NIF. Neither won.

In April 1986, Fr Philip won his seat in Haj Yousif: the first time that any non-Arab had won a constituency in Greater Khartoum. It came as a shock to the political elites.

In parliament, the SNP joined with Southern parties to form the Union of Sudan African Parties (USAP). Fr Philip was the Chairman, Eliaba James Surur was his deputy (and acting chairman when Fr Philip was abroad for medical treatment in 1988-9). The main activities of USAP were campaigning for the repeal of the 1983 "September" Islamic laws, pushing for a peaceful settlement to the war and calling for a constitutional conference to determine a more equitable distribution of wealth and power in Sudan.

However, Nuba parliamentary politics continued to be divisive, concerned with personal ambition and power games as much as representation of the people's interests. Many Nuba became increasingly frustrated, not only with the direction of Sudan's democracy under Prime Minister Sadiq el Mahdi, but also the manner in which the Nuba political leadership, especially the SNP, seemed unable to challenge this effectively. This scepticism about parliamentary politics was intensified when, in 1988, one of the SNP MPs, Haroun Kafi, was arrested and detained in defiance of his parliamentary immunity, as part of a deepening crackdown against the Nuba leadership.

II

WAR IN THE NUBA MOUNTAINS

For nine years we have not seen any peace.

Kabashi Karkandu Jellab, a nurse from
Lagowa, interviewed in Achiron, 7 May
1995.

War came to the Nuba Mountains in July 1985. There were two
nearly simultaneous events, neither of them directly connected with
the Nuba, that were to have a profound impact on the future of the
Nuba. One was a raid by an SPLA unit based in the South, just over
the internal border at Gardud. The SPLA unit, which did not contain
Nuba troops, attacked a camp of Baggara Arabs and killed sixty and
wounded 82, including both militiamen and civilians. As on other
occasions when the war has crossed into the North, the reaction of
the government was immediate and strong. The Baggara were
assisted and armed, and a wave of anti-SPLA sentiment was
whipped up.

The second event was the decision of the ruling Transitional
Military Council to arm the Baggara, specifically the Misiriya Zurug
and Humr. In a series of meetings, the then-Minister of Defence,
Fadallah Burma Nasir, who is himself a Misiriya Zurug, created the
Misiriya militia, widely known as the Murahaliin, and renowned for
its ferocity. For several years, there had already been an informal
Misiriya militia, partly created by landowning interests and partly as
an "oilfields special force" to protect Chevron's oil installations. The
drought and famine of 1983-5 had also impoverished many Baggara
cattle herders, encouraging many young men to turn to violence in
their search for a source of income. From 1985 onwards, the

Murahaliin were to become a powerful force, initially directed against the Dinka, but subsequently also against the Nuba.

THE WAR BEGINS, 1985-88

The militia policy set in place by Fadallah Burma in 1985 was continued during the 1986-9 parliamentary period, when Kordofan was ruled by men with close links to the militia. During 1987-9 the Governor was Abdel Rasoul el Nur. A Misiriya and Sadiq el Mahdi's former personal secretary, he was jointly responsible for the Murahaliin policy along with Fadallah Burma (who remained powerful and was appointed Minister of State and advisor to the Ministry of Defence in 1988) and Hireka Izz el Din (chairman of the Umma parliamentary group 1986-9). The then-Minister of the Interior, Mubarak al Fadl, is an Umma stalwart who is seen by many as the architect of the militia policy. Another important Umma hard-liner was Abdel Rahman Abu al Bashar, a merchant and party leader in Kadugli. Not a militia leader as such, he co-operated closely with military intelligence in their operations.

Brig. Hamed el Sheikh was posted to the Nuba Mountains in 1987, as military commander of the 18th Brigade. He is also a Baggara Arab. Another significant appointment in 1987 was Lt.-Col. Ahmed Khamis to military intelligence. Ahmed Khamis has since been promoted to head of military intelligence in South Kordofan, and is consistently named by former detainees as responsible for detentions, torture and execution. His origins are obscure: he has told people that he is a Misiriya Arab, but he is widely believed to be at least partly Nuba, according to different versions from Abu Januq and Shawabna.

The Murahaliin

The arming of the Misiriya Baggara immediately created fear in many parts of the Nuba Mountains. At the outset, it was a charter for Arab nomads to become more violent and aggressive in their dealings with the Nuba. Although the Misiriya were present in largest numbers on the western side, the impact of the creation of the Murahaliin was even felt in the north-eastern Kawalib mountains. Two residents described how the war began:[1]

> When the militia of Fadallah Burma was formed, immediately our Arab neighbours began to become very aggressive and rob us. The first incident was when Mohamed Barbur was shot in the leg. He had to have his leg amputated afterwards. Barbur lived in Andona village and his whole herd of cattle, 75 in total, were robbed. That was in September 1986. The responsible ones were a joint group of Ayatigha and Awlad Ghabbush. The Kawalib people mobilised themselves and followed the Arabs. But the Arabs were well armed and with their volume of fire, the Nuba were repulsed. Four people were killed: the brother of Barbur, his wife and their twin children.
>
> There was no court and no chance for getting recourse through the law.
>
> By that time we were strangers to each other. If you went to their *fariq* [nomadic camp] you would not return. And if one of them came to our village, he wouldn't go back.
>
> There was a sequence of events in Delami rural council. We can tell you one. In the rainy season of 1987, all the young boys who took the cows to graze in the plains, in areas also used by the Arabs, were taken. They were abducted with their cattle and not allowed to return. They have still not returned up to today. The boys were between ten and fifteen years when they were taken; we don't know the number but they were many. They had nearly three-quarters of all the Delami Nuba cows with them.
>
> Other incidents were sudden attacks, when they kill and rob. It was armed robbery.

The Miri also had problems with the militia—compounded by the attitude of their chief.[2]

> Another big problem was the question of arms. In 1985, we were called by our mek, Mohamed el Zaki, who told us to register our arms so we could be given ammunition. But it was a trick. All the

---

[1] Ahmed Sayed Nur and el Amin Omer Gardud, interviewed in Tira Limon, 20 May 1995.
[2] Musa Kuwa Jabir Tiya, interviewed in Um Dulu, 17 May 1995.

ammunition was given to the Arabs. And in 1987, when the SPLA came, the Government came and confiscated all the rifles.

The problems really intensified in 1985. You would be in your farm, when Arabs would come to your farm with their cattle. You are forced to be quiet and watch the cows eat. There were many incidents. I recall one. An Arab came to our village and spoke to a woman. When I passed by, she said that the Arab wanted to buy a donkey. The Arab said to me, 'Actually this is my donkey.' I objected: 'This donkey was born here. It has a history here. We know it.' He threatened us with his gun, it was a G3, so he took the donkey. We went to the police and reported a case of theft and intimidation. The police did nothing.

No-one would stand up for us in the police force or with the local administration. No-one was sympathetic.

After the SPLA came to the mountains in 1987, the government came to search for guns. They started with their list of 1985. If you had a gun, they would arrest you. They also made a special force comprised of the Murahaliin and the army, whose work was to disarm the Miri. This force also started stealing cows.

The SPLA first entered the Miri land only in June 1989.

In December 1987, the army and Murahaliin came to Fama, in the Shatt Damam area, and also forcibly disarmed the population. During the operation, three people were reported killed by the militia and thirteen were detained and beaten by the army. The militia also killed five civilians and burned many houses in Shatt Damam itself at that time. In February-March 1988, there was another militia assault, in which Kwololo, Um Muzariq and Hajar el Dabib were burned, and four people killed. The people from the burned villages ran to Shatt Damam, which lies in the hills and is more easily defensible.

Even where the Murahaliin did not penetrate, their activities had an impact, in terms of creating Nuba solidarity. For example, this was the case among the Nyima.[3]

In 1985, the start of the Murahaliin had an impact. The Murahaliin of Fadallah Burma were concentrated on Lagowa, not Dilling. Our

---

[3] Interviewed in Um Dulu, 19 May 1995.

63

Arabs were Shanabla and Hamar, not Misiriya. So the immediate impact was in the economy. There was an interruption of trade due to fear. Trade fell away. But socially, the Nuba people of the western side stood together against the practices being followed by the Arabs in Lagowa. This solidarity even affected the meks! The youths decided to ask for arms to defend the Lagowa people.

The knowledge that the SPLA was recruiting among the Nuba gave the militia the pretext for stepping up their raids. Although there was no SPLA presence in the western jebels until July 1989, the fact that well-known Nuba from the area had joined the movement was reason enough for attacks. A nurse from Lagowa summarised what had happened:[4]

> For nine years we have not seen any peace. Originally, our relations with the Arabs were good, to the extent that our farms were next to each other. Immediately when the SPLA came and they saw sons from the area, like [Commander] Ismail [Khamis Jellab], they began to be hostile and accused us all to be rebels. The Arabs closest to us, Dar Heimad, Nimat and Awlad Surur [a branch of the Humr], all became hostile to us.
>
> When they started to be hostile they came to our village and shot into the air at night to frighten us. When they saw we were not frightened, they went ahead and brought their cattle into our farms. When we saw the cows were eating our crops and they were not ready to get them out, we assembled and decided to fight them.
>
> They had modern guns. We had old guns, *marmatons*, but we still chased them. From then the relationship worsened. The Arabs left and brought the army, and armed themselves more. The government began to attack us and continued attacking us. The problems never stopped.

The various Murahaliin groups were active raiding cattle, burning and killing Nuba civilians in ones and twos from 1985 onwards. On one occasion at least, they escalated their activities and perpetrated a massacre, on the pretext of SPLA presence. This was in March 1987 at Saburi, just east of Kadugli. The Rawawga, Fukhara

---

[4] Kabashi Karkandu Jellab, interviewed in Achiron, 7 May 1995.

and Dar Bilal sections of the Hawazma militia were responsible. Mudir Dafallah Kapsaleb is a native of Saburi, who described what happened:[5]

> Daldum of the [SPLA] Volcano Battalion went to the village on his way towards Kadugli. He stopped at Deldako, near Rosires, near Kadugli. This information was passed to the Murahaliin in Kadugli. So the Murahaliin of Hilat Goz, under the command of Mohamed el Kelas, overall commander of the militia in Kadugli sector, went to Rosires. There was another group of Murahaliin, from Abu Safifa, ahead of them who robbed Rosires village and stole the cattle. The villagers sent a delegation of three to Kadugli to inform the authorities. Kelas met them on the road at 3 p.m. He also saw villagers running after their cattle. Kelas killed the three. They were: Mohamed Musa, Hussein Bringi and Omer Kano. He left the bodies and cordoned off Rosires village. The Murahaliin started shooting, and killed 83 men, women and children. The dead included Sheikh Khamis Kori. Among my direct family there were: Hamad al Mudir, Hussein Deldum, Hamad Atta, Mohamed Belal, Attiya Kori, my older sister Hikmat Dafallah, my aunt Fatima Musa, Toto Kafi, Khadija Hamid, Kanu Tiya, my fiancée Selma Hamad, and many more.
> The village was burned and looted. The remaining people ran to Hajar el Mek, or to the Moro areas of Kurichi and Um Sirdiba.

The area of Saburi, Rosires and Laguri was also subjected to army and militia attacks in November 1989 (31 people killed, most of them shot after being tied up by the PDF[6]), October 1990, November 1991 (forty people abducted who have not been seen since) and November 1992 (fourteen people abducted).

SPLA Recruitment

In 1986, a tiny "Jebels Task Force" clandestinely entered the Nuba Mountains to recruit for the SPLA. Up to that time, all Nuba recruits

---

[5] Interviewed in Kauda, 11-12 May 1995.
[6] Petition from Um Lawya chiefs to Sudan Government, 22 November 1989.

to the SPLA had gone through Khartoum or Gedaref, where there was a covert pipeline for smuggling volunteers to Ethiopia. The "Jebels Task Force" was present in the Achiron mountains during the rains of 1986, before going south again.

The first SPLA fighting force to enter the Nuba Mountains came the following rainy season. Under Commander Abdel Aziz al Hilu the Volcano Battalion came to organise large-scale recruitment, before returning South with the recruits for training in Ethiopia. Yousif Kuwa was another of the commanders, who left for the Nuba Mountains in May 1987. The first battle between the Nuba battalion of the SPLA and the Sudan army took place in June, at Rimla (in the south of Tira Limon). There were further engagements in Um Dorein and Um Dulu, but the main purpose of the incursion was to mobilise the recruits who had trekked to the Achiron mountains to volunteer for the SPLA. Small scouting groups were sent throughout the southern and eastern jebels.

The main force of Volcano Battalion returned south again after the rains, leaving just a few troops under Abdel Aziz al Hilu. It was not until January 1989 that the New Kush Division, six battalions commanded by Yousif Kuwa Mekki, entered the Nuba Mountains.

The Army Wreaks Vengeance

The Sudan Armed Forces undertook relatively few military operations in the first years of the war. Hardly any of these were directed against the SPLA, which had no permanent presence in the area, and no military bases. The southern jebels, which lay on the route used by the SPLA to enter the mountains, were the first to suffer. Hamad Tutu Dabah, now chairman of the civil administration of Buram County, explained that the area of Hajar el Dabib had already suffered a militia attack in January 1986. A year later, the army took pre-emptive action ahead of the SPLA advance:[7]

> Buram area was first attacked by the government on 14 January 1987. The government troops came from Kadugli and burned the

---

[7] Interviewed in Um Dulu, 17 May 1995.

villages. Forty-two persons were killed and fifteen were arrested in Gotang. On 20 April 1987 the army burned the village of Kwololo. In 1988, Kwololo and Tarawi were burned again, on 17 May.

During 1987, SPLA recruitment was centred in the mountains of Tira Limon. Jibreel Tutu Jiran, a Deacon of the Roman Catholic Church, explained that this was previously a very isolated area, and how it reaped the vengeance of the Sudan army:[8]

> In Tira Limon, we used to have almost no contact with the Arabs. All our original houses were in the mountains. After our numbers increased, some of us later came down into the plains, for example to Rimla, al Goz and Kandermi. Of these places, now only Rimla remains.
>
> Only the Kandermi people had any contact with the Arabs. Some Jellaba came and settled there, and some nomads came—Awlad Ghabbush and Shanabla. So the Kandermi people were mostly becoming Moslems.
>
> The problems began in 1986 when our relations with the government and the Arabs turned bad, because of the SPLA camp in our mountains. The Arabs turned hostile and started burning.
>
> At the end of 1987, the SPLA had left, so the army could now go to the mountains. They burned many villages. The first was al Goz, burned in December 1987. Karkar was also burned that December, along with Delebaya, which is part of Rimla. They went on into the mountains themselves and burned some villages up there, including Lodo, Chanyaro, Tojoro and Topey. They also burned Achiron, in the mountains.
>
> In 1988, the only village to be burned was Kureha. But there was widespread detention and torture and looting. Nearly all the villages of Tira Limon were robbed, by day and by night. Many people were executed. For example, Fakali Chupa, brother of the mek, was handed over to the government and killed. Another was Tabanya, a man whose house was at the top of a big hill, so he could see the army coming before others. He used to go and warn people of the attacks, so he was captured and killed. Another killed was Haroun.

---

[8] Interviewed in Tira Limon, 22 May 1995.

Korongo Abdalla also sent recruits to the SPLA, and duly suffered in 1987, when army officers called upon the militia for assistance:[9]

> In that year, the army attacked and destroyed Abu Sunun, Kursi, Kufa, Churaro and Sogole. They killed two civilians. The Arab Murahaliin knew the places and went ahead, the army followed them. The Murahaliin know every village and every house, that is why the army always operates with them.

Yagoub Osman Kaloka's account of how Tira el Akhdar farmers resisted the alienation of their land for mechanised farms has been presented in Chapter I. His brother, the sheikh, was also arrested and murdered by the government (see below). The inevitable result of antagonism from the government was that the youth turned to the SPLA:[10]

> In 1986, more than one hundred Tira youths joined the SPLA. The garrison at Heiban put Tira, especially Lubi, on the blacklist: 'These people are rebels.' At that time, they were not burning villages, but they were killing. In July, a force went from Kalkada and arrested Ibrahim, and two from Otoro, Kauda, and took them to Heiban and slaughtered them there.
>   In 1987, the Volcano Battalion came and found all the youth in the area ready to join. More than one thousand Tira youths joined the SPLA in 1987. They returned to Ethiopia and then came back with the Kush Division in 1989.

The villagers of Lubi were to find out what being "blacklisted" meant. Their village was the first to be destroyed in the Tira el Akhdar area.

> On Tuesday 11 July 1988, soldiers from Heiban and Mendi were sent. They met at Kalkada, and proceeded to Tajura, Timbera and on to Karandel. There was a big market meeting that day. They stayed in the market the whole day, as though they were doing

---

[9] Interviewed in Um Dulu, 17 May 1995.
[10] Interviewed in Tira Limon, 23 May 1995.

nothing. Then in the evening they started to search for youths to arrest them. But almost all of the Lubi youths had run away when they saw the army there. The soldiers moved from the market around 4 or 5 p.m. and went to Lubi village. They arrived just before sunset and deployed themselves in the village marketplace.

The soldiers summoned the sheikh, who donated them two sheep. They slept the night there. The villagers served them with food and water. But the Lubi people were also suspicious, and that evening they quietly evacuated their houses and slept outside the village.

In the early morning of the next day, the soldiers formed a big line and started moving through the village, breaking down the doors of shops and houses. Whatever was movable was looted, whatever was not lootable was burned. The remainder of the people in the village fled. The soldiers searched the whole village and then burned the entire place. They looted every house. They took two thousand cows, 32 bicycles and all sorts of personal possessions. But no-one was killed, not even injured. That was not their aim. There was no SPLA in the area, and no-one to fight.

The cows, sheep, the metal beds, the chairs, etc, they loaded them onto their lorries. Then using their 16mm gun they started to shell randomly at the surrounding area. After that they drove off to Um Derafi, near Kauda. There they looted again, but didn't burn. The officers stopped the men, saying that their mission was only to burn Lubi as those people are rebels. But they took some of the Um Derafi people to Talodi. One was called Ibrahim, he was tied up and tortured and nearly died. Later he was released, though his hands are nearly paralysed.

After that, whoever was left went to the SPLA. Even the elders and the mothers said, 'It's better to join the SPLA than stay here and be killed. The elders may die, but you go and take a rifle.' So many Tira were ready to go to the SPLA. Even small children joined the SPLA, and went with them to Ethiopia hoping to go to school. Some of them are still with Riek [Machar], and some are in Uganda or Kenya. Nobody knows. Some have joined the SPLA as fighters. Even my brother's son, who was then aged nine, left. Now, no-one knows where he is.

As the SPLA moved units further north, in search of recruits, the army followed with indiscriminate reprisals. The Kawalib tribe in the eastern jebels provided many early recruits. Ahmed Sayed and Omer el Amin described the government reaction:[11]

> By that time the SPLA had some reconnaissance groups in the area and the army was accusing people of feeding and protecting the SPLA.
> The first village to be burned in Delami was in April 1987. In March, Tundili was burned, just over the border in Heiban county. Then in April the army came and burned Lambere. They came and surrounded the village. They put twenty people in a hut, including a church elder, and burned it down. Thomas, his family and the other people all burned to death. The commander of that operation was Hamed Ibrahim, nicknamed 'Tundili' after the village he had destroyed just before. He also burned Idang village.

But this was just a foretaste of what was to come in 1988, when many people had to run to the mountains, to caves—many of which are in fact just clefts in the rock or hollows under rocks, that do not keep out the rain.

> The SPLA commander at that time was Yunis Abu Sudur, who infiltrated up to Kalara. On 28 May [1988], the government sent a big convoy that moved to Kalara and then up to Jebel Nukri. They burned Kalara village, al Ided, Sanjak, Nukri, Abyad, el Murra, Rijl el Zireiga, Gardud el Basham, el Ginei, Mardeis, Saraya, Gardud Aris, Gardud Humed, Dere, Idang, Lambere, Abri, Kulurina, Sabat, Aren and Urmi. In two weeks they destroyed 21 villages. It was complete destruction. People were abducted. We know of thirteen. They burned all the churches, but left the mosques—they had not started burning mosques at that time. Luckily only eleven people were killed. In one case, Aris el Biri, after he was dead they pulled out his eyes and teeth.
> Most of the people ran to the caves. In the rainy season we were confident that the army would not come back, so most people started to rebuild their houses.
> After the rains the trouble continued. On 25 September, an Arab militia group led by Yousif Hamdan Adi, joined by the Awlad Ghabbush led by Sheikh Kuku el Kumbula, attacked Omo village.

---

[11] Interviewed in Tira Limon, 20 May 1995.

They burned it down and killed seven people. The seven included the sheikh of Kwishi, Ibrahim Brema. We have all the names. One was the small daughter of Kuchi Dafallah. They abducted many people and took them to Fayo. After Fayo, they were moved again, but we don't know where as there has been no news from them.

THE WAR INTENSIFIES, 1989-91

In 1989, the war was escalated by both sides. The SPLA New Kush Division entered the Nuba Mountains between January and March 1989. As SPLA attacks came close to Kadugli in April, the regional government came close to panic. Shortly beforehand, the government of Sadiq el Mahdi began to talk about forming the "Popular Defence Forces"—a euphemism for legitimising the Murahaliin as a paramilitary force in close co-ordination with the army. Although the PDF Act was not formally promulgated until October 1989, by the military government, the PDF were in *de facto* existence in South Kordofan from April.

On 14 April, following a congress of Baggara tribes at the Umma Party headquarters in Omdurman, also attended by a senior military commander and at least one MP, the decision was taken to form the "Popular Defence Force." Fifteen thousand Misiriya militiamen were to be armed and organised, with the plan to double the size soon.[12] This proposal flew directly in the face of the stand taken by the high command of the Sudan Armed Forces, which was hostile to the idea of ethnic militias. In May, Sadiq tried to introduce a "people's defence law" into parliament, to legalise militias, but was forced to drop the proposal in the face of strong parliamentary opposition. However, the Prime Minister still clandestinely went ahead with his proposal. At the end of the month, Governor Abdel Rasoul el Nur told the press that the army and "civilian defence forces" had engaged in five joint operations since March.[13]

---

[12] Details in *Sudan Times*, 19 April 1989.
[13] *Sudan Times*, 1 June 1989.

While a ceasefire was signed in the South in April 1989, the war continued in the Nuba Mountains. While the Sudan Government, the SPLA and western donors agreed to Operation Lifeline Sudan for the war-affected areas at the same moment, the Nuba Mountains was overlooked.

The National Salvation Revolutionary Command Council (RCC) of Lt.-Gen. Omer al Bashir seized power on 30 June 1989. The RCC initially included a prominent Nyima Nuba, Brigadier Ibrahim Nayel Idam, as head of Security. Many Nuba welcomed the coup, as the leaders promised an end to ethnic militias, released some Nuba detainees, and detained a number of the prominent Umma Party leaders who had been most active in encouraging the militia, including Abdel Rasoul el Nur and Fadallah Burma. Another politician much feared by the Nuba, the Minister of the Interior, Mubarak al Fadl, fled into exile.

But the encouragement to the Nuba was short-lived. Brigadier Ibrahim Nayel Idam was rapidly demoted from being responsible for security to the portfolio of youth and sports. The familiar alliance between Khartoum and the Baggara militias reasserted itself. The NIF had itself been active in trying to win the Murahaliin away from Umma Party loyalty, in part through the activities of the Committee for the Defence of Islam and the Nation, an extremist, pro-militia organization that included among its leadership General Abdel Rahman Suwar el Dahab, the former head of the Transitional Military Council. The alliance was sealed in October, when the government passed the Popular Defence Act. Hireka Izz el Din and Abdel Rahman Abu al Bashar were among the former Umma hard-liners who joined the government. In February 1990, Mubarak al Fadl, on behalf of the Umma Party in opposition, called upon the militia to turn their guns on the new government. Despite the close links between Mubarak al Fadl and the militias, they ignored his call.

Lt.-Gen. Sayed Abdel Karim al Husseini was made Governor of Kordofan following the coup. He is a Shaygiya, previously a naval commander in Port Sudan. Abdel Wahab Abdel Rahman Ali, a well-known hard-line administrative officer, was appointed Commissioner of South Kordofan.

Murahaliin to PDF: The Lagowa Killings

In late 1989 and 1990, there was a series of killings and burnings of villages in Lagowa district. It was a complex series of events, which at the time only reached the outside world in simplified and distorted form, as the "Lagowa massacre" in which 98 people were alleged to have been killed.

Residents of Lagowa have investigated the incidents. As Hassan Osman Tutu explained, the killings had their roots in the militia policy, and the events that followed illustrate how the militia policy evolved into a comprehensive counter-insurgency strategy involving systematic violence against the entire civilian population:[14]

> Before 1985, the Arabs were not well-armed. They had spears and we had spears. There were a few old guns—*kartush*—but they were not effective. If there was a conflict between the Misiriya and our people, it was taken to the government for resolution. The Arabs would always try to bribe or influence the officials or judges.
>
> But in 1985, Fadallah Burma brought weapons to the Misiriya. For some years there was not a high level of militia activity. But by 1988, the Misiriya started threatening the Tima and other Nuba in the Lagowa area. They said, 'The mountains are for the Nuba, but now that we are armed, we the Misiriya will come and put our hands on the mountains.'
>
> The Misiriya Humr went to the South, to Gogrial and Abyei, immediately from 1985. When they were pushed out of the South, they went to Babanusa and el Fula. We did not see them for a long time. But during this period the Misiriya Zurug were also slowly being armed.
>
> Mohamed Ali Tiya was one of the first SPLA officers from Tima. After he returned from his training, in December 1988 he went to his village. When the Arabs heard of this, they said that the rebellion has entered Tima. The Misiriya Zurug immediately began to come and threaten civilians, saying that they will come and attack Tima and capture it, and chase all the civilians away. The Duhreymat clan of Fadallah Burma was especially responsible for this.

---

[14] Interviewed in Tira Limon, 23 May 1995.

This threatening continued up to May 1989. That was just before the rainy season, when the Misiriya migrate from Tima to North Kordofan with their families and their cattle. After they had left, only a few armed men remained, in Nukr, without their women and children, and without their cattle.

Throughout this period, the arming of the Murahaliin remained semi-clandestine. But it was not difficult for the citizens to observe what was happening.

In June, I went with the omda of Tima to el Obeid to collect some medicines allocated to Tima by the government. On the way, in Salara, we saw a big lorry loaded high and covered with a tarpaulin. We didn't know what was in it. While we were in el Obeid, the coup of Omer al Bashir took place. We took our medicine and returned back to Tima. When we arrived we learned that the lorry was loaded with weapons, with some other items on top to disguise the cargo. The police in Tima had reported to Lagowa that there was a lorry loaded with suspicious items. When the lorry was in Lagowa, it was parked in the Duhreymat quarter, outside the house of Jibreel Mohamed. The administration in Lagowa took no action; they let the lorry stay. During the night, the weapons were unloaded, only the civilian items remained. In the morning the police came and checked the lorry. They confiscated the remaining items, which were distributed to the police themselves and other senior figures. It was bribery.

By then, the Misiriya had begun mobilisation. They started by organising the teachers, about ten of them. Fadallah Burma was the one giving the orders. The teachers were made into [military] ranks. The school director, al Shafi Dei el Nur, was given the rank of First Lieutenant in the PDF. He was responsible for the PDF groups, and had a camp in Nukr, between Tima and Tullishi.

1989: Militia Killings

The Murahaliin were extremely confident. On 6 August, a group of militia led by Hamid Mohamed el Faggiri led a large armed group towards Jebel Abu Januq, the most north-westerly of the Nuba hills, far away from the nearest SPLA activity. Hamid el Faggiri had reportedly announced in an Umma Party meeting on 18 May that he intended to lead an invasion of Abu Januq and take it over for Misiriya occupation. The attack was stopped by the intervention of another Arab militia group, the Awlad Samar, who had an agreement with the Abu Januq Nuba.[15]

The Misiriya Duhreymat were the best-connected and best-armed militia group, and began their actions a fortnight later. African Rights has received accounts from different residents, and from letters and petitions written on the government side, which all concur. The first militia actions began close to Nukr, their base. On 23 August, they ambushed and killed four farmers in two separate incidents in the plains close to Jebel Tullishi. Two days later, the police came from Lagowa to "investigate" the incident. Their partiality can be gauged from the fact that they were guided to the spot by militiamen. On the way, they killed a woman at Serafaya. On the way back, they shot three people in Kamda, one of whom died. On 2 September, three more Tullishi people were killed by the militia. In early October, they attacked Um Dernu village in Kamda, and reportedly killed thirteen villagers.

The Murahaliin began to range more widely. In October they raided southwards, and attacked some Daju villages. Some Misiriya were killed as the Daju resisted. This escalation brought the conflict to the attention of some government officials and army officers, who were determined to swim against the tide, and try to prevent descent into all-out war. They called a conference in Lagowa. Hassan Osman Tutu was one who attended:[16]

[The conference] was chaired by Major [Mohamed Ibrahim] Kabbashi and it began on 15 October. The agenda of the conference was to resolve the Misiriya-Nuba-Daju conflict. But the issue was not to be resolved in that meeting. Instead they were to plan a second conference, and decide on the agenda for that conference.

When we were negotiating, the Misiriya accused the Tima of rebellion. Major Kabbashi turned to them and asked them to prove

---

[15] Petition from Abu Januq chiefs to Brigadier Ibrahim Nayel Idam, RCC, 30 August 1989.
[16] Interviewed in Tira Limon, 23 May 1995.

it. He said, 'Bring me the proof. I am not ready to fight and kill innocent people. This happened to me in Nasir when I followed false information.' All the negotiations finished after three days without resolving a single problem. We planned to reconvene in January. Major Kabbashi gave orders to the tribes that they should not attack each other.

The Tima were indeed sympathetic to the SPLA, and a small SPLA unit under Commander Ismail Khamis Jellab had entered the Julud hills (the southern part of the Tima range) in August. But the militia actions had all been well to the south-west of Julud, in Tullishi and Kamda. Major Kabbashi is reported to have climbed Jebel Tullishi himself, and, finding he met with no opposition, to have declared the area free of the SPLA. The Nuba delegates were certainly impressed with his even-handedness. The conference lasted three days and set a date for a major reconciliation conference of 1 January 1990. But it was quickly overtaken by events. In Khartoum, the RCC decreed the Popular Defence Act: the Murahaliin were now officially recognised as "People's Defence Forces" (PDF). The Murahaliin needed no more encouragement: they attacked Tima itself. Hassan Osman continues:

> On 27 October, the Misiriya came, returning from the north after the rains, and came to attack Tumu village in Tima. They killed 33 people in total, including women and children. They took a pregnant woman, killed here and opened her stomach and threw the child out. They burned the village.
> The Misiriya then mobilised for a big offensive. In Lagowa town they began to burn houses in the residential areas dominated by the Nuba, including Thawra, Amara, Ladi, Debakaya Atala, and Fugara. That started on 30 October.

Lists compiled by residents of Lagowa at the time include the names of 35 people killed and thirteen wounded between 27-30 October in Tumu and neighbouring villages, and ten killed and eight wounded in the attack that began on 30 October. On 6 November, the Murahaliin attacked Nimr Shago, in Kamda. Four days later there was an attack on Keiga, killing fourteen people.

The Nuba and Daju representatives had lost much confidence in the Misiriya, but the conference opened on schedule nonetheless. Shortly afterwards, the Nuba were to lose all their remaining confidence in the Sudan Government. In 1990, the government and army took the lead in attacking the western Nuba.

On 1 January the conference reconvened. This conference agreed to compensate the Nuba for the loss of properties, and payment of *diya* for the loss of lives: LS 20,000 for a man and LS 10,000 for a woman. A period of eight months was agreed to make the payment.

Before the resolutions could be implemented, there was a combined Misiriya Humr and Zurug militia attack, that also included Fellata. The Fellata were using bows and arrows, the Humr were using horses—this was the first time for these militias to come, and for us to see these things. That was in February. They attacked Kamda Tariin and killed 42 people.

Straight after that, the government called all the chiefs to Lagowa. The chiefs of Kamda and Tullishi went; the Tima and others refused. The government arrested all the chiefs and took them to Nimr Shago, tied them up and shot them. They were fourteen.

Nine of the names of the murdered sheikhs have been recorded:

1.   Ahmed al Izeriq, sheikh of Nimr Shago (Kamda);
2.   Mahmoud Dahir Mualla, sheikh of Nimr Shago;
3.   Mohamed Adam, sheikh of Kamda;
4.   Mohamed Suleiman;
5.   Fadl el Nabi al Izeriq;
6.   Biresa Tutu, court chief, Ras el Fil;
7.   Musa Kuwa, Sheikh of Karalanya, Tullishi;
8.   Khawaja Kalewa, Tullishi;
9.   el Feys.

One of the reasons why the Tima refused to respond to the government's summons was that in January, the army had arrested seventeen Tima, from Saraf al Akhdar and Kallandi, and one Ghulfan man living in Kallandi. Six of them were executed, including Sheikh Jibreel Tabalo and Sheikh Seed Sharra, both from Kallanda.

Straight after the fourteen were killed, the army and militia launched attacks on a series of villages across the entire area. The SPLA had no base in the district, so the attacks were exclusively against civilian targets. In Tullishi, seven following villages were burned: Lao, Karalanya, Timbili, Serafaya, Saada, Shuwa and Lambo. Only Tirdi village escaped. In Tima, Balol and Taya were burned. In Katla and Julud, all the villages were affected. In Kamda, part of Nimr Shago was burned. The attacks were rapid: the army and Murahaliin would burn for one or two days and then return to their garrisons. The whole operation was completed in April.

Hassan Osman describes how the offensive had the explicit aim of depopulating the rural areas: it was far more systematic and sophisticated than the militia burnings of the previous autumn. Roadblocks were set up by the army to control people's movement. Hassan Osman continued his account:

> In March 1990, the people of Tima, Tullishi and Tabak were all given places inside the town. But most people refused to be drawn into the town. So the army and Murahaliin came and took some people by force. The army surrounded an area in daylight and took anyone who was present. Only those in the hills escaped. The villages that were affected include Shingil, Karkar and almost every village in Kamda and Tabak. No village escaped.
>
> People were taken to Abu Zabad and other places further north. First they were taken to Murahaliin camps in the area. People have not returned. This was the first time people were taken out of the region.
>
> The famine began at that time. But it was not yet a killing famine. People were slaughtering animals to eat, eating green leaves. In Tabak, people left to go to the towns. In Kamda, some went inside Lagowa town.

Government forces continued their attacks during and after the rainy season. African Rights has large number of reports from different sources of arrests and executions by military intelligence in the second half of 1990, especially in Lagowa and Nimr Shago. However, while it is clear that a crackdown continued, it has not been possible to confirm the details. It is reliably reported that in September, twelve men were detained in Nimr Shago and later executed. In October 1990, Kayo and Balol villages were burned, and five people killed.

1991: Descent into All-Out War

During and after the 1990 rainy season, the SPLA increased its forces in the western jebels. The government sent more troops and militiamen, and launched a joint army and Murahaliin offensive. A spiral of violence set in. Hassan Osman continued:

> A two-pronged offensive began in December 1990 and continued into January 1991. They burned villages in Tullishi and killed many people. When they reached Tima they killed two, Gismallah Mamur and Abdel Gassim Kuwa. They did not burn in Tima: they were blocked by the SPLA before they could enter the villages.
>
> In 1991, Ras el Fil was burned three times. Kayo was burned in July by the army. Tumu village was burned in the same operation and five people were killed.

In August 1991, the army returned to Kamda and ordered the evacuation of a number of villages, including al Amara, Ladmi and Karagadi. Part of al Amara was then burned. The people were temporarily housed in school buildings in Lagowa, but required to leave before the schools reopened. The army prevented them from leaving the town to return to their villages, and tried (unsuccessfully) to enforce their move to displaced camps further away. A number of leading Kamda were arrested, in a campaign of intimidation that intensified before the major offensive that began in the following dry season (see below).

Jebel Tabak was first attacked 1990/91. African Rights was unable to locate a resident of the area, but Hassan Osman recalled the campaign:[17]

> They abducted people, who were taken with all their cattle. The cows were taken on one side, the owners to another side. The people who remained in the village left for Tima and remain there. Tabak was left empty and still there is no-one there.

These atrocities drove rural people straight to the SPLA. Rabih Hussein Ali is from Julud Basha. He joined the SPLA in 1991:[18]

> At the time I was in Khartoum, working as a lorry mechanic in the industrial area of Bahri. I came on leave to my area.
> When I reached my village, I found that people were in bad condition. All the houses had been burned by the army. All the youth had gone to the SPLA to have guns and freedom. So I decided to go too. I heard that the SPLA was around, and reported to them in Tullishi.

By the end of 1991, the conflict in the western jebels was to culminate in the largest military confrontation of the whole war in the Nuba Mountains, and the government's declaration of *Jihad* (see below).

The New Kush Division

In 1989, the SPLA re-entered the Nuba Mountains, this time to stay. Five battalions came overland from South Sudan to join the Volcano Battalion that had remained inside, temporarily based in the Korongo Abdalla area. The new troops were a mixture of Southerners (chiefly Dinka, almost all of whom returned to the South in 1991-2) and Nuba. At that time, no villages were under SPLA control except Fama in the far south-east. For the whole of 1989, the SPLA had no permanent base: the commanders moved between Tira Limon and

---

[17] Osman Hassan Tutu, interviewed in Tira Limon, 23 May 1995.
[18] Interviewed in Tira Limon, 21 May 1995.

the Otoro hills, before finally establishing a headquarters at Chanyaro in Achiron in December.

SPLA forces were also sent to the western jebels at this time, and penetrated the Miri hills, coming very close to Kadugli. The army appears to have initially been taken by surprise by the speed of the SPLA penetration—within a few months, the guerrillas had free movement throughout a wide arc including the western, eastern and southern mountains.

The SPLA forces committed many human rights abuses at that time, a fact that is readily admitted by their commanders. There were numerous incidents of looting, and some cases of killing those who resisted being looted. This occurred even in villages known to be very sympathetic to the SPLA. There were also instances of forced conscription of youths in 1989, at Lake Abyad close to the Southern border and in the western jebels. Commander Yousif Kuwa has admitted that a fair number of soldiers "rampaged" at that time:[19] "Not all my soldiers are angels. We were tough in 1989 when my soldiers began to loot and kill people. Some were court martialled and executed."

The SPLA record is examined in more detail in Chapter V. Yousif Kuwa and other commanders claim that their harsh disciplinary code has reduced such abuses, a claim that was confirmed by civilians who spoke with African Rights.

South and West of Kadugli

Everywhere where the SPLA penetrated in some form, the government responded with a massive scorched earth policy. It was a simple and brutal method of counter-insurgency. The aim was to destroy the rural economy by burning the villages, devastating the crops, stealing the livestock, and driving the people out. It was a massive over-reaction to the military threat of the SPLA, and unleashed unprecedented suffering on Nuba civilians.

The southern jebels were the first to suffer. Amsal Tutu Tiya, aged 41, a catechist in the Anglican church from Tabanya in Angolo,

---

[19] Interviewed by the BBC in Kapanguria, 1 May 1995.

described one of the first official joint army-Murahaliin operations in South Kordofan:[20]

> On 24 February 1989 Elmaij Dud, an old man of sixty years was arrested by the army and slaughtered in front of his home at 11:00 a.m. They took his cows—about three hundred—twelve stores full of sorghum, and three bags of money to Kadugli. They also burned his village, Hagirat
>
> On 27 March 1989 the army and the Murahaliin jointly and for the first time attacked Angolo. The Murahaliin were composed of Misiriya and Agaira Arabs. Angolo village was burned, including two churches. The army looted the area taking 3,500 cows and 1,700 goats. Sixty-seven persons were killed and 79 injured.

The nearby village of el Dar was also attacked, as described by Jibreel Ismail Kuwa, a 48-year-old farmer of the Korongo Angolo tribe:[21]

> In April 1989, the enemy attacked Dar and killed the daughter of Sheikh Okobri Mani, and his grandson. Another girl was injured. A total of 460 cattle were taken. Twenty-nine cows and 115 goats were taken from me alone.

This area was the first to be secured by the SPLA, leading to relative peace until an unexpected offensive in February 1993 (see below) and the government reoccupation of Buram in December 1993. But isolated army attacks continued into 1990:[22]

> In 1990 a convoy came from Kadugli and attacked Tabuli, Bilenya and Daloka. All the huts were burned but no people were killed or abducted or injured. Also no cattle or goats were taken, only two donkeys.

The reprisals taken further north were far more comprehensive and savage. As the SPLA units came into close proximity to

---

[20] Interviewed in Um Dulu, 17 May 1995.
[21] Interviewed in Um Dulu, 17 May 1995.
[22] Hamad Tutu Dabah, interviewed in Um Dulu, 17 May 1995.

Kadugli, the government reacted fiercely. Korongo Abdalla, immediately south of Kadugli, bore the brunt. Three residents told African Rights:[23]

> In February 1989, the SPLA came. It withdrew the same month. [In April] the army then came and started to burn the villages. They burned Seraf Charnog, Shatt Tebeldi, and Korongo Juwa. In the Katcha area they burned Hay el Suq, including the big church there, and Tuna, where they also completely destroyed the church, and burned all the books. They specially burned any books in the local language. In Tuna, one man and one girl were captured. In Kafina, they abducted two women. In Tuma,[24] they took another man and a woman. All these people are still missing.
>
> This man [Abdel Gadir] alone lost 188 cows in that operation. Up to three quarters of the Korongo cattle were taken by the army and the Murahaliin. From then on until 1993 was a time of hunger. Many people died. 1990 was also a year of drought, and the army burned all the sorghum. The army .attacked and burned; the Murahaliin raided the cattle.

This wanton brutality had the effect of driving rural people straight into the arms of the SPLA. By the end of 1989, many youth had joined the SPLA or were co-operating with it, and the government forces were not able to move in the rural areas with the same ease. The Korongo farmers continued:

> From 1990 onwards there was a new pattern. The army always came from Kadugli. Each attack started with them shelling out of Kadugli, and then the attack comes through Keilak.
>
> In March 1991 the army came with 35 lorries and four tanks from Kadugli. They went to Seraf al Gharnoub and Shatt Tebeldi. We blocked the road with stones but they removed the stones and passed. They stayed in Korongo one day. All the time they were active—shooting at random, shelling, covering every mountain with their gunfire. Skirmishers were shooting at any mountain.

---

[23] Jaafar al Fadl, Abdel Gadir Abdel Rahman and Suleiman Kafi, interviewed in Um Dulu, 17 May 1995.
[24] Not to be confused with Tuna.

While the army was trying to proceed to Shimondo, it was ambushed by the SPLA and returned to Kadugli.

After one failed operation in the Korongo Abdalla area in 1990, the army abducted two villagers on their return to Kadugli. On the orders of the Commissioner, Abdel Wahab Abdel Rahman, a public meeting was called in Freedom Square, so that the residents could witness the "captured rebels." The Commissioner addressed the crowd and told them the "rebels" deserved the appropriate punishment. The captives were executed on the spot, in public, and their bodies displayed on the back of a vehicle.

The destruction of Miri was more comprehensive. It began a few months later, as explained by a local farmer, Musa Kuwa Jabir Tiya:[25]

The SPLA first entered the Miri land in June 1989. The Government then started burning villages and killing people. In October the army started a big offensive, and destroyed ten of the twelve villages of Miri. Keiga was the first village to be burned. They attacked at 4 a.m. when people were asleep, so people were burned in their houses. They also shot to kill. Eighteen people died. All the cattle were raided too. They went on to Miri Juwa where they killed two old people. They continued to burn Lima, Kanga, Abu Sunun, Kufa, Mashisha, al Akhwal and Luba. It was the work of a joint army-Murahaliin task force of four thousand men. People were driven to Kadugli; pregnant women aborted on the way. Crops were left standing in the fields. The shops in the markets were just abandoned, and the Arabs looted them. When burning, the army would break the 'donkey' water tanks, and if they found a donkey or a cow, they would slaughter it and throw it into the well.

Only two large villages—Miri Bara and Kuhaliyat—escaped, because the people had already moved to Kadugli before the offensive.

After that, most of the Miri people were in Kadugli, especially in Mayom area on the north side. Some went on to Khartoum. Only the people of Abu Sunun did not run. On the government side, only

---

[25] Interviewed in Um Dulu, 17 May 1995.

Miri Bara and Kuhaliyat had people. The other areas were under SPLA control, with some people remaining there.

Three small villages, Kadia, Kadoda and Umdago also escaped the burning. These details were confirmed in accounts written by Miri residents living in Kadugli. Musa Kuwa continued:

In March 1991, the army went and attacked Keiga and Kufa, and burned them. Two people were killed in Kufa and four in Keiga, and seven women were abducted. All this burning caused severe hunger and in Kufa alone thirty people died from starvation.

The Eastern Jebels

The Eastern Jebels did not escape the scorched earth policy of the government, though the destruction was less comprehensive than on the western side. As elsewhere, it was a combination of militia (now re-formed as PDF) and army that were responsible. The first attacks were carried out by the army in Tira Limon, pre-empting the arrival of the SPLA:[26]

At the beginning of 1989, the SPLA arrived in the southern jebels, on its way to Tira Limon. It arrived in Tira Limon in April. In March, the army started burning. A big convoy came out of Talodi—there was no garrison at Mendi at that time, it was established later in that year. Tabri was burned on 23 March and one person was killed. Achiron was burned on the same day and Kerker was burned on the next day. In April, the army tried to attack Achiron again and started burning the outlying villages, but it was repulsed with a lot of casualties and prisoners. Some of the prisoners died of their wounds and some were killed by the SPLA.

In the dry season of 1990 the army tried to attack again. They burned Rimla but when the SPLA came they withdrew. After that the army did not try to come to Tira Limon again until 1993.

---

[26] Jibreel Tutu Jiran, interviewed in Tira Limon, 22 May 1995.

Further to the north, in Tira el Akhdar, the pattern was the more familiar one of joint Murahaliin-PDF and army operations. One Tira village that suffered particularly was Kalkada. It has been burned many times. Three residents explained:[27]

We have seen Kalkada destroyed four times. The first occasion was on 5 July 1989.

Some days before this attack, the Um Bororo[28] Murahaliin came from the east onto the farms. They abducted one woman, Hassaniya Madeli and her husband, Osman Medawi, who were going to farm. They took them to Mendi. The Murahaliin were acting as scouts for the army, they were sent to get information. Later, people saw them in Mendi. The Murahaliin had handed them to the army. Later they were killed.

Then the army came from Mendi and attacked the village. Four adult women and two children were killed. The women were Jenni Hamoda, Jebra Hamoda, her sister, Kachi Rahmatallah and Naya Kumir. About five hundred houses were destroyed, more than half of the area, and anything left inside those houses was destroyed. Twenty people were abducted. Two men were killed and eighteen women taken to the garrison and distributed among the soldiers. The men killed were Hassan Rahman and Ali Shalo. Four of them were later transferred to Liri. The older children, who were not breastfeeding, were taken away from their mothers and taken to an unknown place.

The second attack came seven days later. At 2 p.m. they came, while people were in the mosque. When I came out of the mosque first, I found the soldiers outside. They started shooting at me. I ran back inside and out through the other door. Everyone inside also ran. The Imam, Omer Ali Juma, stayed behind, and he was killed— he went out through the main door. The soldiers looted the mosque, they came in with their boots on and took the mats, prayer jugs and Korans. But because it was a concrete building they could not burn it easily.

---

[27] Hassan Ramadan Zakaria, head of Kalkada village, Mekki Lechu Rumbek, secretary of the village, and Suleiman Dafalla Zakaria, interviewed in Um Dulu, 16 May 1995.
[28] The Um Bororo are a pastoralist Fellata group that ranges across South Kordofan and South Darfur.

86

Then they went to the village and started looting all the properties inside the houses—chairs, beds, mattresses, kitchen utensils. They didn't take any sorghum but they took everything else. When they had completed their looting they burned the houses in the village, all those that had remained from the previous attack. Most people were in their farms at that time. All the other people ran; they only captured one old woman, Nani, who could not run.

Then they turned to the market and started breaking down the shops. The four Jellaba shops were left untouched, but they took everything from the 36 permanent shops belonging to the local people. Even the metal doors of the shops were removed. They took the small operating parts of grinding machines, and smashed up the parts they could not remove. There were more than one hundred stalls built of wood and straw, and they destroyed those.

Apart from the Jellaba, people did not emigrate yet. We built up houses in the village again.

The third time Kalkada was destroyed was in September 1990. Again they came from Mendi, on foot. They came at 6 a.m., using the forest route to take us by surprise. When they entered, they started shooting. They shot down a small girl, Tutu Khalil, aged nine. They shot a woman, Titi Murjan, and cut her arm off with the bullets. She is still alive. They shot Idris Kuman and Mohamed Abu Nur, and killed them both. They also killed Tulu Lesho and his brother Boror, and Hussein Abbas.

At that morning, we were supposed to bury a small boy, Azhari, who had died. When we heard the shooting, we just covered his body with a sheet and ran. The soldiers even came and looted the sheet, leaving him uncovered. Seven other people were killed—we have their names.

After that they abducted women.

One of the three interviewees, Suleiman Dafallah Zakaria, continued:

The first one they took was my wife, Asha Hari, and our three children, Delal, aged six, Safiya, aged four and Asia, two. They are in Mendi, still alive. Asha's parents are in Mendi so we are hoping that they are well-treated.

They took Hawa Nur and her child of six days, and her mother Hamya, who was helping her after giving birth. They took Nasa

Shumu and her fourteen-year-old daughter Um Jereida Yousif, and a little girl of two, Kaka Komeli. In all they abducted twenty women and children. We have no news of any of them.

The soldiers stole everything. They did not leave a single animal in the whole area. All the huts were burned, everything was destroyed. But they did not go to the farms and destroy the crops standing in the fields, so we stayed in the area until after the harvest. We did not build permanent houses again, just shelters for the rainy season so that we could cultivate again.

The story of Kalkada is continued in later sections.

In Delami county, the Kawalib people were spared major army activity in 1989, but suffered militia attacks, and later the familiar pattern of joint operations. As elsewhere, the result was famine. Ahmed Sayed and El Amin Omer, explained:[29]

Because of the burning [of 1988], there was serious famine in the whole area into 1989. Many people had to go to the mechanised farms to look for gleanings of sorghum, or to look for work.

The army left us alone in 1989. But the Arab militia were coming all the time to loot and rob. There were so many incidents we cannot count them. But none of them were big attacks, the Arabs were only interested in taking cattle. Life got a bit better that year, as we could cultivate and there was some food.

Some of the militia incidents were reported in a petition by twelve Delami leaders, who complained that "They [the militia] are not afraid. They even raid in daytime, feeling they are above the law."[30] They reported two cattle raids on 29 and 30 April, and another raid in May in which they killed a Nuba herdsman, Mohamed Idris, and stole his cattle: "The Arab tribes do this and then go to security and tell them they have killed an SPLA man." In attacks starting on 5 June, three farmers were killed. Later, in October, the militia of the Awlad Ghabbush attacked farm labourers

---

[29] Interviewed in Tira Limon, 20 May 1995.
[30] Letter to Commander of the 19th Division, Dilling, July 1989.

on the Kortala mechanised scheme, killing nine migrant Dinka workers.[31]

In 1990 there was a major, two-pronged army offensive. One military convoy came on the Dondor road, from Kadugli and Dilling. It entered Delami county up to Kamand, and burned Kamand. Then it went south towards Shwaya and to Luchulu, burning on the way. A simultaneous offensive was launched from Dilling towards Delami, through Habila, burning several Kawalib villages including Dere, Nukri and Abyad. It met up with the other force at Hajar el Attab. Ahmed Sayed and Omer el Amin continued:

> Then in 1990 things began to be worse again. In May, a big force, joint army and PDF, came from Habila. They attacked Gardud al Basham, killing two civilians, Abdalla Somi and Lasara Kodi, and injuring three. One was a child of two, who they shot in the leg, another was an old woman whom they shot and paralysed. One of the injured, Kokandi, died later. They burned the whole village and took all the goats—there were no cattle left after the Arabs had done their raids. One person was abducted.
>
> From the end of 1990 to 1993 we were in continuous famine, because of instability and the destruction of our crops and houses. The militias carried on their raids without interrupting, and the army came back in 1991.

The most exposed Kawalib people were those living in isolated jebels to the west of the main Kawalib mountain range. By 1991, many of these communities no longer existed, as they had been forced out by repeated militia attacks. In one incident in late-1991, a large group of villagers from the Um Heitan area moved first to Kurgol on the main Kadugli-Dilling road, intending to migrate north. There they were intercepted by the army and many of the men were killed. Later, nine villagers were arrested and detained.

Even more exposed were the Kaduru people, who live in an isolated range of hills far to the north. African Rights has been unable to obtain detailed information about this area. Kaduru was

---

[31] Petition from the Nuba Mountains People's High Committee for Peace and Development to the Chairman of the RCC, 30 November 1989.

always under government control and was never infiltrated by the SPLA. However, in October 1989, villages in Kaduru were reported to have been attacked.

A POLICY OF FAMINE

The depredations of the army and the militias combined with drought in the summer of 1990 to create severe famine in the Nuba Mountains. This built upon the disruptions visited on the rural economy in the previous years, including the decline in trade and the fall-off in support from migrant workers.

Siddiq al Tom Obi, the mek of Kuchama West in Otoro, explained how the war and government abuses had driven people into the mountains. His brief account includes references to the way in which government actions have forced people to abandon their farms, how they are unable to maintain their livestock in the mountains, and how trade has been disrupted.[32]

> The enemy harasses us a lot in Kuchama. Especially they come to the places where we collect water, and people are abducted to Heiban. Some can escape, but most don't know how to escape and they are still there. In March and April this year, 24 people were abducted from Kuchama.
>
> Before the war I was a farmer, in Jigheba near el Azraq. When the war began I left to come here in the mountains. The government was attacking the rural areas down there. My brother Abdel Rahman Idris had the neighbouring farm, and he was shot by them in April 1991. After that I ran into the mountains.
>
> The first sign of the fighting is when the army starts firing mortars into the bush and the farms. That makes it difficult for us to stay in the farms, so people began to move up to the mountains, especially to the caves. 1993 was the worst year, when the enemy started to move to different places to attack people.
>
> In 1985, problems didn't reach this area, they were only to the south. The SPLA was still behind the mountains. Even so, we had doubts. The Sudan Government began to arrest chiefs and educated

---

[32] Interviewed in Kujur el Sha'abiya, 13 May 1995.

people. They tortured them, beat them and accused them of collaborating with the SPLA. Since that time, when a chief is tortured and he says, 'So-and-so has a son in the SPLA, etc,' then that person would be arrested, tortured and even killed.

So from that time a lot of people went to the hills with their animals, but because the animals could not adapt to the climate of the hills, they had to come down to the plains again. In the plains they were attacked and looted, and the herders were often captured. There is no chance for us to move down into the plains these days.

Many of the testimonies given above refer to the intense hunger that followed the burnings of 1989-91. The abandonment of "far farms" in the valleys and plains was equally disastrous, as it removed the main source of food supplies. In normal circumstances, rural people would have responded to harvest failure by selling animals, migrating to towns for work and charity from relatives, scouring the forests for wild foods, and working for money on farms. The war made all of these survival strategies difficult if not impossible. Many people ran to the towns, exactly as the government intended. But many people searched for any means of survival that would keep them away from the government they feared so much. Yagoub Osman Kaloka described how the famine struck in Tira el Akhdar:[33]

> The period 1990-91 was the worst time for the Tira. The Baggara militia came and started to burn houses randomly. There were Shanabla—actually the Shanabla came with camels—and others. People were killed randomly. 1990 was also a year of drought, and it contributed to make a serious famine. There was nothing to eat. People deserted their villages completely.
>
> During that time the government and Arabs burned so many villages. They destroyed Muhela, Timbera, Karandel, Lubi (again), al Bata, al Farish, Tajura and Um Derdu. In these last two the people ran to the mountains. These villages are still without human life.
>
> Later on due to hunger, people left the area completely. Many went to Regifi or Um Dulu. About a quarter of the population in

---

[33] Yagoub Osman Kaloka, interviewed in Tira Limon, 22 May 1995.

that area is Tira el Akhdar. Others went to Buram, some went right up to Fariang.

The army and the Shanabla militia were responsible. the Shanabla attacked in small numbers, with small raids. Sometimes a big army convoy would move from Abu Jibeha or Kalogi. A small convoy came in November 1991 from Abu Jibeha. It entered Lubi, which was empty, and shelled the mountains, and burned some huts nearby. It clashed with the SPLA and then went back. Seven civilians were killed in Lubi area, and three SPLA soldiers died in the battle.

During this time, the Shanabla were always present. In fact, there were many different Arab groups in the militia, including Baggara, PDF and anyone on a camel, not just the Shanabla. For the people of Tira, 'Shanabla' just means 'looters.'

Since 1987, the Sudan Government has followed a policy of blocking trade with the SPLA-held areas. At first, the policy was not consistent, and those able to bribe the military have tended to operate with freedom. Indeed, in 1988, opposition newspapers in Khartoum accused the army itself of profiteering from trade with the SPLA.[34] Nuba traders were targetted, though. Many of the testimonies in this report include descriptions of attacks on Nuba traders, or the destruction of Nuba shops and marketplaces. In late-1989, residents of Kalogi wrote:[35]

> There are some merchants who have recently been kidnapped and no-one knows where they are now. They were accused of supplying the SPLA with essential commodities, although some Arab tribes have been trading directly with the mutineers and they have not at any time been questioned. This has taken place in Kowaya which lies fifteen miles north of Kalogi.

The main impediment to trade at that time was the evacuation of Jellaba traders, fearing attacks from the SPLA. Most Jellaba simply ran when the SPLA was in the vicinity, and there were a number of

---

[34] *El Ra'i*, Khartoum, 11 July 1988.
[35] Petition from Kalogi youth to Brigadier Ibrahim Nayel Idam, 23 November 1989.

incidents in which the SPLA ambushed commercial trucks or looted rural shops. Mechanised farms were also attacked and tractors burned. In June 1989, three lorries of the Nuba Mountains Agricultural Corporation were looted and burned. The majority of mechanised schemes were closed by 1990, leading to a collapse in the market for casual labour. In early 1989, as the war escalated, foreign aid organizations also withdrew from the Nuba Mountains.

After 1989, the government's determination to seal off the SPLA-controlled areas increased, as did the SPLA's determination to break the blockade. During 1992-3, the SPLA negotiated a truce with the some sections of the Misiriya in the southern jebels. This opened up a trade route into Buram and the adjacent areas (under SPLA administration) from the west. Using camels, Misiriya traders brought in essential goods such as salt, soap, matches, clothes and medicines. They also brought in food. This commercial activity, limited though it was, created a vital market for the exchange of commodities, and helped Buram avoid the worst of the famine. In fact, Buram attracted refugees from other parts of the Nuba Mountains. Government forces however did their utmost to block this trade route, and ambushed Misiriya traders on many occasions. While this did not prevent the trade, it severely limited it: this is a clear instance of the government strategy of denying the Nuba in SPLA-held areas access to essential goods. The Buram trade continued until the end of 1993, when the government recapture of Buram, and the looting of Misiriya shops by local people immediately before the recapture, brought it to an abrupt halt.

The creation of famine was a deliberate government military policy. The widespread burning of villages and food crops and stealing of livestock could have no other effect. There can be no doubt that, having emerged so recently from the drought-famine of 1984-5 in Kordofan and Darfur, and the war-famine of 1987-8 in Bahr el Ghazal, that politicians and generals were fully aware of what they were doing when they launched the scorched earth strategy in the Nuba Mountains in 1989. The famine, no less than the killings, was a crime.

Joseph Aloga Jargi, another resident of Tira el Akhdar described the impact of the famine:[36]

> In 1990 and 1991 the army and the militia came and burned Timbera, Karandel, Lao and Um Derdu, where the people had deserted to the mountains. The enemy burned all the 1990 harvest and then prevented people from cultivating during 1991 by patrolling and burning.
>
> By 1992 there was severe hunger. People sold their cattle and all other things, even clothes, to buy food. People moved even as far as Fariang. Many people died. I remember that one whole family of twenty people died from starvation; I remember because I was one of those who found them lying dead when we opened the house.
>
> The 1993 famine was less severe than that of 1991 and 1992. Some of the people were able to cultivate. Some were even able to store food. Many people who migrated to Nagorban or Buram were able to find food or some trade. Buram had much commercial activity then. The people have mostly now returned. 1994 was a better year. But the people are without clothes.

As this account suggests, the effects of the famine are still evident. Tens of thousands of people are displaced within the SPLA-controlled areas. Many people have sold their household possessions and livestock, even their clothes, and are left in a state of destitution. When the visitor to the non-government areas of the Nuba Mountains sees almost all ordinary people dressed in rags, or even naked, this is not "normal" poverty—it is the direct and deliberate result of government military tactics.

Many people died. Estimating famine mortality is a notoriously difficult exercise, and is particularly difficult in a place with such poor and controversial population statistics as the Nuba Mountains. But Nuba from all parts of the region are adamant that the period 1990-93 was a famine that killed. It is certain that the fatalities—most of whom were children—can be numbered in the tens of thousands. More than two hundred people are reported to have died in the one village of Kiwe alone, in the Tima hills. Mek

---

[36] Interviewed in Tira Limon, 21 May 1995.

Hussein Karbus el Ehemier of Delami county summarised the sufferings of the Kawalib people:[37]

> After the Gardud incident [July 1985] we feared a serious political polarization. Some people began to move for safety, moving out of areas close to where the Arabs lived. Abri, Jumazaya and Um Daraba were all vacated. Also Um Bechat. The Arabs came and looted these places, but they didn't settle.
>
> This affected the trade. The merchants put up prices. The price of salt especially went very high. Salt and soap became expensive, and also risky to buy, so people began to forget about them. Because of the raids, some people began to climb the mountains to go to caves.
>
> Since the SPLA came, the Arabs now come as complete enemies, to shoot and to loot. When the SPLA came, those who supported the SPLA remained in their villages. The others went to towns. At first, almost everyone was with the SPLA. But with the very harsh conditions—lack of food, no medicine, shortage of clothes—more people went to the towns. But still the majority are on this side.
>
> The critical years were 1991-93. We reached the stage of eating leaves. The *doleib* fruit was finished. People were surrounded and forced to move from place to place, so they could not cultivate. This also followed on from a bad drought. Many people died in Delami county. We did not count them but we think perhaps it was ten thousand.

ELIMINATION OF THE EDUCATED AND COMMUNITY LEADERS

From the beginning of the war, one of the main strategies of the Sudan Government was the elimination of Nuba leadership. The initial targets included government chiefs—their "disloyalty" to the government made the authorities especially vengeful—and members

---

[37] Interviewed in Um Dulu, 16 May 1995.

of Nuba political organisations, and then expanded to include any educated Nuba that did not support the government.

Killings of Community Leaders

Well before the entry of the SPLA, the village of Lubi in Tira el Akhdar was considered troublesome by the government, especially after their take-over of the nearby mechanised farm. For the year 1984 they were left in peace. But, as Yagoub Osman Kaloka explained, "The government was planning countermeasures":[38]

> By 1985 the Governor and the administrator in Heiban found it difficult to let the Tira people continue in this way. So, at the end of August, at 3 a.m. one night, they sent a force to Lubi and arrested six men, including Sheikh Daud Osman, my elder brother (who was a Moslem) and took them to Heiban. That same day they tied them up and shot them. My elder brother said to them, 'I know I am going to die, I just want to pray, then you can kill me.' They refused and said, 'You cannot be a Moslem if you support the rebels.' They shot all six, and then slaughtered them with knives after the shooting.

Kaloka was in el Obeid at the time, and had to leave for Cairo to avoid the attentions of the security forces.

Over the next few years, any chief who was suspected of sympathies with the SPLA was targetted by military intelligence. The government's aim was simple: to eliminate all chiefs who refused to co-operate, and to terrorise the remainder into supporting the government. In this they succeeded, but dozens of chiefs paid with their lives.

One who very narrowly escaped death at the hands of military intelligence is Mek Defan Arno Kepi, son of a famous Otoro chief and an important community leader in his own right. He lived in Eri, on the south-western slopes of the Otoro mountains.[39]

---

[38] Interviewed in Tira Limon, 23 May 1995.
[39] Interviewed in Tira Limon, 22 May 1995.

In July 1988 many sheikhs and omdas in the Nuba Mountains were called for a conference in Kadugli. When we were summoned, we were afraid. The SPLA had come among us, and we were hiding the SPLA in our area. The Governor, Abdel Rasoul el Nur, had warned us that he will deal with anyone who has SPLA in his area. We were already fed up with our treatment from the government. Some sheikhs had already been killed—in that year they had already killed Sheikh Habil Ariya, Sheikh Adam Khidir and Sheikh Tamshir Umbashu, and two other sheikhs, I can't remember their names. Many others had been arrested. Two of our villages had already been burned: Kelpu was the first, destroyed by the Murahaliin, and Shawri the second, destroyed by the army.

We were 36 sheikhs and omdas who went, and one teacher. We were from all parts. Twelve were from Kadugli itself. We were seven from Otoro. Three were from Rashad and Delami, two from Shatt Safiya, two from Shatt Damam. There was only one from Moro, as the Moro people were very suspicious. Others were from Abri and other places. I also went with money to buy some goods for my shop while I was there. But we were all arrested and taken to prison. They took from me LS 46,000 and the clothes, blankets, watches and things I had bought for my shop.

I spent 59 days in prison. Colonel Ahmed Khamis was responsible for our interrogation there. Another one who was responsible is Sheikh Ismail Dana, he was sheikh of Debi but he became a government informer in Kadugli.

While we were in prison, some of us were taken out at night, and killed. A group of seventeen was taken. Ours was the second group, numbering six. We were taken to a place near Katcha at about 11 p.m. by a group of soldiers. There were six of them, plus the driver.

We were tied with our hands behind us, and lined up, with our backs to the soldiers. They were close, some ten metres away. Ahmed Khamis was supervising the procedure.

Then they shot us—ta-ta-ta-ta-ta-ta. Immediately, with automatic guns. I was hit here [in the back of the head] and the bullet exited here [through the jaw]. I fell on my face. My face was all blood. I fell but I didn't die. I knew that if I made any move, they will come and finish me off. I heard more shots as they were poking about, finishing off the others. While I heard this final shooting I pretended to be dead. The soldiers came and kicked me with their boots. They even stood on me with their boots. I held my

97

breath and just pretended to be dead. One said, 'This one is not yet dead.' The other said, 'Let's leave him, he's dead.' The first fellow was not convinced and shot at me with a pistol. It fell just in front of my face on the left side. The one who shot at me personally was [corporal] Ahmed Gideil, who is half Shawabna and half Arab.[40]

They went back to their lorry. I heard the door shut and the engine start, and the sound of it driving away.

When the sound of the lorry died away, I got up, to a sitting position. Because I was tied with my hands behind my back, I cleaned the blood from my face by wiping my face on my knees. I looked around and found that all my colleagues were dead. Then I left. I walked for a long distance in the wilderness until I found a small hut, all on its own, in the fields.

I called out, 'Salaam alekum.' I said, 'You people inside, come out and help me. Don't be afraid when you see me, I am a Nuba like you.' A woman looked out. She was frightened and went back inside and spoke to her husband, 'There is someone outside who seems to have been knifed.' When the man came out he was also frightened and about to run away. I told him, 'Please don't run, I am a Nuba like you.' He asked, 'Which Nuba [tribe] are you?' I said, 'I am a Nuba from Eri.' He said, 'Then why are you here?' I said, 'I was brought by the army and shot.' He said, 'Are the shots we heard earlier this evening the ones you are talking about?' I said, 'Yes.' He said, 'The army comes every night and shoots people in this place. The smell of the dead bodies is disturbing us and we cannot even stay here.' I said to him, 'I do not want anything from you except for you to come and untie my hands.' Which he did.

I thanked the man and said, 'As far as you have freed my hands, now I will not die.' Because the ropes were very tight and painful, the blood was not moving in my veins. The blood even burst one vein [higher up] on my left arm.

The farmer immediately took me to his sheikh. The sheikh said, 'It is better that you stay here with us for ten days, and we look for medicine. Then we can take you back to your own people.' But after four days, the sheikh came and said they had received a message from the army in Kadugli, saying that they had shot six but only found five [bodies], and if the one who is alive is being kept hidden in your villages, we are coming to burn all the villages in

---

[40] Corporal Gideil has been repeatedly named by former detainees for his involvement in executions.

your area. I told the sheikh, 'I cannot be the cause of all your villages being burned and you being killed. Take me away. Throw me into any forest and I will see what will happen to me.'

They took me that night to the bush. It was August and it was raining. I spent four days in the bush, eating only dust mixed with water. Some of this would go inside, down my throat, and some would spill outside, because my jaw was open [on account of the bullet wound]. After four days I reached Eri. I was already exhausted. I had no energy to walk all this way. Since we had been in prison we had been underfed—we were given just one [piece of] bread every day, and you eat one third for breakfast, one third for lunch and one third for supper, with only water.

I arrived in Eri and found my family. They did not recognise me. When I called my mother, she said, 'Who is that who is calling me like that, in a strange voice?' By that time, the damage to my tongue and my jaw had disturbed my speech. I said, 'It is your son, Defan.'

My daughter recognised my voice. After they recognised me, they came to me crying. I said, 'Don't cry, I am already with you.' I immediately asked my wife and daughter, 'Did any soldiers come here?' They said, 'Yesterday there were three soldiers in the house, two on the veranda and one patrolling around the house.' When I heard this I went immediately to the SPLA camp in the mountains, to Juma Kabbi.

After I left the house, eight soldiers came to the house. I left a message with my family not to tell anyone of my whereabouts. Messages had come from Kadugli to the police post that they had to find me.

My wound has healed. But even today I cannot eat proper food, I can only take soup and other liquids.

"Nihna Kadugli"

One of the Kadugli MPs, Haroun Abdel Rasoul Kafi, visited his constituency in August 1988 to investigate complaints of mysterious arrests and disappearances. He too was arrested, and 38 other educated Nuba, including civil servants, local government officials, nurses and one football player, were detained in the next stage of the crackdown. The government said nothing. Haroun Kafi was supposed to have parliamentary immunity.

When the Union of Sudan African Parties challenged Prime Minister Sadiq el Mahdi, the reply was that the MP was involved in subversion against the state, and an investigation was ongoing. The investigation continued for ten months and was only halted when the Prime Minister was overthrown. Parliamentary immunity was lifted two months after Haroun Kafi's arrest, and he spent most of his detention in the military headquarters in Kadugli.

In September, Governor Abdel Rasoul el Nur claimed to have uncovered the existence of a secret organization named "Nihna Kadugli" ("We, Kadugli"). He described it as "subversive" and accused it of "trying to enlist citizens for espionage."[41] He alleged that Haroun Kafi was the leader of this clandestine organisation.

Challenged by Haroun Kafi's lawyers, the government failed to produce a single piece of evidence to substantiate their allegations. The existence of the supposed "Nihna Kadugli" organisation and Haroun Kafi's alleged involvement remained completely speculative. The reality appears to be that the Governor conspired with some leading Jellaba traders in Kadugli and military intelligence to create the allegations. One of those most prominent in organising the crackdown was Captain Yunis al Rihaima, a Baggara from Hamra, who has since been promoted to head of military intelligence for Kadugli town. They first invented a subversive Nuba organisation called "al Sakhar al Aswad" ("The Black Rock"), allegedly formed by Yousif Kuwa in 1980 before he joined the SPLA. When intelligence investigations failed to substantiate the existence of this organisation, another organisation was invented, "Nihna Kadugli." Because of lack of evidence, the military intelligence resisted handing Haroun Kafi over to the police for a trial.

The irony is that there were Komolo cells existing in Kadugli at the time, which were active in facilitating the passage of SPLA recruits to the Nuba Mountains and the South. Some of those arrested in the "Nihna Kadugli" crackdown were Komolo members and in fact the organisation was crushed at the time, with many

---

[41] Quoted in *Sudan Times*, 30 September 1988.

members killed. But there is no evidence that Haroun Kafi, and many of the other victims, were ever members of Komolo.

The Crackdown Widens

The case of Haroun Kafi was well-known, but there were many, many other victims. The definition of "leaders" was very wide, and included all manner of individuals of social and cultural importance. In the southern jebels, traditional wrestlers have a high status, and were among the priority victims for the government. Amsal Tutu Tiya, aged 41, is a catechist in the Anglican church from Tabanya in Angolo, in the far south of the Nuba Mountains. He said:[42]

In 1987 a small force military force came from Turoji to Angolo and abducted eight people, among them Kuku Tutu. When they were abducted I followed them from a distance. In the Alafin area between Kadugli and el Ehimir the army stopped. I saw the eight people being shot by firing squad.

Again, in September 1987 twelve persons among them two famous wrestlers, Kiyaim Kuku and Keis Tiya, were arrested in Angolo village by an army [unit] coming from Kadugli. All of us were called to an open space in the village by the commanding officer. He was a one-star officer. We were ordered to sit down. Kiyaim, known also as Kuyu, was tied up and a military tank ran him over. He didn't die. The tank passed over him three times but each time he was alive. At last the soldiers axed him and beat him with heavy sticks. Others were slaughtered in front of their homes. The army told us not to bury them. This happened in the morning. In the afternoon the army went back to Kadugli. In the evening we buried the twelve deceased.

In the same year 1987 the sheikh of Tabanya (the assistant of Omda Kuku Talodi) and two catechists were arrested by the army from Kadugli. The catechists were Matta Bosh of Tabanya church and Gabriel Tutu Alim Nur of Angolo church. All were taken to Kadugli. After some months the catechists were released and came home with paralysed hands because of torture. Gabriel Tutu later left the church and joined the SPLA. He is now in west Kadugli.

---

[42] Interviewed in Um Dulu, 17 May 1995.

Teachers, civil servants and merchants were also targetted. Most of the Nuba elite who lived and worked in towns were transferred, or they saw what was likely to happen to them and fled to Khartoum or abroad. Those in rural areas were more likely to be detained or killed.

Sherab Lima Kodi is an Otoro merchant who was fortunate to escape in the crackdown.[43]

In 1987 the army started by arresting people, especially leading civilians, accusing them of co-operating with the SPLA. I was arrested twice. The first time I was captured and handed over to a military officer I know, Michael Korio. That was June 1987, in el Azraq. He investigated my case. He accused me: 'You are an Anyanya.' I said no. He said: 'You co-operate with them.' I denied it. I was released without incident.

At the time I was a merchant with a shop, in el Azraq. When the war started, the government confiscated my shop. I listed all the things in my diary that they took, the total was LS 72,000 which in those days was a lot of money. Trade was good.

Not only was my shop taken—all the shops in that area were taken, because we were in a zone of SPLA activity. So they suspected us of co-operating with the SPLA. The Jellaba had run away to el Obeid and Khartoum immediately when the SPLA came. There were four Jellaba and they all left. So only the local traders remained. We were three. So the Arabs were not wanting to take over the trade, they were just wanting to loot our goods. They took all the shops, and then loaded all the goods on cars and took them north. The area of the market is now bush, all the shops have gone.

After my shop was closed, I went to the mountains with my cows and goats, and cultivated my farm. But my animals died in the mountains because the climate was not good for them. It is not possible to trade in this area because people have no money.

The second time I was arrested was in July 1987. It was also in el Azraq. I was taken to Heiban and handed to an officer, Mohamed Hussein. I knew him well. He asked me, 'Do you want to remain with us or go to the SPLA? If you remain with us, stay here.' He let me go and I came to this side at once. Mohamed Hussein was a

---

[43] Interviewed in Tira Limon, 23 May 1995.

friend of mine from before, and his father was a trader who had co-operated with me. That was why he released me.

Any area where youths had joined the SPLA was a target, with the elders accused of organising the recruitment. Korongo Abdalla was one such place. Jaafar al Fadl described how some of the important local figures were victims of the crackdown:[44]

In 1987 an order was issued banning public meetings. Then on 25 April they arrested and shot three people. Their bodies were thrown away. They were accused of inciting civilians. They were: (1) Tutu Mis, a nurse, shot at Khor el Afna; (2) Sikkin Kuku, a tailor, shot at Katcha and (3) Ibrahim Tutu, head of the co-operative society, shot at Khor el Afna.

In 1987-88 many of our people were arrested. Six teachers from our area were arrested and put in prison. One escaped and ran to the South. The other five, we have not heard any news from them. In general, people were not confident. They knew they were being monitored by the government.

We had a co-operative but in 1987 the government refused to supply the goods we needed, such as sugar and soap. The Shawabna traders left. It seems that the reason why the supplies were stopped is that one of them accused the head of our co-operative of collaborating with the SPLA.

In nearby Shatt Damam, the story was similar. In 1988, several chiefs and others detained and executed, including Sultan Jok Muwan, from Kutang, and Tito Tiya, from Hajar el Dabib.

The 1989-91 Arrests and Disappearances

During 1989 the crackdown escalated into a major assault on all educated sections of Nuba society, culminating in 1990-1 with a programme of arrest and detention, torture and killing. For many Nuba communities, the elimination of their few educated people was

---

[44] Interviewed in Um Dulu, 17 May 1995.

even more disastrous than the scorched earth policies in the rural areas. This was said by a Miri farmer, Musa Kuwa Jabir Tiya:[45]

> The worst part of that period was eliminating the educated. So many were arrested and killed. Al Nur Kuwa, a farmer who was educated, was arrested and killed. Khalid Musa, a post office worker, was arrested and killed. Also Berer Khalifa, a primary school teacher. There were many in Kadugli, I do not know all the names.

In April 1989, there were over two hundred arrests in Kadugli, including many SNP members. Soldiers belonging to the pro-government Anyanya II militia were stationed in Kadugli at the time, and were used by Military Intelligence as an extra wing of the security forces, rapidly gaining a reputation for ruthlessness. The hunt for educated Nuba continued after the June coup. One of those who was caught in it, and was fortunate to survive, was a merchant, Munir Sheikh el Din, who was arrested on 10 November 1989. He now lives in Jeddah.[46]

> Just before the June [1989] coup I went to Khartoum. In November I returned, but I was arrested in the bus on 10 November before I reached my village. Four armed soldiers with G3 guns cordoned off the bus and asked for me by name. The commander of them was a fifth man, Mahdi Mamur Nito, a leader of a PDF battalion. He is a Nuba and a former member of the SNP who was dismissed for corruption. Formal charges were laid against him in Port Sudan. He ran to Dilling in June 1989 and worked for military intelligence before they made him into a PDF leader. They enlisted his help to target the educated Nuba.
>
> I was taken to the 19th Battalion [in Dilling], to the intelligence office. I was searched and taken to the cells. Then they made much propaganda, saying they had captured a colonel in the SPLA. While I was in the cell, army officers kept coming to look at this famous SPLA colonel. I had previously worked as a seaman, and they accused me of being with the SPLA at that time.

---

[45] Interviewed in Um Dulu, 17 May 1995.
[46] Interviewed in Cairo, November 1992.

The army took a Doshka [Soviet-made military vehicle] to my village. They searched my home, destroyed some books and stole some. After they returned they started questioning me. Sergeant Abul Gassim Hamad, a Hawazma, was doing the interrogation. I was made to sit on the floor. He said, 'You're a colonel in the SPLA.' I denied it. I was then hit from behind by another one, Sergeant Ali Kombo. He was drunk. He is a notorious man who is responsible for killing some Nuba people in Kadugli. Then his colleagues stopped Ali Kombo and I was taken back to my cell. I was taken again at midnight and questioned until the morning. Most of the questions were about the SPLA. I was hit again, this time by Abul Gassim. The soldiers hit me whenever I denied anything or resisted. The kicked me and hit me with the butts of guns. They called me 'Slave.' They said, 'When did the Nuba become human beings?' They called me a sodomite. They pressed their fingers into my eyes.

In the morning I was taken to a small cell. Sleeping was difficult. I was not given food every day and the water was not enough. This continued for one month. There was harsh interrogation. Sometimes they would send people who would speak to me in soft, kind language.

I was returned for interrogation by Sergeant Hassan Abu Nur, another Hawazma intelligence officer. He had three Nuba men in his office. The three said they were members of the SPLA who had been recruited by me, and I was their leader. The interrogating sergeant turned to me and said, 'You will be executed today. You will go to Kadugli and be taken to Um Dorein to be executed.' At that time many executions were in Um Dorein. They took the three men out and I was transferred to another office. There I found Colonel Ahmed Abdalla, head of Military Intelligence in that place, an internal security man, the director of Dilling prison, the head of the police, the resident magistrate (Ahmad Abu Zaid) and some other Military Intelligence people. They brought in the three Nuba men, and started listening to their testimony. They repeated their story that I had recruited them to the SPLA. Then I was asked to reply. I said, 'Show me the documents. Unless you can prove it, this is nonsense. They are telling lies. These men are not SPLA.'

This degree of formality in interrogation is highly unusual. Rather than the whole Security Committee, it is more common for an intelligence officer to do the investigation, come to his conclusions, and then detain without charge or execute the prisoner. The reason for the formality appears to be that the authorities wanted to make publicity out of the capture of an alleged SPLA colonel. There was also another unexpected element in the interrogation.

I thought it was unusual for the resident magistrate to be part of the Security Committee of the town. But Ahmad Abu Zaid is a notorious judge. There are reports that he visits the battalion [headquarters] secretly, evaluates the evidence, and on his advice the Military Intelligence take people out and execute them. There are many complaints against him from the Dilling people. After these complaints he was summoned to el Obeid for some investigation. But [Chief Justice] Jalal Ali Lutfi ordered his appointment as President of the Special Court.

They interrogated me. During this interrogation the head of the police, el Amin, was supporting me. Then I was ordered out of the office and taken back to my cell. On the way back, some of the soldiers were asking me for money to help me get out. I refused.

The torture started again. There was a three day programme. I was hit with a whip, with sticks and with hands. This went on from midnight to 6 a.m. Then from 6 a.m. to midnight I was put in a small cell with other people. I could hardly sleep. Then after three days I was left alone. I was treated decently, sometimes even given better treatment than the others.

Twice I was taken to a firing squad when I was in that prison. Their procedure was that they would take two prisoners to a place outside the town, stand them up as if to kill them both, and then the officer would shoot one only. The first time they killed a Moro man called Suleiman, I don't know his father's name. The second time they killed Suleiman Ismail from Julud. At least fifteen people were killed in this way.

I spent four months in the battalion [headquarters]. I was transferred to many places and questioned by many different people. Then they transferred me to Dilling prison for two months. I was chained, tied with iron across my wrists. There was more propaganda about this SPLA colonel whom they had captured. More people came to look at me. There was no torture. After one month there they began to allow me some occasional visitors.

After those two months I was transferred to el Obeid prison. At first I was put in with the ordinary criminals, and then taken to the cells of the political detainees. I spent more than twelve months in el Obeid prison, including five months in the hospital. Then, there were about thirty-to-sixty people on average under detention. At one point there were ninety. Three of those detainees died. Others died too.

I was released from hospital by the general prosecution department. A lawyer filed a petition for me, and the attorney-general ordered my case papers. I was released on 22 June 1991.

The large group of detainees that Munir refers to were arrested at different times between 1989 and 1991. Nine of them are known to have died, including:

* Abashir Ali Gaddal;
* Ibrahim Basha (eighty years old);
* Ismail Sultan
* Mohamed Hamad;
* Sheikh Hamedein Fadul;
* Mek Kurtubeir Basha (mek of Julud);
* Omer al Luban;
* Makina Kheir;
* Hassan al Keif.

Abdel Rahim Mohamed Haroun is also reported to have died in prison at this time.

Three of those reported to have been executed at Um Dorein in December 1991, shortly after Munir's arrest, are:

* Hassan al Rimla, a teacher at Um Dorein intermediate school;
* Zakaria Hassan Komi, a teacher at Um Jabralla primary school;
* Hassan Kuku, a medical assistant.

From 1990 onwards the lists of names of educated Nuba who "disappeared" are simply too long. to print.[47] Every tribe lost

---

[47] Long but not exhaustive lists can be obtained from the organization Nuba Mountains Solidarity Abroad.

members; most villages had someone detained or killed. In a community with few educated people, the loss of a few can leave the people without any articulate spokesmen. Starting in September 1990 onwards, there was a major crackdown with many disappearances. Thirty-two educated Nuba are known to have disappeared. It was at this time that the campaign against Nuba leaders and intellectuals began to come to the attention of the international community, on account of the efforts of Nuba living abroad. For example, the Nuba Mountains Solidarity Abroad was founded at this time. Arrests and detentions continued in 1991.[48] In July, Hamdan Hassan Koury, a lawyer from Laguri living in Kadugli, was arrested, released and re-arrested together with his father, a prisons service officer, and later executed. A total of 37 "disappeared" in June-July 1991; more than one hundred were arrested in September. Some of those who "disappeared" in 1990-1 include:

*   Mohamed Nowar Aso, a dentist and a member of the Sudan Doctors' Union;
*   Ismat Hassan Kheir Saeed, a teacher at Kadugli Secondary School, from Miri;
*   Yousif Galgadoun, a teacher at Kadugli Secondary School, from Dilling;
*   al Sir Abdel Nabi Malik, an employee of the soil survey department;
*   Kamal Kano Kafi Haloof, a radio technician;
*   Ibrahim Marmatoun, an employee of the water department;
*   Abu Zaid Shelal, a teacher.

Also in 1990-1, 24 Nuba serving in the army with ranks of Major and above were dismissed from the military, along with a number of other lower ranking officers. Nine senior Nuba police officers and two colonels in the prison service were also required to take early retirement.

---

[48] For some cases see: Amnesty International, "Sudan: The Ravages of War: Political killings and humanitarian disaster," London, September 1993, pp. 11-14.

Although these detentions, murders and "disappearances" are much smaller in the number of victims than killings carried out in the course of military operations, their impact was devastating. The death of well-known members of the community spread fear, and the absence of educated people and community leaders—those most familiar with the workings of government, able to mobilise the people, and exert pressure—left many Nuba communities without their first line of defence in the onslaught that was coming. It also removed their means of recourse: it was these people who spoke on their behalf, nationally and internationally. The rationale was explained clearly by Khalid Abdel Karim al Husseini, the former head of the security branch in the Office of the Governor of Kordofan (and younger brother of the governor), who left Sudan and sought asylum in Europe in 1993.[49] He said that the government was "taking the intellectuals, taking the professionals, to ensure that the Nuba were so primitive that they couldn't speak for themselves."

Finally, the campaign of elimination created a leadership vacuum in which the government could begin to impose its own leaders.

THE *JIHAD*, 1992-93

The Government of Sudan is embarrassed by the fact that it launched a *Jihad* (Holy War) in the Nuba Mountains in 1992, and tries to explain to foreign visitors that this is mere disinformation by enemies of the country. Gáspár Bíró, the UN Special Rapporteur on Sudan, wrote:[50]

> The Special Rapporteur notes that the mere existence of any organization called 'militia', or persons called 'mujahidin' is strongly denied by Government of Sudan officials, as well as the fact of the declaration of jihad. As a matter of fact, there is, on a hill situated along the road between Dilling and Kadugli, approximately 8 km

---

[49] Interviewed by th BBC in Switzerland, 13 June 1995.
[50] Special Rapporteur of the Commission on Human Rights, "Interim report on the situation of human rights in the Sudan," submitted to the UN General Assembly, 18 November 1993, p. 21.

from Kadugli, a large white inscription in Arabic 'Kadugli the jihad' which can be seen from some distance by those who are travelling on this route. The inscription can also be seen very well during the day also by people of displaced camps around Kadugli.

The fact is that in January 1992, the Governor of Kordofan, Lt.-Gen. Sayed Abdel Karim al Husseini, together with the head of the PDF, formally declared a *Jihad* in South Kordofan. Two months later, while the military offensive was raging in Tullishi, the government held a 'Conference of Tribal Leaders' in el Obeid. All the Arab tribes in Kordofan were represented. None of the Nuba were there. Khalid Abdel Karim el Husseini had just taken up his post of head of security in the Governor's office. He said, "By virtue of this position I was in direct contact with the Governor. I used to read all the correspondence to and from the Governor's office... I was eyewitness to military operations in the region."[51] He described the conference:

> The conference was attended by Major-General el Zubeir Mohamed Salih, the Vice-President of the RCC. The principal aim of this conference was to mobilize these tribes by reviving the Native Administration and endorsing NIF plans to create tribal disharmony in the Mountains. The NIF ploy was to talk about the loyalty of Nuba to the SPLA, and their preparations to rebel and separate the Nuba Mountains from the rest of the region, and the Sudan. The NIF succeeded in their ploy and the conference resolved on an Islamic *Jihad* against the 'rebel infidels,' the 'Enemies of Religion and the Nation.'
>
> After this conference finished its deliberations, Field Marshal Omer al Bashir, the Chairman of the RCC, arrived in el Obeid to attend the Conference. On that occasion, a big military parade was made for the chiefs and their followers, where el Beshir was proclaimed the *Imam al Jihad.* El Beshir in turn named the *Wali* [Governor] of Kordofan the *Amir al Jihad* and the tribal leaders were each named *Amir al Jihad* in his area. The new amirs were given an automatic gun and a Landcruiser. They were also

---

[51] Statement to Sudan Human Rights Organisation, Switzerland, 19 October 1993.

promised that any of their followers who volunteer in the PDF will be armed.

Khalid el Husseini went on to describe how the government obtained the support of the Kordofan Arab tribal leaders for the *Jihad*, by a combination of lavish bribery and implicit threat:

> To assure the loyalty of the tribal leaders, the plan was executed in two stages. The first stage was the provision of generous material incentives to the tribal leaders. In addition to the car and the gun, they were given large amounts of money. The government built luxurious guest houses for them, each in the area of his choice. The guest houses were provided with modern communication facilities. The amirs were given extensive powers which they never dreamt of even during the British colonial rule.
>
> The second stage was the use of coercion and threats by the intensive presence of National Security and Revolutionary Security [forces] around the tribal leaders. These security organs were openly reminding them that their privileges were linked with their loyalty to the system.
>
> Naturally, the backwardness, ignorance, superstition and the strength of the tribal administration in the region made the grounds for the success of tribal agitation. Once the loyalty of these tribal and sectarian leaders have been assured it was natural for these tribes to support these devilish plans.

The Sudan Government is bankrupt, but funds were found for this massive war effort. Special taxes were levied and contributions were solicited from Islamic institutions and pro-government Sudanese expatriates in the Arab states. The social security fund was used to provide food and finance for the Mujahidiin. The *Jihad* was all quite open: in fact, media propaganda was an integral aspect of the campaign, and a new radio station was opened in Kadugli.

> All these were announced on the radio and television. It was also officially announced that the year 1992 is the 'Year of *Jihad*' in Kordofan to liberate it from the infidel rebels. After that the *Jihad* support committees were created all over the country, to enhance the *Jihad* in Kordofan. Convoys loaded with materials in kind were

sent to the Mujahdiin in Kordofan. In Kordofan itself they started implementing the conference resolutions by establishing PDF camps in all the provinces of the region, and with every tribe separately. Additional tax was levied upon the citizens in the region under the slogan 'Financing the *Jihad*', while the central government supplied the military hardware. The region was flooded with various types of arms.

The declaration of *Jihad* was no aberration: Hassan al Turabi had been publicly calling for a *Jihad* for years. Three weeks before the 1989 coup, he openly called for the government of Sadiq el Mahdi to fall, to "safeguard national unity" and to "resurrect the spirit of confrontation and resistance."[52]

Further mobilisation and endorsement for the *Jihad* continued during 1992 and into the following year. On 27 April 1992, following a meeting in the Popular Committee Hall in el Obeid, six prominent pro-government Imams declared a *Fatwa* against the SPLA and its sympathisers in the Nuba Mountains. This was the most explicit attempt to obtain religious legitimation for the campaign (see Chapter IV).

The declaration of the *Jihad* was more than the despatch of religiously-motivated soldiers to the front line. It reflected the much wider programme for social transformation undertaken by the ruling National Islamic Front, known as the Comprehensive Call, or *el Da'awa el Shamla*. This has six main components:[53]

(1) religious indoctrination and the imposition of Islam on non-Moslems;
(2) political, social and economic favouritism for Nuba Moslems and their instigation to head the campaign;
(3) *Jihad* against all those who defy the Call, whether Moslems or non-Moslems;
(4) isolation of Nuba Christians and intimidation of church leaders, also isolation of the region from international human rights, humanitarian or solidarity organizations;

---

[52] *Al Rayah*, 7 June 1989.
[53] Mohamed A. M. Salih, "Resistance and response: Ethnocide and genocide in the Nuba Mountains, Sudan," *GeoJournal*, 1995, in press.

Conscripts to the PDF training in Kadugli.
Photo: Nuba Mountains Solidarity Abroad.

Jebel Kadugli marked with the words: *Kadugli al Jihad.*
Photo: Nuba Mountains Solidarity Abroad.

(5) resettlement in peace villages to help achieve objectives (1) and (2);

(6) crackdown on all Nuba, inside or outside the Nuba Mountains, who oppose the campaign.

Governor el Husseini is the individual primarily responsible for the South Kordofan *Jihad*, though there is absolutely no question that he had the full backing of President Omer al Bashir and Vice-President Zubeir Mohamed Saleh. Another key figure was the Commissioner of South Kordofan, Abdel Wahab Abdel Rahman Ali. At the time of the *Jihad* he was promoted to Minister of Health in the Regional Government, to take special responsibility for the *Jihad*, and also temporarily resumed his responsibilities as Commissioner for South Kordofan during the height of the relocations programme. Later, Abdel Wahab was transferred out of the region, and he subsequently met his death in a car accident.

In October 1991, the Nuba Mountains was sealed off by the government. No foreigners were permitted access, and Sudanese citizens needed to obtain passes from the military authorities to travel there. The genocide was to be perpetrated in silence. Khalid Abdel Karim explained:[54]

The policy of the Islamic Front government is to prevent any information leaving the area, which indicates that there is a savage war and many infringements of rights in the Nuba Mountains. The government does not want anybody to know what is happening in the area.

At that date, under the general auspices of the PDF, a new military force known as Mujahidiin was mobilised, mainly in North Kordofan. Members of the NIF and their sympathisers were recruited in large numbers and given a rudimentary military training, and despatched to the front line. Their ideological commitment to the war was deep, and their loyalty unquestionable. The months of the offensive were full of exhortations in the national media for men

---

[54] Interviewed by the BBC in Switzerland, 13 June 1995.

to join the Mujahidiin, and accounts of their progress in recruitment and training. For example:

> Mosque attendees and Moslem *Ulema* [clerics] in Kordofan region will receive training in modern warfare tactics, medical first aid and driving trucks. The registration starts immediately in the office of Religious Affairs in el Obeid town and at the headquarters of various other provinces. The Secretary for the Mosque Attendees' Union, el Sheikh Ahmed Hajeir clarified that this order, which has been issued by the Governor of the region, came as a result of his belief that mosque attendees, as an important section of society, can play an important role in leading the masses to *Jihad*.[55]

There is little doubt that the Iranian model of "human wave" attacks, deployed during the war with Iraq, was in the minds of the military planners. In fact, Iranian military advisors were involved in the training and deployment of the Mujahidiin.

The military component of the *Jihad* had two elements. One was a purge within the army, removing all officers who were not considered supportive. The second was a military offensive of unprecedented size, under the direct control of Army Headquarters in Khartoum, into the western jebels.

The Tullishi Offensive

In November 1991 the Sudan Government began what was to become its largest military operations in the Nuba Mountains to date. In January 1992, the Hajana Division in el Obeid was augmented by several brigades from Northern Sudan, including artillery battalions from Atbara, air defence battalions from Khartoum and Port Sudan, and a company of engineers from Omdurman. One infantry company, from Shendi, was to gain a reputation for systematic rape of women. They paraded in front of President Omer al Bashir and Governor el Husseini before being despatched to the front.

The assault was preceded by a round of arrests and detentions in Lagowa, and some summary executions in the garrison. Mukhtar

---

[55] *Al Inqaz al Watani* (government newspaper), 18 February 1992.

Musa was one of those shot dead; Hamza Farajallah was arrested and taken to el Obeid. Later, Lagowa military intelligence requested his return for further questioning. They took him from el Obeid but executed him on the road. Nineteen men (seventeen Kamda, one Tima and one Daju) were arrested and later executed, on 27 November 1991. Others were arrested and taken to el Obeid. This led to a formal protest to President Omer al Bashir from some leading natives of Lagowa resident in Khartoum.

Five men, including three merchants and one teacher, were arrested and detained in Abu Zabad in October 1991. They spent thirteen months in el Obeid prison without charge, before being taken from the prison by military intelligence on the night of 3-4 December 1992. They were taken to Julud and executed; one succeeded in escaping and later reported what had happened.

All previous campaigns in the Nuba Mountains had been directed from Hajana headquarters in el Obeid, or divisional headquarters in Kadugli or district towns. For this offensive, the Vice-President, General Zubeir Mohamed Saleh, came personally from Khartoum to command the forces in Lagowa. Forces were despatched from Lagowa and Dilling to destroy the SPLA forces in the western jebels, and particularly their stronghold in Jebel Tullishi. The entire operation was called *Bishayir al Kheirat* ("Expectation of Blessing"), with the Lagowa operation also called *Tayir al Ababil* ("Birds of Ababil," from the battle, mentioned in the Koran, in which Allah sent birds to protect the Kaaba of Mecca). After the first round of fighting, the army sent further reinforcements, so that the full strength of the government forces totalled 45,000 men. The second, even larger assault on Tullishi was called *Badr el Kubra*, from the Prophet Mohamed's biggest victory against the unbelievers.

In the Tullishi offensive, the government used their new military force, the Mujahidiin, for the first time. The Mujahidiin were well-treated by the government, but proved themselves a military liability. If they were in the vanguard, their "human wave" assaults were easy prey for the well-dug in SPLA in the hills. If they were integrated with a force of trained soldiers, they obstructed the soldiers either by charging forwards or by retreating in disarray. The SPLA captured many weapons from the Mujahidiin.

The Tullishi offensive included Iranian military advisors. The Sudan Government has repeatedly been accused by opposition forces and some western countries of hosting Middle Eastern terrorists, either in training camps or within the Sudanese armed forces. Most of these accusations are groundless. But evidence from a range of sources indicates that a number of Iranian advisors were stationed in Lagowa district for this offensive. The SPLA forces captured two of them, whom they promptly executed—much to the anger of the commander, who realised that his soldiers' summary killing had cost the SPLA a propaganda coup. All Iranian advisors were withdrawn immediately after this incident.

The assault continued for six months without ceasing, but the three thousand SPLA soldiers on the mountain, led by Commander Ismail Khamis Jellab and Alternate Commander Mohamed Juma Nayel, remained undefeated. The Mujahidiin were never used in the same way again.

The government also encouraged the Murahaliin to raid the neighbouring hills. Hassan Osman Tutu was in Tima during the Tullishi offensive. There, the army did not directly attack but the people felt the force of the militia raids on the flanks of the main offensive. Tima was largely unprotected by the SPLA, and the militia who came included the Misiriya Humr, who had hardly been seen in the Nuba Mountains before. Hassan said:[56]

The biggest offensive was 1992. The Government of Sudan attacked Tullishi. Forces came from el Obeid and surrounded the mountain. They were fighting the SPLA, but they would shoot anyone who was in front of them. All the civilians ran from the area. The army stayed, taking all the food and all the cows, burning the villages. The whole of Tullishi was burned, not a single village escaped.

They seized people by force. At that time there were no peace camps. When they took a person to Lagowa, they just left him there. So the people were migrating to other places. In addition, they used dead animals to poison the wells.

---

[56] Interviewed in Tira Limon, 23 May 1995.

116

The SPLA held Jebel Tullishi. The number of civilians who stayed on the mountain is not known, but there was serious famine. Many people died on the road due to hunger.

I was in Tima at the time. In that offensive, it was our first time to see the Misiriya Humr. They came with horses, in February-March. It was just them, there was no army. The Tullishi people used to come to Tima because the Tullishi water had been poisoned. If the Misiriya Humr caught them on the way, they killed them. The Humr destroyed Maryam village, but no-one was killed in the attack. But people died of hunger afterwards. There was also shelling from the army attacking Tullishi, which affected the Tima people. It forced people to move to Katla. But in Katla there was also famine, although there were no attacks on Katla at that time. The whole area was affected by famine.

Because of this, there was only little farming in 1992, and the famine continued into 1993.

The offensive included the use of aerial bombardment, both against SPLA positions in Jebel Tullishi and civilian targets in the surrounding area. Helicopter gunships, MiG-23 fighter-bombers and Antonov aircraft were all used. One of the civilian targets hit was the market at Um Balol, which was witnessed by a resident. She gave African Rights the names of the eight people who were killed:[57]

> Himera Kafi and her two children; Umama Tiyok (a child); Kaka Deldum and Babay Deldum (sisters); al Nur Mohamed; Khadija Regeyig was wounded and died later. I saw these people dead and we even buried them together. Tiyuh al Himera's leg was cut off by a bomb. There were no SPLA in the market.

The massive attack on Jebel Tullishi was not successful. The army was beaten off, and in May, before the rainy season gave the advantage to the guerrillas, the huge force withdrew. No offensive on the same scale has been witnessed again in the Nuba Mountains. But immediately afterwards the army and militia turned to nearby Nuba tribes and attacked them. In one incident, soldiers arrested six women who were coming to farms in Tima to work as wage

---

[57] Toma Akwa Bele, interviewed in Achiron, 7 May 1995.

labourers. The soldiers killed them with knives and left the bodies there on the farms.[58] Another incident was in June, reported by a resident:[59]

Traders from Abu Januq used to trade with the SPLA. Thirteen traders were active between there and Abu Zabad. All the traders were Nuba. They were captured and sent to el Obeid by military intelligence. They spent two weeks there, and then they were sent to Kadugli, but when they reached Doleiba, near Dilling, they were taken down from the lorry and shot. Twelve died, one escaped.

Meanwhile, militia attacks continued:[60]

The Misiriya Zurug militia, after losing many in the battle of Tullishi, came to villages of Kamda and Tima, got hold of people and took them away. They also picked out people from these areas and from Tullishi in Lagowa town, made a special area called Karakadi in Lagowa town and put them there. Then the government instigated the Misiriya Zurug militia to attack Karakadi in the early morning. They started shooting and killed many people. The numbers were never counted but I have heard people speak of between 250 and three hundred. The garrison was very close but did nothing.

African Rights was unable to confirm this estimate for the number of people who died in the Karakadi killing, but residents of the area all agreed that the number was large, in the hundreds.

Wali, Nyima, Abu Januq, Ghulfan

Wali was virtually completely destroyed in the single military campaign of 1991-2. The countdown to the destruction began when the mek, Abdel Hamid Mohamed Zahra, was instigated to form a government militia. This militia targetted and destroyed the houses of families where youths had gone to join the SPLA. Since promoted

---

[58] Najib Musa Berdo, interviewed in Achiron, 7 May 1995.
[59] Suleiman Jabona, Interviewed in Tira Limon, 22 May 1995.
[60] Suleiman Jabona, interviewed in Achiron, 7 May 1995.

to the government Amir of Salara and Wali, Abdel Hamid Mohamed has admitted that he played such a role: "In 1989, someone came to recruit people to join the rebels. I arrested him and handed him over to the government."[61] (In return, when the SPLA entered the area, it targetted the houses of the Mek and his main followers.) The first burning was in August 1989. In the dry season of 1991-2, the army completely destroyed the Wali villages, burning Abu Sayeda, Baboya, Wali Suq, Um Kurum and Kurunda (a village that had been famous for the number of cattle). A resident of the area told African Rights, "A few people remain in the hills. Most have gone to the towns. No villages remain."[62]

Much of Nyimang was also burned in the same season. The Nyima jebels had escaped the war until 1991, but in the 1991/2 dry season the PDF entered with a vengeance. Their first target was Salara, where Anglican missionaries had built their first church and school. Salara also sent the first pioneers to the SPLA from among the Nyima. The troops destroyed the village, church and school, and subsequently established a garrison. Tundiya was also burned and the people removed. Hajar Sultan, the home of Father Philip Abbas Ghabboush, was destroyed and remains deserted, as was Abu Seyba and a host of small villages. The whole area was then subject to a curfew and tight restrictions on travel; no-one was allowed to leave the area without permission from the authorities.

Jebel Abu Januq is an outlying hill to the west of the main Nyimang range. Though far from any SPLA activity, it was depopulated by force. In March 1992, the people of Abu Januq were told that they must relocate to a camp at Sanut, fifteen kilometres to the north, within 72 hours. Ten people were arrested.

Government attacks continued into the rainy season, after the main offensive was over. On 25 June 1992, after an SPLA unit entered the area, unidentified armed men entered el Faus village in Nyimang, accused people of collaborating with the SPLA, and shot a

---

[61] Speaking at a televised conference of South Kordofan chiefs, Khartoum, October 1993.
[62] Interviewed in Um Dulu, 19 May 1995.

number of young men. Initial reports spoke of a hundred dead, but only sixteen names could be confirmed.

Arguably the most complete destruction and evacuation in 1991-2 was undertaken in the Ghulfan jebels, in the north-centre of the Nuba Mountains. All the villages were destroyed: Karakandi, Kabela, Tikiri, Kalendi, Bardab, Atto, Esho, Dileiba and Shongor. According to one resident,[63]

> All the areas were forcibly evacuated by the army and PDF, turning it into a no-man's land. A few people are now living in the hills. The small SPLA force in the area in 1991 was unable to resist.
>
> Many Ghulfan people who are displaced are recruited to the PDF. Their leader is Amir Mohamed Ismail Bogen. Previously he was a farmer and a soldier. He is believed to be responsible for much of the destruction. Because of him, the Ghulfan were believed to be pro-Arab, but the Ghulfan area was still burned and looted by the Arabs.

Forced Relocation and "Peace Villages"

Perhaps the most dramatic human rights abuse perpetrated by the Sudan Government during the *Jihad* period was the massive forced relocation of Nuba people out of the Nuba Mountains. This was the clearest indication to date of a master plan of the complete social and political transformation of the Nuba Mountains, a re-drawing of the map. At the time, it was labelled "ethnic cleansing". The label was appropriate.

The first evidence for the relocation programme came with stories of children being abducted and forcibly Islamized in a camp run by the PDF at Sheikan, near el Obeid in North Kordofan. These reports were published in strongly anti-Sudan government newspapers and journals, but subsequent events proved that they

---

[63] Suleiman Jabona, interviewed in Um Dulu, 19 May 1995.

contained a strong element of truth.[64] Later, it became clear that the plan for massive removal had existed since the beginning of 1991. In April 1991, the Peace and Resettlement Administration for South Kordofan was established.[65] It was headed by Omer Suleiman Adam.

In February 1992, Omer Suleiman declared that 22 "peace villages" had been prepared, for seventy thousand "returnees" from the SPLA. (The term "returnees" has since been used for all those enticed into government-held towns, abducted by government forces or living in SPLA-controlled areas overrun by the government.) He then spoke of plans for resettling 500,000 people—equivalent to the entire population in the areas controlled by the SPLA and in the rural areas contested between the SPLA and the government. It was a plan for titanic social engineering and political repression on a scale never before seen in Sudan. However, the government's concurrent programme of mass demolition and relocation of squatters and displaced people around Khartoum, which had affected over 500,000 people by that date, was an indication of the scale of what the government was willing to try.

At this stage, the programme of forced removal had two main components. One was evacuation by the military. During the big *Jihad* offensive in the western jebels, tens of thousands of people were driven from their villages. The second was the forced relocation of tens of thousands of people who were already living in displaced camps in and around towns in the Nuba Mountains, principally Kadugli. This component was initially held up by the objections of the then-Commissioner of South Kordofan, Mohamed al Tayeb Fadl (see below). However, between June and August, Governor el Husseini contrived to remove Mohamed al Tayeb, and went personally to Kadugli for some weeks to coordinate the

---

[64] "National Islamic Front abducts children from the Nuba Mountains and places then in a Popular Defence Forces Camp," *El Sudan*, 28 November 1991; also *al Wafd*, 29 December 1991.

[65] See, *inter alia*, Special Rapporteur of the Commission on Human Rights, "Interim report on the situation of human rights in the Sudan," submitted to the UN General Assembly, 18 November 1993, p. 19.

removals. Meanwhile, el Husseini brought back Abdel Wahab Abdel Rahman to be Acting Commissioner.

The idea of the *Dar el Salaam* or "peace camp" or "peace village" had been mooted as far back as 1988, when the Sudan government began to float proposals for resettling displaced people from Southern Sudan. Prime Minister Sadiq el Mahdi darkly hinted at the possible need to replicate "colonial" anti-guerrilla tactics, implying the forcible evacuation of civilian areas.[66] But it was only with the military regime of Omer al Bashir, and the determination of Governor el Husseini and his lieutenants, that such a policy could be put into practice.

Between June and August 1992 at least forty thousand people were moved by force to North Kordofan. They suffered appalling hardship: without adequate food or medical care, they were taken in long journeys over rough roads and simply dumped, in the middle of the rainy season, in "camps" in an alien region.

For many, the first port of call was the regional capital, el Obeid. Convoys of lorries carrying relocated people transited at el Obeid hospital or at displaced camps. In August, 635 people arrived on six trucks from Lagowa. Many of them were very ill. The army asked for 25 to be transfered to hospital, and two died on the way. The next morning, the six lorries continued with their human cargo to Bara, where the people were offloaded at the secondary school. There they joined several previous convoy-loads. The first had arrived in July, consisting of 135 people removed from Lagowa. When these people arrived, the citizens of Bara were appalled at the human cargo that had been dumped in their sleepy little oasis town, and quickly organised to bring water, food, blankets and medicine to the Nuba people. Some came with their cameras to record the scene, but security officers intervened and sent them away. The security also prevented the townspeople from providing assistance, and began to restrict access to the camp. Within a few weeks, the camp had grown to 2,300 people, who stayed until the school was due to re-open, whereupon they were abruptly transferred elsewhere.

---

[66] Quoted in *Sudan Times*, 1 February 1989.

Similar stories can be told from any one of the camps in North Kordofan. The camp in Um Ruwaba was fifteen kilometres outside the town, and in July an estimated five-to-ten people were dying each day from a population of 5,500. Other camps existed in Sheikan near el Obeid (population initially 3,700), en Nahud (2,100), Sidra (3,200), Khor Taggat secondary school, Fanjuja, Hamrat el Sheikh, Nitta and al Mazrub. A number of sources also spoke of the existence of a camp in Sodiri, but others have denied this. The reality is unclear, but some reports indicate that a transit camp for abducted young Nuba boys existed there.

In South Kordofan there were camps at Angarko (near Dilling), Rashad and six camps in the vicinity of Kadugli. Visitors to the Kadugli camps reported them well organised, and run by Da'awa al Islamiya (Islamic Call, an extremist Islamic relief agency), the Sudanese Red Crescent and other Islamic agencies. Of the 33,000 displaced in these camps, over seventeen thousand were moved to el Obeid after a process of screening. Healthy people were earmarked for sending to "production sites", weaker ones to "hospitable families" in North Kordofan (in the event, this demarcation was never fully implemented).

A student from Nyima passed through Nitil, Kurmuti, Salara and Tendiya shortly after the 1992 *Jihad* offensive during his vacation. He detailed what he saw:[67]

There was a concentrated offensive on Wali, Tima, Katla and Julud. Nyimang was also attacked at the same time, and many people were killed in that area. The Tendiya and Salara people emigrated.

Those who escaped are in the peace camp at Angarko, south of Dilling. There are about 3,500 people there, most of them women and old men. I spent ten days in Angarko looking for my relatives. The basic necessities are not there, the only food is sorghum distributed by the NIF youth organization, *Shabab al Watan* [literally: Youth of the Nation]. There is no grinding machine to pound the sorghum grains into flour, so people can only boil and eat it. This is causing many stomach problems and some people died. There is no health service. Most people were nearly naked.

---

[67] Interviewed in Cairo, November 1992.

They said the PDF had come and burned their villages and forced them to leave. Many were killed, they said. In fact, I saw lorries going from Dilling to el Obeid, and others coming from Kadugli bringing people from the southern areas.

I saw one mosque; inside they teach 360 children between the ages of four and eight. They are training the children so that they will become Mujahadiin.

The largest camp is Sheikan, which is fifty kilometres south of el Obeid. There are about fifteen thousand people there including five thousand children. Many children are being taught in the *khalwa* [Koranic school] and trained to be Mujahidiin. People there are also suffering. In one day they buried 34 corpses. Most of the deaths were because of poor food—they give one quarter of a *malwa* [bowl] per day only. Only the *Shabab al Watan* are allowed in the camp, others are prevented.

People are transferred in trucks originally designed for cattle. They are trucks with trailers, with extended high sides. They stop sometimes for water, but people are not allowed off the truck to drink. Also the people are naked and don't want to get down naked. The transfer of people from these camps has started.

Dead bodies are an ordinary sight in these camps, and in el Obeid. Sometimes dogs will bring human parts to the house. The dogs have developed a taste for human flesh—there was one case where dogs attacked a living person who was lying under a tree. In Um Heitan, even the chickens are turning savage. Death is now something normal in the Nuba Mountains.

The government Amir of Nyima, Ramadhan Tayara, later gave the official version of events:[68]

The relocated people were welcomed by the North Kordofan citizens with open hearts. The rebels had entered their villages, killed what they could kill, looted what they could loot, and raped what they could rape. So people went to the Peace Department of Kordofan, and the Peace Department decided to gather them in one place for safety. Our brothers in North Kordofan welcomed them,

---

[68] Speaking at a televised conference of South Kordofan chiefs, Khartoum, October 1993.

and said they would contribute willingly to their welfare. They even gave them shelter and *khalwas*.

The number who died as a result of the relocation programme is not known. But residents of el Obeid and Bara have described vividly the stench of dead bodies on the trucks that brought the relocated people—so that it was difficult even to approach the vehicles. Malnutrition rates in the camps were reported at between 60% and 80% of children under five.[69]

The relocations policy brought into the open the rift within the Sudan Government between the hard-liners, such as Governor el Husseini, Abdel Wahab Abdel Rahman and Military Intelligence, and others who were equally determined to crush Nuba resistance, but were not ready to use such draconian methods. The latter group was headed by Mohamed al Tayeb, briefly Commissioner of South Kordofan. When large numbers of forcibly displaced people were removed to North Kordofan, the atrocities being perpetrated in South Kordofan could no longer be kept secret. There was an outcry, first within Sudan—many residents of towns (including the local authorities) in North Kordofan were deeply shocked, and the Kordofan Drought Relief Operations Group, that coordinates relief efforts, was caught by surprise by its new human burden. There was also an international outcry. Ambassador Jan Eliason, the then-UN Under Secretary General for Humanitarian Affairs, visited Sudan in September and the Nuba issue was forced onto his agenda by international pressure. In October the US Congress passed a resolution condemning human rights abuses in Sudan and mentioning the Nuba Mountains in particular. Relief agencies expressed shock at the appalling living conditions in the relocation camps: visible starvation among the displaced had a more profound and immediate effect than years of human rights violations.

In addition, the Islamic relief agencies and the regional government were having difficulty coping with the sheer numbers of relocated people. Their plans for absorbing the boys into Islamic

---

[69] USAID, OFDA, "Sudan—Drought/Civil Strife," Situation Report no. 55, 7 October 1992, p. 5.

schools were simply too ambitious, and the food began to run out. One Nuba resident in North Kordofan wrote at the time:[70]

> Children were sent to Sheikan and Khor Taggat to be taught the Koran in *Khalwas*. This was not an ordinary education. Later, there was a lack of food in the *Khalwas*. Accordingly, those responsible for them have dismissed the children. Some of the families came and reclaimed their sons. The orphans are left alone without care and are wandering aimlessly in the cities of el Obeid and Um Ruwaba, begging.

The response of the Sudan Government was to mitigate the worst symptoms of the relocation policy without changing its essence. The idea of relocating all the Nuba people outside South Kordofan was abandoned, and instead the peace camp strategy was revised. Henceforth, almost all peace camps were to remain within South Kordofan, attached to towns and mechanised farming schemes. Henceforth, only selected categories of people, such as conscripts to the PDF, were removed from South Kordofan. But this did not mean that people remained close to their homes—South Kordofan is a huge area and people could still be moved long distances within their home region.

In September 1992, the regional government announced that it had set up 91 peace villages with 167,265 people. The people transferred to North Kordofan began to be re-organised. Most were despatched to "production sites", which were large camps close to mechanised farming schemes. The main such camps were Sidra, Rahmaniya and Abu Jibeha. Others, mainly women, were sent back to peace camps adjacent to towns in South Kordofan. Youths were conscripted into PDF training camps, and young boys sent to Islamic schools. In October, for example, most of the camp population at en Nahud was screened and removed in several different directions, the largest number being transported to Sidra and Rahmaniya.

Meanwhile, with less intense military operations, the rate of abduction of villagers slowed. In April 1993, Hussein Karshoum, Director of Peace Villages for South Kordofan, said that there were

---

[70] Letter, 11 October 1992.

163,000 people in peace villages—a number slightly lower than six months previously. (The drop can be accounted for by the removal of boys to *khalwas* and youths to PDF camps.) He also said that eighty tractors had been provided. In reality, rather than a gift to support the displaced, the tractors were controlled by the merchant farmers whose mechanised schemes demanded plentiful cheap labour.

Thereafter, the peace camp strategy has had two main components. One is as the classic counter-insurgency measure of "protected hamlets" employed in, among other places, Malaya,[71] Vietnam, Algeria, Rhodesia, Ethiopia and Guatemala. Small, tightly-controlled settlements are established next to garrisons. The second component is labour camps to provide workers, particularly at peak times, to mechanised farms.

One of the first areas to have small garrison peace camps was the Miri hills. The beginnings of this were described by a Miri farmer:[72]

> Starting in 1992, the Government began to move the displaced to peace camps, in Miri Bara, Kadi (for 1,500 Miri Bara people) and Kuhaliyat (for three thousand people) in 1992. Miri Bara is the biggest camp with ten thousand. In 1993 they moved people to Keiga, which has about one thousand people, and Mashisha—this camp is about seven thousand people and has people from Korongo and Shatt as well as Miri. Keiga is divided in two, part is under the SPLA and part is a Government peace camp with one thousand people. Mohamed el Zaki has become the Government Amir of the Miri. He is a Government servant, trained to obey orders.

The labour camp strategy is familiar from decades of labour policy in Sudan, and is also being implemented as part of the programme of relocating displaced people from Khartoum.[73] It is also related to the privatization of state-owned farms following the promulgation of the "Economic Salvation Programme" in 1990. This

---

[71] Lt.-Gen. Omer al Bashir received military training in Malaysia.

[72] Musa Kuwa Jabir Tiya, interviewed in Um Dulu, 17 May 1995.

[73] African Rights, *Sudan's Invisible Citizens: The Policy of Abuse against the Displaced People in the North*, February 1995.

programme included a special fund of LS 1 billion to finance agricultural development. The privatisation of the Nuba Mountains Agricultural Corporation was one of the priorities of this programme, which was duly implemented. This meant that credit for buying tractors could now be extended much more widely, to well-connected Northern merchants and officials. But, as before, the main impediment to the profitability of mechanised farming is lack of labour at key times in the agricultural cycle: hence the creation of a captive labour force.

Fought to a Standstill

By the middle of 1992, the two sides had fought each other to a standstill. The SPLA had repulsed the largest-ever offensive mounted by the government, but massive military action by the army and PDF had likewise halted the expansion of the SPLA.

The *Jihad* was never abandoned—indeed it was re-affirmed by regular public statements. However, the military strategy of massive conventional assault was not tried again. The main reason was that it simply did not work. Too many soldiers, militiamen and Mujahidiin were killed, and too much weaponry fell into the hands of the SPLA.

A secondary reason was some discontent within the armed forces. The offensive caused considerable unhappiness among Nuba non-commissioned officers and policemen. On 11 April 1992, 101 NCOs and policemen, most of them Nuba, were arrested and accused of planning a "racial coup" under the leadership of Abdel Rahman Idris. Eighty three of them were released shortly afterwards but eighteen (twelve Nuba, one from Darfur and five Southerners) were kept in prolonged detention in Suakin prison on the Red Sea coast.

Meanwhile, the SPLA was suffering its own problems, due primarily to the August 1991 split in the (Southern) SPLA. Before the split, the SPLA in the Nuba Mountains had been supplied through Upper Nile. This area was now under the control of the Nasir faction, and resupply had to take a much longer and more hazardous route through Bahr el Ghazal. In 1992, the SPLA made four attempts to send ammunition to the Nuba Mountains. Only one succeeded. One attempt never even approached the Nuba Mountains.

One was blocked by the SPLA commander at Fariang, Meyik Jau, who has always been unsympathetic to the Nuba.[74] A third attempt ended in disaster when more than half of the four hundred troops died of thirst when forced to make a detour through waterless country near Fariang. A fourth attempt reached the Nuba Mountains but more than one hundred soldiers were drowned in floods on the return journey.

On both sides, the sheer scale of human suffering was causing commanders and administrators to ask the question of whether they could continue the war, or whether it was better to negotiate. This led to the first—and last—real negotiations for a ceasefire in the Nuba Mountains.

Early in 1992, the hard-line Commissioner of South Kordofan, Abdel Wahab Abdel Rahman Ali, was promoted to Minister of Health in the Regional Government. He was replaced as Commissioner by Mohamed al Tayeb Fadl, a Hamar from Abu Zabad. He was an active military officer who took a more conventional approach to the war than his predecessor, and indeed than his superior, Governor el Husseini. While the Mujahidiin attacked Tullishi, Mohamed al Tayeb took responsibilities for the southern jebels and followed a policy of local peace, including opening negotiations with Yousif Kuwa.

On the SPLA side, Commander Ismail Khamis Jellab was despatched to respond to the Commissioner's offer. He gave an account of the short-lived talks:[75]

> In 1992 we began to talk to the Kadugli regional government about a ceasefire. The first meeting was in Um Sirdiba, and then in Bilenya. During these talks, some of the citizens thought that an agreement for a ceasefire had been reached. So people began to go to the towns, such as Kadugli and Hamra. They went to buy things and return. But the government reversed its policy. It stopped them returning and took all the things they had bought. The peace talks

---

[74] In May 1995 Commander Meyik surrendered Fariang to the Sudan Government. He had been ordered to report to SPLA headquarters and suspected that he would be charged with a number of disciplinary offences.
[75] Interviewed in Um Dulu, 19 May 1995.

collapsed with no agreement. The people who were affected by this were only in Korongo and Buram; the western side was not affected.

The Bilenya talks collapsed in May. Meanwhile, Commissioner Mohamed al Tayeb had clashed with Governor el Husseini and in June, he was ordered to go on the pilgrimage to Mecca. Abdel Wahab was put in charge of South Kordofan once more, and immediately on his arrival in Kadugli began organizing the mass removal of displaced Nuba from the town. Many of those he proposed to remove were the villagers who had been lured into the town by the illusory ceasefire, and then trapped there when the talks were abruptly terminated. Abdel Wahab succeeded in relocating about seventeen thousand people, but this action led him into a dispute with the Kadugli Security Committee, that had been supportive of the peace efforts. The Security Committee complained to Khartoum. After his return from Mecca, Mohamed al Tayeb was briefly put under house arrest, on the instructions of Abdel Wahab Abdel Rahman. Vice President, Zubeir Mohamed Saleh intervened and sent Mohamed al Tayeb back to Kadugli, but with much reduced powers. The relocations to North Kordofan were halted. But the reprieve was brief. Two months later, Mohamed al Tayeb was replaced by Habib al Mukhtum, a prominent NIF civilian from Darfur. Real power remains with in Khartoum and el Obeid.

At the height of the outcry, the head of National Security, Dr Naafi Ali Naafi, held a series of five meetings with Nuba representatives. The final meeting, in August, was held at the Immigration Social Service Club in Khartoum and was attended by about seventy Nuba leaders and intellectuals. They presented a series of demands, which were all rejected by Dr Naafi. Despite promises of safety, more than twelve of the representatives were later arrested.[76]

The debate within the government was resolved against the relocations to the north, but also against peace. By November, the

---

[76] See: *Sudan Update*, "Chronology: Conflict in the Nuba Mountains 1972-1993," 4.11, Spring-Summer 1993.

army and PDF in Kordofan were back on a war footing, and a major offensive in the eastern jebels was launched (see below).

At the same time, the SPLA in the Nuba Mountains also engaged in a debate over whether the war should continue. In the rainy season of 1992, Commander Yousif Kuwa Mekki proposed that an "Advisory Council" be convened to discuss the matter. Invitations were sent to all communities under SPLA administration or in contested areas. Two hundred representatives met in Debi on 30 September 1992. There was one agenda item: whether or not to continue the struggle.

On the first day of the five-day conference, Commander Yousif Kuwa presented a lengthy history of the Nuba people and their political struggles, including the roles of GUN and Komolo. On the second day he concluded:[77]

> Up to today, 1 October 1992, I am responsible. I take responsibility
> for everything that has happened in the Nuba Mountains up to now.
> But, from today, I will not be responsible. If we are to continue the
> war, then this must be our collective decision.

The floor was then opened for the delegates to express their opinions. They did so, in what all who were present agreed was a remarkably frank manner. Alternate Commander Telefon Kuku Abu Jelha was the main advocate for peace. Yousif Kuwa argued against him, saying that he did not object to peace, but that no-one should trust the government to stick to its promises.

On the final day, the Advisory Council voted overwhelmingly to continue the war. Telefon Kuku promised to abide by the collective decision. He retained his command and returned to lead his forces in his home area of Buram. However, over the next twelve months he established contact with the Sudan government. In December 1993, as a Sudan army force advanced towards Buram, Commander Telefon agreed to surrender the town without a fight. He also protested in a letter to Yousif Kuwa that peace with the government was the only alternative. He was arrested and charged on four

---

[77] Interviewed in Tira Limon, 23 May 1995.

counts, including mutiny. Commander Telefon was in detention awaiting court martial at the time of African Rights' visit.

The 1992-3 Dry Season in The Western Jebels

After the massive destruction of the first five months of 1992, the rainy season came as a relief. Militarily, it was quiet. But much of the western jebels had been reduced to a wasteland, as all the harvest from the previous season had been burned, and most farmers were displaced and could not plant. In Tullishi alone, 1,842 people were recorded by as having died of hunger. Many more people went to the towns.

"Quiet" is a relative term: raids, detentions and killings carried on. A group of more than forty men was arrested on 16 July and taken to el Obeid, where 35 of them were brought to court under charges of armed robbery. Their trial was delayed until November, and they were convicted but sentenced only to short prison terms, and released on the grounds that they had already served them. In the intervening months, national and international pressure had embarrassed the Sudan Government into some symbolic shows of leniency.

In December the SPLA counter-attacked at Lagowa, descending from Jebel Tullishi to attack the PDF forces in the first of a series of raids. In response, at the end of January 1993, the army went on the offensive again, as reported by Hassan Osman Tutu:

> In February 1993 there was an army offensive to Tima. The army occupied it for one month, and burned Koya, Balol and Maryam villages. All the small villages around Koya were burned, and thirteen people were killed, including the sheikh, four women and one small child. They were shot down while trying to run away.

Most of the people succeeded in escaping from the government forces and later re-occupied some of the depopulated areas. A large number of women and girls were abducted and taken to el Obeid, where residents who saw them reported that many were pregnant on account of rape.

The Southern Jebels Offensives

Smaller military actions were launched southwards from Kadugli during the *Jihad* period. The attacks were preceded by a round of detentions, particularly in Kadugli. A battle on 25 September 1991 at Shaeer, just north of Kadugli on the road to Dilling, in which the SPLA inflicted heavy casualties on the PDF and killed Mohamed el Kelas and another militia commander, was the spark for the crackdown. More than one hundred civilians were arrested shortly afterwards, accused of being the SPLA's "fifth column."[78] But, due to the peace overtures of Mohamed al Tayeb, military activities did not begin until July. Korongo Abdalla was one of the areas that suffered:[79]

In July 1992, the army came from Kadugli, round through Keilak, to attack Korongo. They attacked Korongo for four days. They took over the town, and then took over the SPLA camp at Shatt Tebeldi, and stormed the mountains where we were hiding. For four days we were hunted in the mountains. But then the SPLA encircled them and forced them out. When they were searching the ground after the battle, the SPLA found one civilian who had been burned to death in his house—grass had been put in the doorway and set alight—and three others dead on the hillside.

In April 1993, a big convoy came through Sama to Hajar Anaba. They left their lorries behind and went to Anaba village and burned it. They found no civilians there. Then they went on to Bilenya, which is a big village. They took all the cows and burned some of the houses, before they returned to Kadugli.

In July that year, the army destroyed Shatt Tebeldi, Seraf al Gharnoub and Bilenya [around Shatt Damam]. They tried to go further but they were checked by the SPLA. They also burned Keiga, and all the civilians in Keiga lost everything and went to

---

[78] The anti-government newspaper *al Watan al Arabi* claimed in its 8 November 1991 edition that over one hundred civilians were massacred in reprisals at Shaeer, but African Rights has been unable to confirm this.
[79] Jaafar al Fadl, Abdel Gadir Abdel Rahman and Suleiman Kafi, interviewed in Um Dulu, 17 May 1995.

Kadugli. Only twenty came to our side, plus another five who escaped from Kadugli.

The largest attack on the southern jebels was launched in February 1993, from el Muglad in south-west Kordofan round the southern edge of the Nuba Mountains to Lake Abyad and Turoji. This was an unexpected route which took many people by surprise, particularly the tens of thousands of famine refugees who had congregated in the area.

During this operation there was a major massacre, which residents of the area believe to be the single largest incident of mass killing in the history of the war. Among the people of the southern jebels, it is widely believed that up to 1,900 people were killed or died of hunger and thirst while running away from the killing. African Rights has been unable to verify these numbers. The following testimony, of Amsal Tutu Tiya, from Tabanya in Angolo, gives an overview of what happened:[80]

In February 1993 the enemy came from el Muglad and attacked el Abyad. The attack took people by surprise. Many were killed by the enemy and by thirst. Not less than 1,900 people were killed and twelve thousand cows were taken by the army. Osman Kuku, Jedi Tia and Tatu Kuwa from Jebel Kuwa were killed. Tutu Kuwa Albared, from Shatt Safiya was also killed in that incident. Some survivors reached us in Angolo the same day. The attack was at noon and some reached us before the sunset in Angolo. I and others were pouring water on them before they could drink any water. Yet some died. Among the survivors known to me are, Abdalla Musa from Shatt Safiya, Sheikh Kodoko, Kuwa Rakuba Tia and Kuku Kuwa Hakim from Turoji.

El Abyad was a big settlement. People had migrated to el Abyad from Otoro, Tira, Kawalib, Moro, Delami, Shatt, Korongo Abdalla, as well as Dinka from Fariang. All came there with their cattle and goats during the severe hunger of 1992. The hunger was caused by the burning of food crops and farms by the enemy. That was the time they had that big attack on Tullishi. El Abyad was chosen as an appropriate settlement because there was plenty of

---

[80] Interviewed in Um Dulu, 17 May 1995.

fish, *nabag, lalub, ardeib* [all types of wild fruit], *beji* [edible roots] and *kurtal* [wild berries that must be soaked in water for four days]. Fariang area had good harvest that year and most of the Dinka in el Abyad were traders.

The enemy spent two days in el Abyad and proceeded to Turoji. After attacking Turoji the enemy went back to el Muglad through el Abyad.

African Rights is undertaking further investigations into the details and number of fatalities in the el Abyad massacre.

The Heiban Offensive 1992-3

The second major offensive launched by government forces in 1992 began in December, in the eastern sector. It was centred on Heiban. Shortly afterwards, reports began to trickle out of a major massacre at Heiban itself, in which up to six thousand people had been killed at Christmas and buried in mass graves. African Rights' investigations indicate that this is a simplification of a much more complex series of events. Though the offensive involved many acts of violence against the civilian population of the area, it is very unlikely that such a large number of civilians were killed by Sudan Government soldiers.

The offensive started early in December and lasted for about sixty days. Two military convoys left Abu Jibeha. One operated in el Azraq and the other in Luchulu. There was also an offensive out of Mendi, which targeted the southern parts of Otoro and Tira el Akhdar. Most of the devastation and killing of civilians that was reported occured in this zone. Simultaneously, the Heiban garrison started shelling any villages within range. They shelled Abol, Oya, Karakir, Luchulu and Kuchama village. The main aim of the shelling was to pin down the SPLA forces in the district, but the shells caused numerous civilian casualties, particularly in Kuchama and Abol. African Rights was unable to obtain reliable figures for deaths, but is undertaking further investigations into the human cost of this offensive.

135

Another aspect of the offensive was the widespread abduction of people, particularly to Heiban and Mendi garrisons. Many of those abducted were never seen again. Kuchama village, just south of Heiban, was one that suffered. A resident, Sherab Lima Kodi, said:[81]

> And at the end of 1992, the Government came to capture people. At Christmas they came to Kuchama and abducted many people, who were tortured and killed inside Heiban. The number is not known.

Kalkada was one of the villages that bore the brunt of the assault from Mendi. The village had already been burned on three occasions (described above). The head of the village, Hassan Ramadan Zakaria, described how they escaped the first onslaught of the "Christmas offensive", only to suffer at the end:[82]

> The fourth attack was on 4 February 1993. The soldiers came with 21 lorries and cars and one tank. Again they came from Mendi.
> This time, we had information that they were coming. All of us moved in advance to Kumu. The only houses they found were the shelters we had built for the rainy season. They burned them down. No-one was killed but whatever food they found, they burned it.
> People emigrated. They went to Kumu, to Eri, Regifi, Um Dulu, Reika, Kurchi, Buram, Korang, Seraf Jamous, Tamanya and even as far as Fariang. We had absolutely no food. Many many people died because of hunger and displacement.

An attack from Dilling through Habila to the Kawalib areas followed at the end of January 1993, which affected much of the Kawalib area.

---

[81] Interviewed in Kujur el Sha'abiya, 13 May 1995.
[82] Interviewed in Um Dulu, 16 May 1995.

III

THE NUBA TODAY:

GENOCIDE BY ATTRITION

The ongoing order given to the troops is to kill anything that is alive, that is to say to kill anybody, to destroy the area, to implement a scorched earth policy, to destroy everything, to burn the area, so that nothing can exist there. Those are the orders of the troops there fighting in the area.

Khalid Abdel Karim Saleh, former head of security in the Office of the Governor of Kordofan, interviewed in Switzerland, 13 June 1995.

Since late-1993, the Government of Sudan has followed a new military-political strategy. There are no frontal assaults on SPLA positions, and fewer large massacres. The dramatic "ethnic cleansing" of 1992 has been modified to the more innocuous sounding programme of "peace camps". But there are ways of dismembering a society other than killing every one of its members, and the combination of practices employed by the Sudan Government are still aimed at the same objective: crushing the SPLA goes hand-in-hand with obliterating Nuba society as it has existed up to now. It is genocide by attrition.

The current campaign has three main elements. One is political and much publicised: *Salaam min al Dakhal* ("Peace from Within"). *Salaam min al Dakhal* refers primarily to the mobilisation of prominent Nuba, mainly meks and people appointed as meks, as

137

political and military leaders. Secondarily, it refers to the attempts to win SPLA commanders over to the government side.

The second element is a new means of obtaining resources, human and material, to fight the war. It is also publicised, though the details of how it is implemented are suppressed. This is *Nafir al Sha'abi* ("Popular Mobilisation"). Under *Nafir al Sha'abi*, rather than relying primarily on the army and the Arab Murahaliin-PDF, the plan is to create *Nuba* pro-government militias. The Mujahidiin used in the 1992 Tullishi campaign had proved a costly failure. The Arab Murahaliin were proving unreliable—some had negotiated their own truces with the SPLA (for example the Misiriya who engaged in the Buram trade), while Umma Party leaders in exile were calling on them to turn their guns against the government. Creating militias from among the Nuba themselves promised to be a means of building an army at low financial cost and low political risk.

The third main component is a new strategy of low-intensity warfare, known as *tamshit* ("combing"). Small forces move out from a network of garrisons, aiming at civilian targets: primarily villages but also farms, cattle camps or places of refuge such as caves. Everything necessary to sustain life is destroyed or removed. People are abducted. "Pseudo-guerrillas" also infiltrate the SPLM-administered areas to burn, raid, assassinate and abduct. Though all government announcements speak of the destruction of "rebel camps" and the capture of "rebels", these in fact refer to villages and civilians. Meanwhile, resources are provided to the garrison towns and the attached "peace camps" to entice people to live there. It is the classic counter-insurgency strategy of "draining the sea to catch the fish". Another rationale for this plan is that it minimises direct military confrontation with the SPLA, reducing the danger of casualties or losses of equipment.

The main military campaign in the 1993-4 dry season was *Misk al Khitam* ("Final seal"[1]). It was a two-pronged offensive aimed at Buram, with one force coming from Kadugli and one from Abu Jibeha, through Talodi. There was much publicity in advance, which should have aroused suspicions that all was not what it seemed. The

---

[1] The name was repeated in 1994-5 for the defence of Kapoeta.

138

forces duly captured Buram, and the government made much propaganda out of their victory. The reality was that a deal had been struck in advance with Alternate Commander Telefon Kuku Abu Jelha that he would surrender the town without a fight.

The 1994-5 dry season offensive was named *Seif al Salaam* ("Sword of Peace"). The largest military components of this were an armoured column that travelled south from Heiban down the Kauda valley, destroying a number of villages and briefly occupying Kauda town, and a similar operation in the Tima area. In June 1995 the government also proudly announced the capture of Fariang, the link point between the South and the Nuba Mountains: as with Buram eighteen months earlier, this "victory" was in fact due to the defection of the SPLA Commander Meyik Jau. Although a two-month ceasefire was announced between the Government and the SPLA on 28 March, after approaches to both sides by former U.S. President Jimmy Carter, this did not impede the programme of destruction in the slightest. The Sudan Government issued instructions to its forces that the ceasefire was to apply only in the South.

It is important to stress that, although the use of the Mujahidiin as a major component of military strategy ended in 1992, the *Jihad* as such did not end. The components of the "Comprehensive Call" package remain. In particular, element (2), "political, social and economic favouritism for Nuba Moslems and their instigation to head the campaign," has been promoted.

"SALAAM MIN AL DAKHAL": ACCOMPLICES IN THEIR OWN DESTRUCTION

The most insidious policy of the Sudan Government is to co-opt the Nuba people to be accomplices in their own destruction: *Salaam min al Dakhal* or "Peace from Within". The NIF has copied the British strategy for "indirect rule" in the Nuba Mountains, and has bought off existing chiefs and promoted other corrupt or corruptible figures to be new government chiefs. It is important to recall that almost all

Nuba tribes do not have a tradition of chieftancy. Chiefs should primarily be seen as government-appointed civil servants.

A combination of reward and coercion is used to obtain the loyalty of the government-appointed amirs of the Nuba. It is the chance for opportunists. Meanwhile, some other prominent Nuba have, out of despair or resignation, opted to cast their lot in with the government. The groundwork for this strategy was laid with the sustained crackdown on Nuba leaders and intellectuals: by 1993, all those who could have provided a voice for the Nuba cause within government-held Sudan were dead, detained, abroad or terrorised into silence.

Some of the prominent Nuba in the "Peace from Within" include:

*   Abdel Hamid Mohamed Zahra, Amir of Salara (Nyima) and Wali. As Mek of Wali, he was one of the first chiefs to agree to form a pro-government militia, in 1989, and rapidly gained a reputation for ruthlessness in directing his militiamen to attack the families of youths who had joined the SPLA.

*   Mohamed Rahma Lashu, Amir of the Central Nuba Emirate-Heiban. He is a Tira. In the 1980s, he led the crackdown on Christian communities and the Roman Catholic Church among the Tira el Akhdar. More recently, Mohamed Rahma has created one of the most violent and abusive PDF forces in the entire region, and his headquarters in Mendi is one of the most feared of all government garrisons. His supporters are almost exclusively from Tira Mendi and to a lesser extent Tira el Akhdar: very few from Tira Limon have joined *Salaam min al Dakhal*. In early 1995, Mohamed Rahma was injured in a land mine incident and temporarily incapacitated.

*   Idris Kaluwa is the government Mek of Tira el Akhdar in Heiban.

*   Farouk Orem is an Otoro mek. He was promoted by the government from his former employment as a ticket seller at a lorry station.

*   Osman Kunda is the Mek of Abol and Lira, based in Heiban. He is a former merchant.

*   Angelo Abu Rasein is a former teacher from Heiban. Originally a Christian, he has converted to Islam (and has changed his name accordingly), and become a fervent supporter of the NIF.

*   Kafi Tayara el Bedin, Amir of Shatt, was renowned for his readiness to be bought by the authorities and the Misiriya Arabs in the 1980s. He played a role in blocking resolution of the major Shatt-Misiriya dispute in 1987. He formed a pro-government militia in Kadugli, and after a disastrous PDF mission to Shatt in early 1993, he was detained by the authorities there. He was back in action and reinstated as Amir by October, running a *khalwa* in Kadugli and a relief organization financed by Da'awa al Islamiya in el Obeid. Kafi Tayara is widely believed to be involved in the sale of Nuba children in Kadugli.

*   Shahad Abu Anja Tutu is the Amir of Korongo Abdalla. He is based in Kadugli and has built up his support and forces there. He is described as making excellent business out of the displaced, for example charging a levy on all Korongo people in Kadugli who are recruited as labourers.

*   Riyad Tiya is the government sheikh of Angolo, who was responsible for much of the burning and looting of the area in March 1995.

*   Ramadhan Tayara, formerly the Mek of Nyimang, is now the government Amir.

*   Mohamed Ismail Bogen, an Amir of Ghulfan. Previously he was a farmer and a soldier, and formed a pro-government militia in 1989.

*   Fadil Habila, another Amir of Ghulfan. He has been prominent in the government media (see below).

*   Mamur Nyeto, Amir of Dilling. He has been Mek since colonial days and is described by residents as a faithful government servant.

141

*   Nabil Sayed is the Amir of Kawalib. The Kawalib provided many early recruits to the SPLA. The *Salaam min al Dakhal* among the Kawalib was launched with big meeting only in January 1994, and the meeting was held in Dilling, rather than Delami itself. Compared to other Amirs, Nabil Sayed has a reputation for moderation and has reportedly tried to restrain some of the abuses of the army and PDF in the Kawalib area, and also tolerates Christian churches. There are recent reports that he has run into trouble with higher authorities for this policy.

*   Hamad Abu Sudur, a former MP and merchant farmer, is the Mek of Dere, in the Kawalib area.

*   Al Hadi Sayed, an official in the MFC in Dilling and a former politician, and Merkazu Kuku, a former MP, and some teachers are also involved in Delami county. Mohamed Merkazu, a merchant farmer, led military forces in the February-March 1995 "combing" operation in Delami.

*   Mohamed el Zaki Ali, Amir of Miri. He has been one of the most enthusiastic implementors of the government policies of establishing peace camps and PDF forces.

*   Mandu Ismail Libreke, Amir of Moro in Um Sirdiba. He has made little headway in mobilising the Moro and forming a PDF force.

*   Dedan Kuway, Amir of Katcha.

*   Mohamed Ibrahim Shumshum, Amir of Talodi.

*   Hazim Yagoub Rahhal, Amir of Kadugli.

*   Hamad Rahhal Mohamed Rahhal, Mek of Kadugli.

One of the important tasks of the leaders of the *Salaam min al Dakhal* is to "represent" the Nuba to foreign visitors and in the national media. One instance of this was a public conference held in Khartoum in October 1993, designed to "refute" the evidence presented by Gáspár Bíró, the U.N. Special Rapporteur on Human Rights in Sudan. Mr Bíró had recently visited Kadugli (but was prevented from visiting the rural Nuba Mountains) and was due to issue his report in November.

The speeches were almost entirely scripted, and were both tedious and repetitive, blaming everything on the SPLA while also claiming that peace had been established. Fadil Habila, Amir of Ghulfan, took a prominent role in the conference. He said:

> We hear a lot of allegations and accusations of racial discrimination. It may be just differences of religious interpretation. We hereby confirm that we live, despite our differences, in harmony without discrimination.

Mohamed el Zaki Ali's speech was typical. He said repeatedly, "There is no reason at all for the rebellion." Referring to the Nuba Mountains Solidarity Abroad, he said that any international Nuba organisations that claimed to speak for the Nuba only spoke for disgruntled and ill-informed individuals, not for the people themselves. Kafi Tayara el Bedin's presentation, though at times lapsing into incoherence, was one of the more memorable. Having blamed the rebellion on Yousif Kuwa Mekki's personal quarrel with the former Governor, el Fatih Bushara, he continued:

> Even the Nuba boys who joined [the SPLA] do not know why they joined. Yousif Kuwa just came to the Nuba Mountains to loot and take our cattle to feed his forces. Nobody has killed the sons of Nuba except Yousif Kuwa and John Garang. Our sons abroad, in Washington D.C. and in America are just trading on [i.e. making money from] our case. We the sons of the Nuba are present, we have not gone anywhere. You can see our people who were harassed by the rebels have come to Kadugli and Rahmaniya and the government has made camps for them and is feeding them. There are no Nuba who have been killed by the Government of Sudan. The Nuba people abroad just want to line their pockets, they are not speaking on behalf of the people who are dead [sic].

A number of prominent Nuba in Khartoum have also actively supported the government. They include:

*   Dr Kabshur Kuku Gimbil, formerly head of the department of psychology at the University of Khartoum and chair of the Social Affairs Committee, is currently Minister of Education. He is from Delami. A former member of GUN, he is regarded as a political opportunist.

*   Bishop Boutros Kuwa of the Episcopal Church of Sudan denied the existence of human rights abuses in the Nuba Mountains. A Moro, he was a consistent advocate of the government line and a regular government delegate to peace talks, before his death by thirst in the northern desert in 1994 when his car lost the road. The incident has never been satisfactorily explained.

Another component of this strategy is to use the Nuba officers in the Sudan army to lead military operations in their home areas. For example, in early 1994, Lt.-Col. Bashir Abdel Bein was transferred from Khartoum to Delami to supervise the *Nafir el Sha'abi* and lead the military operations where necessary.

Some of the Baggara Arab chiefs are sometimes presented by the government as "Nuba leaders." They are in fact men who have been implicated in the militia strategy since 1985. Leading Baggara chiefs include:

*   Hireka Izz el Din is Amir of Lagowa and head of the PDF in the district. He is a Misiriya Zurug and was Chairman of the Umma Parliamentary Group during Sadiq el Mahdi's premiership, 1986-9, and was one of the architects of the Murahaliin.

*   Osman Bilal Hamid is the Hawazma Amir of the Kadugli area. The position of nazir was formerly held by his father. He had been prominent in government propaganda efforts.

This list is far from exhaustive. There are many other civil servants, meks, omdas and sheikhs, teachers and merchants who have joined with the policy of "Peace from Within." Their rewards

144

include salaries, a share in the loot of what is captured by PDF "combing" missions, business opportunities, and the opportunity to obtain leases in mechanised farms. Lacking finance, the government has proved extremely adept at using its one plentiful resource—land—to obtain support. A resident of Nyimang described how the policy of selling off leases to mechanised farms was both a way of rewarding the NIF's paymasters and co-opting the Nuba leadership:[2]

> The NIF decided to privatise the older mechanised farms, such as Habila. In Nyimang, the NIF cells were given the facilities to allocate the farms, to give them influence, now or in the future.
>
> The areas with farms are Nyitil and Kurmuti. These farms were made by taking land from the people. Some were given to Nyimang elites, but mostly the merchants from el Obeid and Kosti then come and buy them up off the Nyimang elites. In the past, meks and chiefs owned big areas of land and objected to people cultivating them. As owners of mechanised schemes, all tribes are represented: Kawalib, Ghulfan, Hawazma. Among the Nuba, the Nyimang may be the majority. This is creating a new class affiliated to the NIF. Any NIF businessman has the opportunity, whatever area he is from.
>
> There are also new mechanised farms along the Dilling-Kadugli road and in the Ghulfan area. Initially these were small experimental farms. Since 1989 they have become permanent farms.

The same strategy has been followed in Kawalib, where some of the most prominent leaders of the PDF are the owners of mechanised farms.

The government has used all its diplomatic skills to capitalise on the demoralisation of some SPLA commanders. Some have wanted peace at almost any price, for instance Alternate Commander Telefon Kuku, who surrendered Buram in December 1993. Some have felt that the SPLA leadership in the South has abandoned them. This feeling was particularly strong after Commander Yousif Kuwa, who left the Nuba Mountains to attend the Abuja peace talks in May

---

[2] Interviewed in Um Dulu, 19 May 1995.

1993, was repeatedly delayed in his attempts to return. Nobody in the SPLA forces was quite sure why the commander was remaining for so long in the South and in Kenya, and rumours abounded. Others, such as Commander Meyik Jau, a Dinka controlling his home area of Fariang, were recalled to SPLA Headquarters on account of repeated infractions against the disciplinary code, and preferred the enticements of the government "Peace from Within" to the prospect of SPLA discipline. Meyik Jau handed Fariang to the government in May 1995, amid much government celebration on the national media.

Other have resisted. Alternate Commander Yousif Karra Haroun, in command of the Heiban zone, rejected an advance from the government. In April 1994, he received a delegation, bearing a letter from the leading NIF politician, Ali el Haj. The letter invited him to join the "Peace from Within" and discuss his grievances. The delegation was headed by a former MP, Ali Gadim Juru, and included the supervisor of education from Kadugli, Mekadi Kuku Angelo and a teacher from el Obeid, Mohamed Ismail Abu Salib. Lt.-Col. Bashir Abdel Bein facilitated the mission. Some of the members of the delegation were Yousif Karra's own relatives, who tried to argue that his position in the SPLA was harming his extended family in the government-held areas. Yousif Karra rebuffed the advance, writing back that "these are not family grievances to be settled in a discussion between relatives," and requesting that future peace overtures be directed to the leadership of the SPLA through the diplomatic channels established by the regional heads of state.

"NAFIR EL SHA'ABI": INSTITUTIONALISING FRATRICIDE

The government of Sudan has announced victory in the Nuba Mountains, and some Nuba have believed that such a victory is, if not actual, then all-but-inevitable. The SPLA-administered areas of the Nuba Mountains are extremely isolated. Since 1991 there has been no SPLA radio, whereas the government has not only Radio Omdurman but also a local radio station transmitting from Kadugli.

Between 1992 and 1995 there were no supplies of arms, while the government garrisons were all re-supplied. In May 1993, Commander Yousif Kuwa was summoned to participate in the Abuja peace talks, and was absent for two years, without a definite promise that he would return. Senior government leaders have regularly toured the region; most recently President Omer al Bashir visited Kadugli and Talodi in April-May 1995. Since the war began there have been no humanitarian programmes in the SPLA-held areas, and people have been locked into a cycle of deprivation and famine without even a gesture of assistance from outside. By contrast, starting in 1993, international relief organizations began operating in Kadugli and other government towns, supplementing the Islamic organizations already providing much assistance there.

These have all contributed to the demoralisation of the Nuba resistance—and the opportunity for the *Nafir el Sha'abi*, or "Popular Mobilisation."

Enticement with Relief

The government has no illusions that it is well-liked by rural Nuba. But it counts on the realism of a people who have, over the centuries, become accustomed to defeat and repression. Believing that government victory is only a matter of time, many rural Nuba people have decided that their best—or least bad—option is to accept the government invitation to come over.

During the severe famine of 1990-93, thousands of Nuba villagers were forced to abandon their homes and seek sustenance in the towns. Now, hunger is less acute, despite the best efforts of the government at burning crops and foodstores and stealing livestock. Education, medical care and above all clothes are now the main factors that entice rural people into the garrisons and their attached peace camps.

Rural Nuba people recognise this clearly. A farmer in Dabker village, that had been burned less than two weeks earlier by the Sudan Government, told African Rights:[3]

---

[3] Daniel Abu Rafas Angusa, interviewed in Dabker, 8 May 1995.

Because they have not defeated us they are burning our villages so we will go to their towns and become their slaves. We are convinced that the final aim of the government is to destroy us, so we are made to believe that our boys who are carrying arms for us are weak and we will go back to their towns. They want us to be poor and weak and go to them. Even this burning has made a few faint hearts go and join them. We who are the majority will stay here.

Rural people are extremely reluctant to leave their land and join the government peace camps. However, due to lack of essentials, many have done so. Others have retreated further into the mountains, or migrated to parts of the SPLA-administered areas that are more fertile.

Najwa Abu Anja al Kadro is in her early twenties and lives in the Dabker area of the Moro hills. Tired of dressing only in rags, in April 1995 she decided to go to the nearby garrison to see if she could obtain free clothes.[4]

I went to Um Dorein two weeks ago, and stayed there for eight days. I said, 'I have come to buy clothes.' I was sent to the peace camp. When I reported to the peace camp I was taken to the army barracks, where I was interrogated: 'Why did you come?' I said, 'I am coming to stay here. Especially, I have no clothes.' I was registered at the barracks. After that I was given some clothes, one shirt and one *tarka* [head scarf] and told to go and stay in the peace camp.

I wasn't told to go to a particular place. They just said, 'If you have anyone you know, go and stay with them.' Everyone who stays there has to build his or her own hut. The government doesn't assist them. They just gave me a *malwa* [bowl] of sorghum and told me to look for any relatives I might have in the camp.

But the harassment and deprivation of life in the peace camp, outweighed the attractions of receiving clothing and meagre food ration.

---

[4] Interviewed in Dabker, 8 May 1995.

Most of the women in the camp were adding to their rations, which were small, by working. For example they carry water or thatch houses. Especially those who carry water for the army are given some money.

After I was put in the peace camp I escaped at night. I had only gone there to get some clothes. The soldiers openly demanded from me that they wanted to sleep with me. They were demanding it from me, and sometimes they forced the women to have sex.

I was lucky because I didn't stay long so I was not noticed by many soldiers. But other women said that the soldiers tell them to carry water to the barracks, and then they force them to have sex. In Um Dorein the water is available only from one 'donkey' pump,[5] so what the soldiers do is they stand beside the pump and only allow the women they want to fill their water containers. So you can stay there a long time without getting water unless you agree with them. The soldiers supervise the whole camp, but particularly they are around the 'donkey' pump.

Most people there are there against their will. But there are always armed people about. The people are frightened of the Arabs. If they are given the chance to come out, they will come out.

Najwa's account is fairly typical. More details of life and death in peace camps will be presented below.

Many people are abducted by force, taken to garrisons, and then enticed to stay with offers of relief. It takes a strong will to resist the combination of threat and the offer of modest but real material assistance. One Nuba lady who had the strength of will to resist both the intimidation and the blandishments is Fawzia Kuku Komi, aged thirty-five. She is a Lira who was abducted by force along with more than thirty other people in April 1995. Among those who were taken with her were Jibreel al Nur Kuku, aged 21 years, his brother Zaki, aged fifteen, and Suleiman Ibrahim Suleiman, aged twelve. Fawzia told her story to African Rights:[6]

---

[5] A deep bore hole with a diesel-powered pump.
[6] Interviewed in Debi, 10 May 1995.

It was about 3 p.m., we went to the place of water in the *khor* [river bed], next to the garden. We put all our water containers down near the wells and we entered the garden to have some mangoes. The government forces came into the garden and ordered everyone to stand still. They were both soldiers and PDF. We were about 33 people. After that they asked us, 'Is there any Anyanya [i.e. SPLA] with you in the garden or not?' We said that Anyanya was there some time back but they had all gone. All of us there were civilians. They began to ask us about the wells where the cows and goats used to drink. One of the men with us, Baggari, told them where the cows and goats drink from. After he told them the soldiers started pushing him. He was told to lead them to where the wells were. One soldier and two PDF took Baggari away. The rest remained to guard the 32 people.

From the garden we were taken to the bush. They said, 'If we find the animals we are looking for we will leave you. If not we will take you with us to Heiban.' When the soldier and the two PDF who took Baggari returned with him but without any animals, the group decided to take us all to Heiban. Before we reached Heiban they beat us and chased us ahead of them. When we were close to Heiban, Jibreel was tied with his hands behind his back and a gun was pointed on his head. They said, 'We are going to shoot you.' They also said, 'We will also kill you with the *marmaton* [old rifle] you were carrying.' They had tied him up. When they were about to shoot him they changed their minds. They said, 'We will shoot a bird with that bullet instead.' We were driven into Heiban. Jibreel was only untied later.

We were interrogated. They asked, 'How many Anyanyas are there in your area?' We said we didn't know. They showed us a parade of their army. They said: 'Is their number the same as this?' We said, 'Our number that has been brought here [33]—the number of Anyanya is more than us.' We said that in our village there are only four people with arms.

We were taken to prison. It had brick walls and a cement floor. Men were put in one room and women in another room. After we were separated, the soldiers came into our women's section and began talking to us, making advances and demanding sex. We were 23 women and girls. They called two women to follow them. I told them in our Lira language not to follow them. One was Sumeya Mahana and the other was Amina Hussein. I said, 'Don't go. Don't go.' When they saw I was talking to the women, the soldiers turned

150

to me in anger and pointed their guns at me. I bent down and carried on talking: 'If it is to be death, let us die with honour, Don't go with them.'

They told us: 'We are coming to tie you up and take you by force.' They called Amina: 'If you don't get up and come with us, we will tie you up and take you by force.' Amina didn't move. They said the same to Sumeya. I told Sumeya: 'Let them tie you up.' Sumeya said: 'Bring the rope and tie me.' Then they saw that it was difficult, so they left us.

The next day the captives were subject to an interrogation which included crude but characteristic propaganda about the resources in the hands of the government compared to the SPLA.

The next morning we were taken to the Council of Heiban, men and women together. The Administrative Officer of the Council, who was a Nuba, said, 'Take your [new] clothes and don't go back to your village. Stay in Heiban.' We refused the clothes. They said: 'Anyone who wants to go back, stand on one side. The others, stand on the other side, so we can give you clothes and you can stay.' No-one went to the side of the clothes. The Administrative Officer pointed at me and said: 'You are the agitator. You don't want people to have clothes and stay in Heiban.' I told him, 'If you are fed up of our children, it is up to you. Us, in our hearts, we want to go back to our children and our village.' They said, 'You who are in villages are deceived by the Anyanya. They are deceiving you that they have good relations with the *khawajat* [foreigners, international community]. But the *khawajat* will never help you. The *khawajat* are in agreement with us. They send clothes and food to us. Where are the clothes and food they send to the Anyanya?' We said, 'We have not seen [any] clothes.' They said, 'They are deceiving you. And the Anyanya will run out of ammunition and go back to the South and leave you. Soon, we will bring weapons, even if you are in your caves it will force you to come out. If you don't come out before May, you will see death like you have never seen before.' We replied, 'If this is the will of God, he will do what he wants.' The Administrative Officer gave an order: 'Return them all to prison.'

We spent eighteen days in prison, in police cells. After some days, we were taken back to the Council. Then we were asked, 'Do

151

you want to go back or stay?' We said that we wanted to stay. It was a way to get out. They were very happy and took the boys to be registered in school. They were given their school uniform of *damuriya* [cotton cloth]. Jibreel and Baggari were ordered to go for military training. From there, all of us were given clothes, except for Jibreel and Baggari, who were going to receive their military uniforms later.

They said, 'Now, we have dressed you. John Garang has run away and all his guns have been taken by the sons of Omer al Bashir. We have all the guns of Garang. Yousif Kuwa—where is he? He is not coming back. He has decided to deny you and he has gone to the South.' We said, 'It is only God who knows, we can't say anything.' They were happy.

We were released to be free inside Heiban. Someone called Issa Duma was made responsible for us and we stayed in his compound. He gave us rations—sorghum, two *malwas* for a month.

After sixteen days, I told Jibreel that we have to plan a way of escape. I said that he should go ahead with the small boys. I told them that we will follow. At 3 p.m. Jibreel left Heiban quietly with the boys. When we were sure they were not noticed, fourteen women moved that night. Some of us remained in Heiban: Baggari, five boys, nine women. Three of those women who stayed escaped later.

Central to the government's strategy is attracting international assistance to the garrison towns and peace camps. It has made health facilities in Kadugli a priority, to the extent that staff of international agencies have considered the town exceptionally well-catered for and not in need of international medical assistance. Elsewhere it has succeeded in obtaining some international assistance. UNICEF has a programme in the government-held areas, although Operation Lifeline Sudan (which is headed by UNICEF) has been prohibited from operating in the SPLA-held areas. A delegate from the International Committee of the Red Cross made a tour of the government-held parts of the region in November 1994, but the ICRC has not yet reached an agreement with the government. In April 1995, a delegation from the World Food Programme of the UN, the Islamic African Relief Agency and the Sudanese Red Crescent toured garrison towns including Talodi, Um Dorein and

Um Sirdiba, to assess the needs of what the government calls "returnees" in the peace camps. In this report, these people are referred to as "internees" or "captives."

The "Popular Defence Force"

President Omer al Bashir has repeatedly called for the creation of a "million-strong militia" in Sudan to fight the SPLA. During his visit to Kadugli and Talodi in April-May he attended rallies in which thousands of newly-graduated militiamen applauded him as he announced victory in the Nuba Mountains. He regularly attends similar ceremonies throughout Sudan. The centre of this plan is the mobilisation of all available adult males into the "Popular Defence Force."

The Popular Defence Force in the Nuba Mountains consists of the regularised Arab militias (Murahaliin) and the more-recently formed Nuba PDF battalions. The Nuba PDF are recruited in several ways. Some young men are picked up in regular sweeps in towns. Others are picked up as boys, sent to "acculturation camps" where they are given new identities, and then transferred to PDF training camps when they are old enough.[7] Others volunteer because of lack of any other options. A large number are forcibly conscripted after sweeps of rural areas.

The idea of obtaining military recruits by force is not new in Sudan. Historically, the ruling elites of Egypt and Sudan maintained armies of slaves, many of them forcibly captured. These armies were then used to subdue the very regions from which the captives originated.[8] Such soldiers might be expected to sympathise with the people they were required to fight against, and desert at the earliest opportunity. But this happened surprisingly rarely: the slave soldiers were fiercely disciplined and were given economic rewards for participation in campaigns and raids. Many also became Moslems,

---

[7] See: African Rights, *Sudan's Invisible Citizens: The Policy of Abuse Against the Displaced People in the North*, February 1995, pp. 17-22.

[8] See, e.g., D. H. Johnson, "Sudanese military slavery from the eighteenth to the twentieth century," in L. J. Archer (ed.) *Slavery and Other Forms of Unfree Labour*, London, Routledge, 1988.

changing their identities and coming to identify, at least in part, with their new overlords. The local regiments of the British army in colonial Sudan, while technically "free", followed this tradition.

The existence of the Nuba PDF has to be seen in the light of the Sudanese history of slave soldiers, and the strategy of "Peace from Within." If leading Nuba citizens have been drawn to the government side, is it surprising that rural youth are ready to follow the same path? Ahmed Sayed and El Amin Omer explained how the Nuba PDF began in Delami:[9]

> The *Nafir el Sha'abi* started in this area [Delami] in 1994. The big difference is the forcible recruitment of people, who are then sent back to take animals and people from their home villages. People who are captured are taken to Delami, and from there to unknown destinations. Some are taken to the Kortala agricultural schemes. One returnee, Omer Saad, said that while they worked on the schemes all Moslems and Christians were forced to pray together. Others are trained in the PDF.
>
> The PDF is still controlled by the Arabs. The leaders of the military side of the *Nafir el Sha'abi* are all Arabs. But the Murahaliin still exist separately and sometimes they make joint operations with the PDF. If a member of the PDF captures an able-bodied man, he is given LS 10,000 as an incentive. If he captures a woman or an old man, he is given LS 5,000.

Omer Saad Osman is a farmer from Nyingir village, who went with his wife and five children to Delami town hoping for a life free from hunger. When he arrived, he said "the soldiers were all Arabs," but then he saw the PDF in the process of being formed:[10]

> There was no PDF camp when I was first there. The PDF had a training centre situated between the garrison and Delami water tank. They also had a weekly military parade every Saturday in the military garrison, but they took their guns home. One of the famous PDF leaders in Delami is Anter Alabu Kieman.

---

[9] Interviewed in Tira Limon, 20 May 1995.
[10] Interviewed in Tira Limon, 23 May 1995.

I was harassed by Hussien Abu Jalaha, Hassan Kunida and James Komi, my relatives who were in the PDF in Delami. They wanted me to join the PDF. On 22 July all of us fit for service were summoned to a big tree near the police station of Delami. There the leader of the PDF, Anter Alabu, told us to prepare for joining PDF training in October '94. [The delay was] because most of us were cultivating. He told us that all 'returnees' [i.e. internees] have to be armed to fight the rebels. He said, 'Nobody has the right to refuse.'

When I saw that I will end up in the PDF I and my wife decided to return. Everybody in the peace camp who is in good health is waiting for his day of compulsory recruitment into the PDF in Delami.

One night in August [1994] I escaped with my children and wife at about 8:00 p.m. from Delami to Eiden village. The following day I proceeded to Nyingir.

Conscription to the PDF is compulsory: those who object are beaten and detained until they agree. Children as young as twelve may be conscripted, though most recruits are fifteen or over. There are some indications that the Sudan Government prefers to conscript teenagers rather than adult men, presumably because they are more pliable. Yunis Dakum Kucha, a boy of thirteen from Kortol village in Otoro, is one who narrowly escaped. The first part of his testimony tells how he was abducted and interrogated. He spoke in the Otoro language:[11]

I was captured in the bush when I went to cut wood. There were four of us, one boy older than me and two younger ones. We left the house and went and began cutting the trees. At about 10.00 a.m. we were surprised by a large group of soldiers, all of them Arabs. They hadn't captured anyone else, and they hadn't looted any animals. They just took us and made us carry big loads of mangoes. It was about four hours' walk to arrive in Heiban.

As soon as we arrived, we were taken to the office of the security. They asked us, 'Where is the camp of the Anyanya?' They had someone to translate from Arabic to Otoro. We said, 'They walk in the whole area, especially in the mountains.' They beat us

---

[11] Interviewed in Kauda, 12 May 1995.

155

with sticks and the butts of rifles. They said, 'It is better for you to tell the truth.'

We spent four days, and day by day, we were always beaten. Every day, in the morning, we were taken for work. Our work was cleaning the barracks, washing clothes and dishes. Then in the afternoon, after the soldiers had eaten, we were taken for interrogation until about 5 p.m. All four of us were taken together. There were three soldiers investigating, and two others sitting behind us with sticks. When the investigator said, 'You're not telling the truth,' these two would take you outside for a beating. One of the boys was beaten until he was paralysed and unable to work. His name is Kumi Chatika and he is younger than me. I don't know why they picked on him for specially hard beating.

Military Intelligence cannot have expected to obtain much valuable information from a thirteen-year-old boy using such techniques. But part of the rationale for the brutality is simple intimidation: preparing the captives for their future life as PDF conscripts. Yunis continued:

After four days, I was sent to the PDF training centre. The instructor said, 'We will shave your head, give you a khaki uniform, give you boots and then you will start proper training.' There was a batch of PDF recruits that they were training there already. They already had uniforms and shaved heads. They were being trained with guns. I knew some of them from my area—Kalu, Kuku, I don't remember their Arabic names. Most of these trainees were young, some were my age, some were younger, some a bit older. The group from my area was ten boys, but the total number was much larger.

For two days we had a sort of preliminary training. We didn't yet have uniforms or shaved heads or guns. In the morning we started with running. Then we were taught how to assemble and take apart a gun. In the afternoon we were taught how to drill, and various things like crawling on our stomachs. There were between twenty and thirty of us. There were six instructors who spoke the Otoro language, with an Arab in command, and they translated his orders.

We were often beaten. Beating always happens. When you are given an order and do it slowly, or you are not doing something well, or for any reason, they will beat you.

In the evening, we were taken for cleaning the barracks. We cleaned the houses, washed dishes, utensils and clothes, and did the ironing. Those who knew how to iron clothes were selected for ironing.

We slept outside on the verandas of the barracks. Our rations were very little—we were given just one *malwa* of sorghum. We could see that the food for the regular soldiers was much better.

I could see some women they had captured during their operations. When the soldiers came back from an operation, they would divide up the women between them, and each soldier would take the woman he had chosen.

I am a Christian, though I am not yet baptised. When they asked me my religion and I said I was Christian, they said, 'Everyone here is Moslem,' and they took me to the mosque. I was given the name Musa. As I was already circumcised they did not need to circumcise me. There was someone assigned to teach us Islam, he was a Baggara Arab. We were taken to the mosque and he taught us things in Arabic, but as there was no translation, we didn't understand anything.

They said that the total training will last six months, and that after graduation we would be sent to Abu Jibeha.

After two days, I decided to escape, although there were guards all around. If someone was caught escaping, they tortured him badly. I saw one man, a married man from Jongiya village, who had tried to escape, whom I saw tied up in the garrison. He said in our language, 'If I get another chance I will escape again.' His arms were tied behind his back, all the time, even during the night. He was in a cell with a zinc roof, and when the sun is hot during the middle of the day, they brought him outside and put him in the sun without water.

In the middle of the night, I crept between the huts, until I was outside the camp. Then I ran until I got to Luchulu village, and from there I came home.

There is no upper age limit for the PDF. Omer Ashmor Aloki, a farmer from Kauda South, was abducted from his village in January 1995, and taken to Mendi garrison. He is fifty eight—normally much

157

too old for military service First he was interrogated in the military camp, and then taken to the peace camp, which lies a small distance away. He told African Rights:[12]

> After the registration we were shown *rakubas* [shelters] to sleep in and we were given one *malwa* of sorghum for one week per five persons. After fifteen days I was given a 'relief *jellabiya*' with the colour of white. I was told to join the PDF. Many PDF are Baggara Arabs. My name was registered for the PDF. Every able-bodied man in the peace camp was required to join the PDF.

Omer escaped on the eve of his transfer to the training camp in Talodi.

Recruits to the Nuba PDF are subjected to rigorous training, lasting six months (though some reportedly do only a "crash course" of 21 days). The ideological components of the training are probably more significant than the military ones. The conscripts are taught Islamic extremism, and Christians and traditional believers are encouraged or forced to convert to Islam. They are given rations and uniforms, but no pay. Instead, they are rewarded with "incentives" for abducting civilians and bringing them safely to garrisons, and with a share of what they succeed in looting from villages. Usually, seventy per cent of the value is taken by the PDF, with a variable share to the soldiers responsible. The penalties for non-compliance are severe: beating, torture and summary execution.

The first military action of a PDF recruit is usually either as a "guide" for an expedition of regular soldiers, or as the vanguard of an army convoy. Either way, the new recruit is under strict supervision, and can expect summary treatment if he fails to live up to expectations. A resident of Otoro explained:[13]

> Nuba are normally trained as PDF, so they do not have to be paid a salary. Immediately after training, the first thing they are used for is as guides for the forces during an offensive. If the operation succeeds in finding things to loot, the guide is given an incentive. If

---

[12] Interviewed in Kauda, 11 May 1995.
[13] Interviewed in Kauda, 11 May 1995.

it fails, he is beaten, arrested and locked up. Sometimes if soldiers are killed in an SPLA ambush, the guide will be executed. There are cases of guides being killed on the spot. They are always suspected of co-operating with the SPLA.

For example, Awad Dalil was used by the enemy to guide them to the cows and goats at Karakir. But when the army came they found that the people had already evacuated the animals, and then the army unit was ambushed by the SPLA. So they decided that Awad had betrayed them. They returned to Heiban and Awad was executed. That was in August 1994.

Once a recruit has become "blooded" by military action—which usually means looting, abduction or other violence against civilians, often people of the same tribe or even village—he will feel alienated or criminalised, distanced from his former community. The experience of forces that use violent conscription, such as Renamo in Mozambique or the Interahamwe militia in Rwanda, is that such people are then transformed into obedient soldiers, willing to carry out atrocities to order. Though less extreme, the process of induction of the Nuba PDF is comparable. This is one reason why few Nuba PDF have deserted to the SPLA. Other reasons are the widespread SPLA practice of killing captives (see Chapter V) and the fact that PDF captives who are spared are immediately released, and then tend to run straight back to the garrisons. People in the SPLA-controlled areas, including SPLA officers, explain this by saying that the conscripts have become accustomed to their new way of life, which is materially preferable to the hard life in the SPLA areas, and their shame in front of their former communities.

"COMBING": A CAMPAIGN OF SCORCHED EARTH

The rationale of *Tamshit*, "Combing", is simple: the obliteration of everything that exists in the areas not under the direct day-to-day control of the government forces. What can be stolen, is stolen; the rest is destroyed. It could be described as economic warfare, counter-population warfare, or total warfare. It serves the dual purpose of creating utter destitution and demoralisation among the rural Nuba, and enabling the Sudanese army and the PDF to "live off the land."

Burning Villages

The central component of "Combing" is the burning of villages. Before 1993, many villages were burned, either by the army or the Murahaliin-PDF, in their reprisals or military operations. Now, the military forces deliberately avoid engaging the SPLA and simply target villages. On several occasions, African Rights saw burned villages just a few miles away from SPLA camps, which had not been attacked. It is a cruel and cowardly form of war.

Between February and May 1995, African Rights visited villages that had been destroyed by the Sudan Government, and interviewed dozens of people who had suffered from wanton destruction. Information was collected from villagers from all parts of the Nuba Mountains. It became evident that the programme of the Sudan Government is to burn every Nuba village that it does not completely control. The campaigns of 1993-4 and 1994-5 have gradually penetrated more deeply into SPLA-administered areas.

The word "village" in the Nuba Mountains requires explanation. Most villages, particularly in the hills, are settlements strung out across valleys and hillsides, sometimes continuing for several miles. The different sections of a large village may be separated by a hill or a water course, and may have different names. It is also possible for the government to establish a garrison in a village, while the other end of the village, across a valley or mountain, is under SPLA control.

Tira Limon

The largest settlement in Tira Limon is the big village of Seraf Jamous, that used to be spread over two steep valleys, an escarpment, and a substantial area of the plain that separates the Tira Limon-Achiron-Moro mountain range from the hills of Mesakin. Over the last eight years, Seraf Jamous has gradually contracted. First, the permanent market in the plain was abandoned, as the

Jellaba merchants fled. When African Rights visited in May 1995, only a few ruined walls and the remains of a grinding machine were left from two rows of shops, and all the commercial activity in the area now takes place under a single tree. The great majority of the more than two hundred houses on the plains and escarpment are now abandoned, and only those in one narrow valley, completely enclosed by mountains, remain inhabited.

The mek of Tira Limon, Jibreel Alin Kabi, listed the villages that were burned in the 1993-4 dry season: Oya in December 1993, and Rimla, al Tura, Farandala, Arda, and Seraf Jamous, in April 1994.[14] Jibreel Tutu Jiran, a deacon in the Roman Catholic Church, described the burnings of 1994 and 1995, and explained why the people still considered themselves lucky:[15]

> This year they [the army] have been more aggressive, they burned part of Seraf Jamous, Rimla, al Goz and also went to Dabker in the Moro area. That was at the end of April.
>
> Casualties are fewer in this area than in other parts. That is because there are not many government informants here, because contacts with the government were not good beforehand. So there are no Tira Limon people in the PDF and no defectors. There is no Tira Limon Amir under the *Nafir al Sha'abi*; the only candidate was Abdel Salaam Musheri Chupa who was killed.

When African Rights visited Seraf Jamous, it was necessary to stay under a tree and call the people from their hiding places in the hills. Santo Kuku Shangiron, a farmer aged 39, was one who came. He described the 1994 attack:[16]

> The enemy came from Talodi and entered Seraf Jamous at about 10.00 a.m. They started shelling earlier, while they were advancing. The first shells landed at Tori, which is part of Seraf Jamous. They also fired shells into the Achiron Mountains. After that they entered Seraf Jamous and started burning the huts. They used burning shells called *munira*. Some they burned by hand using matches.

---

[14] Interviewed in Achiron, 7 May 1995.

[15] Interviewed in Tira Limon, 22 May 1995.

[16] Interviewed in Seraf Jamous, 8 May 1995.

At that time they burned a total of 139 houses. They burned a lot of sorghum. I can recall that they took nine cows belonging to Trimbi, and one belonging to Albini. Only one woman was killed.

It is clear to me that the government of Sudan wants to come and burn villages so that people go to the towns that they hold. But people don't go. We don't go because we don't trust them and we have no [good] relations with the Arabs.

Omda Abbas Hadira Lipa confirmed the same account, and described the difficulties that ensued:[17]

There was a big government offensive in April 1994. They came and burned villages and killed people. One woman was killed in the hills. She was called Keni Shahid. They burned more than 120 houses and took animals. They took one man who was cultivating. He is called Reme, we have no news from him since that day. The only information is from a boy, Abdullahi Murjan, who was arrested with 28 cows and taken to Talodi, who escaped. The boy said that life is very hard in the military camp and that Reme had been killed.

After the village was burned we cultivated but we faced many problems. We were in a state of fear, so we didn't put our energies into it. We concentrated on the small farms in the hills and left most of the big farms in the plain. Many people went hungry as a result. The hungry people borrowed food from others who had more. Nobody went to the [government] towns.

The Seraf Jamous people did not rebuild the main part of the village. But those who had houses in a wide valley north-west of the plain continued to live there, hopeful that the terrain would protect them. As Santo Kuku Shangiron explained, it did not:[18]

On 27 April 1995 at midday they started shelling and immediately entered the area. But they were afraid to come too far in, too close to the mountains. So they just stayed three hours. They burned seven houses using shells. I counted twelve vehicles, some people

---

[17] Interviewed in Seraf Jamous, 8 May 1995.
[18] Interviewed in Seraf Jamous, 8 May 1995.

162

say thirteen. I saw eight lorries and four jeeps with anti-aircraft guns and launchers. All the lorries were full of soldiers.

No-one was killed. That was because information came on Tuesday [25th] from the SPLA that the enemy was moving in the area. So most of the people went into hiding with their possessions and their cattle. But there were some who were reluctant to believe the information and stayed behind. Luckily they were able to move quickly when they saw the enemy coming.

Omda Abbas had not yet counted the losses of livestock or other possessions at the time of African Rights' visit. He said, "I don't know the number: they took nine from this man, six from him, nine from the other one. Also fifteen cows from someone. They didn't take any people." But any simple list of the animals, furniture, household utensils and clothes that had been destroyed or looted cannot explain the impact of such losses on people who are already pushed right to the economic brink. Khamisa Kodi Arno, a young mother, explained:[19]

On 27 April the Sudan Government attacked our village. They burned the huts in the village and they burned the sorghum. They took my clothes and the clothes of my two children. I have only these clothes I am wearing now. The children have no clothes at all, except the older boy who ran in his underwear. He is four.

We have nothing left. Even the seeds are gone. We are trying to borrow from others, we are eating the aid that is given us by local people, organised by the omda. He goes and asks people to donate. Most people are poor and they can give only one cup of sorghum. So it will not be enough. We are sleeping in the house of a lady called Aratul, which was not burned. Our problem is that we are so many in one house—three women with fourteen children.

But it is better to stay here than to go to the peace camps. I don't want to leave my land and my village: let me stay here, even without clothes. Those who go to the peace camps, no-one has brought news of them.

---

[19] Interviewed in Seraf Jamous, 8 May 1995.

The neighbouring village to Seraf Jamous is Arda. In both 1994 and 1995, Arda was burned the same day as its neighbour, as described by Sheikh Osman Bombey Fadul:[20]

[In April 1994] the government forces came from Talodi, through Seraf Jamous. They arrived in Arda around 3 p.m. It was a very large convoy; there were 53 vehicles going on the road to Um Dorein. When we heard the cars and saw them coming we ran to the mountains.

I saw them come down from the trucks and start shooting artillery. The ones ahead do the shooting, the ones behind do the burning. More than one hundred houses were burned in Arda—the whole village. No-one was killed or wounded. They took many cows, but I can't tell you how many—it is for everyone whose cow has been taken to tell you how many.

Everything was destroyed—sorghum, groundnuts, sesame, pigs. We kept some seeds for planting. We ate mangoes and doleib fruits, and fortunately we had good rains. But the harvest was not so good because of insects, and because we were living in fear.

The story was repeated on 27 April 1995. Though there was less devastation, this attack was even more demoralising, leading people to question whether they could continue to live in their native village.

This year we were attacked again. Again, everyone escaped. Normally our people don't get killed or wounded because we have a good hiding place. So we ran again and didn't lose anyone. They took cows and goats and killed pigs, and one shell killed seven cows belonging to Ibrahim Edam. But it was not as bad as last year. They burned more than sixty houses, but we are rebuilding. We have hidden some small amounts of food.

In the past, our Arab neigbours were Misiriya Zurug and Jellaba. We had good relations with them, just like salt. But now we do not have good relations; nothing can bring us together again. When we didn't have guns, they were colonising us, looting our things. Now we have guns they don't do this. So now the Misiriya Zurug hate us, and they come with the government forces to burn

---

[20] Interviewed in Dabker, 8 May 1995.

us. Even sometimes they know our huts, they call our names. I have heard that some of my Arab friends are with the government forces but I have not seen them here.

We are still afraid. But what can we do? They will burn the houses again and we will build them again. We cannot go to Um Dorein. The news we hear is that people are even hungry in Um Dorein.

But when the Sheikh was asked whether he would seriously consider abandoning Arda for life in a peace camp in Um Dorein, he answered simply: "We want our mountains. God has given us our mountains, and if we cultivate them we shall be rich and happy."

Moro Hills

On 27 April 1995, the same day that the government forces had destroyed the few remaining houses of Seraf Jamous and burned Arda, they continued eastwards towards Dabker. Until that day, Dabker was a village of about ninety houses, lying on the southern escarpment of the Moro hills. That evening, the Talodi force met up with a unit dispatched from Um Dorein garrison, and attacked the village at dawn the next day.

African Rights obtained a copy of the following report deposited with the headquarters of the Hajana Division in el Obeid, which describes the army attack on Dabker village.

> 28 April 1995
> Operation Nida' al Salaam (Call of Peace)
> 18 Operations K 127/K254/Sha'abi Talodi
> Confidential 93
> Situation report no 46
> Covers the period of the last report dated 24 April until 13.00 hrs [today].

Our forces attacked Dabker camp today at 6.00 hrs. We have burned the whole camp, killed three rebels and freed twenty civilians. Our losses: two wounded, no. 330010 Surgeon Mohamed Hassan Mohamed Kuku from Signals Division, lightly wounded;

no. 340742 Lance Corporal Juma al Malach Tutu Nasir, no. K254, seriously wounded.

At 13.00 hrs our forces attacked al Rimla camp and we burned all the huts that had been built and for the first time we opened the road of Um Dorein-Rimla. Our forces have now secured the road properly. The rebels fled to Lado, Farandala and al Tura. We have freed four women. The rebel losses: four dead. Our losses: one wounded, no. 330957 NCO Mumi Tutu Jadalla Kafi, 1st Company 199.

Our forces were able to remove two ambushes between Dabker and al Rimla and between al Rimla and Salamat [an army post close to Talodi]. Our forces arrived at Salamat today at 13.45 hrs. Our wounded have been removed to Talodi hospital. Our morale is very high. Quick recovery to our wounded. Allah hu Akbar. Hajana *foug*! For information.

The "camp" was in fact a village undefended by the SPLA, and the "three rebels" killed were villagers who were too old or infirm to run away. Others were wounded. Lupi Tuti Idris, a blind woman aged about seventy, was unable to climb high into the mountain when the army came. She was shot by a bullet in the right ankle when she tried to flee. She said:[21]

We were four people, left behind in a cave low on the mountain. The soldiers seemed to be following us. They started shooting at us. I don't quite know what happened.

Angata Jani, aged about eighty, also could not escape. The soldiers found him in his hiding place at the foot of the mountain. He was hit by shrapnel and bullets in his shoulders, thigh and knee. Without any medical treatment, his chances of survival are not high.

The sheikh of Dabker, Magreis Suleiman Kori, described how the Sudan Government destroyed his village:[22]

The Sudan Government forces came from Um Dorein. We heard when they attacked al Tura village, which is three hours walk from

---

[21] Interviewed in Dabker, 8 May 1995.
[22] Interviewed in Dabker, 8 May 1995.

here, on 27th. After al Tura was destroyed, we slept in the bush. In the morning, we went to the mountains to monitor what was happening. When we hear a rumour we always try to confirm it by climbing.

We saw thirteen trucks of various types, some large and some small. There were many soldiers.

The Sudan Government entered Dabker at 6 a.m. When they entered, two SPLA soldiers were passing by, who shot at them. Then the vehicles stopped, and the army started shooting in all directions. They advanced, some on foot and some in cars. They started cordoning off areas and searching the whole village. Some started burning the houses, using matches house by house.

I was in the mountain. All the people ran up into the mountains except those who were very old. The soldiers started to burn the sorghum and shoot at the pigs. They killed 21 pigs. They took fourteen cows and lots of goats. Every single house was burned; not a single one was spared. The total is 85.

A few people managed to take their possessions and food into the hills. But the majority had their crops burned. Some ran away with clothes, but most of our clothes were burned. Most of our *angarebs* [wooden beds] were burned. The [two] churches were burned. Most of our food is burned. The few people who have food remaining are sharing it with the others.

We took all the children up. The old people, who were able, also climbed to the top, but some could not climb and stayed down the mountain. Among those who stayed down are the people who are wounded.

The army stayed three hours. During this time they were shooting without stopping. We don't know why they were shooting as there were no people down there.

Adam Khalil Kolanga, a leading layperson in the Dabker congregation of the Sudan Church of Christ, witnessed the military precision with which "Operation Call of Peace" was implemented.[23]

I was next to the church. I saw the army in trucks; I was below the mountains. When they came they dismounted from the trucks, and when I saw them advancing I also moved from my hiding place to

---

[23] Interviewed in Dabker, 8 May 1995.

go up into the mountain. They started burning the houses down here. At the same time they were shelling the mountain with artillery mounted on cars. Then I saw the soldiers using matches burning the houses, until I saw them approach the church and burn it. While one part of the army was advancing and shelling, another part was in the middle, burning the houses. There was a third group stopped, sitting behind with the cars and resting. They were all army, I know the uniform. They were mixed, some Arabs and some blacks.

The Moro-Otoro Valley

One of the main "combing" operations of the 1994-5 dry season was mounted from the garrisons of Um Sirdiba and Aggab. A swathe of Moro and Otoro villages lying in the broad valley between the Moro Hills and the Otoro Hills were burned. The reports submitted by the army unit to the headquarters of the 18th Brigade speak of a succession of "enemy camps" burned, a total of two rifles (one an aged *marmaton*) captured, one or two very minor injuries to the soldiers (probably caused by their own equipment) and, repeatedly, "the losses of the rebels are not yet assessed." Soldiers will recognise the formula for the destruction of defenceless villages.

At 5.30 a.m. on 21 February 1995, forces from Um Sirdiba and Aggab garrisons attacked and burned the village of Karkaraya el Byeara. They shelled the nearby villages of Lupi, Karkaraya and Gardud el Humeid. They withdrew, but the following day they returned and burned those same three villages, and shelled Um Dulu. African Rights visited Karkaraya the afternoon after it was burned and spoke to the sheikh, Simon Madawa Tutu.[24]

> Many people died in the attack. There is a lady called Siema el Kanama and a man called Hussein Kabra, and an elderly woman who died as well; there is a woman who was hit and left with broken legs, and another old man was wounded in his back and now he is dying. They attacked him inside his house, and burned him inside the house. His situation is critical and he is just waiting for his death; he can't walk or even move.

---

[24] Interviewed in Karkaraya, 22 February 1995.

168

All the people fled with their children and are now homeless. The people are afraid; even to go and bring water to your children is a real problem. The homeless people are now suffering as they have deserted their village; adding to their ordeal is that the el Dibeibat area was totally destroyed so people have nowhere to go, and the people of el Dibeibat are suffering as well.

That evening, residents of the burned villages were all fleeing to the mountains. Osman el Dikan el Maki, omda of Karkaraya, and his administrative assistant, Sheikh Yunan Karama Kujam gathered fragmentary information from the refugees.[25] They provisionally estimated that 330 houses had been burned, eight people killed, five injured and four known to be abducted, and numerous pigs and donkeys killed. The mosque was confirmed as burned, and witnesses said that an old man had insisted that the Korans and other books be removed before the burning, but the soldiers refused had his request, and burned everything.

On 23 February, the forces continued to Libis, Tingil, Nugra and Um Sirdiba village (which lies outside the garrison), and burned them all.

The forces then continued eastwards. On 24 and 25 February, the villages of Toror, Zangar and Tebeldiya were attacked in turn. After the first evening, the army unit filed the following report:

> From: Seif al Izz al Taani [Sword of Dignity No. 2]
> To: Hajana 18 Operations
> Repeated to: Mobile Seif al Izz al Awal [Sword of Dignity No. 1]
> Confidential no. 9
> Code Harba 23

> With the will of men and the solidarity of heroes, our forces were able to burn the camp of Toror. Our forces went into battle with the rebels at 16.00 hours. The losses of the rebels are not yet assessed.

The army stayed the night in Toror and left the following afternoon. Mohamed Siddig, sheikh of Toror, spoke to African

---

[25] Interviewed in Regifi, 22 February 1995.

Rights the following day. Still in a state of shock from inspecting the still-burning ruins, he gave his account of the "battle" and his preliminary assessment of the losses:[26]

> The army came from Aggab and attacked us in the afternoon. They came in vehicles from Aggab. They are Omer al Bashir's people; they came with six lorries and two artillery pieces. They burned down the entire village and caused a great deal of loss by burning down the houses and the sorghum. They left us with nothing. In the attack, ten people were killed and eight were wounded, and 68 were taken to Aggab... The whole village was destroyed except the mosque. My people are now homeless, and I don't know the whereabouts of most of them. The people have nothing to eat, and the village is still burning. We buried some people here [points]. Here is a grave, here is a grave. These are the graves of Ismail Kuku and Kuku Kodi, God bless them.

At that time, the number of people abducted was not clear—residents hoped that most people had run to neighbouring villages, and only 68 had been confirmed missing. But in May, African Rights met again with the sheikh and other elders of Toror, and found that they had compiled a list of 250 villagers who had been abducted and taken to Aggab garrison. More than half the captives were children. The reason for the large number of captives was the unusual time of the attack, in the afternoon. Because Toror lies close to Aggab in an area of constant insecurity, the village had not been rebuilt, and the people were living as refugees in the neighbouring villages, such as Eri and Debi. They are facing hunger.

Sheikh Mohamed el Zein and Sheikh el Sid Jaber also inspected the ruins of Toror that evening. Based on the first reports from villagers, they estimated that the Government of Sudan had taken the majority of the crops, cattle and goats, and that five thousand people had been left homeless.[27]

---

[26] Interviewed in Toror, 26 February 1995.
[27] Interviewed in Toror, 26 February 1995.

Toror and the nearby villages were wholly undefended. There were no SPLA forces in the area, and there was no military engagement between the Sudanese army and the SPLA.

Otoro Hills

The Sudan Government mounted almost continuous "combing" operations into the Otoro Hills and the neighbouring Tira el Akhdar areas during the 1994-5 dry season.

In November 1994, forces from Mendi destroyed much of Kodi A village. Three people were killed, and according to records kept by the head of the district administration, Hassan Mahmoud Rende, 387 cows and 265 goats were stolen.[28] Seventy-five people, almost entirely women and children, were captured and taken to Mendi. Among those abducted was a man called Hussein Kiril, who was recruited to the PDF and subsequently became what Hassan called "a notorious guide for the enemy."

A second attack was launched on 31 January, again from Mendi, and lasted until 7 February. The villages of Tuchi, Kodi A (again), and Kodi B were burned. Mek Osman Gamar told African Rights that 350 houses had been burned, ten people killed, 142 goats and 105 cattle looted, and seven thousand people displaced in this attack.[29] In a later interview, he added:[30]

> The aim of the attacks is to force us to join the government, by making us go into their towns—Mendi, Abu Jibeha, Kalogi, Heiban. There are peace camps in all these places.
>
> From the people they captured, they have made some into officials, such as wakil [deputy amir], omda and sheikh. The people were all captured, hardly any went freely. From my tribe, 460 people were taken by force, between November 1994 and now. A few returned forty days ago.
>
> Our biggest problem now is hunger, because of a poor harvest and the destruction of the enemy. People are beginning to go to the

---

[28] Interviewed in Kauda, 11 May 1995.
[29] Interviewed in Tira Limon, 5 March 1995.
[30] Interviewed in Kauda, 11 May 1995.

enemy because of hunger. Some of them do not even have one *malwa* of sorghum.

The administrator, Hassan, apologised that he could not confirm details of the numbers of people killed and livestock looted because his records had all been destroyed in the third assault. However, he described the attack as more devastating than the earlier one. Ali Bagigor Arkada, an Otoro farmer aged 42, lost his cattle in the attack.[31]

I was living in a cattle camp near Kodi A with my cattle. In February 1995, the enemy attacked our cattle camp in the early hours of the morning. I ran away with some of the cattle and the enemy managed to take my thirty cows. They took my cows to Mendi for no reason whatoever.

In March, the enemy came back and attacked Kodi A village. They burned my ten huts. They looted all my household including fourteen sacks of sorghum, ten sacks of groundnuts, five bags of beans and six sacks of sesame.

In April, the enemy came and abducted my mother, Mariam Kodi. They took her away to Mendi. Some people who just escaped from Mendi are saying that my mother is in the peace camp in Mendi.

I have now built four new huts in Kodi A to protect me and my four wives from the rains. I have eighteen children with nothing after the government soldiers looted me.

As Ali's account shows, after February the attacks were virtually non-stop, from both Mendi and Heiban. Several villages on the escarpment south of Heiban were shelled, attacked and burned. Sherab Lima Kodi, from Luchulu village, told African Rights:[32]

On 1 March this year they came to Luchulu and destroyed houses, sorghum, sesame, groundnuts and so on. They looted animals. One person was injured by bullets. People were forced to run away. On the same day they burned houses in Kuchama, burned all the food

---

[31] Interviewed in Kauda, 12 May 1995.
[32] Interviewed in Kujur el Sha'abiya, 13 May 1995.

and took many cows. Six people were injured. Later in March they burned Kwarle in Lira area, and took animals and properties. They also destroyed Abol, burning the houses. Three people were injured. But they didn't take any animals.

Sayed Jerman Lajora is the head of the administration of Kuchama district, appointed in 1993. He is an Otoro from Kola.[33]

Since I took over the responsibility for our six villages a lot of incidents of burning and looting by the enemy from Heiban have taken place. The four villages mainly affected by enemy destruction are Kuchama East and West, Sarobar (Luchulu) and Kauda Foug.

On 10 March 1995 the enemy came from Heiban and attacked Kuchama East and West and Luchulu at about 5:00 a.m. and 5:30 a.m. consecutively. The enemy divided itself into three groups. These three groups attacked Kuchama East and West and Luchulu the same day and at the same time. All the houses in these three villages were burned down completely except the church in Kuchama East. In Luchulu the enemy burned two churches, took 81 cows and a large number of goats. Nineteen people were abducted from Luchulu and taken to Heiban. Their names are: James Kodi, Omdurman Kuku, Halima Labina, Samuel Opalo, Anisa Abdalla, Kushi Abanur, Zenab El Medin, Lochi Marco and Kajera Khater. Seven of these persons escaped from Heiban. Samuel came on 12 April 1995 and Umdurman came on 1 May. The rest arrived as a group on 7 April. All came back to Luchulu.

The enemy looted 55 cows from Kuchama West. These cows were taken from the wells in Khor Kusher in Kuchama.

On 17 March the enemy came again from Heiban and attacked Kuchama East. They burned the church and its compound. It was the only building remaining from their previous attack of 10 March.

Sayed Jerman explained that a major reason for the attacks is so that the PDF and army can supply themselves with food, while simultaneously creating famine among the farmers.

---

[33] Interviewed in Kujur el Sha'abiya, 13 May 1995.

In all these attacks the soldiers will carry away what they can carry from food crops and destroy what they cannot. Cows and goats are driven off to Heiban. Pigs are killed and left behind.

Our farms that are a distance of one to one-and-a-half hours walk from Heiban have been harvested by the government soldiers. The soldiers will come with their civilians who are in the peace camps. They will spend the whole day harvesting our farms and take our crops to Heiban. The enemy also takes away crops already gathered by us in the farms.

These attacks, especially the burning of food crops have created some difficulties. There is now shortage of food and most crops in store are kept as seeds. I hope the enemy doesn't come soon to rob our seeds.

In mid-March there was a much larger operation, launched jointly from Heiban and Mendi. For the first time since 1989, the army came and occupied the small town of Kauda. The army occupied Kauda on 20 March and stayed for three days. The forces comprised one regular army battalion (six hundred men), one battalion of Mujahidiin, and an unknown number of PDF. They had eleven vehicles—seven large trucks, two jeeps mounted with machine guns, one with a 106mm gun, and one water tanker. They also had a long-range howitzer, two light machine guns, and some 82mm mortars. But, despite their numbers are arms, they were very nervous during their brief spell in the town. The trucks remained loaded at all times for a quick retreat.

In Kauda, there was widespread but not comprehensive destruction. The army looted houses and the mosque. Several houses were destroyed, but the permanent buildings of the school, clinic and mission station were not destroyed (contrary to the report received in Hajana headquarters in el Obeid from the army commander), possibly because the soldiers preferred to use these buildings as their own sleeping quarters. In the market, the one operational grinding mill was destroyed. The principal well was poisoned with a dead goat, and it took several days after the removal of the goat for the water to be drinkable again.

African Rights has not obtained the military reports that detail the number of "rebels" killed. But there were civilian casualties, as the army opened fire on anything that moved. One victim is Fatima Kuku Hanisi, a Moslem Otoro from Kauda aged 34:[34]

On 20 March 1995 the enemy surrounded Kauda at around 4:00 a.m. to 5:00 a.m. I escaped the siege with others and went to Kauda Foug—the mountains. I stayed three days in the mountains with my children Naser el Din, Kuwa, Hussein, Kuku and my husband Fadul Mundu. We were not able to carry food with us to the mountains when we escaped.

After three days we felt hungry and thirsty. My son Naser el Din, Jada Arnei, my husband and myself agreed to come to our huts in Kauda to fetch some food. It was early hours of the morning but still dark. Our plan was first to detect whether the enemy have left Kauda. If they have left then we take food up the mountains, otherwise we have to return to our hiding place in the mountains.

When we approached Kauda I heard the sound of bullets: 'tetat-tetat-tetat.' I was shot in the left thigh and fell down. I cried out that I was shot but nobody heard me. My thigh was bleeding and I started crawling back to the mountains. Half way I felt tired and hid myself in a nearby cave. I lay down there for a long time.

At noon, about 12.00 or 1:00 p.m., I saw some young men passing by quietly. I recognised among them Ali Nytambe and Komi Bedawi. I called both of them by name. They came and carried me to Lwere where I had medication. I was treated for six days and allowed home as there was no medicines. I continued traditional treatment. For two months I walk only with an *okaz* [long stick]. Now I can walk but not long distances or carry heavy loads. Long sittings give me acute back pain. I can't also climb mountains or come down from them. If the enemy comes now I will not run. I would let them kill me rather than have more pains and nights of agony.

The army surprisingly did not burn our hut but looted all our property. I and my husband are now living on loans as I have no sorghum to make *merissa* [beer] with. Because we have taken many loans my husband is in Debi village to find some work that could be paid in sorghum.

---

[34] Interviewed in Kauda, 12 May 1995.

175

During this operation, the village of Kauda North (Kauda Foug) was also burned. Yousif Mandlei Kodi, an Otoro farmer from Kauda Foug, aged 37, told African Rights:[35]

On Wednesday 22 March [1995] the enemy came from Mendi and burned our village of Kauda Foug. At about 6:00 a.m. we heard gunshots from the direction of Komoriti. I asked our people of Kauda Foug to evacuate the village as the enemy may likely advance towards us. While people were preparing the things they would run away with, the enemy arrived. They started shooting even before getting close to the village. A lot of artillery shells fell on the village. They were firing from the northern side.

I ran very fast into a nearby cave on the mountain as I was almost outside the village.

I saw nine big vehicles of fourteen tyres. The trucks were green and yellow in colour. The trucks were empty the soldiers were all on foot. The enemy started burning our village at about 8:00 a.m. I saw the soldiers burning the huts of the village by setting them on fire. They will pull the grass from the hut [roof], light it and burn the hut. When the place is far from them or it is closer to the mountains they will fire a *munir* [incendiary]. Once the bullet hits the target it bursts into flames. Most of the huts they burn this way are the ones on the outskirts of the village. I saw them loading their trucks with food crops and other items. All in-built mud stores are emptied—either burned or loaded into the trucks.

After the trucks were loaded they moved ahead and soldiers walked behind the cars. The soldiers spread in a semi-circle moving out of the village. They were driving a lot of cattle and some people with them. The soldiers spent about three hours in the village.

In the afternoon I came down with other elders of the village. I found all our stored food had been destroyed or burned. Fifteen persons were abducted and taken to Mendi. Most of the abducted are old women, men and children primarily those who were not able to escape. The persons abducted were: Ikram Kodi, Nawal Mukhatar, Faisal Kodi, Abdel Moniem Abdel Rahman, Kuku Abdel Moneim, Samia el Tayeb, Keni Lema, Keni Kodi, Kaka Idris, Kacha Kodi, Faisal Sulieman, Hanan Kodi, Keni Kuku, Kuchi el Tayeb and Wadia Komi. Nobody among the abducted returned

---

[35] Interviewed in Kujur el Sha'abiya, 13 May 1995.

and there is no news about them from Mendi. 212 cows were taken from the village.

Kodi A and B were also attacked again. By this time, a total of 1387 houses had been burned in all five villages of Kauda, Kodi and Tuchi.

In another operation on 18 April, the villages of Kernalu, Riil and Luchulu were attacked and many houses were burned, bringing the total number of villages burned in 1995 in Heiban county to sixteen.

Tira el Akhdar

The village of Kalkada lies on the southern edge of Tira el Akhdar, close to the notorious garrison of Mendi. It has been burned many times—five incidents of burning were detailed in Chapter II. It suffered again during 1993-4. Three residents of Kalkada described what happened after they were forced out of their village after these repeated attacks:[36]

> The largest number of people went to Kumu, because it is nearby. Here we were attacked again. That was in February 1994. The army came from Mendi, on foot. They took the cattle belonging to the Kumu people. They killed two of the Kumu people and abducted 36 people. The abducted included some of our Kalkada people, including Omer al Nil and his wife Katcha Hadra and their four children; Musa Majiri and his three children—his wife escaped— Haboba Hassan and her five children, Niri Mahmoud, and Yom al Eid and her two sons. We heard news of them recently from someone who escaped from Mendi. She came last Thursday and said that the people are suffering, still staying in *rakubas* that don't keep out the rain, and that some children have died. We also learned that some of the men had been executed: Ali Shalo, Abdalla Netu and Hamid Shughulu. We are still waiting for more details.

Other people stayed, and were burned again. Aboud Hamad Bako, aged 28, is the Imam of the Ansar el Sunna mosque in

---

[36] Interviewed in Um Dulu, 16 May 1995.

Kalkada. He witnessed the same army unit also attack Kalkada village.[37]

> On 25 February 1994 the enemy attacked at about 2:00 p.m. They began attacking with light weapons first and later followed by heavy artillery. It was a market day. Everybody was in the market that day. It was unexpected. The people in the market ran in panic to all directions. Many people were killed, among them my mother Jabara Kasho, my wife Toma Rahmatalla and my paternal grandmother Keni Tutu. My son Abdel Hamid (one-and-a-half-years-old) was injured. Lako Abdalla, Elnaga Lalo and Kalo Tutu were also killed. They abducted twelve girls and children aged one-to-two years.
>
> There were two mosques in Kalkada. The Government of Sudan looted the mosque with the permanent roof and burned down the mosque with the grass roof. They took the zinc sheet off my mosque's roof and the other 35 zinc sheets stored in the mosque for further extensions. Three iron doors, ten carpets, 45 Holy Korans, twenty Hadith books, a tin of gas, a new Tilly Lamp and a few medicines were all taken. In the main Kalkada mosque, which they burned, they took 145 copies of the Holy Koran, 35 books of el Hadith, fifteen carpets and ten chairs. Twenty mats were burned.
>
> Personally, the enemy looted my property. They took from me one sewing machine, one bag of clothes, ten sacks of sorghum, two sacks of sesame, ten cows and thirty goats.

The 1994-5 dry season was one of near-continuous attacks from Mendi garrison.

> On 10 September 1994, the enemy returned and attacked the village in the morning while people were cultivating in their farms. This time they abducted five women and a man. The man was later killed. His name is Abdalla Toto. Two women were later released, namely Kaka el Omoda and Hawa Hassan. The other three were taken captives. They are now captives in Mendi military garrison and they are Agadi Jakisa, el Zein Jadalla and Neni Kalo. There is no news about there fate.

---

[37] Interviewed in Kauda, 12 May 1995.

On 2 October 1994, the enemy came in the early morning of that day at about 5:00 a.m. They did not fire from a distance as they used to do. They fired when they had already encircled the village completely. Yet I managed to escape with others. In my house they captured two people, Jadalla Hamedein and el Ahmar Angelo. Jadalla was killed there with a bayonet. Angelo was killed in Mendi by firing squad. The eyewitnesses said that after he was killed, his body was thrown in an old well. Hassan Rahma and el Amin Lodi from Kalkada were killed with him in Mendi.

There was a pre-dawn attack on Kalkada on 4 November, in which many houses were burned and people were abducted and taken to Mendi. Aboud was absent. But he suffered again:

The enemy attacked Kalkada in February 1995. They didn't find much to take this time. People have little left from previous raids. The soldiers abducted 150 women and children and took them to Mendi. These people are still there.

Now due to all these frequent attacks we leave Kalkada in the dry season, that is from December to May. We spend the dry season in the mountains. In June we come down and return to Kalkada to cultivate. For our gardens, we usually ask the SPLA to give protection to pick them, especially the mango trees.

Joseph Aloga Jargi, outlined some of the attacks on Um Derdu on the eastern side of the Tira el Akhdar Hills:[38]

In 1994 the government burned Um Derdu. The sorghum was all destroyed by fire, and all the properties burned. The cotton was looted. Two people were killed. One of them was my uncle, Bedey Loicho. One woman and two children were abducted. Kumu was also burned.

In 1995, they burned Um Derdu again, and killed four people and stole all the cattle. It was a joint army and PDF force sent by Mohamed Rahma from Mendi. They also attacked Tajura and took many people to Mendi.

---

[38] Interviewed in Tira Limon, 21 May 1995.

Shambali Bashir Jama, a thirty-year-old farmer from Um Derdu, was a casualty in one of the attacks.[39]

In November 1994, the Sudan Government forces attacked our village of Um Derdu while I was sleeping. The sounds of shooting woke me up. I ran out of my hut and headed towards Um Derdu mountains. Between the mountains and the village I felt some pain. I felt as if I was not running and something was pulling me back. I fell down and saw my left foot bleeding. There I found that I was shot. I was frightened and tried to lie down but the sounds of the gunshots passing over my head made me to have courage. I crawled up to the mountain's foot. Thank God the enemy did not come to search the area otherwise they would have found me. I did not crawl very far from where I was shot. Perhaps it was not my day to die.

The enemy spent about three hours in our village and withdrew after burning it completely.

At about 8:30 a.m. Ibrahim Gadier and Osman Salih found me where I was lying and carried me to the top of Um Derdu mountain. As our village didn't have a health centre our native doctor Halima Adam treated me. She made a traditional bone healing. My foot was tied up with sticks every day for one month and half. After one month and half I was able to walk slowly. I'm not completely healed as my fingers cannot move. Halima told me that the bullets might have cut some veins. I can't run now or climb the mountains. Even I can't clear my farm. Any hard work that needs movement have become extremely difficult. The Sudan Government has looted and burned my house. They left nothing. Now I'm getting it difficult to feed my family and my wife Malika Ibrahim.

Kumu is another Tira village that has been repeatedly attacked. Hamad Berier Jar el Nabi, 38, a farmer in Kumu village, told African Rights:[40]

In the first week of May 1994, the enemy came from Mendi garrison and attacked Kumu at about 4:00 a.m. The enemy burnt all the huts of Jembi, the largest part of Kumu village. They took

---

[39] Interviewed in Kauda, 12 May 1995.
[40] Interviewed in Kujur el Sha'abiya, 13 May 1995.

682 cattle and five hundred goats. Two persons were killed: Hassan Kabashi and Idris Kamli. Thirty six persons were abducted and taken to Mendi.

After a week of the first attack the enemy came and took the remaining cows, about 45 of them. No person was killed or wounded. There were no abductions as by that time many people of Kumu withdrew to Ngabero Mountains. In November 1994 we came down and rebuilt Kumu. New houses were built including a new mosque. Everybody settled and started clearing the farms.

In March 1995, the enemy came from Mendi and attacked Kumu at night. They looted the village. They took 270 cows and 480 goats. They burned the crops in the stores, sorghum, sesame, groundnuts. Persons killed include: Abakar Adam, Ismail Angelo, Adam Tutu, Hussein Ismail, Hussein Adam and Ali Adam. Fifty-five persons were abducted, among them Osman Maregi and Nafisa Ali, Keni Sulieman, Komoka Hussein and her four children, Hussein Lodi, and Ali Shuba.

Delami County

Between 5 February and 30 March 1995, army and PDF units from Dere garrison and Delami attacked a string of villages on the eastern side of the Kawalib hills, entering and destroying much of the large village of Abri, and burning part or all of Dere village, Kamand, Um Jamena, el Laud and Nugor villages. Another operation was mounted to el Laud and Baba on 29 March. Nine villages were destroyed in total. The aim of "combing" this area seems to have been to populate the newly-opened peace camp at Dere and to increase the captive population at Delami. It succeeded. Most of the villages were rendered uninhabitable and more than five hundred people were abducted by force and about seventy were killed. The number of internees in Delami peace camp rose to over nine thousand. This offensive is detailed in the section, "Driven out of places of refuge", pages 215-21, below.

181

Korongo Abdalla

In early April 1995, Sudan Government forces mounted a "combing" operation in the Korongo Abdalla and neighbouring Miri areas. On 3 April they burned the village of Abu Sunun. No-one was killed but four were wounded. On 5 April at 12.00 noon they attacked Korongo Abdalla itself. Mahjoub Ismail, African Rights monitor in the area, submitted the following report:[41]

> On 5 April at 12.00 noon heavy shelling began on the village, forcing many people to run to the mountains and the caves, leaving behind all their properties. After the heavy shelling receded, the Government forces entered the village and looted cattle, burned huts and took away sorghum and groundnuts. Then they began looking for people who had decided to hide nearby.
>
> Seventeen people were captured and five were killed: one woman, three men and one child. Four were wounded.
>
> People have lost all they had and have taken refuge in the mountains nearby.
>
> The names of the dead are:
> *   Bushra Kuku Heiban, aged 29;
> *   Kelinki Kafi Osmar, thirty;
> *   Abdu Tiya Jardeen, 25;
> *   Haura al Tom Kuwa, 23;
> *   Tutu Ibrahim Kafi, three.

The army unit responsible meanwhile submitted its own report. African Rights was passed a copy:

> 6 April 1995
> From Hajana 18 Operations to all units, Hajana Reika.
> Confidential 654

> If God gives you victory, nobody shall defeat you. Al Hamdu li Allah and with his assistance and the will of men.

---

[41] Report from monitor Mahjoub Ismail, dated 7 April 1995.

At 15.00 hrs today our forces Suyuf al Izza (Swords of Dignity) and the PDF of Keilak were able to capture and destroy Korongo Abdalla. [Also] the camps of Shatt Tebeldiya, Tamargi and Abu Sunun. Our losses: five martyrs and twenty wounded. Paradise for our martyrs and quick recovery to our wounded. Moral is very high. Allah hu Akbar. Dignity for the Nation.

The Korongo Abdalla area has the unfortunate distinction of being the sole part of the Nuba Mountains where the Sudan Government has used anti-personnel mines extensively. Before 1994-5, there were only very occasional reports of land mine incidents. One of the few was on 15 March 1992, when Kuku Khalifa stepped on a mine, assumed to have been planted by the army, on the Miri-Kadugli road and was killed. Two of his companions were injured, Nur el Din Khamis and Mohamed Musa Torein. The recent operations in Korongo have involved much more extensive mining. On 10 April 1995, el Amin Tiya was killed by a mine planted at the gate of his house when soldiers withdrew from his village, in the Korongo area.

Buram County

Since the re-occupation of Buram garrison in December 1993, Buram county has been a major focus of government "combing" activities. In addition to Buram, the army established garrisons at Teis (on the road to Kadugli) and Turoji (on the road to Talodi). The forces based there rapidly gained a reputation for violent destruction of the surrounding rural areas. During the 1994-5 *Seif al Salaam* offensive, the Sudan Government refused to engage with the SPLA, and concentrated on, first, burning villages, second, establishing military camps, and third, establishing "peace camps".

African Rights was unable to visit Buram but spoke to community leaders and refugees from the area. The chairman of Buram County is Hamad Tutu Dabah. He recounted how his area, formerly the quietest in the whole of the Nuba Mountains, are now subjected to the Sudan Government's scorched earth tactics. The scattered outlying settlements of Buram town itself were among the first areas to be "combed".[42]

> On 28 December 1994 the army came from Kadugli through el Ehimir to Teis. In Teis they burned 1,200 huts and looted what they could manage to carry. The army entered Buram at 8:00 a.m. and burned about five thousand huts. Many people—around eight hundred—were captured and prevented from leaving Buram. Buram is now turned into a peace camp.

Having established themselves in Teis, the army unit then ventured further afield, burning and abducting:

> This year in February the army attacked Fama, Jebel Kuwa and Shatt Safiya. People abducted from these areas were taken to el Ehimir and Teis. Sheikh Kuwa Miri of Shatt Safiya People's Court and five members of his family, Kafi Sandali Tiya, his daughter and his niece Kaka were abducted from their farms. All were taken to Teis military garrison.
>
> On 15 March the army that had attacked Teis and Buram earlier now attacked Reika. All the houses in Reika were razed to the ground. Nine people were killed in Reika and eight injured. Reika is now turned to a military garrison. The former Reika primary school is the army headquarters. Reika was heavily reinforced with many soldiers and made the base to attack other neighbouring villages.
>
> The army immediately proceeded from Reika and burned the areas of Kelandu, Mesakin Tuwal and Qisar, Tamora, Desari, Desabo and Tadoro. The enemy used burn a group of villages and go back to its base in Reika.

From Buram, the army's target was to move southwards, to destroy Tabanya, Tansa, Damadirga, Tabuli and Angolo—the western side of the Mesakin and Korongo Angolo hills. This operation opened with aerial bombardment using an Antonov in the Tabanya and Turoji rural areas, on 30 December 1994. A ground

---

[42] Interviewed in Um Dulu, 17 May 1995.

attack followed, as described by Amsal Tutu Tiya, a resident of Tabanya:[43]

> On 3 January 1995 the enemy came from Buram and Turoji and attacked Angolo. Our village was already surrounded by the army coming from Buram when the Turoji army started shelling us. We ran to the mountains but many were captured by the army. In the shooting, seventeen people were killed and 35 injured. In all, 198 people were abducted and taken to Buram by the army. Among the people abducted was Sheikh Riyad Tiya of Angolo.
>
> Cows and goats were taken in thousands by the army. Our area of Angolo is one of the rich areas of the Nuba Mountains in terms of cattle. We used to rear cattle for the Arab nomads in peacetime. We used to rear the cattle of Misiriya Zurug, Awlad Surur-Felaita [a branch of Misiriya Humr] and Awlad Jeifel Arabs in return for cows in payment.

The government forces moved on to the third stage of their operation, establishing a permanent army camp and the basis for a local *Nafir el Sha'abi*.

> In March, Sheikh Riyad Tiya, after being recruited as PDF, came as a guide for the attack on our village, Angolo. All able-bodied men abducted from our village are now PDF in either Buram or Turoji. This attack destroyed Angolo completely and made us go to the mountains. The attack was composed of the Buram army, and the PDF of Sheikh Riyad Tiya. The PDF was composed of Misiriya Zurug, Felaita-Awlad Surur and some Nuba formerly abducted from Angolo.
>
> The army and PDF decided to camp in Angolo. They loaded the harvested crops into big trucks and took them to both Turoji and Buram. We could see between three and six trucks each day loaded with our crops, mainly sorghum, sesame and groundnuts, leaving Angolo.
>
> During the day the army in Angolo will shell us on the mountains for hours and hours, while the PDF are gathering crops or loading them in the farms. When we saw that the army and the

---

[43] Interviewed in Um Dulu, 17 May 1995.

PDF intended to stay most of us moved to Tabanya. Angolo until now is under the occupation of the enemy.

At the time of African Rights' visit, no peace camps had yet been established in Teis, Reika or Angolo, but villagers were anticipating this as the next stage.

The second prong of the offensive came from the eastern side, from the army unit in Turoji, which was soon reinforced by troops from Talodi. On 30-31 January 1995, Lado village and the surrounding area were destroyed by the force from Turoji. Daud Kunda, chief of the area, estimated that 420 houses burned, 250 cattle and goats looted, and nine people injured. About three thousand people were displaced in the attack.[44]

This attack widened into a large "combing" operation affecting all of the eastern side Korongo Angolo hills. Hamad Tutu Dabah described how the offensive unfolded:

On 28 February the army came from Talodi and entered Turoji in the morning. Using Turoji as a base, the enemy attacked Dabakaya, Alumhalib, Kordofan, el Dar, Degasi, Jebel Diya, Thaba, Doudi, Kalbubu and Lindu. All these areas starting from Turoji were destroyed. Fifty persons are known to have been killed in these offensives but many lost their lives in the forests while running away from the army of the Sudan Government. Thousands were displaced to areas of Lado, el Abyad, Fariang, Fama, the Galtia mountains around el Dar and Talodi. Some people returned to Turoji and it is now a government peace camp.

What was formerly one of the richest areas of the Nuba Mountains, that provided food not only to its own inhabitants but to many refugees from devastated areas further north, has now been subjected to hunger for the first time. The village of el Dar in the Angolo hills was one that was destroyed. Jibreel Ismail Kuwa, a 48-year-old farmer from el Dar described how the army carried out its plan:[45]

---

[44] Interviewed in Um Dulu, 18 February 1995.
[45] Interviewed in Um Dulu, 17 May 1995.

186

On 20 January 1995 the enemy attacked el Dar coming from Turoji. It was early morning when the village was bombarded with heavy artillery by the army. The army was shelling from a distance but the rate of bombs were very high. Not less than two thousand artillery shells were fired by the army. In this attack seven persons were killed. Among them Moya Kafi, Kiki Dhukan with her daughter and a son, Habuba Kaka an old woman of sixty years, and the son of Tiya Kodi and a girl from Turoji related to Tiya Kodi's wife. Six persons were injured. My wife Mastura Kuchi was abducted and taken to Abu Jibeha. Other persons abducted and taken with her are Tutu Merkaz and Kafi Kaftera. The enemy stayed four hours and withdrew from el Dar.

The government had meanwhile decided to establish a garrison and peace camp in el Dar, and additional forces were brought from both Talodi and Buram.

The enemy came back on 7 March 1995. The government troops came from Kadugli, Talodi, Buram and Turoji. I counted 79 cars, lorries, trucks and jeeps from Turoji to el Dar. El Dar was attacked at 8:00 a.m. and occupied by the enemy. El Dar is now a military garrison and a so-called peace camp. Two persons were killed: Salim Dhukan and Yagoub Kuwa (Shatt by tribe). Fifteen persons were abducted and taken to Turoji. Six persons were injured: Kuku Jadom, Saloma Tiya, Hawa Hanij, Daud Kuku—his left leg was later on amputated.

The army immediately intensified its "combing" operations, to depopulate the surrounding villages and hills, and populate the new peace camp.

Many people of el Dar entered the caves in the mountains. Yet the enemy will come at night to take people out of the caves. The army will come at night to the mountains and fire flares or signal bullets into the air. The whole area gets bright. People are frightened and get out of their caves to run away. Then people are abducted trying to escape from the caves and taken to Turoji. Four persons who were abducted from the caves returned recently from Turoji. They are Taliq Kafi, Kuku Tiya, Ibrahim Murkab and Tiya Darjaula.

187

Other areas near to el Dar like Tawili and Lindu are still being raided by the government from both Turoji and Buram. Recently, Assistant Sheikh Tutu Idris was killed by the enemy and others were abducted from Lindu. Kurkel Talha and Tiya Tawer were taken to Turoji. Tutu Tiya, Juwa Tutu (son of Tutu Tiya), Musaran Dudu and Dudu el Faraj were abducted and taken to Talodi through Turoji.

There is no news about the persons abducted except from a few who manage to escape from the government centres. I heard that Sheikh Tubo Riyal, his brother Tigani Riyal, Tutu Jamon, his mother Diya and Tutu Talha have been killed in Buram. Nobody can tell us when were they killed. The people returning will just tell us these people must be dead as they just disappear from the peace camp. I hope the enemy might have transferred them to another place as they have many peace camps and labour centres. The government can do anything they want with them. They have been killing us like dogs and even without graves. I tell you the government army will order us not to bury our people whom they have killed. I have seen many bad things and buried many who were supposed not to be buried.

Personally I have no news of my wife [who was] abducted by the enemy. When my daughter Keni asks me as to when her mother is coming home I answer her in tears. Frankly I don't know what to say. I only pray that one day she will come. God is Great.

In Buram county, in a period of four months, the Sudan Government has succeeded in establishing a stranglehold of garrisons. It has done this at the cost of destroying the economic foundations of a formerly wealthy agricultural area, and forcibly displacing its people. The human cost cannot be calculated.

The Western Jebels

African Rights was unable to visit the western jebels, partly because of the ongoing army and PDF operations against villages in the area. Government forces have overrun most of the area, but have been unable to hold many of the mountains.

The Tima hills have been the focus of most military activity during 1994-5. At 6.30 a.m. on 31 October 1994, the PDF attacked

Tumu, and burned the entire village of more than three hundred huts. Thirty civilians were either shot dead or burned in their houses, among them Shang Taha and her five children, who were burned to death in their house. Most of the livestock in the village was stolen. On 5 January 1995, the PDF attacked Karkar village; they did not burn but they looted cows. They killed one child, el Ehimir Ali Kuku, and wounded two adults.

Kabashi Karkandu Jellab is a male nurse in Lagowa, who is originally from Tima. He witnessed one of the government's "combing" operations in his home area:[46]

I came on leave from Lagowa to my home, Tima, in December [1994]. I spent twelve days there. One night, at about 7 p.m., the army and PDF attacked Tima village. They burned all the huts of the village and killed fifteen people with bullets. One of the dead is Idris Magren Fafa, another is Osman an Nur Subahi.

They captured people; they ran after people into caves and took them. They took Fatma Barballa, Toma Injili, Fatma Tiyuh and her three children. From the men they took el Ehimir Babu and Tutu Regeyig. They must have taken eight or nine people, all those they could find. They also took cows, but not goats. I ran away.

We have no further news of the people they took. Normally we don't hear anything. No-one has escaped and come to us.

Since I came here in February, I have heard that there was another attack and the PDF captured some fifty people. I don't know the names.

The assault that Kabashi refers to was launched at the end of January, from Dilling garrison towards the Julud and Tima hills. On 4 February, the army and PDF burned Mandei, Julud Basha and Karkar, after forcing the people to evacuate to the peace camp at Majda. Accustomed to such attacks, residents described the casualties as "few". Many cattle and goats were looted.[47] At the same time, the Misiriya Murahaliin came to Kayo and Karkar villages, where they killed a cowherd aged fifteen and stole all the cows they could find.

---

[46] Interviewed in Achiron, 7 May 1995.
[47] Mohamed Tutu Tiya, interviewed in Um Dulu, 18 February 1995.

On 19 March, the villages of Kiwe and Tomond were attacked and burned. Thirteen people were killed, including two young children and the sheikh, Abdel Hamid Juma.

In April, the army attacked and captured Tima itself. According to residents who escaped the attack, the aim was to take civilians, with the accusation that they were supporting the SPLA, and remove them. The soldiers burned and looted extensively and took people to a peace camp. At the time of African Rights' visit, no more detailed information was available. In May the army was forced to evacuate Tima, which was re-occupied by SPLA forces.

There have also been military engagements and army and PDF attacks in Tullishi, Kamda and Nyima in early 1995, though details are not currently available.

Raiding Cattle

Along with farming, raising cattle and goats is the central economic activity of the Nuba. Livestock not only supply milk and meat, but are the major store of wealth. In times of shortage, farmers can sell or barter their animals to obtain staple food. The loss of livestock is a devastating blow to rural people. In line with the Sudan Government strategy of encouraging its forces to "live off the land", while creating destitution and hunger among the people in SPLA-held areas, raiding cattle is a major component of "combing".

Yagoub Telamir Kuwa, aged 45 and an elder of the Sudan Church of Christ, used to be a major cattle-owner in the Seraf Jamous area of Tira Limon. Because cows have difficulty surviving in the mountains, Yagoub was herding them in the plains, where they were vulnerable to government raids. He was raided in November 1994, in the early hours of the morning:[48]

> I was in my *zariba* [livestock enclosure], with cows and goats, close to Seraf Jamous, south of the village at the end by the market. At about 4 a.m. the army came. They got me when I was sleeping. We were surrounded. I was awoken by them. They told me to take the cows and goats, I was put ahead of the soldiers. I was with my

---

[48] Interviewed in Jibreha, 8 May 1995.

son, Abil, who is eleven. They took him too. They stole 35 cows, belonging to me and my family, and twelve goats.

They abducted Osman Marat from the same *zariba*, and they killed him on the road. He was guarding seventeen cows belonging to his brother Abdel Rahman, which they took. He was also shot on the way between Seraf Jamous and Rimla. I don't know how exactly; he was behind me and I just heard the shot. When I asked they said, 'It is Osman.' They were talking among themselves, 'We have finished with this Anyanya.' Two others were shot in another *zariba* near us. They went in and shot them immediately before they came to our *zariba* and captured us. One was Ibrahim, my elder brother, and the other was Daud, his son, aged ten. They took their cows too.

We just took a forest route. They were on foot, about four hundred men, all armed. They were PDF. The commander was a Nuba from Liri; there were only two Arabs among them. I knew one of them, Hassan, who is a Moro like me, also from Seraf Jamous. He went to live in Mafulu a long time ago, before the war. His family are here—they don't say anything, but they are not happy with him.

When we reached the bush they stopped. One said, 'He is one of the Anyanya, there is no need to take him, let us kill him.' They asked me if I had a gun. I said, 'I don't have one.' They said, 'Even if you don't have a gun, you are an Anyanya.' Then others said, 'Take him to Talodi.' We went on, then stopped. The same argument ensued again. When they were talking, some SPLA fired on the group. There was an exchange of bullets. In that exchange two PDF were wounded.

One of the wounded said, 'If you don't want to kill him, let him carry us to Talodi.' At last, I was forced to carry the wounded. There were four wounded. [Two other soldiers had been wounded earlier, before Yagoub was abducted.] I carried one, three others were carried by the PDF. When they got tired, they changed themselves, but they decided I shouldn't be changed. It took two hours up to a place called Mafulu, an army outpost of Talodi. I carried a wounded man all this time.

A favoured location for the government to mount their ambushes is at wells. They hope to capture animals as they come to drink.

Abdel Bagi Fadul Katin, an Otoro from Kuchama East, lost his livestock in this way.[49]

> I was looking after my cows and goats in Khor Duluie. It was on 1 May [1995], in the morning. The cows and goats were drinking water. Some women were also around. At about 9 a.m., the government soldiers ambushed us. The women taking water managed to run away. I was surrounded and caught. My hands were not tied but they just simply ordered me to go ahead of them with my fourteen cows and my 28 goats. We headed towards Heiban. The soldiers were behind me when I crossed the last *khor* to Heiban. There I started to run and the soldiers shot me on my right knee. I managed to enter the grass and hid myself. The soldiers searched the whole area but didn't get me. I saw them going away taking the road to Heiban.
>
> At about 12:00 midday I heard people passing by talking in my language, Otoro. I saw these people carrying firewood. I recognized them and called for them. They were Abdel Karim Beshir, Beshir el Nur, el Khalil Hameid and Mohamed Tamilala. They carried me up to Abol where I got some medicine. I spent 35 days in Abol taking treatment. I have improved a lot now. I don't have any news of my cows and goats in Heiban.

If they fail to capture animals at the wells, the government forces abduct people and then try, using any means, to obtain the locations of the animals from them. One farmer who experienced this is Ibrahim Kunda Atir, aged 44, a Lira from Kwarle near to Heiban.[50]

> Twenty four days ago, I was in a place in our village where people and animals drink water; a *khor* [dry river bed] with wells we have dug. I went there to bathe at about 5 p.m. As I had arrived I saw some women doing the same. So I withdrew to give the women a chance to put on their clothes. At that moment the soldiers of the Sudan Government saw me. When I came back to take my bath I heard a voice saying, '*Sabit, sabit*'—'Stop, stop.' When I turned I found a gun pointed at me. When I saw the gun I was frightened and started to run. Then I found I was surrounded, so I gave myself

---

[49] Interviewed in Kujur el Sha'abiya, 13 May 1995.
[50] Interviewed in Debi, 10 May 1995.

up. The cordon was tight and there was no way to escape. They immediately closed in on me. They were five in number, Nuba from Dingir, PDF in Heiban garrison. They took hold of me. The first beating was on my head. I fell down, and lost consciousness. While I was dizzy I saw blood coming from my head.

I came round. The first question they asked me was, 'Where are the cows?' I said, 'I haven't seen any cows drinking here.' After that, they told me to go and be their guide to take them to the cows. They continued to beat me. They continued pushing me, telling me to move. They hit me with the butt of the gun here [on the side of the head]. When they took me away from the wells they tied me up. These are the marks of the ropes [on the elbows]. They tied my hands behind me. I was kept like that for nearly an hour. While I was tied I lay on my back and they continued to beat me. Even now I can't use my fingers properly. It has made my fingernails black. There was no blood in my hands—no feeling. Four of them went ahead and I was left tied up with one man to guard me.

The four went off and robbed cows and goats. They came back with animals and three children they had captured. I didn't know the children, but later I learned that they were from Urmi village in Lira area. Adam al Diyir reported that his son was missing.

They immediately decided to untie me and ask me to go ahead with them. I refused to go, I said my body cannot move after all this beating and tying. Then they told me to go home. I said the same: 'I can't walk.' They left me. After they had gone I got up and tried to go home. After I reached home I tried to look for medicine, but I have still not found any.

In areas where there is no SPLA presence, the army and PDF simply send out small parties to comb the bush for flocks of goats that are herded by young boys. One case is that of four boys from Tuda in Shwaya, Izz el Din Muhedin Abdalla, aged fifteen, Khamis Jadia Hamad, aged fourteen, Dafalla Adam el Rubu, aged thirteen and el Rashid Niter el Bederi, aged twelve.[51]

In April [1995], while we were rearing our goats in the forest of Lekia in Shwaya, we heard a voice telling us to stop. When we turned we saw one Arab soldier pointing his gun at us. We tried to

---

[51] Interviewed in Kauda, 11 May 1995.

run and another two soldiers appeared from hiding, pointing their guns also at us and ordering us not to move. We stopped and they started beating us with their hands and belts. Our hands were tied behind us and we were ordered to move ahead of them. Our goats were escorted with us to Aggab military garrison.

We slept the night a room in the garrison with our hands tied. The following morning a soldier came to untie us. After we were untied the soldier told us that we will stay in the barracks until tomorrow where he will come to take us for the military training. We told him that we have no objection. We spent six days in Aggab thinking how to escape. During that time we saw our goats being slaughtered and eaten by the army. A boy from Otoro called el Nur was made to join us so that we were given one *malwa* [of sorghum] for five persons as a food ration per week. El Nur told us he was abducted from Otoro forest with his fifty cows.

On the seventh day at night we escaped from the room as it was unlocked. We took the direction of the peace camp and we penetrated the garrison fence, which was made of grass. We started running from there until the forest of Khor Aggab. The following morning we reached our village of Shwaya.

Livestock, especially cattle, are so important that Nuba villagers will risk their lives trying to defend them, and SPLA units are ready to use their precious ammunition in trying to recover raided cattle. Adam Angolo Mindan, a 65-year-old farmer from Lira near Heiban, was raided on the night of 7/8 May 1995. African Rights met him at Debi Nursing School, where he had gone in the hope of obtaining medical treatment for the wounds he received in defending his cattle:[52]

I was sleeping in my *rakuba* [shelter], outside in the courtyard. In the middle of the night I heard the sound of boots, people walking in my *zariba* [livestock enclosure]. I have a gate that I always close after the cows are inside. In the moonlight I saw about five people removing the thorn bush that is the gate. They stopped, before reaching me in my *rakuba*. At that time I was very tired and I had put my gun near the door—normally I put it by my mat. I felt that these people were coming to rob my cattle. So I tried to look for my

---

[52] Interviewed in Debi, 10 May 1995.

gun, but I did not find it. My heart told me that if I have to die, I must die alone and not with my children. So I slipped quickly into the house and told my wife that people are coming for bad things. 'Let the children sleep on the ground, not on beds,' I said, 'Where did I put my *abu ashara?'* ['Father of ten', an old rifle]. She said, 'It is outside.'

When I returned to the door I immediately saw the gun, but when I tried to come and get it I was attacked. I heard bullets—ta-ta-ta-ta-ta—frequent shooting like machine guns from two men. And they rounded up the cows. Sixty cows and calves. I went ahead to get the gun but when I was about to raise it to shoot I felt unable. My left arm was as if it was not part of my body. I found that it had four bullet wounds in it. It was broken. I went back inside and told my wife to take the gun. I informed her that I was already shot.

When I came out I found that these are the government forces because they were close to me and I could see them as they took positions surrounding the place. My wife and some other people were pulling me back saying, 'Don't attack them.' I said. 'Let me go to them so they can finish me off.' I was angry and began insulting them. 'Is this the Government of Sudan? What kind of government is it that robs people's things like this?' By that time I was bleeding and I nearly fainted.

The women went and told the SPLA. After that the SPLA sent a force to ambush them on their way to Heiban. God was great. The men escorting the cows were ambushed and the cows ran in disarray. All of the cows came back except one that was shot by a bullet.

When I was fainting, people said they wanted to take me to a clinic, Nashab. I said, take me to Kaldro. I was brought to Kaldro, where I found some medicine and they amputated my left arm.

The day after the attack the government again sent a force to my place to capture me and my cows, or, if I am dead, just to bring the cows. They didn't get me or my cows. So they arrested Naima, the wife of my cousin Ibrahim Kuku Suleiman, and took her to Heiban. She was interrogated about my cows, and about whether I was alive or dead. Naima spent one month in detention in Heiban and only escaped when she said she was going to bring the rest of her family.

KILLING

The genocide in the Nuba Mountains is not a policy of massacres: there are other ways of committing genocide. Large killings in which a hundred or more people are killed in a single day are not a feature of the current policy of the Government of Sudan. The aim of "combing" is not to kill all the inhabitants of the villages that are attacked. Moreover, with the exception of the Lake Abyad massacre in February 1993, all the main massacres were the work of the Murahaliin and took place in the late-1980s.

But the killing has not stopped. The killing of Nuba citizens takes two main forms: assassination by death squads, and casual and indiscriminate killing during military operations. Captives—both civilian and military—are also often executed in garrisons.

Death Squads in the Nuba Mountains

Abduction and assassination squads have been operating in the Nuba Mountains since the late-1980s. When they began, their principal targets were the educated Nuba living in government-held areas (see Chapter II). But they also targetted leaders in rural areas. A resident of Shatt Damam told African Rights:[53]

> Abduction squads were active in our area from early. In 1988, Sultan Jok Muwan was taken from his village, Kutang, by force, and killed in Kadugli. Tito Tiya was abducted from Hajar el Dabib, also in 1988, and killed in Kadugli.

By 1992, the campaign of arrests, detentions and "disappearances" had been so successful that the few remaining Nuba intellectuals and community leaders living in government-held towns were terrorised into silence, or had joined the "Peace from Within." Government efforts at abduction and killing are now

---

[53] Kuku Idris al Izerig Kafi, interviewed in Tira Limon, 20 May 1995.

focussed on rural areas held by the SPLA. Mahjoub Ismail, a pharmacist from Buram, explained:[54]

> The most common problem is abductions. The Sudan Government is abducting educated Nuba in my area, accusing them of being the brains behind the rebellion, and having influence over uneducated people. So the Government takes them and eliminates them, so that the people are 'not confused' by them. We have lost many educated people, abducted and killed. Even some of these educated people are farmers. Some are employees of the government itself. We are handicapped, we don't have the means to go and find out before they are killed, how they are being treated. We have no means to help prevent abduction. The only confirmation is their absence. Most are killed. This now raises the issue inside among the Nuba: the lack of Nuba leaders internally who can defend their rights, and speak on behalf of those who are abducted.
>
> This thing has taken place over a long time, starting with the entry of the SPLA. It is easy to label anyone 'fifth column.' Many people have lost their lives in this way.

Hamad Tutu Dabah, the chairman of Buram County, confirmed this:[55]

> The government has started to assassinate community leaders who are refusing to join them. The sheikh of Fama village, Kuku Kafi, was assassinated in house at night by government militia sent from Turoji.

Abduction and assassination squads are at work throughout the Nuba Mountains. One of their main centres is the garrison at Heiban. Although these death squads started only recently—in July 1994—they have pursued their work with vigour. The first victims were in Kernalu. Ali Idris Kuku, the deputy head of the civil administration in the area, recounted what happened:[56]

---

[54] Interviewed in Um Dulu, 18 May 1995.
[55] Interviewed in Um Dulu, 17 May 1995.
[56] Interviewed in Kujur el Sha'abiya, 13 May 1995.

One day we were having a meeting with the [SPLM] government. On that day we returned back and met with four SPLA soldiers, and told them to stay the night with us. We went to the house of the chief of Kernalu, Omer Komi. We ate with him. When it was time to go to sleep, the chief said, 'I'm going to sleep away from here.' We asked him, 'Why?' He insisted and went to sleep in another place, leaving the four soldiers to sleep in his house. That night the enemy came to take the chief, but found the soldiers instead. They killed three of them and injured one—they shot him as he was running away. He died later.

Later in the month, the army succeeded in finding who they wanted. Sherab Lima Kodi, a resident of Luchulu, told African Rights:[57]

The Heiban army comes to take animals and abduct people by night. They choose the prominent citizens. Meks, omdas, sheikhs—we don't sleep in our houses at night, because we fear abduction. My former court clerk, Hassan Bashir, has been taken, and also one *mandug* [SPLM representative], Abdel Rahman Kodi was taken to prison, where he was beaten and tortured. These two men were taken off to an unknown place in August 1994.

Another *mandug* was killed in his *zariba*. He was Ibrahim Kuku, and he died last month [April 1995]. Even in the mountains, they can come and abduct you because they have guides, and they can send some soldiers with the guide to come and abduct.

The third attack was in September, in Ali Idris Kuku's own village of Badwa. Attacks continued. Ali Idris added, "Ibrahim Adlan, the administrative representative in the village [Badwa], was assassinated in September 1994. Since then I sleep away from my house, because I am afraid to be taken."

Another victim, killed in October 1994, was Hajar Medani. The death squad came with the aim of assassinating the head of the civil administration in the county, Khamis Kundara. Instead they met his bodyguard, Hajar. Just as Hajar was about to warn Khamis, he was shot and killed. Khamis escaped.

---

[57] Interviewed in Kujur el Sha'abiya, 13 May 1995.

The next victim was Izz el Din Kukuman, who was abducted but is not known to have been killed. He is a member of the Advisory Council, and was abducted from his house with his wife and children, also in October. On the way to Heiban, his wife and children were released. Izz el Din was taken to Heiban and later transferred to Abu Jibeha.

Information from various sources indicates that the Government of Sudan is implementing a programme designed to eliminate all civilian administrators, especially the meks, omdas and heads of counties. In Heiban, the co-ordinator of the death squads was reportedly Captain Hamed Humur, the commander of the garrison. He was recently shot and killed by his own bodyguard.

In Delami, Ahmed Sayed and El Amin Omer Gardud, reported a similar pattern of assassinations of community leaders and administrators, and gave one example:[58]

> They are assassinating prominent citizens. The Mek of Dere, Kanani Nyimba, was killed in July 1994. He was shot down in broad daylight on his farm by a group of assassins from Um Birembeita. One woman was killed with him.

The murder of the Mek of Dere means that there is no competitor for the Sudan Government's nominee for the position, Hamad Abu Sudur, one of the leaders of "Peace from Within."

When the army captures civilians during "combing" operations, security officers rapidly screen the captives to find out if any of them are prominent citizens, and especially if any are on the death list. Such people may be executed on the spot. Omer Ashmor Aloki, a farmer from Kauda South, described one such incident:[59]

> In January 1995, the enemy entered Kauda while we were away in the Kauda Mountains. At 4:30 a.m. we quietly entered our village of Kauda to take food, utensils and other items that we need for our hiding. I was with my wife Khamisa Tariela and my daughter Saida. After we collected our our things we left our house but

---

[58] Interviewed in Tira Limon, 20 May 1995.
[59] Interviewed in Kauda, 11 May 1995.

suddenly found the Sudan Government army has surrounded our village. The army told us to stop and inquired at gunpoint whether I had a gun. I told them, 'I'm a civilian with no gun.' The army escorted me and my wife to their base in Kauda primary school. I asked the officer to allow my wife and daughter to leave as my wife has a child of one-and-a-half years starving without food or milk. The officer told me that my wife will only be allowed to bring the child here. I told my wife in dialect not to return.

After my wife left, I was put in a room in Kauda primary school and found other eleven people. The only person I knew in the room was Kuku Abdel Hamid and his wife Kaka el Tom. Others were from different areas and I don't know their names. At about 3:00 p.m. all of us twelve were given things to carry and were ordered to march ahead. I was given an iron bed to carry. When we reached the forest of Kalkada we were stopped. Four persons who were already tied up were executed in front of us. Among the executed was the sheikh of Angamu, Omer Mardu (from Kauda Jebel).

It is probable that the sheikh had already been targetted for execution by the government.

One of the most common aims of interrogation of captives is to help the assassination squads locate their victims. Jibreel al Nur Kuku, aged fifteen, was abducted with Fawzia Kuku Komi, whose testimony is presented on pages 149-52, and taken to Heiban. Jibreel added:[60]

While I was in prison, someone called Isam, a police officer, was interrogating me. When I said I was a member of the Sudan Church of Christ, he became very angry and said, 'Where can I find the pastor?' I said, 'He doesn't sleep in his house.' He also asked about the sheikh of the village, Mohamed Kodi. I said that he also doesn't sleep in his house.

Isam ordered me to step forward. He had drawn a red cross on the ground. He said, 'You deserve to die.'

---

[60] Interviewed in Debi, 10 May 1995.

Ismail Abdalla Tutu, who lost his foot in an army attack and was denied treatment in Mendi garrison. His testimony is on page 254. *Photo: Alex de Waal.*

Toror village after burning. *Photo: Julie Flint.*

Casual, Indiscriminate Killing

There may not be a policy of massacre. But government forces in the Nuba Mountains are able to act with complete impunity. They routinely murder civilians whom they capture, including young children and old and infirm people. If the army or PDF attacks and occupies a village before the inhabitants have the chance to flee, there are almost invariably people killed—in ones and twos, or in dozens and twenties. Some are murdered in cold blood, others shot while running, others killed by the shelling of villages and mountainsides.

Sayed Duha Zubeir is a farmer in Kalkada, whose baby son was murdered by the Government of Sudan on 5 November 1994.[61]

The army came at 5 a.m. My house is at the edge of the village. When the army came, one soldier entered in the room and told my family to wake up. My wife and eleven children were all there. We were taken out of the house and beaten, under a mango tree some way away from the house.

Five of my children ran away. Six were taken by the soldiers. A second lieutenant, Mohamed Tortor, was responsible for killing my youngest child, Khalid, who was one-and-a-half. I know him. He is from Talodi, and used to work in the forestry department there before the war. When he saw me he became angry because I had become his enemy. He said, 'You are a betrayer, I will finish you. I will take your children, your animals and all your property.'

Tortor went to my wife and tried to snatch the child. My wife said to him, 'My son—you leave this baby.' He took Khalid and threw him away. My wife ran after the little boy but found that he had a big wound on his head. He died five minutes later.

The soldiers hit me with the butt of a gun on my lower back and leg until my hip became dislocated. I fell down unconscious.

When I came round, the sun was shining on me. Perhaps it was 11 a.m. The soldiers had all gone. I could not move. When the SPLA came, they helped me and carried me to another house some way away. I saw that all the village had been burned. They took my

---

[61] Interviewed in Kauda, 12 May 1995.

45 cows, twenty sheep and fifteen goats. Seventy chickens were burned inside their chicken coops. They took three beds, but all my other properties were burned. All our food stocks were taken: one-and-a-half sacks of sesame, four sacks of sorghum, four sacks of of groundnuts.

The members of my family who were abducted are: Hawa Musa, my wife; Selwa, aged 21; Khamisa, aged eighteen; Sadia, aged thirteen; Huda, aged nine; Amira, aged six; and Abdu, aged three. They were taken to Mendi. I have no news of them.

I still have five children. I cannot feed them properly. I am only given a little food by the mosque committee, but it is not enough.

There are rewards for captives, but the Government of Sudan gives its soldiers smaller incentives, or no incentives at all, for the abduction of an old person. Elderly people are often found dead after an army or PDF attack on a village. One case was Luna Kollela Bakheit, aged 66 years, from Ngolo village in the Otoro hills. His nephew, Bakri Omer Bakheit, a tailor aged 36 from Kauda town, spoke to African Rights:[62]

On Sunday 19 March 1995, the enemy attacked Kodi A and Kodi B. On 22 March the enemy attacked our village of Ngolo, in Kauda county. As I was worried that the enemy seemed to be advancing I took my three wives, Muna Mundu, Medina Beshir and Khadija Adam and my sewing machine to Kujur el Sha'abiya for hiding with my cattle and goats.

I slept the night in Ngolo on Tuesday to protect my crops from local thieves and stray animals. At early hours of the morning of Wednesday, I was going to the nearby bush to relieve myself when I saw people in uniform standing nearby. The time was about 6:15 a.m. A group of them immediately advanced towards me ordering me to stop. They were shouting: 'Stop, you slave!' I was running with an old rifle in my hand. They started firing at me but I did not stop. I continued running until I reached Kujur el Sha'abiya.

At 2:00 p.m. I returned to Ngolo village as I thought the enemy might have left. I found my hut, my crops, three bicycles and a [weighing] scale burned or looted.

---

[62] Interviewed in Kauda, 11 May 1995.

On Thursday after breakfast I found my uncle Luna Kollela Bakheit, aged 66 years, dead in the grass, a chicken in his right hand and a bag of groundnuts in his left hand. I counted seventeen bullets in his head. We recognised him only from his white tetron *araagi* [short *jellabiya*]. The body was already swollen to the extent that once it is touched it tears apart. To bury him, I and others had to use a spade and wood to lower him into the grave near where he was shot by the enemy. I'm now responsible for his wife and four children.

An elderly woman, Seredi Akucha, was murdered by the Sudan Government forces on 20 March 1995 in Kauda. Her son, el Amin Bedawi Kuku, told African Rights:[63]

The enemy attacked Kauda that day. My mother, Seredi Akucha, was very old and cannot run away, and we could not carry her. My sister, Kusha Malika, is mentally retarded and cannot be persuaded to run. So they stayed at home. When the Government of Sudan found them in the house, they shot my mother and killed her, and abducted my sister. The house was not burned but all the properties were looted, and also all the animals, including even the chickens.

Soldiers are able to do exactly what they like. They kill for no apparent reason. One victim was Idris Kuku Jabari, a farmer from Kodi B village in the Otoro mountains, leaving his wife and seven children. Having no other clothes, his widow, Asia el Jerada Kuku Bakheit, was wearing his bullet-riddled shirt at the time of the interview:[64]

[One day] in November 1994 at about 4 a.m., somebody called Mohamed Idris cried out that the houses are on fire. When I ran out of the hut with my husband Idris all the village was on fire. My husband Idris ran carrying our daughter Nimat on his shoulder and I was carrying our younger daughter Miriama in my arms. Some distance from our house we found the government soldiers have surrounded the village of Kodi A. The army that attacked our

---

[63] Interviewed in Kauda, 11 May 1995.
[64] Interviewed in Kauda, 11 May 1995.

village came on foot. They were not using trucks but they looted our property.

My husband was ahead of me when two soldiers caught him. I stopped and heard one of the soldiers telling my husband, 'Come with us.' My husband asked, 'Where do you want me to come with you?' They replied, 'To Mendi. And if you refuse we will shoot you.' Before my husband replied to them, they shot him. I saw my husband falling in front of me with our daughter Nimat on his shoulders. My husband was shot in the stomach and chest with a machine gun. I screamed and was also shot and here are my wounds on the left arm and shoulder. I fell unconscious. I did not know what happened after that around me.

After I regained consciousness I found my daughter Nimat sitting near her father and calling 'Baba Baba,' trying to awaken him. I looked around and there were no people except me, my dead husband and my two children. I tried my hardest to crawl and got a leaf of a doleib tree. I tied my wounds with that leaf. I turned to my husband. I saw his bowels and kidney out in the grass. My children also were looking at me. I took my children to a shade under a nearby tree and went look around for a bed. I found a *angareb* in the compound of Juma. I put my husband onto the *angareb* and suddenly I found out that I cannot bury him alone. I started crying, not knowing what to do. I even forgot that I was wounded myself. I asked The Almighty to let me die together with my husband.

In the afternoon some women from the village came back. Awatif and Hawa helped me to carry the body of my husband into one unburned hut. Men later on came around and buried my husband before sunset. My other five children who were with my sister Romeya in Kodi B on the day of the attack came for the burial of their father.

Other persons were killed the same day. I remember two of them were guests who slept the night in our village. I don't know their names. They came from Tira, Um Derdu and Kumu villages.

I was in turn brought to Kauda health centre for treatment. My wounds healed after two months and half.

Abdalla, my brother-in-law, is the only one helping after the death of my husband despite of his own difficulties. I have now migrated to Kodi B as Abdalla is leaving here. I cannot survive on my own with seven children. All my children, Omer, Kodi, Kalo, Nagawa, Kasho, Nimat and Mariama are in the house of Abdalla. Abdalla himself is now responsible for six families. Suleiman his brother was also tortured to death in Mendi by the government army and left two wives.

The government had made my life miserable. Now I have nothing after they looted our house. Even this cloth I'm wearing now was the one worn by my husband the day he was killed. You can see the bullets' holes here in it. I wanted to bury my husband with this shirt by then but I now discovered that if I did that I would be naked today. I would have been unable to come out of my hut or see you. I thank Allah that I didn't.

The Nuba people hold the Government of Sudan responsible for the deaths of those who die of hunger and thirst, as well as the murder of people captured in villages and those killed by shells. Buna al Tom al Imam Kuku, a father of four in his late twenties from Kauda, described how three family members died in the government attack:[65]

In the morning of 20 March, the enemy came. It was a convoy of twelve lorries, filled with soldiers. They started by firing artillery from a long way off and then the entered the area. When we heard shooting we ran to the top of the mountain. At that time my father was still in the house. He went into the pigsty to hide, with the pigs. But he was discovered and captured by the soldiers. They took him to their temporary headquarters in the school. Then, three days later, when they were retreating, they took him into the bush and shot him dead.

The enemy took everything we owned. They took three goats and three sheep, chickens, sorghum, groundnuts, beans, our table and furniture. They killed our two pigs.

I ran with my wife and four children to the mountains, and we lived there for four days while the soldiers occupied Kauda. When the enemy started shelling, I ran with just one *malwa* of groundnuts, one *malwa* of sorghum and a container of water. Nothing else. When we ran, we found all the people there. We stayed four days without any other water. Some children began to die from hunger and thirst. My smallest child, Kuku, who was six months old, died on the mountain.

---

[65] Interviewed in Kauda, 12 May 1995.

We ran to Jebel Karga, the big mountain behind the first line of mountains. Then the enemy shelled Karga. One of my uncles was killed in the shelling. His name is Kodi Lona Juber. We were sheltering under stones. One shell exploded near Kodi, killing him at once. But we only found his body three days later. Luckily he was the only one killed by the shells.

We ran to Kolo, where we got a small quantity of water from the locals. But then we suffered from thirst. Three children overall died from hunger and thirst.

After the enemy was driven out we were afraid to search for bodies. The soldiers had killed people and dumped their bodies in different places.

African Rights was not able to visit the western jebels. But information from recent arrivals from the area indicates that the army and militias are still killing villagers regularly. A resident of Katla detailed some incidents from 1994.[66] In March, the army killed Artile Reme, Taleb Jaburi and Kuku Reme in Katla. In June, the army killed 25 people on the road as they tried to escape from the peace camp at Kujuriya (see page 247). In July, the Misiriya militia passed through farms in Katla and abducted some women, whose fate is not known. They include Nyongole Titi and her three small children and Hamuma Shasha. At least one person was also killed.

FORCIBLE ABDUCTION: A GOVERNMENT KIDNAPS ITS OWN CITIZENS

One of the main objectives of the "combing" strategy is to depopulate the SPLA areas, and to provide captives for the peace camps, labour camps and the PDF. Jaafar al Fadl recounts the experience of Korongo Abdalla since the launch of the *Nafir al Sha'abi*:[67]

By that time [late-1993], military convoys were picking civilians one by one and taking them to Kadugli. But the major attacks

---

[66] Jeilani Hamad Anduma, interviewed in Achiron, 7 May 1995.
[67] Interviewed in Um Dulu, 17 May 1995.

stopped. They would come by night in small groups to seize people from their houses and abduct them. If you refused, they would shoot you. So during 1994 there were no big attacks. But they raided cows from Katcha three times. They took many people, in small groups.

This year, the Government returned to burning villages in our area. In March, they came out of Kadugli. Bilenya was burned on 1 April and all the sorghum was taken to Kadugli. Then they came out again and captured Korongo. Evey house in Korongo was burned on 5 April. Abu Sunun was burned just before. Choror was burned on 10 April. Some troops remain in Korongo and Bilenya. The civilians are staying in the hills around, but thirst has forced some of them to go into the town and surrender. They have planted the whole of Korongo with anti-personnel land mines.

When the people are taken to Kadugli, the women are forced to work in houses. Most recently they have been involved in work on building sites. There is an area, Mayom, newly established, where the women are assembled. The son of our chief, Shahad Abu Anja, sells them to merchants to work on farms. A truck is filled with people and a certain fee is paid to him, as a tax. The men are conscripted and sent to other fronts. Some of them are also forced to work as gravediggers.

Many instances of abduction have been described in outline in earlier sections: thousands of people have been captured by government forces and taken to garrisons and peace camps during "combing" operations, and hundreds have been abducted with their animals. This section highlights a few · more aspects of this programme of "combing" for human beings.

Abduction during "Combing"

Every time a man, woman or child leaves his or her village, to herd animals, tend the fields, walk to another village or a market, or collect firewood or water, there is a chance that he or she will never be seen again. Explaining that "we have a problem with abductions," a deacon of the Roman Catholic Church, Jibreel Tutu Jiran, told African Rights:[68]

> A recent case, six days ago, was Sherabi Ibrahim and his wife Kachi Andora, who were taken at Kwiha. They were going to take thatching grass which they had gathered and placed near the wells. We did not see them again and someone who went to the well saw the bootprints of the army.

At the other end of the scale are wholesale forced evacuations from entire villages or towns. A number of cases are detailed above and below. The abduction of 250 people, most of them children, from Toror village on 24-25 February was the largest instance during African Rights' visit to the region. Most common are the abductions of people in groups of up to fifty, when there is an attack on a village. The survivors of such attacks find that the disappearance of their family members and friends is the most disturbing part of the attack. El Fadil Ismail el Zubeir, aged 61, was constantly preoccupied with the fate of his two sons who had been captured by the government:[69]

> I used to be the Imam of Elkok village until I ran away with my family to Kumu. I came to Kumu to escape the governments attacks.
> In July 1994, the enemy came and attacked our village of Elkok at night. I was sleeping with my wife in our hut. My father was sleeping in his hut near us. When I heard the gunshots I asked my wife as to which direction were the shots coming from. My wife was not sure. I, my wife and the children ran out of the hut. We were running and the bullets were flying over our heads. My father came out of his hut and tried to run towards my hut to awake me but he was shot.
> My father Ismail el Zubeir was shot in the head and died instantly. Another six people were also killed, they were: Ahmed el Zubeir (my uncle); Ibrahim Komi; Musa Hamoda; Ziya el Nur Ali;

---

[68] Interviewed in Tira Limon, 22 May 1995
[69] Interviewed in Kauda on 12 May 1995.

Suleiman el Tahir and el Safie Badawi. All these people killed are Moslems who used to pray with me in the mosque.

Many people were abducted in this attack among them el Faki Tahir, Mohmed Abdalla, Sulieman Abdalla, el Kwarti Ali, Ahmed Umbada, Angelo Benadagi and Bakheit Ismail. They were taken by force to Mendi.

The soldiers burned the whole village including my mosque. In my mosque they burned the Holy Koran and other Islamic books including Friday's Preaching Book. They took fifteen sacks of sorghum from the mosque. This sorghum was part of el zakat [the Islamic tithe]. Personally, the enemy took from me 57 cows and 25 goats.

I moved to Kalkada after the attack. I spent some time in Kalkada. I built three huts for my family. But at the end of last year the enemy attacked Kalkada. Again my huts were burned with the rest of the village together. The enemy took my clothes and the clothes of my wife. Worst of all, my two sons were abducted by the enemy. We were running when they remained behind. They lost our tracks when we entered the caves. My two sons abducted are Mohamed, who is twelve years old and Yunis, seven years old. The enemy took them to Mendi. The news I hear about them is that they are staying in the military barracks. They are doing washing and cleaning for the army. I'm informed that my son Mohamed has been told to prepare himself for military training. I don't know whether he will be trained as soldier proper or PDF. I'm worried as to what will happen to my younger son Yunis if his brother Mohamed separates from him and joins the military training.

I hear our people are suffering there in Mendi. There is nothing I can do to help my sons and get them out of Mendi. Allah is Merciful, He may help them. I leave it to Him!

Now I have moved from Kalkada to Kumu with my wife Umjuma Angelo Toto. I am old now as you can see but I have to start all over again. I have to build a house and clear a farm before the rainy season.

Many Nuba have been forced to watch while their loved ones are taken away by the army or PDF, and never seen again. Ali Kodi

Agbi, an Otoro farmer from Kodi A, escaped the army by running into the mountains. His family was not so quick.[70]

On 19 March [1995], the army attacked our village of Kodi A just after breakfast. I had just taken my *asida* [porridge] when I heard the first shell falling onto our village. After that the heavy artillery was followed by machine guns. I immediately guessed they were coming from Mendi. I ran to the mountains in front of me. High on the mountain I saw my father Kodi Agbi, his younger wife Kaka Kodi and my half-sister Kaka Kodi being rounded up by the enemy. All of them were carrying some items on their head. My half-sister Kaka was clearly carrying three chairs. I could recognise them as my father's chairs. I saw the enemy burning the village, looting it and walking away with the abducted persons.

There was no news of my father, my step-mother and my half-sister until this morning. Umsalama Adam escaped from Mendi yesterday and confirmed to me this morning that they are in Mendi alive. According to her they are staying in the peace camp, where they are suffering form lack of food and shelter.

At least Ali had an idea of his family's fate. Bashir Kunda Opali, aged 29, is the Imam of the mosque in Kodi A. His mother was nowhere to be found after the army occupied the village.[71]

In the morning the enemy attacked Kodi A and Kodi B with heavy artillery. I ran and hid myself in the Tira [el Akhdar] mountains where I was seeing the army vehicles firing at both villages. I left my mother, Kaka Aya, behind in my house in Kodi A as she was too old to run with me to the mountains. I slept the night in the Tira mountains.

In the morning of the 21st I went home and did not find my mother. My hut had been burned and my things looted. They looted my two beds, two sacks of sorghum, four sacks of groundnuts, one sack of sesame, house utensils, twelve Islamic books and LS 700. Birth certificates of my children were torn into pieces and thrown on the floor.

---

[70] Interviewed in Kauda, 12 May 1995.
[71] Interviewed in Kauda, 12 May 1995.

I searched the whole village and the surrounding bushes and mountains for my mother but did not find her. I lost hope and thought she might have died a distance far away.

For more than a month, Imam Bashir did not know if his mother was alive or dead, her body lying unburied in the bush.

It was only recently when somebody called Omer Apera from Kodi A returned from Mendi then he told me that my mother was abducted with him. Omer informed me that my mother was in the peace camp in Mendi. Omer himself told me that he spent one month in captivity in Mendi.

Again this morning a lady called Umsalama who just escaped from Mendi confirmed my mother is in the peace camp in Mendi. I'm worried that she may not be getting any care as she is now blind and approaching eighty years of age. In all my five prayers I always pray that they may release her to come home.

Many of those who are abducted are children, who are separated from their families. There have been repeated reports that many of these children are later sold into slavery. El Amin Omer Gardud had been alerted to two cases, which he was investigating:[72]

Three children, two boys and one girl, were snatched in Dere in July 1994 and put in a *jurab* [leather basket]. The militia of the Hamar from al Feyt were responsible. The children were abducted and taken to a place outside el Feyt. The information we received was that the Hamar were planning to take them to Bara and sell them with camels. They were carried on camels. One day they were covered with canvas so they could not look out and see the place. Two escaped: this information was given to me by one of them, a boy called Kallu.

Last week, on 8 May, two girls were abducted from Abyad. One is Nawal Mehana who is about seventeen, the other is Kaka Omer Kuku, who is eight or nine. They were snatched by the PDF from Hadra, when they were going to the wells. We have no news of their fate.

---

[72] Interviewed in Tira Limon, 20 May 1995.

There are indications that the government has recently begun to focus its efforts on abducting children. Many residents of the Otoro hills reported that children were being snatched in larger numbers than before, especially in the villages of Luchulu, Kuchama, Dingir, Jigheba and Laro. Community leaders said that, since April, the army seems to have a new strategy of concentrating on children aged between seven and fifteen, and that a total of over four hundred boys and girls had been taken. A former teacher from Lira, Angelo Abu Rasein, now a Moslem Brother, is reported to be co-ordinating this campaign.

Ambushing the Hungry and Thirsty

The government is using rural people's need for food and water to entrap them. For example, during the March operation along the Kauda valley, the army unit filed the following report to Hajana headquarters in el Obeid:

> 20 March
> From Nida' al Salaam to Operations HQ el Obeid. For information, repeated Operations Medani/18/19/all sectors. Confidential 145.
> Code: Abu Anja
> Report no. 20. Covers from the latest report until 8.00 hrs today.

After burning and destroying the camps of Kauda, Karga and Kuchama, the rebels are now without shelter and food. They have resorted to infiltration tactics into the gardens of el Azraq and Heiban to collect mangoes as an alternative food. Our forces are in control of el Azraq and Heiban gardens through patrols and ambushes. Three citizens have given themselves up to our forces. Osman Digna has made our forces reach Kassala today.[73] The situation is quiet. Our forces are intact.

---

[73] 'Osman Digna' and 'Kassala' are code names, which were not explained by African Rights' source.

The "rebels" who "resorted to infiltration tactics" to collect mangoes included the villagers Fawzia Kuku Komi, aged thirty-five, Jibreel al Nur Kuku, aged 21 years, and his brother Zaki, aged fifteen, and Suleiman Ibrahim Suleiman, aged twelve (see pages 149-52). Another was Michael Hassan Tutu, an eighteen-year-old farmer from Kumu, who was abducted with a large group of boys and girls, most of them younger than him.[74]

Last Sunday [7 May], I was going to get mangoes at Kubrungor in the morning. In the place where there are mango trees, I was surrounded by soldiers. Most of them were Arabs; they had only a few blacks with them. We were many people—I don't know the number. The soldiers divided us into two groups, and took the men and boys to one side, and the women and girls on the other side. From time to time, the soldiers came to take the girls in ones and twos to the bush, for one or two hours. They chose the pretty ones. I can't tell you how many soldiers there were, or how many girls they took, but there were many. Then they came back. When a girl came back, on the back of her head, she had grass in her hair.

We were captured at about 9 a.m. and kept there until 3 p.m. One of the soldiers said, 'Let's shoot and kill all these people.' But the others said no and they didn't shoot.

We were taken to Heiban. They selected three girls and three boys to take with them. They said, 'When we get to Heiban, the three girls will marry. The three boys will go for military training.' The girls were loaded with mangoes and the boys with heavy firewood.

We arrived in Heiban nearly at sunset. The girls were immediately taken to the peace camp—a citizen from this area took them to his house. We have had no news from then since. The boys were taken to the barracks and they interrogated us. They asked, 'Where is the camp of the Anyanya?' We said, 'We don't know.' The soldiers asked us: 'Are you Moslems or Christians?' We said, 'We are Christians.' We were beaten. They beat us with sticks and the butt of a rifle; one of the boys was seriously affected. One of the Arab soldiers said, 'Put them in prison.' One soldier was from the Tira tribe, and he said, 'No, leave these people with me.' After some

---

[74] Interviewed in Kauda, 12 May 1995.

minutes, this soldier came to us and spoke to us in the Tira language, saying, 'After some time I will help you escape.'

Later that night, the Tira soldier came and took us to a place from where we escaped.

Abduction at water points is also common. Control of water supplies has become an integral part of the government strategy for trying to control the rural population. Ahmed Sayed el Nur, from Delami county, explained:[75]

Another area of concern is denying water resources to the people. Once the government attacks an area, they seal off the people from the water source. Water pumps are dismantled and taken away or destroyed. They may ambush people near water places, to deter them.

Elizabeth Terielo Tamri, an Otoro from Kuchama East, was abducted at a well and later told by an army officer: "You are rebels, if you want water, join us."[76]

I went to Khor Duluie to take water and let my four goats drink. I was with Kunu Beshir, Ember Nyalo a boy called el Tugil Ali Jaber. Others I found them in the *khor*. That was about 11:00 a.m. After I filled my three tins of water and I was preparing to come home, I saw the enemy coming upon us in the *khor*. I tried to run but the soldiers shouted at me to stop. They were shouting, 'Stop or we shoot!' I was rounded up with others and they asked us to empty our tins which we did. We were then ordered to go with them and escort our goats to Heiban. By then I was with nine others. When we approached Heiban the army ordered us to run into Heiban and they started beating us with sticks. We entered the military garrison at noon.

At the garrison I and the others were ordered to sit down in the sun. A two-star officer came and talked to us. He told us, 'The Nuba should come here to have clothes, because all your clothes now are full of lice. As for your rebels, we are going to defeat them. We will arrest everybody soon who doesn't come to us in the peace camp.

---

[75] Interviewed in Tira Limon, 20 May 1995.
[76] Interviewed in Kujur el Sha'abiya, 13 May 1995.

You are deceived by the *khawajas* [white people, i.e. international community], as they are helping us and not you.' Nobody among us talked. We kept silent. We only asked him to give us water to drink as we were very thirsty. The officer refused to give us water saying that, 'You are rebels, if you want water, join us.' Finally the officer asked us, 'Who wants to remain and who wants to go back?' Four people among us stood up that they wanted to go back to Kuchama. The four included me, Jaber, Kunu Beshir and somebody I don't know his name. He looked at us and ordered us to sit down saying, 'There is no going back.' He went to his office. We spent a long time in the sun until late afternoon.

One of my relatives who is a soldier recognized me and called me. I went to him and he told me, 'An order has been made that there is no going back to the village.' He warned me not to insist on going back. He told me, 'When the northerners go to play or parade I will tell you to run away.'

He brought other two soldiers who were both Arabs. At about 5:00 p.m. I heard a whistle, and the two Arab soldiers went away. I could see them joining the parade. My relative remained behind guarding us. He told us in our language that anybody who wants to go should go now. I got up and the three followed me. We immediately entered the forest near the garrison. The forest is just east of the garrison. We ran until we reached Kuchama.

I left my goats and my plastic water cans with the soldiers in the garrison. I didn't hear about them again. I think my goats might have been slaughtered by now.

Driven out of Places of Refuge

Nuba people have few places to run where they can be safe. This is particularly true in places, such as the northern Kawalib hills, where government forces are stationed nearby. One elderly farmer explained:[77]

> I live on the border with the enemy. We are attacked by the army from time to time. They have taken everything we have, not even

---

[77] John Daud Khalil, from Kamand, interviewed in Tira Limon, 23 May 1995.

one bed remains. Now we are sitting under the stones of mountains. I cannot count the attacks we have suffered. Maybe four or five times a month. Our only protector is the mountain. We have a lookout every day from early morning until sunset. If we see the enemy or we hear shooting we run away. Otherwise we can stay and work on our farms.

Unfortunately, the mountain was to prove an unreliable protector. Hunger and thirst are the Sudan Government's most reliable weapons to entice people out of their strongholds, but they have others too. One case was in Kamand, in the northern part of the Kawalib mountains. The attack began on Sunday 5 February 1995. Hamdan el Amin Komi, a farmer in Dere, escaped:[78]

Government forces were coming from Delami and attacked Dere village at 6 a.m. We ran to Nyingir mountain. About 2,500 people ran. Then many of them—about one thousand maybe—returned to the village to collect food. We ran to two sets of caves, in Dere and Kamand. Then we were pushed by hunger to leave the caves. People were captured. The capturing started that same evening and is continuing up to now.

Al Tahir al Nur Jibreel, a farmer in Kamand, ran to the caves on the mountain. In that attack, the troops did not abduct villagers from Kamand:[79]

Early in the morning I went to trap animals in the bush. I came back after dawn, and at about 8 a.m. I was sitting in my house drinking water, and the enemy attacked us. I saw them. They came with fourteen lorries.

All the people of Kamand scattered to the bush. Some climbed Kamand mountain. The soldiers started burning all the huts and pouring out the sorghum onto the ground. Some of it was burned. They took the beds and other furniture out of the houses, and shot the chickens. The other animals were not present at the time. The army proceeded to Dere.

---

[78] Interviewed in Um Dulu, 16 May 1995.
[79] Interviewed in Tira Limon, 23 May 1995.

In that attack, nothing was left. The clay pots were broken. The cooking pots and pans were all taken. The good *angarebs* were taken and the bad ones thrown on the fire.

After that attack, we stayed in caves and between the big rocks on the mountain. A large cave can take seven, eight or nine people and protect you from the rain. We knew that if we built at that time [i.e. in the dry season] we would just be burned again. When there was no sign of soldiers, we stayed at the foot of the hill to be closer to our farms.

One week later, the army returned. Before dawn, they occupied the village of Abri, and captured 62 people, who were all taken by force with the soldiers. The army unit reported to Hajana headquarters in el Obeid:

> From: Mobile Brigade 19, Abri
> To: El Obeid Headquarters Operations/Intelligence
> Repeated: Hajana 19 Operations
> Confidential No. 1
>
> Our forces captured Abri today. The force has established its defences around the village. We visited our forces at 13.00 hours. The morale is high. We discussed the arrangements regarding the population with Governor and Peace Department.

African Rights' sources did not have details on the contents of the discussions between the army and the governor concerning the civilian population of the area. But, over the following three weeks, hundreds of civilians were forcibly abducted and taken to garrison towns and peace camps in a large "combing" operation. That same day, Kamand was attacked again, and this time the Sudan Government had come to abduct the citizens.

> At about 8 a.m., the army returned from Dere. When they reached Kamand they attacked us again. Our people ran again, into the bush and up the mountain into the caves. My family ran into the caves. The soldiers followed us up the mountain. They saw us when we were climbing and followed us. When they came up they had lost us, they weren't sure which caves the people had entered. So they

217

fired tear gas, to see where people cry and where people cough, and so that we come out and they can take us.

So they threw tear gas into the caves. The children began to cry. From my own family, eight were taken. My wife, Miriam Abdel Salaam, was taken. My five children, al Nur, aged six, Khalid, four, Rafa, three, Yasir, two and Jalal, who is breastfeeding, were taken. My sister Hawa and her son Jameis, aged about twelve, were taken. The total number of people in the village who were taken was so many. Others can tell you the names.

I cannot tell you exactly how they were found. When they [the soldiers] first started shooting we scattered and everyone chose his own place to hide. I chose my own place and I was on the other side of the mountain, not affected by the tear gas.

After the army left, I came round to the other side of the mountain and searched for them. I called their names. They didn't appear. I carried on calling out. But I saw their footprints and the boot marks of the soldiers who had taken them. I have heard that they are in Dere peace camp.

Still we have not decided to rebuild the village. We are living in caves.

Asha Shawgi Kunda, a mother of five children, was hiding in another cave. She was a victim of the tear gas. She told her story:[80]

On Sunday morning we took breakfast and we were ready to go to church. We were staying on the slope of the hill, sleeping between rocks. One girl climbed the hill, and when she climbed she saw the government forces coming, and ran and told us that they are coming. So we ran. We ran and entered the caves.

We had no houses because they had been burned before. The soldiers just poured out the sorghum from the pots and big sacks, and other soldiers brought dry grass and put it on top of the sorghum and burned it.

We were thirteen hiding in one cave. It was a deep cave. If you enter here, you can go in a distance of up to that tree over there [about fifteen metres]. There was a man, Hassan Daud, who was captured earlier who was with them. He knows that cave because

---

[80] Interviewed in Tira Limon, 23 May 1995.

we always used to hide in it. He was with the soldiers, showing them the cave.

When Hassan showed them our place, they ordered him to talk to us in our language. He called us a long time in the Kawalib language but we were silent. He entered the cave and came over to our place and started calling, saying 'Come out, nothing bad will happen to you.' But we were silent. Some of the very small children were sleeping. The other children were very afraid.

After we didn't appear, Hassan went out. The soldiers said, 'Didn't you find them?' He said, 'They're not there.' They told him, 'Say, announce, you must follow us!' in a loud voice. He said that and we stayed silent. Then, when they were ready to leave, they threw a tear gas [canister], by hand, into the cave. When it exploded, the tear gas affected all thirteen of us. The little children were vomiting and shitting, and even the adults, our eyes were crying. It affected the throat and the head. We were unable to breathe, especially the children.

Some of us came out. We said to those ones, 'Go and say that you are out and no-one remains.' But really four of us remained inside. I was one of them, with one other woman and my two children. But, because of fear, those who went out said that there were some other people remaining inside.

The soldiers called, 'Either you come out or this time we will throw in a hand grenade. It will not be tear gas this time.' When we heard this, we came out.

When we came out, they said, 'Don't fear. Beating and killing is stopped. We don't to that now. But we are going to a place of the government.' They took us and we walked for some distance, and we found a very big lorry. There were many of us put in the lorry—the thirteen of us, also some civilians brought with them as guides, and many soldiers. So the lorry was full.

Magamdam Hassan Daud, a forty-year-old farmer, was also on the mountain hiding close to his family, and suffered from the tear gas:[81]

I smelt some but I endured it, but I immediately heard the cries of women and my children. I could distinguish the cries of Sadia and

---

[81] Interviewed in Tira Limon, 23 May 1995.

Habiel my youngest children. The more they cried the more intensive the tear gassing became to their cave. I heard the enemy threatening in loud voices saying, 'You *awlad el haram* [bastards], if you don't come out we will shoot you with RPG [rocket-propelled grenades]. You get out.' I saw the people in the cave coming out. In my family alone there were twelve people who came out of that cave. They were captured.

The enemy came with ten trucks, two artillery carriers, two jeeps and one tank. At 12:00 noon people were loaded into the trucks. I saw my wife, children, father and mother going into one truck. Other villagers entered different lorries including Asha and some of her relatives. Other lorries were loaded with looted properties, goats and cows' carcasses. All people and property were taken to Dere military garrison. I recognised Abdalla Karger Angelo, head of Dere PDF, talking and laughing with the soldiers.

Asha and the other captives were taken to Dere garrison and peace camp (see pages 250-1). Asha's husband, John Daud Khalil, was hiding in the cave next to her, and escaped capture.[82]

My cave and the cave of my wife were separated by one stone. They fired tear gas into the cave with my wife. The small children cried, so they called them to come out. I didn't come out. They took my wife Asha Shawgi and two of our sons, Abdel Hamid who is seven and Tantous who is three.

They were captured on Sunday and taken to Dere. But they didn't stay long. The next day my wife was released, sent with a letter to come and collect us to go in. She left the two boys with my brother's wife, who was also abducted. When Asha reached us and told us that we are wanted there in Dere, we left Kamand to go to Nyingir. In Kamand we have only one place for water, and we fear the enemy may make an ambush and capture us there. But in Nyingir we face famine. We came with only our bodies, we have nothing.

The army offensive in Kawalib did not stop at Kamand. Two days later the army continued to Um Jamena. Fifteen people were abducted and the entire food supply of the village was destroyed or

---

[82] Interviewed in Tira Limon, 23 May 1995.

looted. On 23 February, an army unit from Dere surrounded el Laud village, stole goats, and abducted two complete families and two individuals. On 1 March, they attacked Nugor village and abducted four people, who were taken to Dere. One man was shot while trying to escape and died from his wounds later the same day. Four days later, the army surrounded the wells of Andona village, where they abducted six people, one of them a child of less than seven years. They also took cattle and goats. The largest attack was mounted before dawn on 29 March, when the villages of Baba and el Laud (again) were surrounded, and more than one hundred people were abducted and taken to Dere.

A POLICY OF RAPE

The rape of Nuba women and girls by soldiers of the Sudan Government is a matter of policy. The evidence collected by African Rights points overwhelmingly and consistently to this conclusion. Soldiers and militiamen are given a license to rape Nuba women and girls during "combing", during abductions, and in garrisons and peace camps. The entire power structure of peace camps is designed to compel women and girls to submit to rape. The soldiers often force themselves on the women, or may coerce women into sex with threats, by withholding food, clothes or access to water, or may punish women who refuse to submit. As a matter of policy, soldiers are also encouraged to take temporary "wives" from the Nuba captives.

The policy of rape is comprehensive. Often, every single one of the women who are captured or abducted from a village are raped. Every woman interviewed by African Rights who has been taken to a peace camp has been raped or threatened with rape.

The policy of rape serves several functions for the Government of Sudan. First, it is seen as an "incentive" to soldiers and militiamen. Secondly, it terrorises and humiliates Nuba communities. This aspect has been present since the war intensified in the late-1980s. For example, a community leader from Korongo Abdalla told African Rights:[83]

> Soldiers started to rape women as a way of intimidating us. The first major incident was in July 1987, when two soldiers dragged Khalida Abdalla[84] out and raped her in the middle of the day. We found her crying. Her son has come to the SPLA.

Thirdly, rape destroys the very basis of the community. It breaks the fundamental bond of the family, the relationship between husband and wife, and breaks down the trust, confidence and sense of identity not just of the woman who has been raped, but the family and community. When women bear children as a result of rape, they do not have a known, legitimate patrilineage—and so they lack an acceptable social identity. Rape is thus an instrument of genocide.

During the 1992-3 *Jihad*, there were accounts that indicated that the political and military leaders of the campaign intended to use the separation of Nuba men and women, and mass rape as a means of destroying the possibility of another Nuba generation. Khalid el Husseini indicated that this was the policy of the Governor of Kordofan:[85] "The reason for the men and women being distributed in different camps is to prevent them marrying, the reason being that if the men and women are together and get married and have children, that itself is contrary to government policy." He continued, "the members of the Arab tribes are allowed [encouraged] to marry them in order to eliminate the Nuba identity."

The separation of men and women captives continues, as does the policy of rape. But African Rights could not find evidence for a current policy of creating a new generation entirely of mixed Arab-Nuba children, conceived through rape. The reason is that, under the *Nafir el Sha'abi*, Nuba men are forced to join the PDF, and the PDF itself is a mechanism of mass rape. This is one of the most insidious effects of the government policy—Nuba men are coerced to rape Nuba women; they are turned into criminals. The children that result

---

[83] Jaafar al Fadl, interviewed in Um Dulu, 17 May 1995.
[84] All the names of rape victims have been changed.
[85] Interviewed by the BBC in Switzerland, 13 June 1995.

may be ethnic "Nuba," but that does not give them a secure identity. Their fathers may not be known, nor their fathers' tribes. Such children are deracinated to the same extent as children whose rapist fathers are non-Nuba. Even though "Nuba" children are born from the policy of rape, the fabric of Nuba communities—or rather, Tira, Moro, Tima, Otoro, etc, communities—is being torn apart. The fact that many of the rapists are themselves Nuba in no way lessens the fact that the aim of the policy of rape is genocide.

Identifying and interviewing rape victims is difficult in any society, because of the deep shame that is associated with the crime. In the Nuba Mountains it is doubly difficult, because relatively few rape victims escape from peace camps and garrisons. Often, it is only possible to obtain testimonies such as that of Kafi Yunis, whose daughter was raped. Yunis is a farmer from Kauda in his fifties, who was abducted and taken to Mendi, but managed to escape one month later:[86]

> I escaped from Mendi alone without my daughter Tabitha. Only eight days after arriving in Mendi my daughter Tabitha was taken from me by a soldier called Abdalla. I still remember how she was taken from me as if it has just happened this morning. Let me tell you what happened. As I told you earlier, on the eighth day a soldier called Abdalla approached me while I was with my daughter in the *rakuba* at the military headquarters. Abdalla told me he was going somewhere with my daughter. When I asked him, 'Where?' and 'Why?' Abdalla told me to shut my mouth, as though he is carrying out his official duty. People around me in the *rakuba* shouted at me to be silent. I kept quiet and thought she was being investigated. My daughter Tabitha by then was twenty years old.
>
> From that day I did not see my daughter. Whenever I asked about her, other soldiers and camp residents they will always tell me not to look for trouble. They tell me she is married and alive. They will also add that I should thank God she is alive. I felt angry and sad that a government army should do this to my daughter.

---

[86] Interviewed in Kauda, 11 May 1995. His identity and that of his daughter have been changed.

When I left Mendi I started running from Mendi at about 4:00 p.m. and arrived in Kauda before the cockcrow. At home I found all my things have been looted by the enemy.

It is one month now since I returned from Mendi and have no news of Tabitha. I don't know whether she is still in Mendi or taken somewhere by Abdalla—whom I don't even know his father's name. What happened to my daughter is rape not marriage. While I was in Mendi peace camp I met women without husbands [who were] pregnant, some even do have children with either the soldiers or PDF. Some of these women told me frankly about that, when I asked them about my daughter.

Many women and girls who have been raped do not even try to escape. Once they have been raped, and especially if they are pregnant as a result, some feel too ashamed to return to their villages. It is yet another indication of how rape changes identities, and is a weapon of war and genocide.

Rape during Abduction

The nature of many of the Sudan army's military operations in the Nuba Mountains is indicated by the fact that the soldiers are able to spend many hours raping the women and girls they have captured. One incident of mass rape that was confirmed by several interviewees was perpetrated on Sunday 7 May 1995. One of the victims was Miriam Haroun Kuku (not her real name), a Tira girl aged twelve years old.[87]

Last Sunday we were going with other girls—about fifty—and twenty boys from Kumu to Heiban to collect mangoes from the gardens. We left Kumu in the early morning and at about 7:00 a.m. we entered the gardens of Heiban. When we were about to put our baskets down to collect the mangoes we were immediately surrounded by the enemy soldiers.

I found myself with about forty people surrounded by the enemy who ordered us to sit down. We sat down with guns pointed at us. The soldiers separated us from the boys. In turn we girls were

---

[87] Interviewed in Kauda, 12 May 1995.

also divided into groups. Every group of three girls was guarded by a soldier. The soldier guarding me with other two girls took us to a *khor* near the garden and ordered us to sit down. The two girls with me were Rhoda and Halima.

When we sat down five soldiers came to us. Three soldiers ordered us to lie down to have sex with them. I was surprised and tried to resist but I was beaten by all of them. They beat me with heavy sticks they were carrying. While I and other girls were being raped by three soldiers, some other three soldiers stood guard over us. One of the soldiers on guard after a long time cried out saying *'khalas!'* ['enough' or 'finished'] and the three raping us got up. I was about to get up when I heard another soldier ordering me to stay in the position I was in. He came and raped me. The other two girls were also raped. It was now the turn of the soldiers on guard. The soldiers continued raping us in turns for a long time. I can say we were raped from morning until just a little before sunset.

All the girls captured in the garden were raped. The men were beaten badly as they were being called cowards and rebels.

Before sunset I was selected with other five persons to carry the mangoes to Heiban. We were three girls and three boys. The soldiers allowed the others to go back to the village. Most of the youth with us had escaped when they discovered the enemy in the gardens. Other people caught with us were old people. I and the two girls, Rhoda and Halima carried the mangoes and the three boys were carried firewood. We arrived at Heiban military garrison when it was almost dark. Heiban was not far from where we were abducted. I was walking slowly as I was feeling extreme pains of rape. The other two girls were also in pain.

Miriam was fortunate that inside Heiban there was a member of the PDF who was sympathetic to her plight.

In Heiban we were asked whether we knew anybody in Heiban garrison. We replied that we didn't know anybody. One of the soldiers who raped me took the six of us to the civilian quarters where we were handed over to Juma[88] and Daud from Kumu village.

---

[88] The names of people inside garrisons who assisted captives have been changed to protect their identities.

Juma asked us whether we wanted to stay in Heiban or go back. I told him we wanted to go back to the village. Juma told us he will arrange how we can escape from Heiban. At about 5:00 p.m Juma took us out of Heiban. While coming out of Heiban we met an Arab soldier who asked Juma as to where he was taking us. Juma deceived him that he was ordered to release us and take us home. Juma who is a brother-in-law of one of the three abducted boys accompanied us up to near Dingir. Juma went back to Heiban and we slept in Dingir. On 8 May we reached Kumu.

At home I told my father and mother what happened. My father told me not to go to look for mangoes in Heiban area again. He said, 'Let us die of hunger if we have to live on Heiban mangoes.'

Since I came back from Heiban I didn't get medication because of the lack of medicine here in our area. Rhoda and Halima were not able to come here because their wounds of rape are not yet healed. Halima my age mate is still suffering seriously. My mother is the one treating me with hot water every day to cure my injuries.

Coercion for Sex

Nira Suleiman Bashir has investigated many cases of rape. She described how the policy of rape was modified in al Atmur and Um Sirdiba garrisons as the season's "combing" operations ended, and the captives were held in the peace camps.[89]

Rape was common when many women were abducted during the dry season offensive in February and March. Now they are developing a new policy [in the garrisons]: starving women, withholding food and clothes so the soldiers can give them money or gifts in return for sex. Most of the people are living without shelter, sleeping in the open. The soldiers come at night with their torches and begin to touch the women, so they can choose the young ones and take them for sex. In case they don't get young girls they go for adult women.

---

[89] Interviewed in Um Dulu, 18 May 1995.

Karima Marinya Aria, from the village of Kodi B, described how the soldiers of Mendi garrison used all the means at their disposal to coerce women and girls into submitting to sex. She is a mother of six children; five were living with her and one was in Khartoum at the time of her capture. Her testimony begins with one of the most explicit descriptions of how the Sudan Government divides its captives on the basis of age and sex: choosing women and children, and killing men:[90]

I was taken to Mendi on 31 January 1995. One of my children was taken to Mendi and remains there. He is Seifur Ali, aged six.

The enemy surrounded Kodi B at 6 in the morning. When we heard the shooting we got out of our houses and tried to run, but every way was blocked. We were surrounded by army and PDF. After we were captured, all the materials—chairs, tables, cooking implements—were loaded up by the soldiers. The enemy surrounded three villages and took many people. They had no cars; they came on foot and we went on foot. We were more than seventy women, and the soldiers made us carry all the things they had looted. They abducted only three men, and they killed them on the way. I don't know their names, they were from another village. They were just taken off into the bush and shot. The number of children who were abducted—I cannot count them.

We walked to a place near to Mendi garrison, where we got thirsty and sat under some trees. Some PDF came with water. Then we were taken inside Mendi and taken to the peace camp.

Karima detailed some of the strategies used by the soldiers to force the girls to submit to them.

After we were put in the peace camp, the army came and selected all the girls. They said, 'We need all the girls to serve us in the houses of the soldiers.' The girls refused. The soldiers said, 'We need girls to come and collect firewood for us.' The girls refused again. The soldiers' idea was this: any girl who refused had to do hard work, carrying [22.5 kilogramme] tins or even sacks of

---

[90] Interviewed in Kauda, 11 May 1995.

sorghum from a long distance up to town. But when a girl agreed to go with a soldier, she didn't have to carry the tins of sorghum.

In Mendi, medical treatment was done in a divided way. The people of the town were treated in the hospital. All of the blacks were treated under the trees. When we objected to this, they said, 'You are the women of the Anyanya, so we will punish you.' After this continued, without the soldiers succeeding to get the women to do what they wanted, the soldiers came up with another plan. They came out to the peace camp in the night to collect the women they want. If the women refuse, they beat them up.

I know many women who were taken as 'wives' by the soldiers. When a woman is taken, the soldier says, 'Your husband was an Anyanya, so we will marry you again.' If the woman has children, the new 'husband' takes all the children. Every woman who refuses to 'marry' has to work as a servant, escorted by soldiers from one place to another, doing hard work. The soldiers always look for a chance to rape her by force. If there is any service, clothes or food or water or firewood, you have to get it from the government, or with an escort of soldiers. And they are continuously daily attacking and raping the women. If you refuse, they make you work hard, carrying heavy things, always beaten and always escorted.

The young women were also always escorted by soldiers, to stop them escaping. Also, all the young children were collected and kept separately from their mothers in one house, to stop the women from escaping. All the people there want to escape. But if you are 'married' to a soldier you don't have a chance of escaping.

Your husband who remains in the village, he can't do anything. He may be expecting his wife to return. But he asks, 'How long can I wait? Better to marry another one.' But a woman who returns will be taken back by her husband.

Karima said that it would take the whole day and night to detail all the hardships the people suffered in Mendi. But she gave a brief summary, explaining that her words could not do justice to the people's experience.

I am a Moslem. When we went in, if you are a Moslem, they welcome you. If you are a Christian, they interrogate you: 'Why are you a Christian?' In the end, they force you to become Moslem.

We were given one set of clothes per person. When we reached there they said, 'The rebels have no clothes. So here is one set each.' We were given food; one *malwa* of sorghum for ten people. After that, there was no ration. You had to work to get food.

After spending some time in Mendi peace camp, most people are taken to Ngurtu and Um Duwal peace camps, near Talodi. These are a long way away from home so people cannot escape easily. The people captured from our area in November had all been taken to Ngurtu and Um Duwal when we arrived.

All the bad things in Mendi mounted up, so I decided to escape. I spent thirteen days there.

Other people tried to escape. If you were caught escaping, you were killed immediately. Many tried to escape but were ambushed and killed in the bushes. Especially from Kumu village, many people tried.

At first, everyone was gathered together in one room, which continued for a long time. Then we were put in one hut each. Anyone they suspect, fearing desertion, they keep them in the big room. Children were kept separately for a while, and only when they believed there would be no desertion, then they reunited the children with their mothers.

Finally, Karima had to make a terrible choice, between her child in Mendi and her children at home.

Only one of my children was taken. Four remained at home. I decided that I would go for my four children and leave my one, Seifur, behind. The whole garrison was surrounded with guards, but there was one gap. So one morning at 4 a.m. I escaped.

Rape in "Peace Camps"

Fawzia Jibreel is a seventeen-year-old Otoro girl from a village south of Kauda, who spoke to African Rights the day after her return from three months in Mendi peace camp. Her voice was very quiet and she held her head in her hands throughout. Her village was attacked at dawn on 31 January.[91]

Very early in the morning the enemy came and surrounded the whole village. Our family has two compounds—they took sixteen people from just our family. The soldiers said, 'You will come with us to Mendi. If you refuse, you will be killed.' When we had all been gathered, we had no alternative but to go with them so we started to move with the soldiers. We were carrying bags of clothes—the soldiers took all the good clothes, leaving us just with the rags. They gathered us under a tree for the morning, with no food and no water, while they were burning the houses. It took three-and-a-half or four hours. All the houses and most of the furniture were burned. They took cows and goats in large numbers, I don't know the total. They looted the best furniture and other possessions. By the end of the morning we were about 25 women and girls under that tree.

After finishing their operation at midday, the soldiers started making us walk to Mendi. I was made to carry a bed. The sixteen of us were all carrying things looted from people's houses, like big dishes, plates, cups, and so on. On the way they said, 'Something you have never seen before—you will see it in Mendi.'

The prediction was accurate. Fawzia described the nightmare that began later that day:

When we arrived in Mendi, we were taken to the garrison. All the looted properties were put in one place. The people were then divided. The older women were taken to one place, adult women who had one or two children were taken to another place, and unmarried girls were taken to another place. Before we were divided up, the officer said to us, 'Now you have reached here, every one of you will be married. If any one of you refuses, you will be killed.' Then we were given a small amount of flour to cook and told, 'When you are married you will have enough food to eat.'

Five of the women were already married. Three of them I knew: Khaltuma, Nura and Zeinab. Two of them I didn't know. Those of us who were still unmarried, the soldiers came in the

---

[91] Interviewed in Kauda, 12 May 1995.

morning and told us to work, carrying heavy things. Then they demanded sex. Those who refused to have sex were treated badly; they were forced to carry heavy things all day. In the evening, we were brought back to our place in the military camp to sleep.

After dark, the soldiers came and took the girls to their rooms, and raped them. I was taken and raped, but I refused to be 'married' to any of them. The girls who were 'married' were treated better—they stayed in the rooms of their 'husbands'. But, when the soldier is transferred, the woman stays behind, whether she has a child by the soldier or not. I saw some women who were remaining behind, but I don't know their names.

When you have been taken, the soldier who has taken you will do what he wants, then he will go out of the room, you will stay, and another one will come. It continues like this. There is different behaviour. Some lady, if she is raped by four or five soldiers, she will cry from pain. Then, if the soldiers are good, they will leave her. But others will beat her to keep her quiet, and they will carry on.

Every day the raping continued. It continued during the daytime and at night. My sister Leila, aged thirteen, was raped. My father's second wife, Asia, was raped. They wanted to rape my father's third wife, Naima, but she was heavily pregnant and she objected, and in the end nothing happened to her. Another lady, Umjuma, who has six children, was also raped.

It is impossible to count the men who raped me. It was continuous. Perhaps in a week I would have only one day of rest. Sometimes one man will take me for the whole night. Sometimes I will be raped by four or five men per day or night; they will just be changing one for another.

Fawzia could not estimate the number of times she had been raped, but repeated that it was rare for her to pass the night without being violated at least once. She was in the camp from the afternoon of 31 January to the afternoon of 11 May: exactly one hundred nights. Nor were the daylight hours much of an improvement: every activity seemed to be designed so that the soldiers could exercise their arbitrary power over their women captives' bodies.

We were made to work. There were different types of work. Some of us were made to go to the garrison to clean the compound, the rooms and the offices. Sometimes we were sent to Ngurtu, which is one-and-a-half hours away, to bring sorghum. When we are carrying sorghum, each lady would carry two tins. Older women with children were also made to work. Then, afterwards, they had to prepare food for their children. These women were taken to the peace camp, where they also had to build their own houses. All women, whether they have children or not, are given the same ration, of one cup of sorghum for breakfast and supper. So they worked for money or food. If there was no work available, they are forced to become prostitutes, so that they can get something to feed to their children. Many women were forced to sell themselves for money.

No clothes were distributed to us. But any soldier can bring clothes and use them as a bribe or a payment for sex.

The only water in Mendi is from handpumps that are just outside the garrison, about five or seven minutes' walk away. The women go with guards to collect water. On the way, or when women are going outside to collect firewood, the guards are saying, 'Why are you talking about going back to the Anyanya? Life here for you is comfortable. So don't refuse if one wants to marry you or sleep with you.'

From Fawzia's description, there can be no doubt that Mendi peace camp is designed to destroy utterly the pre-existing social relations of the "returnees".

I did not see any people who had been in the peace camp for a long time. People are taken somewhere else after a while. But we heard that there are other peace camps where people stay for a long time.

Three men were taken from our village. One was carrying a bicycle on the way to Mendi. When we were inside, they were taken straight to the PDF for training. We never saw them again. Inside the town, men and women are completely separated.

There is a school, which teaches the Islamic religion only. All the Christians who are taken there become Moslems. There were some Christians with our group, and when we reached Mendi, they went to pray under a tree. The soldiers went and called them and said, 'Don't repeat this. There can be no Christian prayers. There are only Moslems here.' But the Christian women objected, and prayed again. The soldiers called again, and gave them a threat, 'If you

232

pray again you will be killed.' The Christians didn't pray after that, but they also did not go to the mosque.
There is a hospital, but it was not for us. There is no medicine if you become sick. I stayed there three-and-a-half months, but I never saw any pregnant woman. It is unusual. Perhaps there were some at the early stages, before the stomach becomes big.

Fawzia did not believe herself to be pregnant at the time of the interview. In fact, it is remarkable how few of the raped women and girls are pregnant as a result. This was also remarked upon by Nira Suleiman Bashir, who had investigated rape in al Atmur and Um Sirdiba peace camps,[92] and by other women who had spent time in Heiban, Aggab and other peace camps. This is a mystery: one possibility is that the sheer stress of life in these camps has rendered the women captives infertile.

By 11 May, Fawzia had reached her limit of endurance. She knew the penalty of being caught while escaping, but took her chances.

Yesterday, at 5 p.m., I thought about escaping. I talked to my younger sister Leila, I told her, 'Let us escape.' My sister said, 'How?' I said, 'We will try, God will help.' I told my sister, 'Go to the handpump as though you are going to bathe. After that, we will escape, because when you are bathing, you will not be monitored too much.' I went ahead with the bucket, my sister was to follow. But she delayed, and so I decided to go alone. I entered the bush there as though I was taking a bath, and escaped.

Such extremes of sexual violence are not uncommon. All African Rights' evidence points to the fact that, on the contrary, repeated gang rape is the rule.
Hanan Mohamed Adam, aged nineteen, a Moslem girl from the Shwaya tribe, is another victim of the Sudan Government's policy of rape inflicted on Nuba women. She told African Rights:[93]

---

[92] Interviewed in Um Dulu, 18 May 1995.
[93] Interviewed in Kauda, 11 May 1995.

233

On the last week of February [1995], we went to al Atmur market from Shwaya village. We were twelve, six men and six women. We were going to sell our goods, okra and dried tomatoes, in al Atmur Sunday market. Men were carrying ropes and *angarebs* for sale. We left Shwaya after breakfast and slept the night in the open between Shwaya and al Atmur. After we have just moved a short distance from where we slept the night I saw soldiers and warned the group that there are soldiers coming towards us.

Two of the soldiers immediately went to one side of the road and ordered us to stop. We stopped and they searched our goods. They did not take anything from us but they ordered to go ahead of them to Aggab. Some of us, like Ali Abeta, Abdel Rahman Magedi, Said and Leila refused to go at first, and were beaten up badly. We were escorted to Aggab military garrison by the two soldiers. On arrival we were taken immediately to an officer who interrogated all of us together. Our names was registered in a big book. The investigation was concentrated on the questions as to why we are refusing to come to the peace camps where there are clothes, medicine and food.

The other question was the whereabouts of the SPLA in our area. And we told the officer that we are alright in our village and do not know the whereabouts of the SPLA.

The officer handed to another person who took us to what we later found out was the peace camp. We slept the night in the open air. The following morning we were told by the army officer to go and cut grass to build our *rakubas*, which we did. We were issued with Reagan *dura*[94] mixed with wheat. Five persons were given a tin of sorghum for a week. Lentils were issued to us but nobody ate it because it it was yellow and makes stomach trouble. It happened to me personally, especially diarrhoea and vomiting each time I eat these yellow lentils.

The peace camp is inside Aggab military garrison. Every day, at 6:00 a.m. we are taken to clean, carry water and do other duties for the soldiers. Men are asked to wash soldiers' clothes and iron them. At 6 p.m. another whistle is blown and we are escorted back to our *rakubas*. No civilian is allowed to build a hut. Where we slept there were no blankets or plastic sheet or anything; we slept on the floor.

---

[94] This is a reference to sorghum donated by USAID, which since the 1984-5 famine has been known as "Reagan dura".

Regarding clothes, we were given one dress each, the one I'm now wearing. This one dress you wear it, work with it and sleep with it as bed sheet or blanket. In Aggab I saw a military health centre where we were not allowed to go. For the school they teach the children only the Holy Book, the Koran.

My husband Ibrahim was captured with me and I left him in Aggab being trained to join the army. As soon as we arrived they took him away from me.

In Aggab garrison, the policy of rape is implemented in precise conformity with the military hierarchy. Officers and soldiers choose the women in turns in accordance with their rank. Hanan continued:

I was raped every night. Six to seven soldiers will rape me in turn every night. Even when I sleep with their commander they will wait for me and demand their turn. Ismail Gandoul, the bodyguard of the commander will come and pick me up for the commander (a captain) and after that el Zaki of intelligence and Ali el Hindi will rape me, in that order every day apart from other junior soldiers. They rape me and others anywhere they choose. El Zaki and Ali el Hindi raped me many times in their houses. Other soldiers will take me to the barracks rooms known as 'Anaber'.

I ran away because of this rape. I cannot bear it any longer. I was more worried when I saw some women from our area becoming pregnant. Batul, Khadija and Selwa were made pregnant by the soldiers in Aggab.

The day I escaped we were taken for grass cutting in the morning. Ten soldiers were guarding us. I was in the middle of the group. When we reached the bush I ran away. The soldiers fired many bullets at me but I continued running until Amazera near Shwaya. In Amazera I met Hassan el Mahdi who took me to Shwaya.

It is now fifteen days now since I ran away from Aggab. I have no news of my husband Ibrahim in Aggab but even if he comes or sends for me I can't go back to him. I'm no longer his wife because other men have seen me. I'm ashamed.

Escapees from every peace camp tell similar stories. Rachel Kuku describes the life in al Atmur peace camp:[95]

> I was abducted by soldiers when our village Karkaraya el Beayara was attacked on 21 February. I was first taken with others to Aggab garrison. Later I was transferred with other groups of women to al Atmur camp peace village.
>
> In al Atmur we were put in a hall which happens to be an old school dormitory. All looked quiet and normal that day. We were given clothes, cooking oil, flour and one piece of washing soap.
>
> The following day we were separated from each other, Christians on one side and Moslems on the other side. We Christians were asked to renounce Christianity and convert to Islam, or they said we would be dealt with accordingly as wives of rebels. Most of us were frightened and kept silent. Islamic preaching started immediately.
>
> On the third day I discovered soldiers checking on us at bed time. Some women were called out of the hall by these soldiers. We were told at the time that women were being interrogated. When my turn came, I was surprised to find soldiers under mosquito nets behind our building. One soldier told me to enter his mosquito net. I resisted, but at last I slept with him. There were another twelve mosquito nets in the place with other soldiers and women in them.
>
> One morning I was taken with other women to collect firewood and there I got the opportunity to escape. The conditions there in al Atmur and the way people are handled is very bad. Many will escape once they get the chance. I have no words for it, it is very bad.

Enforced "Marriage" to Soldiers

Soldiers and militiamen of the Sudan Government have adopted a practice of taking their chosen women as captive concubines. They call it "marriage" but it is not. According to Sudanese custom and Maliki law, a marriage can only be considered legitimate if there is an opportunity for the woman to say no, and if the woman's parent or

---

[95] Interviewed in Eri, 3 March 1995.

guardian is present. Neither of these conditions apply. No ceremony is followed. In no sense is it a contract freely entered into by the woman. Insofar as it resembles any form of marriage, it is akin to the illegal practice of "slave marriage" or "slave concubinage".

Mawlana Najib Musa Berdo, the judge of the central court in Lagowa county, has looked into the legality of "marriage" in peace camps. He has no doubts that this "marriage" has no legal status—not least because most of the "wives" are never told the full names of their "husbands". In short, it is rape. *Mawlana* Najib summarised the practice:[96]

> In Majda, girls are 'married' to soldiers for three months. After three months, the soldiers are free to 'divorce' or pass them on to their colleagues. If the girls get pregnant, they don't have a name for the father.

If proof of the forcible nature of such "marriage" were needed, it is provided by the testimonies of the "wives" themselves. Afrah Ashmur, a mother of two aged about twenty from the Otoro hills, was abducted by the Government of Sudan on 10 March 1995 while collecting water.[97]

> I went to the *khor* to collect water early in the morning. At that moment there was an army attack coming to Kuchama. We were four women, and we were all captured. Some soldiers were put to guard us. After the attack on Kuchama, the government lost many soldiers, and they came back angry. They said, 'We lost men in Kuchama, you tell us why. Where are the Anyanya? You must tell us where your people are living, why you are in one place with the Anyanya. Tell us the truth or we will kill you at once.'
>
> They took us to Heiban. They had looted some sixteen cows and a lot of furniture. We were made to carry the furniture. We took beds, chairs, buckets, bags full of clothes. I had to carry a table, two buckets and a big dish for washing. It was two hours' walk to Heiban.

---

[96] Interviewed in Achiron, 7 May 1995.
[97] Interviewed in Kauda, 11 May 1995.

Afrah's status as a wife and mother was of no import to her captors. Her "wedding" ceremony was extremely brief.

> When we arrived in Heiban barracks, the commander said to me, 'From these four, you are the youngest.' Then he told the soldiers, 'Release the three old women but keep this young one as her husband is an Anyanya rebel.' When the three old women had gone, the commander turned to one soldier and said, 'This woman is your wife. You keep her. If she tries to escape, shoot her down.' The soldier I was given to was an Otoro originally from my village, Idris Jabir.[98]
>
> When the commander said this, I did not refuse because I knew him from before: he had a hard reputation. Idris took me to his house. We spent two days as 'husband' and 'wife'.

Afrah was reluctant to discuss her "married" life, but she described the general conditions in Heiban.

> When I was in Heiban I was not given any clothes. I only got one ration, which was one *malwa* of sorghum on the day my 'husband' was sent out on his mission.
>
> I saw that the captured people were working hard building the peace camp. Every morning, all the people—men and women, youths and girls—are assembled to go to the bush. The men do the cutting, the women do the carrying, until the afternoon. They are escorted by soldiers all the time. The first day I was there I went with them. The second day, my 'husband' was leaving so I didn't go.
>
> In Heiban, there is a rule. If you are sitting doing nothing, like this, a soldier will come and say, 'Come with me for sex.' If you refuse you are beaten. The first day this happened to me and I was beaten. The soldier said, 'This is a woman of the rebels.'
>
> My 'husband' Idris Jabir had a house with a zinc roof in the old market. In that place, all the shops and houses are given to soldiers. All the soldiers and officers there have 'wives' from the region. I knew some; Asha Mohamed, Amina Ali, who were abducted before, in 1993. Asha was well dressed and had a child. Amina was in old clothes and pregnant. Both were 'married' to Arabs. But I did not spend time talking to them.

---

[98] His name has been changed to protect her identity.

I learned that if the 'husbands' are transferred, the women are sent to the peace camp in Abu Jibeha. Their children are sent too. They do not get transferred with their 'husbands'.

Afrah took her first opportunity to escape, despite the threat from her "husband".

After those two days, Idris was chosen to go to Abbasiya to bring some spare parts to Heiban. When Idris left, he said, 'You wait for me in the house. If you desert, we will make an attack on Kuchama area and I will kill you just like that.' In the same night, I left. There were other women, the 'wives' of soldiers, always going outside Heiban to take mangoes, so I went up to the mango trees and escaped from there.

When I was taken, I had left my husband and two children at home. When I came back I found the small one, Huweida, who was breastfeeding, was very sick. She was refusing to drink milk again.

When I returned back, my husband welcomed me. He said, 'This is our condition. There is no problem about what has happened.'

Some rape victims are ostracised or rejected; more often they feel ashamed to try to return to their families and communities. The case of Hanan, above, is one. But, African Rights was also impressed with the readiness of many Nuba women and men to overcome their prejudice against rape victims and accept them back. Afrah is one case. Another is Awadiya Kodi, who is in her late teens. Before she was captured by the Sudan Government in April 1994, Awadiya was engaged to be married. She was "married" in Heiban garrison, but after her escape, her fiancé agreed to resume the engagement.[99]

The enemy came very early in the morning and surrounded our village and started shooting. I came out from our house and tried to run away, but I fell into the hands of the enemy and I was abducted and taken. They were all wearing khaki uniforms, I don't know if they were the army or the PDF. There was a large number of them, and they were looting, taking all the good *angarebs*, chairs, clothes,

---

[99] Interviewed in Kujur el Sha'abiya, 13 May 1995.

239

all sorts of possessions. Then they started to burn the houses, and take the cows and goats. After choosing all the good chairs and beds, they told the abducted people to carry them to a place where some lorries were waiting. The lorries were stopped some distance away, so we couldn't hear them as they arrived, and be warned and run away.

Four girls were abducted. There was me, Awadiya. There was Sara, who is married, but she has no children yet. There was Hamadi, who is older than me but not married. The last one was Selma, who is nine years old.

In our house we had fifteen or twenty sacks of sorghum stored in a big granary. The soldiers opened the granary with one big blow, so that the sorghum started pouring out on to the ground through the hole. Then they set fire to the granary.

When the soldiers had finished putting the things we were carrying in the lorries, we all went back on foot, carrying more things they had looted. The soldiers carried on taking things they had taken out of the houses, and taking them to load up the lorries. We continued to bring tables and chairs to the lorries, until they were full up. Then they made us walk to Heiban. I carried a table and a chair.

Awadiya's captors made their intentions clear well before they reached the garrison. It was like a market. The fate of each of the girls—including nine-year-old Selma—was decided.

When we got half way to Heiban, it became very hot and we put our things down and waited under a tree until the afternoon. While we were sitting there the soldiers were talking to us, looking us over, saying, 'I will marry you,' and 'I will marry *you*.' But they did nothing to us. Most of those soldiers were Arabs but some were Nuba.

Then when it was nearly evening we walked on to Heiban. It was another one-and-a-half hours.

As soon as we reached Heiban we were sent to the prison. We stayed there for three days. In the morning, we were brought out to grind flour for the soldiers. The guards came in to take us by force to rape us. They even took Selma, who was small. The day she was raped, Selma cried. We heard her crying outside, and afterwards we

240

heard that she had been taken to the hospital. I don't have any news of what happened to her after that.

I was taken and raped for two days continuously. Only one day we slept without being raped. Two men took each girl. One man got on top of me, the other man guarded. Then they changed places.

After the rape in the garrison came "marriage" in the peace camp. As Awadiya makes clear, it was in fact a form of slavery.

After those three days, we were taken to the peace camp, to be 'married.' We were made to work, washing for the soldiers, carrying firewood, cleaning the military compound, also grinding flour for them. The three of us were given one hut. For food, our ration was half a *malwa* for three of us for seven days. Water we took from the 'donkey' pump; one of the soldiers would escort one of us to the pump to bring water. If one of us was sick, one of the soldiers would go and bring medicine. We were all given clothes.

All three of us were Christians. When they asked us our religion, they then said that everyone in Heiban is a Moslem. 'From now on, there is nothing called "Christian",' they said. But they didn't give us new Moslem names. We were ordered to go to the mosque, but we refused. They did not force us.

Three soldiers came to select us. Each one chose one of us and said, 'You are my wife.' But we stayed living in that hut. When they had no duties, those soldiers used to come and spend time with us, and sleep with us. My 'husband' was Bashir, an Arab. I don't even know his father's name. Sara was 'married' to al Nur, another Arab, and Hamadi had another Bashir, also an Arab. If a woman is 'married' and taken to a soldier's home, then after that no other soldiers will come from outside to rape her.

Those soldiers used to eat in their mess, not with us. They did not give us any extra rations or money. So we just continued with the same rations as before, sorghum with a little beans or lentils for sauce. There was nothing in the market to buy, even if we had money. I saw two women who had children by their 'husbands', and even they did not get any special food or extra rations. There was no milk for the children.

In Heiban, I didn't see any civilians there except those who had been abducted by force. Life is really hard in Heiban. There are shortages of everything. There is not enough food. We were

241

deceived that we could get salt and nice clothes, but we never received them. In the work camp at Rahmaniya people said it was even worse. But the number one bad thing was the raping that was taking place all the time.

Many people are taken to the prison in Heiban. Most people are taken there as soon as they arrive after being abducted. There they are tortured and beaten, we could hear the cries coming from inside the prison. The prisoners are also brought outside when the sun is hot, between midday and 2 p.m., and beaten outside in the hot sun.

I was four months in Heiban. As I was a 'wife', I was not monitored so much as other women. One day, I took a jerrycan as if I was going to the 'donkey' pump to bring water. The 'donkey' was at a high place next to the river bed. I put the jerrycan down, went to the river bed, and then started running until I entered the bush. Then I came back to my village.

Before I was abducted I was engaged to be married. Our engagement is still on, my fiancé understands that what happened was because of the war and not because of my will. We plan to be married.

The evidence from rape victims alone indicates that the Sudan Government is pursuing a policy intended to destroy the existing communities of Nuba people in Sudan. If, as the Sudan Government intends, all the rural population of the Nuba Mountains is resettled in peace camps, *all* Nuba women now living in villages will be raped or "married" to soldiers.

"Peace Camps": A Life of Fear

The official position of the Government of Sudan is that its "peace camps" are inhabited by "returnees" from the SPLA, who have either voluntarily joined the peace camps, or have been "liberated" during military operations against the rebels. The Government also claims that the peace camps are centres for the provision of relief assistance and even development.

The truth is very different. Since the peace camp strategy was first implemented in 1992, government critics have consistently accused the government of a range of abuses including "ethnic cleansing" and forcible Islamisation and Arabisation. Not all the charges are true. But the realities of life in peace camps are sufficiently horrible: the inmates are kept there against their will, they forced to work for low wages or no wages, men are forced to become members of the PDF, women are raped, and children have their identities changed. It is all part of the programme for dismembering Nuba society.

Ahmed Sayed el Nur summarised the information he had obtained about peace camps in his area:[100]

> In Delami people tend to be [abducted] in large numbers. When they are taken to government-controlled areas, many end up in labour camps for mechanised farms. Some are taken as families, and then the wives are separated from the husbands. No family reunion is permitted afterwards. Some who go voluntarily to join them, with their properties, find that once they arrive, their properties are taken. When someone who is abducted wants a family reunion, they are first given a mission to return to the village and persuade more people to come. Anyone who refuses is called a 'fifth column[ist]' and is punished. If you succeed to bring them, and they take them to peace camps, the reward is LS 10,000 per able-bodied adult.
>
> The situation in camps is like being in prison. You are not allowed to move freely. Small children are separated from their parents and taken to the *khalwa*. When they grow up they are taken to the PDF or the army. Some of those who are abducted are used as guides for the army and PDF to return to the villages and loot cows. If they refuse, they are denied any incentives or rations. You are kept there as a hostage, and to be used as a soldier.

It is also widely held that the peace camps are kept as a "human shield" to discourage SPLA attacks. It is certainly the case that the presence of a peace camp puts civilians at great risk if the SPLA attempts a frontal attack on a garrison. SPLA commanders say that their attack on Mendi in 1993 was thwarted for this reason: they decided to open the attack by shelling from a distance, thus giving a

---

[100] Interviewed in Um Dulu, 18 May 1995.

warning to the civilians so that they would have a chance to run away. The shelling of course also gave warning to the government troops.

For the most part, the "human shield" strategy does not seem to be a strong motivation for peace camps. Most do not surround the garrisons, and some are at a distance away. The army seems to be more afraid of the peace camp inmates running away than the SPLA is afraid of exposing them to risk during a battle. For example, in May 1995, when the army learned of an imminent SPLA attack on Um Dorein, they removed most of the peace camp before the attack, fearing that they would escape once the raid started.

Forcible Detention

"Peace camps" are prison camps in one vitally important respect: the inmates are kept there against their will. The following testimony makes this abundantly clear.

Khamisa Abdel Rahman Monu is aged nineteen. She lives in the Otoro hills. When she was abducted and taken to Heiban peace camp, she was separated from her baby of two months old. All the time she was in Heiban, her only thought was for the baby she had left behind.[101]

On 17 March [1995] the enemy came for operations in Kumula. We had gone to collect water. We were four: my sister Hanan, who is six, Susan Omer, who is also six, and Ngama, who is the same age as me. When we had filled our pots with water, we carried them on our heads back towards the village. While we were on the way, we met with soldiers. When we saw them, we threw our water pots and ran. But the soldiers ran after us and captured us.

They started to beat us. We were tied, with our hands behind our backs, and beaten from that place to inside Heiban, which was a walk of two-and-a-half hours. When we reached inside the garrison, we were untied and taken to the commander for interrogation. He asked us, 'Are you the wives of the Anyanya? Where are they?' But the government people found nothing from us. So we were sent to

---

[101] Interviewed in Kujur el Sha'abiya, 13 May 1995.

the peace camp that same day. We were handed to one person there and told that we should stay with him until someone would come and take us to a labour camp at Rahmaniya.

There was a soldier called Sabit el Amin, from the same village as us. Sabit protected us from any harm, from the bad things that we expected to be done to us by the rest of the soldiers. Other soldiers came and wanted to rape us but Sabit said, 'These are my sisters.' So they respected him and we were not harmed.

At the time I was abducted, I had a baby of two months left at home. I was only thinking of my baby. As soon as I reached the peace camp, I told them that I had to go home to be with my baby. They refused. Then I told Sabit that I had to go and be with my baby. Sabit took me to the military administration and said, 'Release this woman to go and be with her baby.' The commander refused, he said, 'Let the baby die. I am not responsible for that.' This was repeated three times. Then Sabit said to me, 'I have failed to help you.' Other soldiers used to come and talk to me and say, 'What are you thinking of? If you are thinking about your baby, and about your village, we will destroy it, and your baby will die. So forget about that and you will soon get another baby here.'

My sisters were taken to school to be taught the Islamic religion. But i didn't go. One day all the soldiers went out to attack Abol, and only a few remained. Even Sabit went with them, and told his wife to look after me, and not to let me escape because there were strict orders that if I escaped, Sabit would be imprisoned. That same day, Sabit's wife was planning to brew beer and so she went with Sabit's sister to collect water. Twice she brought water. Then we went together to collect firewood. In the place where we were cutting wood I decided to escape, and succeeded.

On my way back I met a reconnaissance group of soldiers returning to Heiban. They said, 'Is this not the girl we captured last time?' When I heard this, I ran. They chased me but I was fast. They shot at me with their guns but they missed.

When I reached home I found that my baby had been given to another woman who had a baby of the same age, so that she could feed them both. The two children milked together. But she had become very weak. Also I found that the village had been burned. Nothing remained: no sorghum, no sesame. Our only way to get food is to beg from those who have some food, or to look for work on farms. But at least I reached the place that I wanted.

After I returned my father was abducted from his farm and taken to Heiban, but he also escaped. He came back with the news that those girls are not there, and that they had been taken away to an unknown place.

Escape from peace camps is not permitted. Those who try to escape and are caught may be subjected to a range of penalties ranging from confiscation of all property, including clothes, to torture, to summary execution. Many people have been shot while escaping.

Najib Musa Berdo described one incident in which six people are known to have been killed, and ten children were lost in the bush, when trying to escape from the camp at Majda, south-west of Dilling.[102]

In January 1995 there was a military operation in Julud Basha village. My family—children, aunt and uncle—were snatched and taken to Majda garrison. All the people of Julud Basha were forced out in this operation, and most are now in Majda. The operations covered the whole of Julud area, but people in the other villages got word of the attack and escaped.

They arrested Mek Khalil Bashir and Sheikh Bala Terjemi and tortured at the time of their arrest. Their subsequent fate is not known.

Majda was originally an Arab settlement. The Arabs left when the war began. Now the Government of Sudan is resettling people in a peace camp there. People are put inside a fence and told to build houses for themselves and the PDF. My uncle, aunt and grandfather have all died there. Conditions are very bad, the ration is one teacup of sorghum per person per day. So the government sends missions to seize sorghum from farms.

Because of the hunger in the camp, people were prepared to run and run the risk of being shot. Some people were also shot while trying to escape, including Fatima; Halima Hamdan; Hamdan Direma (an old man, the father of Halima); Korkelen Korkele (an old man); Abbas Adam and Kortokulu Berto (an old man).

---

[102] Interviewed in Achiron, 7 May 1995.

Ten children were also lost when the soldiers fired on the people running away. In the panic they got lost and have not been seen since. But some people did manage to escape.

The people who ran from Majda knew the risk they were running. In June 1994, the army shot and killed 25 people escaping from the camp at Kujuriya, in the nearby Katla hills. One local farmer learned what had happened:[103]

> People were on the road from Katla to Kujuriya because of famine. In Kujuriya there were army and PDF. When people went there, they were taken to the army camp, without tents or any form of shelter, and told to build huts. It was raining. They were not given any food or other sort of assistance, so they were not able to build huts. So they saw that life was difficult, and after fifteen days they decided to walk back to Katla. Thirty-five people went.
>
> As they were leaving Kujuriya, the PDF ran after them and open fire at a place called Wali, which the Arabs call Sir al Ghazal. They killed 25. Idris, his wife and three children. Bakheita, the wife of al Nasr. Al Fil Mamur; Adam Kufa, Nila Mamur and Jaafar Umbili. People were not able to go and bury the dead. They were weak because of no food, so they left them for the birds.

Occasional lenient treatment of would-be escapees was reported from Um Dorein. While some escapees have been shot and killed, Nira Suleiman Bashir had talked to a number of women internees who had merely been robbed of their possessions:[104]

> Some women who go to peace camps, especially Um Dorein, once they escape they fall into the ambushes of reconnaissance groups of soldiers, who take their clothes and all their belongings, and leave them to come naked—or force them to come back to Um Dorein where their things may be returned.

But, the day after Nira filed that report, Hanan Yabsi, aged fifteen, was shot while running away from Um Dorein. Fortunately

---

[103] Jeilani Hamad Anduma, interviewed in Achiron, 7 May 1995.
[104] Interviewed in Um Dulu, 18 May 1995.

she survived to tell the tale. Hanan is from Um Dorein village (which is under SPLA control). She went to Um Dorein government garrison in the hope of obtaining clothes:[105]

I went with other two girls, Shija and Natsia, to Um Dorein (of the government) on Wednesday [17 May]. We left our village on Tuesday evening and arrived Wednesday afternoon in Um Dorein. We didn't have any clothes and we heard from people that there are clothes in Um Dorein peace camp.

When we reached Um Dorein we reported to the military garrison. At the garrison we were asked by a soldier on duty as to what and why we came to Um Dorein. We told him, 'We are in need of clothes.' The soldier asked us whether we want to stay. We answered, 'We would like to go back to the village.' The soldier became very angry and told us to go back. He told us, 'The clothes are for people who are staying here and not clothes for the wives of rebels. You go away from here, now!' I told the soldier that I had money for shoes that I needed to collect from somebody here before going back to Um Dorein village. The soldier told me to collect my money and go away. He told us that we will be arrested if he finds out tomorrow that we are still in Um Dorein. The soldier was a Nuba from Heiban and we felt he was very angry with us. When we left the military garrison I went to look for Simon, whom I gave money earlier to find me shoes. My companions Shija and Natsia were frightened and they told me they couldn't wait for me.

In the evening I got my money and left Um Dorein. I found an elderly woman coming to our village on the way. I was walking with that woman when we found two government soldiers. The soldiers seemed to be lying in wait for people going away from Um Dorein. One of the soldiers immediately caught my hand and started dragging me to a nearby bush. I managed to free myself and began running. The other soldier told his colleague, 'Why don't you leave her if she is refusing.' But that first soldier insisted and came running after me. The elderly woman tried to stop him but she was pushed aside. In that space of time I ran faster. I looked behind while I was running. I saw the soldier had stopped and was aiming carefully at me. I ran faster and heard a sound of bullets. He shot

---

[105] Interviewed in Nagorban, 20 May 1995.

me on the left leg but I ran even faster as I knew he wanted to kill me.

I ran, and pains were growing until I fell down near a water pool close to Um Dorein hills. I was crawling towards the pool when I felt some hands raising me up. I cried, 'I'm thirsty, give me water, give me water!' I could hear distant voices saying, 'No, you are shot, you can't drink otherwise you will die.'

After a while I was able to see. I found out that those voices were youths from my village who brought cows to the pool. I recognised them. I asked them whether they saw any soldiers here. They said, 'No, but we heard the gunshots.' I told them, 'Let's go, I'm sure the soldiers are coming.' They wanted me to rest but I refused. So they carried me home. I was given penicillin injections by the nurse of our village, Simon. Thank God, now I have improved greatly though I still cannot walk. If I knew things were bad like this I wouldn't have gone to Um Dorein. Nobody should tell me again about the good things in Um Dorein. It is enough what I saw with my own eyes. It is enough.

However, for adults with children, the greatest deterrent to escape is not the risk of being shot. It is the choice between their freedom and staying with their children, as it is almost impossible to escape with young children.

Food, Medicine and Clothes

As explained above, the Sudan Government is using its control of essential commodities to try to control the people. For people without clothes, soap, salt, cooking oil, medicine and other basic supplies, even meagre amounts of assistance can be vitally important. But, while some peace camps have become established as "centres of attraction" where people are clothed and fed, others—the majority—are marked by physical deprivation and scarcity.

African Rights spoke to a range of individuals who had been in more than one dozen peace camps. They agreed that the best conditions were to be found in the peace camps in Delami county, for example at Dere. Asha Shawgi Kunda, the mother who was abducted with two of her children from the caves in Kamand mountain using tear gas, described her reception:[106]

> When we reached Dere we were taken to the registration office. They asked what religion we were. The Christians said, 'Christian' and the Moslems said 'Moslem.' The soldiers did not say anything. After being registered, we were taken to the store and given clothes and shoes. The Christians received clothes as well as the Moslems, we did not see any discrimination. Even there is a church in Dere.
>
> After we left the store, they took us to the place where we would stay. They gave us two-and-a-half *malwas* of sorghum, half a *malwa* of wheat and half a pound of oil and some lentils and okra and some onions. We were put in one classroom of a former school. We joined some people who were there already. This was inside the military compound—the trenches of the soldiers surrounded us. At that time, the civilians in Dere were busy building the peace camp; everyone was going and collecting their materials. Now I hear that all the civilians in the garrison have been removed to the peace camp.
>
> I stayed two nights there. They called me to the office again. They asked me, 'Why don't people like to come here? We don't like forcing people, we come as people of peace. Even if SPLA soldiers come, they are welcome.' After that I was sent to go and inform the people in Kamand, to tell them that those who want peace have to come to Dere. I was also given a letter to the SPLA forces in Kamand.

Asha did not report aggressive interrogation, separation of men and women, the children being taken elsewhere, or sexual abuse of women. In every single other camp about which African Rights has information, these abuses were routine. Had Asha stayed a few days longer, she would probably have returned with a different story—and less likelihood of persuading her family to come to the peace camp.

Omer Saad Osman, a farmer from Nyingir, went voluntarily to the peace camp in Delami in June 1994, with his wife and five

---

[106] Interviewed in Tira Limon, 23 May 1995.

children. At first they were relatively well provided for. They were registered and questioned, and then:[107]

> The officer ordered a soldier to take me to the relief office. I was taken to the relief office which was situated in Delami market and I was registered with my family. I was given three and half *malwas* of sorghum, one *rubu* [quarter pound] of *lubia* [beans], one *rotl* [pound] of salt. These items were for seven of us.
>
> No clothes were given. We were then taken to Delami primary school where we were told to stay. In the primary school we found that other people were accommodated there too.

But this did not last. Soon, the internees were required to work for money and food.

> Our food ration continued for fifteen days, but then the relief stopped. The relief officials called us one morning and said every one should look for work to live on. I became a wood-cutter. I sold the wood to merchants, soldiers and citizens for building their compounds and fences. One piece of wood was LS5. In the evening I went back to the primary school to sleep.
>
> After nearly four weeks from the date of our accommodation in the school, the relief officer and the intelligence officer came to the school. They told us to evacuate the school for other returnees to be accommodated. They showed us a place to build only *rakubas*. We were warned not to build permanent huts. We built our *rakubas* in a place called Hay Tambul. I spent nearly one month in the school and one month in Hay Tambul.

Then, abuses began to intensify. Omer was called to register for PDF training, and told that it would start after the rains (see pages 154-5). And the women in this peace camp—which has a reputation for relatively little sexual violence—soon began to realise why they were welcome there. Omer continued:

> While I was still living in the school premises, the military intelligence came every day at 6:00 p.m. They would choose girls and women, whom they would tell, 'You are wanted in the military

---

[107] Interviewed in Tira Limon, 23 May 1995.

garrison.' They take them and bring them back the next morning at about 5:30 or 6:00. I and my wife asked one of our women relatives taken frequently by the intelligence in the evening, as to what happens to them in the garrison. She told us that once they reach the garrison they are distributed to officers and soldiers, who in turn take them to their mess for sex. They are usually given some soap or cooking oil or small amounts of money or second-hand clothes. When I went to the barracks to sell wood [in the daytime] I saw there were very few women. It seems most soldiers in Delami are bachelors.

More recent information from Delami indicates that little has changed. The extremist agency Da'awa al Islamiya is controlling food distribution and enforcing an official policy of Islamisation. Children have been forcibly separated from their parents, and the peace camp has been designated as a model for implementation of the *Da'awa al Shamla* ("Comprehensive Call" for Islamisation—see pages 112-3.)

Along with Delami, the peace camp at Talodi is considered one of the "better" ones. Yagoub Telamir Kuwa was abducted and taken to there in November, where he stayed four weeks.[108]

I spent 29 days in Talodi in the barracks. I saw the army of the government there. The Arabs were not many, they were in ones and twos. The majority were Nuba. The commander at Mafulu was black. The PDF commander in Talodi is a Liri, his name is Hamza. The army commander is a lieutenant-colonel, an Arab. The army and PDF didn't treat people well. I knew the Nuba people there; the people who joined the government were not well treated. Even those who took cows to them had their cows taken away by the PDF. The women are always sexually mistreated.

All the people in Talodi are Moslems. I didn't see any Christians, or any church. There were no Moro there. The people were mostly Tira and Tata. The people in the peace camp seemed content, but I did not talk to them. Their houses were poor and small, but they had a health centre, a school and water. They told us, if you stay longer we will give you clothes. Food was rationed. I

---

[108] Interviewed in Jibreha, 8 May 1995.

sent my son to register and he was given fifteen *malwas* one time and told to wait for the next distribution.

Yagoub escaped in December with his son. Shortly afterwards, the peace camps at Talodi were massively expanded by an influx of people who had been abducted earlier and kept in Mendi peace camp, whereupon conditions reportedly deteriorated.

The system of either cutting back on rations after a week or two, or keeping rations inadequate to feed an individual or a family, is widely used to force the internees to work for very low pay or no pay at all. Samira Argeil Angalo, a Moro from Nagorban, contrasted the provisions given to the internees and the soldiers in Um Dorein peace camp:[109]

> Not enough food and clothes are given to the people. The people are doing a lot of work to live. The army has a grinding mill but they don't allow civilians to grind in it. Very small children are working as servants in the barracks or soldiers' homes. Many of these small children cut doleib tree leaves and sell to the Arabs and the army so to survive.
>
> The army have no problem of food as their rations come from Kadugli. They also have large quantities of soap, both bathing and washing, to the extent that sometimes they pay for service by soap not money. The people in the peace camps are really suffering. There is a church in Um Dorein but sometimes when there is shortage of food it is distributed in the mosque. So many Christians go to the mosque for food as they don't know when the food distribution will take place.

The impressions of Sheikh Yousif Ardan of Regifi, who was briefly in Um Sirdiba peace camp, are typical:[110]

> What I saw in Um Sirdiba was appalling. Our people are but inside a big compound with Arab soldiers on guard. Morning and evening people are taught Islamic religion, including prayers. In the afternoon, some people do manual work, like cleaning the

---

[109] Interviewed in Nagorban, 20 May 1995.
[110] Interviewed in Regifi, 28 February 1995.

compound, building huts for soldiers, collecting wood and cutting grass for thatching. At night the soldiers pick up Nuba girls they want to sleep with. Even girls too young, of the age of ten years, are slept with by the soldiers. The people are badly treated as if they don't belong to this country.

Many former internees in peace camps reported lack of food and medical care. Sometimes these were absent simply because of lack of resources—for example because the garrison had not received supplies for some time. Often, these things were deliberately withheld from peace camp inmates, in order to coerce them into cooperating, as a punitive measure, or through sheer cruelty.

Ismail Abdalla Tutu is a farmer from Kalkada in his thirties. He has lost his left leg below the knee, along with two toes and the adjoining part of his right foot. When he spoke to African Rights, he was walking with great difficulty and pain, using a simple wooden leg, a crutch and a walking stick. It was a laborious interview because of Ismail's evident pain, and his persistent stammer. He started his testimony with the attack by troops from Mendi on his village before dawn on 4 November 1994:[111]

At 5 a.m. the army came and attacked Kalkada. I was inside my house with my wife. My mother and father were in another hut in the compound.

I was shot by bullets, I don't know how many. There were many people shooting. We were still inside our huts. They shot and killed by mother and father inside their hut. My wife and I were in another hut. We started to run. They shot at me with an RPG 7 and hit my leg, cutting it right through. The parts of my legs that were still there were also injured. [Ismail indicated scars from shrapnel.] I fell down. My wife sat down next to me.

I have three children, Suleiman, aged seven, el Amin, aged five and Hussein, who is one-and-a-half. They hid in a hole under the bed. When the soldiers came in to the house, they didn't see them. God was with them—all the houses in Kalkada were burned down except that one. I found out only later that they were alive. Our neighbour is looking after them.

---

[111] Interviewed in Kauda, 12 May 1995.

254

The soldiers came and took us in their car to Mendi. The army had about ten lorries. They took many people and destroyed the whole village. They took cows, goats and all sorts of possessions.

Ismail was bleeding heavily, with parts of his feet and legs hanging off and the bone on his left leg exposed. He expected some treatment.

In Mendi they took me to a place that was part of the hospital. I was not treated well. There was a doctor, but he did not treat me. No medicine was given to me; they just dressed the wound, and then the dressing was not changed. The wound had worms living in it. A whole day could pass without food, and then you are given only a small amount of food. I slept on the ground, without even a mat.

One day I said I was angry and demanded food and treatment. They asked me why and beat me with a bicycle lock chain, on my hip. The soldier struck me five times. The one who did that was al Nur al Jalil.

Three others were injured in the same attack and were with me in Mendi. One was Abdel Rahman Musa, who was shot in the neck. He took two days to die. They did not give him any medicine. Another was Hussein Haroun, who was shot with a bullet in the chest. They gave him no treatment and he died after nine days. When they died, the captives in the camp were ordered to dig a grave and put the body in it. There were no prayers, just the burial. The last injured person was Miriam Abdel Rahman, who was shot through the thigh. Her fracture was fixed in the traditional way by our people. She is still alive.

I was separated off from other people. The women were completely segregated. It is not allowed for men and women to speak to each other. They were not supposed to come and see me but sometimes they managed to come after dark. They said that if you want to speak or ask for anything, you will be beaten or taken off to prison. They said that girls as young as twelve are used for sex by force. Even married women are used for sex. They were forced to sleep at night in the prison, and in the morning taken off for work. They said, if they get a chance they will run.

If I talked with my wife I would be beaten. She could only talk to soldiers. Even bringing firewood for me was secret—they would have been beaten if they had been found out. One night she came crying saying that they had done bad things to her. After that she was put in prison. My wife is still there. I have not had news from her but I hear that she is cooking for the soldiers and serving them.

Ismail survived by displaying the sort of stubborn, enduring strength that has enabled the Nuba people to survive in the face of overwhelming odds.

I stayed there one and a half months. I was not recovered, in fact the bone was sticking out and my wounds were full of worms and were very painful. But I decided to escape because of the ill treatment.

So I ran on my knees. I escaped at night. The guards were sleeping.

It took me one and a half days on my knees to get home to Kalkada. I tied tree bark around my knees. I had no food but I had a small water container and I strapped it to my back. I took short rests but I did not sleep. It would have taken me two days, but when I came near to Kalkada, I found a man called Nur el Din Abdalla, who was cutting wood. He carried me the rest of the way up to the village.

In Kujur el Sha'abiya at last I got some treatment. Omer Haji, our nurse, amputated the wounded part of my leg and Hussein al Nur, who makes mortars for pounding grain, made me a wooded leg. He also made a crutch. I got some medicine too.

I can't work properly, and I do not have enough food to feed the children. The administration is helping me and my children. But we do not have enough. The crutch is causing pain and swelling under my arm, and the wooden leg is very heavy. It is painful: I use it only because there is no alternative.

Shortly after the interview, Ismail travelled by donkey to Debi nurses training college and Um Dulu to look for more medical treatment. But there are no specialists in the SPLA-administered areas of the Nuba Mountains who could provide the needed treatment, and no medicines.

Islamisation

The entire peace camp programme is suffused with the objective of religious and cultural transformation of the internees. Almost every account of life in peace camps describes pressure for Islamisation, ranging from restrictions on Christian worship, through to forcible conversion—all practices deeply offensive to most Sudanese Moslems.

Children are particularly susceptible to the lure of simple material rewards, and the Sudan Government has ruthlessly exploited this in order to promote its programme of Islamic education. The parents' resistance was quickly overcome, as escapees from the peace camps reported to Nira Suleiman:[112]

> For those children staying in Um Dorein and al Atmur [peace camps], now they have schools for them. They are *khalwas* [Koranic schools], and they are only taught Arabic and the Koran. At the beginning, the parents of children refused to allow them to go to the school, because they were only Islamic schools, but the authorities decided to cook *zelabiya* [cake/bread] for them, and also provide tea, so the children began to go of their own accord. After some time, the parents were told, 'We are taking the children to Um Ruwaba for further education so that they can return and take positions of responsibility in the Nuba Mountains.'

The removal of over one hundred children in March was confirmed by other internees of Um Dorein. Most were reportedly aged fifteen or sixteen. They have not been seen since by their parents. However, residents of North Kordofan have reported the children's arrival in Um Ruwaba on 13 April, at about the same as another similar group from Buram district arrived. The children had been told they were going for three years' education. On 21 April the Ministry of Social Affairs held a well-publicised ceremony to inaugurate a new *Khalwa* in the town, where the children were required to study.

---

[112] Interviewed in Um Dulu, 18 May 1995.

The Moro people are mostly Christians, and, according to former internees in Um Dorein, most of the removed children were Christians. After removal, the children were seen by some people who knew them, who reported that many were Christians and they were objecting to their forcible conversion to Islam.

Interrogation, Intimidation and Torture

The Sudan Government's strategy of "combing" requires that the army units know the locations of villages, cattle camps, food stores, wells and the houses of sheikhs, priests and other community leaders. Intelligence officers also try to extract military information such as the SPLA's sources of supply. This information is extracted from ordinary captives by force or the threat of force. Most prisoners know what is in store for them if they do not co-operate, and they do what is required to avoid torture. The following account includes most of the issues normally covered by army officers when they interrogate their captives.

Yagoub Telamir Kuwa, an elder of the Sudan Church of Christ in Seraf Jamous, was abducted with his cattle in November 1994 (part of his testimony is given on pages 190-1). He and his son arrived at Mafulu, an outpost of Talodi garrison, later that day. He said:[113]

> I was taken to the military commander there. I was interrogated by the commander: 'How did I come? Did I have a gun?' I said I didn't. Then I explained to them how I was captured. He said, 'If you didn't have a gun then why did they capture you?' I said, 'I was just taken.'

A lengthy interrogation then followed in which the commander tried to ascertain whether his captive was an SPLA soldier or genuinely a civilian. Apparently satisfied that Yagoub was genuinely a cattle-herder, he asked Yagoub if he wanted to go back. Yagoub refused to provoke his interrogator, and said,"It is your decision. I can go back or stay."

---

[113] Interviewed in Jibreha, 8 May 1995.

Another lengthy interrogation ensued, first about the location of the SPLA bases and then about the guerrillas' military strength. Yagoub again complied:

> He asked me if the SPLA have guns. I said yes. He said, 'What type of guns?' I said, 'There are many types of guns they have, big and small.' He was asking, 'Do they just have Kalashnikov?' I said, 'All types.' I was taken by the commander to see the guns they had in their store. He asked me if they have this type, and this type, this BM. I said, 'Yes, they have all this.' He said, 'Do you know how they shoot it?' I said, 'I don't know but I see them firing it.' The commander said, 'It is better you say the truth, whether the SPLA have guns or not. Others say no.' I said, 'I am telling the truth.' He said, 'Do they have ammunition?' I said yes. He asked, 'From where does it come?' I said, 'From the South.' He asked, 'How do they bring it?' I said, 'On foot, carrying it on their heads.'

Then the interrogation switched tack, and concentrated on civilian items—which are equally central to the government's plans.

> The commander asked, 'Will you go back or will you stay?' I said, 'The decision is with you.' He said, 'You should stay because we are going to capture all your Nuba Mountains.'
> Then he asked me, 'You seem to be in rags, with no good clothes. Does your government [i.e. the SPLA] not give you clothes?' I said, 'They don't have clothes.' He said, 'You have to stay here with us and you will go and bring your family so you all stay here.' Then I said, 'Fine, I will stay with you.'
> In the morning, the force [that abducted me] was going to Talodi with the commander. We went to Talodi and I was asked the same questions there. The only extra question was, 'Why don't you people want to join us here in the camps at Talodi? If you don't like Talodi, why don't you go to Um Dorein?' I said, 'Because we don't know the way.' They said, 'Is your government not allowing you to come?' I said, 'There is no problem. No permission is needed if you know the way.'

The crux of the interrogation came only at the end, when the army commander had decided what purpose Yagoub could serve.

259

The Talodi commander said, 'You the Moro, especially you in Seraf Jamous,[114] you are not good people, not like the people of Korongo [Angolo] who come and stay with us in peace camps. You stay here and I will take you for an army operation to the Moro area, especially Seraf Jamous, so you can take me to show me the location of the food crops, the stores, the cows, the goats, and we can also go and bring people.' I said, 'Okay it is fine.'

A month later, Yagoub succeeded in escaping and returned home, free but destitute. The operation that the Talodi commander promised was carried out in April, and is described on pages 162-3.

Yagoub was very fortunate to escape without even a beating inside Talodi garrison. Barnaba Abdel Rahman Abu Salah was less fortunate. He is a young farmer from the village of Karkaraya on the northern edge of the Moro hills. When he denied being a member of the SPLA, his captors did not believe him, or at least maintained that they did not. At the time of his interview, his wrists and ankles were bearing the wounds from prolonged tying during torture.[115]

It was Wednesday [3 May 1995], and I was in my farm at Lupa near Um Sirdiba. I was clearing the farm in preparation for the rains. At about 4 p.m., some soldiers came, and suddenly I found myself surrounded. They told me not to move. They came and started to beat me. They beat me all the time until we entered the garrison at Um Sirdiba. Then they tied me up. They asked, 'Are you an Anyanya or a civilian?' I said, 'I'm not an Anyanya.'

They took me to a place where there were many holes in the ground, like wells, all covered with zinc sheets and rocks. There were people in these holes, one in each.

My hands were tied behind my back, and tied to my feet, which were also tied together, tight. They call it *rabta tamanya* [the shape of the body resembles the Arabic figure for 8]. Three soldiers came and threw me, like a football, down into a hole. It was a deep hole. I landed on my chest. Then they dragged me out and swung me and threw me in again. They did it six times. Then one of the soldiers came with a stick and started beating me around the testicles. They walked on my chest with their boots and then kicked

---

114 In fact, Yagoub, like the other villagers in Seraf Jamous, is Tira.
115 Interviewed in Um Dulu, 19 May 1995.

260

me so I rolled over and walked on my back with their boots. One of the torturers was called 'Hamar'; he was with military intelligence. Another was called 'Abu Safar.'[116]

A pistol was put in front of my neck. They put a stone in my mouth. They asked again, 'Are you a civilian or an Anyanya?' I said, 'I am a civilian.' They carried on beating me until my eyes were bleeding and my testicles were painful. My chest was also paining me.

Then they threw me into the pit again and left me there. It was about two-and-a-half metres deep: even if you raised your hands they wouldn't reach close to the top. Then the hole was covered with a zinc sheet with a big stone put on top. I stayed there four days. I had no food and hardly any water. I was not even untied: I had to stay in one position, kneeling with my hands tied behind my back, tied to my ankles. The hole was narrow and I didn't have enough space to lie down. I was not taken out. I had to defecate and urinate there in the hole.

After four days they began to see that I was suffering. On the fifth day they brought me out. That day, by good luck, there was someone coming from Khartoum who knew me. He was a relative who is a policeman. He recognised me, and told the soldiers, 'This man is a civilian.' But the soldiers insisted I was an Anyanya. But after they had argued they said, 'Anyway we will release you.' I let out but told to stay in the garrison. But that night I ran to Karkaraya.

My chest is still paining me. If I try to walk a short distance, my feet become tired, and I cannot work with my arms.

Hussein Um Dabalo Angalo had a similar experience at Um Sirdiba garrison. Hussein is forty, a relatively prosperous farmer and the owner of a sesame-oil pressing mill in Nukta village in the Moro hills. He is too old to be suspected of being an SPLA fighter, but is the kind of influential villager whom the government is very keen to eliminate, or at least terrorise. In April 1995, he paid his way through army checkpoints to reach Kadugli:[117]

---

[116] These are nicknames or code names, used so that the tortured person does not know the true identity of the torturer.

[117] Interviewed in Um Dulu, 18 May 1995.

261

I went to Kadugli to buy clothes for my family. I bought four pairs of trousers, four shirts, five pairs of women's shoes, five pairs of men's shoes.... [he continued with the list of items.] I spent just one day in the town. When I came from Kadugli on the road to Um Sirdiba, before reaching the garrison at the bridge, I came across and army post guarding the bridge. I was with my son Abdel Majid who is about eighteen.

I encountered some soldiers at that post, who said that I should wait for some more people to accompany me, and that I cannot go alone. I refused, I said, 'I cannot wait for people I don't know.' The soldier said no, and told me not to move. He sent two girls to the camp, saying to them. 'Bring more force.' The soldier started to interrogate me under the tree, saying, 'Where is your permit?' I didn't have one—sometimes people can go in and out of Kadugli without a permit, if you pay.

The soldiers' first plan was to shoot and kill Hussein on the pretext that he was trying to escape. Hussein was too wily to fall for this ruse.

When the girls came back they brought fourteen soldiers from Um Sirdiba, making a total of fifteen. When they were approaching they started firing, aiming at the tree. The soldier who was with me told me and Abdel Majid to lie down, and then he said, 'Run away!' I told my son, 'If it is our day to die, we die. So don't run away.' Their firing was all in the air, it was not serious—they wanted us to run so they could shoot us down running away. The one soldier was insisting, 'You run, just leave your things.'

The fourteen arrived and decided to search my things. They started beating me with the muzzles of their guns, on all parts of my body. All of them were joining in. The first soldier had an axe and he hit me three times with his axe on my head. It didn't cut the skin, there was swelling but no bleeding.

This made them angry. One of them shouted, 'He must have a *hejab*!'[118] So they searched me and found my *hejab* and cut it off with a knife. After they took the *hejab*, they said 'Now let us test him with the axe again, to see the effect.' When they tried, they hit

_____

[118] A *hejab* is an amulet, typically a leather pouch containing some verses of the Koran, that is believed to act as a lucky charm.

me on the head, a big wound opened here [right on the top of the head in the centre] and I started bleeding. I was also hit with the muzzle of a gun on the left temple and started bleeding.

The soldiers then began their usual routine of interrogation, leading to torture.

After the beating they took us both inside Um Sirdiba garrison, to the security [military intelligence]. The sergeant-major, Abdalla, asked, 'Are you an Anyanya or a civilian?' My son was asked the same question. I said, 'We are both civilians.' The intelligence officer said, 'If you don't tell the truth, we will kill you both now.' I repeated what I had said, insisting that we are only civilians. He told me, 'If you are not telling the truth, we will see.' He picked up a club and hit me on the head, on the same place that had the wound from the axe. It bled more. The intelligence officer said, 'We will tie you up and throw you into a well unless you tell the truth.' He ordered that we should have our arms tied and we should be taken to the well—in fact it was a deep hole that was dry and not a well as such. Which they did: we were tied and thrown into this hole in the garrison.

It was dry and about two metres deep. Abdel Majid and I were thrown in together. After we had been thrown inside they closed the top with a piece of zinc and put a rock on top. The soldiers said, 'Stay there, we are coming in a minute.' It was 5 p.m. when we were put in the hole.

It was thirteen hours later, at 6 a.m., when they came for us. They said, 'If you don't confess we will kill you today.' I insisted, I told them: 'I am a civilian. If it is my day to be killed, let it be.' There were two soldiers. One of them was ordered to untie us. He did. After we were untied they sent the other one to fetch water from inside the garrison, from a pond there. He brought the water in a cup. It was dirty. The other soldier added some wheat flour and told us to drink it. After we drank it the soldier said, 'We have given you time, now think and tell us the truth.' At breakfast time they brought us some *asida* [sorghum porridge]. We ate it. Afterwards, a soldier came and said, 'You have to stay seven days, after that we will consider taking you to a displaced area.' During this seven days we were in the hole. We were never taken out. We took our food and water in the hole. Only when we wanted to go to the toilet we were let out, with two guards. All the time the hole was covered with the zinc. During the day it was extremely hot.

When we were taken out we saw that there were many holes, all covered with zinc. Maybe twenty in all. Some were deeper than ours, you had to shine a torch to see in.

On the eighth day, the officer, Abdalla, came with the sheikh of the displaced, Simon Araya. Abdalla told the sheikh to bail us, on the condition that we should not leave Um Sirdiba. We had to stay in Um Sirdiba. All this time I did not get any medication for my wounds. There is a health centre in Um Sirdiba but there was no medicine for civilians.

For civilians living in contested zones, life is a constant tightrope in which survival depends upon calculation and compromise. Having escaped death by torture, Hussein had to consider his personal finances—he had invested heavily in his visit to the market in Kadugli. Getting his possessions back meant dealing directly with his torturer.

We spent one month with the sheikh. After one month I went to Abdalla and asked for the things that were taken from me on the first day. He took us to the commanding officer, a captain, who pointed at me and told Abdalla, 'This man is feeding the Anyanya. He had an oil press, using a camel, to feed the Anyanya. So he deserves nothing.'

I said, 'If it is feeding the Anyanya, it is because they come to me as a government, they have guns, like you have guns in your place. If this means feeding the Anyanya, let it be so. I am a civilian. I have no option to refuse.'

He looked at me for a long time and then at last he told Abdalla to give me only the four pounds of sugar. I took them. After I took the sugar I went to Abdalla again with my son, and my wife who had come from Nukta to see me. I said, 'This is my wife and my son. The things I bought for them are with you.' Abdalla gave us two pairs of shoes, one for a man and one for a woman. Abdalla said, 'You stay, I will see to your things.' I also had LS 4,700 that was confiscated.

After that we prayed the Eid Dahiya [10 May] together and I had the opportunity to remind him that I was still waiting. He said, 'If you have animals, you go and bring them for sale here. There is nothing I can do.' After that I felt that there was nothing to wait for. So I left and came here three days ago.

Torture by keeping people in holes in the ground for long periods is not confined to Um Sirdiba. African Rights received reports from other garrisons, including Turoji, where Mahjoub Tiya Kuku, a 43-year-old farmer from Lindu village, was treated in this way. Mahjoub told African Rights:[119]

My village is Lindu east of Turoji, about two hours walk. The war situation forced me migrate to Lado. I spent one year and two months in Lado. Due to lack of something to wear, I travelled to Turoji with my wife. I left Lado with my wife on the 18 April 1995 for Turoji. I had LS 1200, two tins of sorghum and eight *malwas* of groundnuts, all to sell and buy clothes with the money. Actually I managed to buy one *jellabiya*, one pair of trousers, one pair of shoes and a dress for my wife.

The day I was supposed to leave Turoji with my wife, one former SPLA soldier surprised me by accusing me to the army of Turoji, saying that I had come from the rebel-controlled areas. He went further and accused me of being a rebel myself. His name is Ibrahim Karaka. I was arrested by the military and taken to prison. In the prison there is a deep hole with a zinc cover. I was first tied up and thrown into the hole. I was kept for a whole three days without food and only a little water. I was given a cup of water once a day at 1.00 p.m.

After three days, I was taken for interrogation. The sergeant who interrogated me, asked me where my gun was! I told him, 'I don't have a gun. Truly I live in the areas of the rebels but I am not an SPLA myself. I could have been recruited but for my poor health and family responsibilities. But I wasn't. I only farm to feed my family. I have three wives and seven children.' During the interrogation, the sergeant wanted me to admit that I was Anyanya. He promised to forgive me and put me into a peace camp instead. He told me that I will be allowed to go home to bring my remaining family to the peace camp.

I didn't change my first statement that I was a civilian in the rebel areas. After interrogation they released on the condition that I

---

[119] Interviewed in Um Dulu, 17 May 1995.

was not leave Turoji. In turn they confiscated all the belongings that I had bought in Turoji. I accepted the release conditions at the time. Once I found that I was not being followed, I escaped to Lado village. I'm now with my wives and children.

Every former internee of a peace camp or garrison has stories of torture, either from personal experience, from observation, or from the tales told by other inmates. References to beating and various forms of deprivation abound in the testimonied presented above and below. Another case is presented here. Omer Munu Kalu is a farmer in his thirties from Umula village in the Otoro hills. He was abducted on 1 April 1995 and taken to Heiban.[120]

I was in my farm, cleaning the sorghum stalks from last year. The stalks were very thick so I couldn't see or hear the army coming. They came very close—then I raised my eyes and saw them. They were many. They said, 'Don't move!' I was afraid to run, thinking they would shoot me, so I surrendered. They took me. On the way, we met a woman carrying sorghum—it was the hungry period. They took her and the sorghum. Also on the way we met a boy, aged about twelve, and a girl, recently married. The soldiers took them. We went ahead and found an old man clearing a farm, and the soldiers also captured him. Now we were six in number.

After walking some way we heard the sound of lorries ahead, and the soldiers told us to stop. There were three lorries and a landrover mounted with a machine gun. When the lorries reached us, they told us to climb into the lorries. They drove into Heiban.

Immediately we got down from the lorry we were taken into the investigation office. They interrogated us: 'Why are you working in the farm? Do you think there is peace? There is no peace!' We were also asked, 'Who planted the land mine that exploded under our car on the road?' I said, 'I am only a farmer, I don't know.' They said, 'If you don't tell us who planted that mine, you won't be released.' We were also asked, 'Where do the planes land?' We said, 'We don't know.' They continued, 'How many times did it land? Did it land in Nyakama?' I said, 'I don't know anything about this.' We were told again, 'If you don't tell us, you won't be

---

[120] Interviewed in Kujur el Sha'abiya, 13 May 1995.

released. We have standing orders, anyone captured should stay here with us and not be released.'

They did not beat me or torture me, but during four days I was not given any food. But then someone I knew came to the prison and said, 'Give me this man, I can take care of him and give him some food.' So I was taken to his place. They told me that I was to be trained in the PDF.

In the prison, there was one man from Dingir, called Yousif, who had been captured carrying a G3 rifle. He was badly tortured—they tied him up and hung him behind a car. He wasn't released from his tying except when they gave him water. His arms were paralysed and he couldn't hold the water in his hands.

Omer escaped shortly afterwards, when two lorryloads of "returnees" and a truck full of raided cattle were leaving for Abu Jibeha, and he was left momentarily unguarded.

The torture of political detainees in military camps, prisons and "ghost houses" continues throughout Sudan, but will not be dealt with in this report.

Forced Labour

One of the reasons for abducting and detaining Nuba civilians is to create and maintain a cheap labour force. There are two major components of this. One is serving the garrisons themselves: internees are required to cook, clean, carry water and cultivate for soldiers. The second is working as manual labourers on mechanised farming schemes, usually on the fringes of the Nuba Mountains.

Most of the forced labour within the garrisons is domestic work imposed upon girls and boys aged between about ten and eighteen. Nura Kabia Chagul, aged seventeen, is a Moslem Otoro girl from Longoro who experienced this.[121]

I and a friend of mine, Batul Umdour, left Kuchama in the afternoon. We were going to the farms to clear weeds in our farm. On the way we met the enemy coming from Delier. I was not aware that they had burned Delier that morning. The enemy stopped us

---

[121] Interviewed in Kujur el Sha'abiya, 13 May 1995.

267

and forced us to carry heavy load of sorghum. It was August last year [1994]. I and Batul carried the load all the way up to Heiban. We reached Heiban in the evening and proceeded to the military garrison. At the garrison we handed over the load of sorghum to soldiers who came with us.

I and Batul were put into a very small room without windows. A soldier locked the room from outside and told us, 'Any noise from you pigs and I will shoot.' I and Batul spent two days in the garrison.

On the third day we were separated. I was taken and handed over to the family of somebody called Idris. I was given half a *malwa* of sorghum as my ration. I didn't know for how long it was supposed to last. I was not given clothes.

Idris is a PDF [soldier]. He is not Otoro. He comes from Lira. Idris has two wives. He showed me to his wives and told them that they should treat me as their servant. Idris told me not to go anywhere without his permission and I should only stay in the house.

I spent seven days in Heiban in the house of Idris. I was working in his house and his farm. I get up every morning at about 4:30 a.m. I clean the compound and prepare breakfast, usually *asida* [sorghum porridge]. At 6:00 a.m. I go to the farm to either clear the weeds or keep the animals away from it. I stay in the farm up to 4:00 p.m. when I return from the farm I go to fetch water from the Heiban water tanker. There I wait for long hours though I should come quickly to cook the super. After the supper at about 8:00 p.m. I wash the utensils. Before I go to sleep in my *rakuba* [shelter] I will go to the elder wife of Idris, Aziza, and ask her as to what I should do the following day.

On my way to the farm every morning I meet many adults who are in the peace camp. They all go to work in the farms. The farms in Heiban belong to the army and the PDF. I can see many of these adults in the farms near to the one of Idris but nobody can talk to the other. I was always thinking of how to escape. I would always weep when I remember my mother, my relatives and my village. Though I was not given enough food to eat by Idris's family I had no appetite. I was always thinking how to come home.

What I saw in Heiban cannot make me go there [again] for any reason whatsoever. I saw how people are suffering for no food, and overworked. I was sad that I was separated from Batul. I have no news of her and I don't know what happened to her in Heiban. I left her behind in the garrison the day I was taken to Idris's family. I was crying to leave her and she doesn't know what happened to me when the soldier took me away that morning.

Among the internees in Heiban, the greatest fear was to be transported to one of the labour camps. This was what most motivated Nura to try to escape.

While I worked in the farm of Idris I used to see people transported in lorries outside Heiban. I didn't know what was happening until Lyila the younger wife of Idris warned me. One evening she called me and told me that I should not accept being transferred to Khartoum. She told me that the PDF will come around one day to deceive me that I was being taken to Khartoum. She said I should not believe them. Nobody is taken to Khartoum from Heiban. They only take them to Abu Jibeha and Rahmaniya agricultural schemes. I will end up in one of those schemes if I believe them. I was more frightened by this information and decided to escape once I had the opportunity.

The morning I escaped Idris told me that I should stay at home. He said that there was a rally in the PDF Square in Heiban and his two wives will go with him. Idris told me to guard the house and his other gun. Idris went away with his wives and the other gun. When I was sure they have gone and everything was quiet I escaped into the nearby sorghum field. It was August and I made sure that I was concealed by sorghum. I started running when I reached the end of farms. I ran without stopping until I reached Khor Heiban. In Khor Heiban I felt afraid that I didn't go very far from Heiban. I started running again avoiding the road. I ran in the bush until I reached Jebel Tomaro. It was there where the direction of Kuchama became clear to me. I could see Medie mountains and Heiban far behind me. I started walking to Kuchama West taking the direction from Jebel Medie as it falls between Kuchama West and Luchulu.

I arrived home before the sunset and everybody was very happy to see me back. My mother was extremely happy but thought the government may follow me from Heiban. I walked with her to Luchulu to sleep the night until she is sure that I was safe. I'm now in Kuchama West. I'm now very happy to be home.

Zeinab el Amin Abu Ras, aged fifteen, is from Kernalu village in the Otoro hills. Her account of her mercifully brief stay in Heiban, eight months after Nura, indicates that nothing had changed in the meantime. She was abducted when Kernalu was attacked on the night of 18 April 1995.[122]

I was abducted at 11.00 or 12.00 at night. The village was surrounded by soldiers when I was sleeping. We were ten, including my mother and three older girls, including me, my sister Samya and my cousin Amal. My father was in Heiban already; he was captured by the army in December. They took our family, and another man, his wife and their two children. No-one was killed. They took all the furniture, everything we had in the house—angarebs, chairs, two sacks of sorghum, all our fourteen goats.

We were taken at night and arrived in Heiban that same night. The soldiers came on foot. They were Arabs from the north, with one or two blacks among them. There was no moon that night, and they had torches to see the way. They ordered us: 'No talking, there is insecurity from the Anyanya.' So we walked in silence.

In the morning, we were taken to the barracks for registering our names. We were told, 'Your father is here, in the [PDF] training centre. So we were taken to his house in the peace camp, for my mother to stay in. Our father was absent at the training centre. In fact, the peace camp was empty, as two or three days before we came, all the people had been taken to Abu Jibeha. The enemy are afraid that if people are kept near to their homes, they will desert, so they take them somewhere else, far away. They go by lorry, I heard.

The soldiers came to us and said: 'Clean our houses and wash our clothes.' They beat us. They said, 'If you have never before slept with a man, today we will show you.'

In the afternoon, they brought our father to us in the house. He said to us, 'If any soldier gives any order to work in the house, you work.' He was being threatened by the soldiers, who were telling him, 'If there is any work, let your daughters do it: washing, cleaning and so on, then they will get their rations.'

---

[122] Interviewed in Kauda, 11 May 1995.

That day, in the evening, three soldiers, all Arabs, came and divided up the three girls and took us away. I escaped later that night. My sister and my cousin remain.

The withholding of food rations to ensure that internees of garrisons and peace camps follow their instructions to work is common across the Nuba Mountains.

Heiban is in the centre of a thickly-populated area, and the "combing" expeditions from the garrison have become one of the government's main sources of captives. Especially during the dry season, week by week, the number of captives in Heiban mounts. Once enough people are assembled, the military authorities there call for a convoy to come from Abu Jibeha labour camp, to the east. Typically the convoys come four times a year, but they are more frequent when there is a major offensive—they come for resupply and go back with the larger-than-normal number of captives. The convoy usually consists of between six and eight large trucks that can carry up to one hundred people each. The convoys never empty Heiban completely; some captives are always left behind for domestic labour, as "wives" for the soldiers, and for training in the PDF.

African Rights was unable to locate any escapees from Abu Jibeha or Rahmaniya labour camps. Returnees from other camps, who had met internees from the labour camps, reported that they were required to work from 6 a.m. until 5 or 6 p.m. and they receive very poor food. Awadiya Kodi, whose testimony recounting her rape and "marriage" is presented on pages 239-41, explained what she had observed:[123]

We saw a lot of women who had been abducted earlier. When the number of abducted women grew too large, they were taken off to Rahmaniya to work on the farms. After the harvest, these women were then brought back to Heiban, to prepare food for the soldiers and to serve them. Some of those who were 'married', their soldier 'husbands' were selected to go with them to guard the people in Rahmaniya. Some women went with their 'husbands'. They were

---

[123] Interviewed in Kujur el Sha'abiya, 13 May 1995.

lucky because they were treated better. If they were not so lucky, they went alone and their 'husbands' stayed in Heiban. When they returned they went back to their 'husbands'.

I didn't go to Rahmaniya, but I spoke to many women who had been there and back. They said that conditions there were bad. The water is bad, and far away—it is brought by tractor. The people work from early morning until sunset. The farms are huge. There is only a break for breakfast at 10.00 a.m. and then people go back to work until 5 p.m., and then they have to go back to their houses and make supper.

When the women are brought back from Rahmaniya after the harvest, the men remain to continue preparing the farms for the cultivation season. Then the women are sent back during the rains.

As well as the big labour camps, there are a large number of small camps attached to small mechanised schemes in the north of the Nuba Mountains. They are not large enough to warrant labour camps in their own right, and instead the labourers are recruited under arrangements with garrison commanders and government chiefs. Since about 1987, the owners of mechanised farms have hired armed guards under contracts with the army. The farmers pay the army on a system known as *allawat al mashari* (scheme allowances or incentives). Meanwhile, merchant farmers regularly visit the peace camps of Kadugli and Dilling with requests for a certain number of labourers. They pay a fee to the authorities controlling the peace camp for each person that is recruited on their behalf. The contract is made between the merchant and the Amir or commander—the labourer is not usually party to it. However, poverty has led many peace camp internees and others to look for work, despite very poor levels of pay, or even just payment in food. It is worth recalling that before the war, migrant labour was a mainstay of the Nuba economy.

Yousif Atti Sayed, a farmer in his mid-thirties, left Sabat village, near Jebel Urmi in eastern Kawalib after the 1994 rainy season. He was nearly destitute and had decided to look for work. His first destination was Delami town, where he arrived on 9 October.[124]

---

[124] Interviewed in Tira Limon, 21 May 1995.

The first thing that you find in Delami is the garrison. Military intelligence takes you and asks you, 'Where are you coming from? Where are you going to? Why' And so on. The officer was wearing plain clothes. I said, 'I am coming from Sabat village. I have left my family there, and I have come to join you.' He asked me, 'Why didn't you bring your family?' I told them, 'I left my wife harvesting and told her to finish the harvest, sell it and then join me.' He asked, 'How many children do you have?' I said, 'Four.' He asked, 'Why did you not come before?' I replied, 'It was difficult for us to come without something in our hands. We couldn't come with children and find they have nothing to eat.' He asked, 'Why don't you come and cultivate the land here?' I said, 'I didn't know you had land for cultivation.' And I was asked all sorts of questions about the Anyanya, their numbers, their guns, the locations of their camps, and so on.

After the interrogation, I was instructed to stay in a hospital ward, with other people who had arrived ahead of me. There were no sick people—it was being used as a dormitory. The army was staying in the intermediate school, us civilians waiting for screening in the hospital wards. They told me, 'Be ready to take a gun and look for your family and your relatives.' I told them again, 'I have already agreed with my wife, and if you wait, they will come.' They insisted, 'You have to take a gun.' I said, 'I am a catechist [in the Sudan Church of Christ]. I am a religious person, I preach for God, and I cannot take a gun. We as Christians, our enemy is Satan, and we fight through prayers.' The security man said, 'There are many Christians carrying guns.' I said, 'Everyone has his faith. In the Ten Commandments we are told not to kill.'

Everyone in Delami is in the PDF. When they go on operations, the whole town is empty. Even the government officials go out on the operations, then they come back and go back to their civilian jobs.

Yousif was not in the end recruited to the PDF as he had feared. He asked permission to find work, as he had come to Delami without any money. He was told: "Fine. But stay in the ward." Yousif described the conditions of work.

273

The next day a merchant came looking for labourers. In Delami, the arrangement is that any merchant who is looking for labourers contacts the garrison, especially the military intelligence, the police officers, the commander of the garrison, the executive officer of the council, and the state security, and brings a permit from them. Then the names of the labourers are attached for the final permission. So this merchant came and registered us. His name was Bedawi and he had a farm on the Mulabak scheme. He wanted 22 labourers.

The whole interrogation and screening process took fourteen days. After that we were taken on a lorry to Mulabak. Bedawi was given a condition, that he was responsible for anyone who escapes. So when we reached Mulabak, we were seated on the ground and handed over to a group of soldiers. Each merchant has his force of regular soldiers on his farm. Bedawi had eight for his farm. Their job was to protect the merchant and his workers from the SPLA, and to guard the workers and stop them from escaping. Even if you disagree with the merchant and try to leave, the soldier can shoot you.

We were taken immediately to Bedawi's scheme. We agreed with Bedawi on a payment of LS 3000 per *mukhamas*.[125] Bedawi grew sesame and sorghum. We worked on the sesame. We were sixteen men and six women. Three were members of the PDF who needed money.[126] The rest were 'returnees' taken from the peace camp in Delami.

The soldiers did not misbehave. They are our boys, there to guard us only, and we did not provoke them. There are many stories of them misbehaving on the schemes, especially with the women, but I did not encounter that. Also it seems that the Amir of the Kawalib, Nabil Sayed, has tried to come to an agreement with the army to restrain the raping of women.

I worked six days in Mulabak. Then I took permission to return to Delami. In Delami, Amir Nabil required the people in the peace camp to build a big shelter for a reception, because the *Wali* [Governor] of South Kordofan was visiting Delami on his way to Rashad. I had finished my contract with Bedawi so I went to him and he paid me for six days—all the payment is made in Delami, not on the spot in Mulabak. This is different from normal, for

---

[125] An area of 180 yards by 120 yards.
[126] PDF members receive no salary.

security. He paid me in his shop. I worked building the shelter. The *Wali* came and had his reception.

Yousif then had to travel to Dilling to accompany a sick relative to hospital. He had great difficulty getting a permit and arrived only a few days before his relative died. Lacking money, Yousif was forced to stay in a quarter of the town inhabited by displaced people. He reported:

> Life is hard in Dilling. There I saw real famine. Many people are not able to eat. I stayed in Redif. The Dilling people themselves are not hungry, but the people who have migrated from other places like Delami are really suffering. I saw the Comboni Sisters giving some assistance to these people, but that is all. Even to buy some oil to heat the *doka* [an iron sheet used for cooking] is LS 100, and I didn't have money for even that. And that was with my close relatives, forced into Dilling by hunger. Those people are miserable. They have no clothes. To buy one shirt is LS 7000.
>
> In the whole of [government-controlled] Sudan, half the people are armed. Only the casual labourers are not carrying guns.

Yousif then travelled to Khartoum to look for work. Due to harassment and fear of forced recruitment to the army he left Khartoum and looked for work in eastern Sudan, travelling as far as New Halfa. But the level of intimidation was such that in January 1995 he opted to return to the Nuba Mountains and live in the SPLA-administered areas once again.

THE OFFICIAL STORY

The Government of Sudan argues simultaneously or alternately that there is complete peace and tranquility in the Nuba Mountains, and that all the problems there are the work of the SPLA; and that it is fighting a *Jihad* and that it is a tolerant, multi-religious government simply putting down a rebellion.

While African Rights was conducting its research, Hassan al Turabi spoke at length on the situation in Sudan, including the Nuba

275

Mountains, to the Netherlands newspaper *Trouw*.[127] Some of the interview runs:

> *Trouw: What happened last year in the Nuba Mountains?*
>
> *Turabi:* Now you can go and see for yourself that 95 per cent of the citizens have returned to their homes and left the camps. One part where there were pockets of SPLA activity has been liberated and now the area is in complete peace.
>
> *Trouw: According to statements made by people fleeing the Nuba Mountains, there are tens of thousands of people killed and women forced into prostitution.*
>
> *Turabi:* (incredulously) In an Islamic State?!
>
> *Trouw: Will you allow international observers to investigate the incidents in the Nuba Mountains?*
>
> *Turabi:* They are welcome, provided that they do not have a prejudice against Sudan or against Islam.[128]

Trouw then showed Turabi some information on the genocide in the Nuba Mountains, published by the newspaper in February. Turabi denied everything:

> What does destruction mean? You cannot destroy villages. There are no buildings to destroy, there are only huts... What is this? Graves? It's natural that there should be graves. Killing fields! Excuse me—this is madness.

Dr Turabi is not telling the truth. Moreover, the information available to *Trouw* at the time of the interview was only a fraction of the reality. The following Chapter details the depths of the Sudan

---

[127] 'Soedan is niet perfect, er zijn een paar politieke gevangenen," *Trouw*, 27 May 1995.

[128] The Sudan Government has declared the UN Special Rapporteur on Human Rights in Sudan, Gáspár Bíró, *persona non grata* on the pretext that he has a hostility towards Islam.

Government's hypocrisy, and Turabi's extraordinary inversion of the truth.

IV

ATTACK ON CHRISTIANITY; ATTACK ON ISLAM

This government has made our lives miserable in the name of Jihad. I don't believe that theirs is a holy war. They avoid the SPLA and come to attack us. They are just thieves and criminals.

> Aboud Hamad Bako, Imam of the Ansar el Sunna mosque in Kalkada, which was destroyed by the Government of Sudan on 25 February 1994. Interviewed in Kauda, 12 May 1995.

A TRADITION OF TOLERANCE

The Nuba include Moslems, Christians and followers of traditional religions. The numbers who profess each faith are a matter of dispute. What is not in dispute is that the Nuba have a strong tradition of religious tolerance. It is not uncommon to have followers of three different religions within the same family. A leading anthropologist of the Miri Nuba has written:

> All Miri people, villagers and migrants alike, are free in their religious practice... they are obliged, however, to respect their fellows' emphasis on other religious practices.
> Thus a villager is free to build his own mosque, as has happened in Umduiu village, and is free to go on the pilgrimage, as has been done by a farmer in Miri Bara. He is not free, however, to demand of others to follow his example, or to deprecate their reluctance. Nor is he free to opt out of the priestly rituals and

natural observances that within each village maintain the order of nature. Conversely, a farmer may be more than usually conscientious in the performance of non-Islamic ritual and may even on occasion revive one that has been neglected by the community at large. Yet, he is firmly expected to keep the current Muslim practices, and not denigrate the zeal of others.[1]

This tradition of respect and tolerance has been eroded by the Sudan Government in the last decade, but it remains strong in areas not under government control.

Islam has been present in the Nuba Mountains since at least the fourteenth century. The Kingdom of Tegali was founded by a Moslem and always had Moslem rulers. But it was not until the nineteenth century that Islam began to spread beyond the small circle of elites in the northern jebels who were most exposed to contact with neighbouring Moslem peoples. Then, Islam was spread by two main means: the presence of Moslem Arab communities in places such as Dilling, Talodi and the western jebels, and probably more importantly, the return to the Nuba Mountains of Nuba who had served under the Turco-Egyptian and Mahdist states as soldiers. Despite colonial policies intended to isolate the Nuba from Arab-Moslem influence, the most rapid spread of Islam occurred this century, starting under British rule. Nuba Moslems are mostly followers of Sufi sects such as the Gadiriya, but there are also strong communities of the Ansar el Sunna and other Moslem sects. Sudanese Islam has two contrasting traditions: of messianic zeal, and Sufist tolerance. Nuba Moslems in general fall squarely into the second, tolerant tradition.

Christian missionary activity began in the Nuba Mountains with the visit of Daniel Comboni in 1874. These first efforts were interrupted by the Mahdiya, and it was not until the 1920s and '30s that the missions began to establish themselves fully, with schools, clinics and churches. While some groups, such as the Kawalib and Otoro, embraced Christianity, others such as the Katcha proved very resistant to its appeals, despite the presence of nearby mission

---

[1] Gerd Baumann, *National Integration and Local Integrity: The Miri of the Nuba Mountains in the Sudan*, Oxford, Clarendon Press, 1987, p. 172.

stations. The missions were vital in introducing education to the Nuba, and they did so in a way designed to minimise the influence of Islam—notably they refused to use the Arabic script for as long as possible. Some missionaries saw their role as competing for adherents with the Moslem preachers.

By Independence, the Nuba tradition of tolerance was thus overlain with religious politics. It has continued this way. Successive Sudanese governments have sought to restrict the activities of Christian missions, while the most prominent Nuba politician, Philip Abbas Ghabboush, is an ordained Christian priest, and Christianity has been attractive to some Nuba youth precisely because it is not favoured by the government. While many Nuba have turned to Islam in the last forty years, Christianity has also been on the increase, notably through individual conversions among the youth.

A former catechist from Tira el Akhdar, Yagoub Osman Kaloka, explained some of the tensions that arose when he and others from his village converted to Christianity in the 1970s:[2]

> In the past, the Tira people had many conflicts with the Arabs. But at the same time we adopted parts of the Arab culture and about two thirds of the Tira became Moslems. Christianity was not strong, it only started in our area in the 1970s with the coming of the Roman Catholic Church. (Kauda mission was concerned with the Otoro people only, not us.) So I converted and became a Roman Catholic. But when Christianity came it caused problems, because many of the youth became Christians, while the elders were mostly Moslems. My own father is a Moslem.
>
> I was in school in Kalkada from 1965 onwards. Then I went to Khartoum, and then my elder brother took me to the Comboni school in el Obeid. Most of the pupils there were Christians, and read Christian books. So I also read the Christian books. So I compared the religions, and found that I preferred Christianity.
>
> In our village, the Moslem leaders told people that their children should be Moslem, and that if they disagreed, they should declare a *jihad* against them. Our elders quarrelled with us, telling us we should be Moslems. On my return, I met with the elders and said that religion is a matter between the individual and God. These

---

[2] Interviewed in Tira Limon, 23 May 1995.

280

problems continued up to about 1975 or '76. But by the late 1970s, the great majority of elders accepted us. Only a few were still aggressively Islamic.

By the 1980s, the locus of aggressive or extremist Islam had shifted from a few village Imams and teachers to the state itself. This process culminated in the declaration of *Jihad* in 1992. One of its consequences was to open the eyes of Nuba Moslems to the manipulation of religion for political ends. In non-government controlled areas, there is now greater religious tolerance than for many years (see below).

THE ATTACK ON CHRISTIANITY

A selective crackdown on Nuba Christians began before the war even reached the Nuba Mountains. It was the work of the security forces operating in a polarised political context, with Islamic extremism in the ascendant. Local politics also played its part. For instance, the repression of Tira Christians was instigated in part by an ambitious Tira politician, Mohamed Rahma, who has since become Amir under the *Nafir el Sha'abi*.

Agostino al Nur Ibrahim Shamila is now a judge in the civil administration under the SPLM. He was one of the first victims of the crackdown, in 1983. The pretext for the crackdown was that churchpeople were supporting the SPLA. It was a self-fulfilling prediction.[3]

> I am a Christian, but my father was a Moslem. At first, I was a Moslem (my name was al Nur) but I became a Christian in Khartoum after I began to study the Bible at evening classes. That was in 1968. For me it is a matter of personal conviction, for the Moslem Brothers it is a matter of *ridda* [apostasy, a crime under Islamic law punishable by death]. My family—at the beginning they were not so happy. They called me and I talked to them; they saw my behaviour and how I had changed. They were impressed.

---

[3] Interviewed in Achiron, 7 May 1995.

I saw segregation and discrimination in our society. I have felt this since 1963 when I was in primary school in Kauda. At the time when I entered school, the treatment of the Nuba children and the Arab children was not fair. We were living together in a dormitory, but we were not treated equally. I can remember many incidents. For example, when there was a noise in the dormitory, the head teacher would call the prefect, and if the prefect said the person who is beaten and is crying is a Nuba, the head teacher would ignore the matter. He would not come and see what was happening. But if the one crying is an Arab boy, he would come and lash all the Nubas.

These incidents continued all the time. We felt we were not needed, that we were not part of the school.

I was in Lubi, in the region of Tira [el Akhdar], which was my place. I was a [Roman Catholic] catechist at Lubi church. Since the start of the SPLA, persecution against the church intensified. We were being accused either as SPLA or as supporters of SPLA. I myself was detained three times by the State Security.

The first time was in December 1983, in Heiban. I was kept three weeks. There was no charge. The second time was in early 1985. There were two charges; first that I was co-operating with the SPLA, then second that I was myself an SPLA [member]. The third time was also in 1985, with the same accusations. I was kept for three months in detention in Kadugli by the security; I was never shown in court. I was released on 15 September 1985, with the condition that I cannot go back to the church. All the churches were closed to me; I had no chance to exercise any church activities in South Kordofan, and especially in Lubi. So I decided to go to Khartoum.

In Khartoum I discovered I was being followed by State Security. Many people from my tribe were facing the same situation. I continued evading the security forces, waiting for the rainy season. When the rains of 1986 came, I went to el Obeid, then to Lubi village.

Security was informed after one week that I had violated the conditions of my release and gone back to Lubi. So a force was sent from Talodi to arrest me in our village. The army came to Um Bera, between Talodi and our village. People ran to inform me that there was a force sent to arrest me. I left, leaving my wife and three children in the house. I went to the mountains. That was 12 July 1986. At 3 p.m. the army came, surrounded the house and entered it. All the houses of my relatives were surrounded. When they did not get me they started torturing people. My wife was beaten with a cane and the daughter of my brother was also beaten up. They were asked to say where I had gone. When they said they didn't know, they were beaten more. I had left a message that they should say I was with the cattle. They were beaten all night.

In the morning, all the chiefs were called. The head chief said I had gone with the cattle. So the army told the chiefs that I must be arrested and brought to the government. They took all my possessions, such as clothes, with them. The chiefs were given three days to arrest me.

The army went to Kalkada. When three days passed, my elder brother, Ahmad and our chief, Sheikh Hamoda Murjan, went to Kalkada to tell the government. My brother Ahmad was arrested at once. The order was passed that all our cattle and goats should be confiscated at once. An army [unit] came and took everything. They also arrested my father. The order was passed: if I am found, I must be shot.

I had nowhere to go. I decided to go to the SPLA, to defend myself and defend my property. I went to the SPLA on 16 August 1986. First, I reported to the SPLA base on Um Jarbralla mountain [near Um Dorein]. From there I went south, to Bilfam for training. I joined Volcano Battalion.

A catechist from the nearby village of Um Derdu, Joseph Aloga Jargi, confirmed that the assault on the church preceded any other problems in the Tira area.[4] While many Nuba tribes suffered militia raids from 1985 onwards, Joseph said that "there was no fighting in our area. In fact our relations with the Arabs did not deteriorate until very late." He continued:

The government began by burning churches. In August 1985, the army came and burned the church at Um Derdu. Jimmu Teima was killed on the spot. A church elder, al Nur Hamoda, was taken to Heiban and killed there. Daud and Abbas were taken and slaughtered with knives.

Lubi was the most dominant Christian village. The Mek, Mohamed Rahma, was very hostile to the natives of Lubi. So the

---

[4] Interviewed in Tira Limon, 21 May 1995.

Lubi youths accused him of many mistakes, and of making an alliance with the Arabs. The Lubi youth had an early crisis with the Arabs, and began to go to the SPLA.

When Mohamed Rahma saw this, he decided to rob the Lubi people by using the Arab militia. The first village to be burned was Lubi, which was burned by the army of Mendi in 1988.[5] The raiders took the cattle, furniture, clothes, everything. Then the youth of Um Derdu saw what was happening and followed those of Lubi to the SPLA.

Similar assaults on Christian churches were common throughout the Mountains. In the western jebels, six Christians were imprisoned in Tullishi in April 1988, for opening a church without government permission.[6] When the SPLA entered the area a year later, the churches were the first target of reprisals, by the government and by NIF cadres. The Christian centre at Salara was attacked and destroyed, along with all the books and furniture. In Tullishi, the people managed to protect the churches for long enough so that they were still intact when the SPLA forces reached the mountain at the end of the year.

The destruction of churches has become so commonplace in the war that most people interviewed by African Rights did not even bother to mention it. When asked if the church was burned when such-and-such a village was destroyed, the answer was always, "Of course!" The descriptions of peace camps in the previous chapter have also detailed discrimination against Christians, including forcible conversion.

The burning of churches continues. Churches were burned by troops from Um Sirdiba and Aggab in their February 1995 "combing" operation. Yousif Haroun, a catechist in Karkaraya, inspected the ruins of his church, the afternoon after it had been burned, accompanied by African Rights:[7]

---

[5] See paages 68-9.
[6] *Sudan Times*, 24 May 1988.
[7] Interviewed in Karkaraya, 22 February 1995.

The army burned the church down and broke the office; they took all the church's documents, such as the notebooks, money and all the other properties such as chairs and books. They burnt everything, and there is nothing inside the church now.

Several churches were destroyed in the assaults in Tira el Akhdar and Otoro between January and March 1995. One of them was in Kuchama East, as described by Butrus el Amin Tibra, a 28-year-old Roman Catholic catechist.[8]

The army came from Heiban and attacked our village of Kuchama East on 17 March. The attack took place at 2:00 p.m. The enemy burned the whole village including the Catholic church. They also burned the Catholic church guest house, the school, store and three residential houses. The soldiers looted ten sacks of sorghum, five sacks of beans, six sacks of groundnuts, ten chairs, six wooden beds and two choir drums.

It is the first time the church was burned in our area. Previously they use to burn the village but not the church or the mosque. This time they burned both the church and the mosque. I think they want us either to move away completely to other areas or report to their peace camps. We will try to build the church again though it will be very expensive. Our priority now is rebuilding the school. I appeal to the world to help us with school materials. Our children need education and they are the future of the Mountains.

In the burning of Dabker on 28 April 1995, the churches of the Roman Catholics and the Sudan Church of Christ were completely destroyed.

The Sudan Government is eager to enlist Islam as a legitimation for its war effort. But in reality the war is about power and wealth, and the government's target is wider than Christianity. As Butrus mentioned, the mosque in Kuchama East was also destroyed—a testimony from the Imam is reproduced below. Barnaba Angelo, head of the New Sudan Council of Churches in the Nuba Mountains, explained:[9]

---

[8] Interviewed in Kujur el Sha'abiya, 13 May 1995.
[9] Interviewed by the BBC in Debi, 10 May 1995.

285

When the government started the war it was against the church as it believed that the church was behind the rebellion in the Nuba Mountains. The government burned the churches and launched a *jihad* against them, telling the Moslems that church people [i.e. Christians] do not believe in God and are the people who are going to destroy the country... But when the government saw Moslems were not keen to support its actions, and when Moslems did not join the government's campaign against the church, government troops started burning mosques too.

This is perhaps the Sudan Government's darkest secret in the Nuba Mountains: it is systematically desecrating mosques.

THE ATTACK ON ISLAM

Ali Tutu Atrun is the Imam of the mosque in Kodi B in the Otoro hills. He described how his mosque was desecrated and his Holy Books, his prayer mats and other possessions of the mosque were deliberately destroyed by the Sudan Government.[10]

One morning in January [1995], the enemy attacked Kodi B. They were shelling the village by using heavy artillery while they were advancing. I was in Kodi A when I heard the shelling. It was 9:30 a.m. by then, exactly, [I knew] as I had a watch. Immediately I ran to a mountain between Kodi A and Kodi B. On that mountain I could see everything in Kodi B very clearly. I took a good position and saw the Sudan Government forces going towards the mosque in Kodi B market. They were running and spreading out across the whole village.

After they burned the area adjacent to the mosque I saw them moving towards the mosque. They entered the mosque with their shoes on. They took some time and they came out carrying books, chairs, a table and a carpet from the mosque. I saw six of them taking positions around the mosque's *rakuba* and the library. The six soldiers pulled out matches from their bags and in minutes the mosque's *rakuba* and the library were on fire. Then I heard a

---

[10] Interviewed in Kauda, 12 May 1995.

gunshot and saw the fire at the top of the mosque. The mosque started burning from top to bottom. I couldn't believe my eyes. I counted the soldiers burning the mosque and its surroundings. They were twenty five in number.

I saw the enemy leaving Kodi B at about 10:30 a.m. It was a big force of over three hundred men all in military uniform. At 12:00 noon I came down to check the destruction. We were fourteen persons including Sheikh Yousif Omer. I was the first to enter the mosque. Inside the mosque I found writings on the wall. The writing reads 'If you want to be Moslems, join *Dar el Islam* in Mendi.'[11] I found some books including two copies of the Holy Koran burned. I checked the mosque's contents and found out that some items were taken by the soldiers. They took 52 books of the Holy Koran, 62 other [articles of] Islamic literature, one office table, three chairs and one carpet of six by three metres. One sack of *zakat*[12] sorghum was scattered inside and outside the mosque. To rebuild this mosque needs a large sum of money between LS 50,000 and 60,000.

This incident of burning the mosque made me completely unhappy. My feeling is that the Government of Sudan forces are racist and not Moslems because I can't imagine a Moslem burning a mosque. Moreover burning the Holy Koran—the Book of God! Allah is anywhere—we need not go to Mendi to be good Moslems. I know the government think we do not know enough Islam but they are wrong. I will not go to Mendi and will continue stay here as there is no Islam in Mendi. I refuse their version of Islam, their Islam of looting, burning and killing. I believe we are the true Moslems and al Hamdu li Allah.

The graffiti left by the soldiers is instructive: the Sudan Government has told them that Islam exists only in the areas controlled by the government. Imam Ali of course found this a tragic absurdity.

---

11 The Prophet Mohamed divided the world into *Dar el Islam*, the land of Islam, and *Dar el Harb*, the land of war.
12 The *zakat* is the Islamic tithe collected for distribution to the poor and needy.

Islamic Law and the 1992 *Fatwa*

Islamic law was first decreed in Sudan in September 1983, though the previous five years had witnessed a steady Islamisation of many areas of political life. The "September Laws" contained a provision prohibiting *ridda* (apostasy, renouncing Islam) and imposing the death penalty on those convicted of this alleged crime who refused to return to Islam. The prominent philosopher and politician Ustaz Mahmoud Mohamed Taha was executed for apostasy in January 1985, for preaching a version of Islam (tolerant and reformist) that was antithetical to the extremism of President Jaafar Nimeiri and his allies among the Moslem Brothers. Under this extreme definition, very many Nuba are guilty of apostasy. A significant number have converted from Islam to Christianity (and some to traditional religions), and most Nuba Moslems practise or tolerate practices that the ruling extremists consider un-Islamic.

Many leading Nuba Moslems are opposed to the imposition of Islamic Law on the Nuba Mountains. One is Imam Adam Tutu Atrun, a leading Nuba Islamic scholar. Imam Adam studied in the prestigious Hay Abdel Moniem school in Khartoum, and then went abroad to Saudi Arabia for seven years, where he studied the Islamic religion in Mecca. In December 1994, he headed the Islamic delegation to the conference on religious dialogue held in the SPLA-held areas of the Nuba Mountains (see below). Imam Adam argues that it would be wrong to impose the *Sharia* in a land where there are followers of different religions.

The rebellion in the Nuba Mountains intensified the problem of Islamic law and the question of *ridda*. Despite the fact that the SPLA forces in the Nuba Mountains have been very largely led by Moslems, successive governments have portrayed the guerrillas as fighting against Islam. In order to do so they have withdrawn the legitimacy of Islam in the SPLA-held areas, in effect declaring all Moslems who are not with them to be infidels, and thus the legitimate target for a *Jihad*.

This became explicit with the *Jihad* declared in January 1992 and confirmed by *Fatwa* shortly afterwards. Though the Mujahidiin

288

are not currently significant as military forces in the Nuba Mountains, the *Jihad* and *Fatwa* remain in force. The full text of the *Fatwa* reads:

In the name of Allah, the Beneficent, the Merciful, a Fatwa to fight the rebels.

May the peace and blessings of Allah be upon His Prophet. In their conference which was held in the Popular Committee Hall in el Obeid on 27 April 1992 (Shawaal 24, 1413 AH), the religious leaders, Imams of mosques and sufists of Kordofan State issued the adduced *fatwa* to legalize the *jihad* in South Kordofan State and Southern Sudan.

The rebels in South Kordofan and Southern Sudan started their rebellion against the state and declared war against the Moslems. Their main aims are: killing the Moslems, desecrating mosques, burning and defiling the Koran, and raping Moslem women. In so doing, they are encouraged by the enemies of Islam and Moslems: these foes are the Zionists, the Christians and the arrogant people who provide them with provisions and arms. Therefore, *an insurgent who was previously a Moslem is now an apostate; and a non-Moslem is a non-believer standing as a bulwark against the spread of Islam, and Islam has granted the freedom of killing both of them*[13] according to the following words of Allah:

(1) Allah says:

O ye who believe! Whoso of you becometh a renegade from his religion, (know that in his stead) Allah will bring a people whom He loveth and who love Him, humble towards believers, stern towards disbelievers, striving in the way of Allah, and fearing not the blame of any blamer. Such is the grace of Allah which He giveth unto whom He will. Allah is All-Embracing, All-Knowing. (5:54)

(2) Also, Allah says:

---

[13] Emphasis added.

And they will not cease from fighting against you until they have made you renegades from your religion, if they can. And whoso becometh a renegade and dieth in his disbelief such are they whose works have fallen both in the world and the Hereafter. Such are rightful owners of the flames of Hell: they will abide therein. (2:217)

(3) On the legality of fighting the disbelievers, Allah says:

O Prophet! Strive against the disbelievers and the hypocrites, and be stern with them. Hell will be their home, a hapless journey's end. (66.9)

(4) For the affidavit of combating the rebels, Prophet Mohamed (may the peace and blessings of Allah be upon him) said:

'Whoever comes to you (united in opinion) and tried to divide you (to incite *fitna*), kill him.' Retold by Moslem on behalf of the venerable Companion Arfaja ibn Shurayh.

(5) Our paragon in fighting the apostates is the first Caliph Abu Bakr al Sideiq (may Allah be pleased with him). When Prophet Mohamed had died and some Arab tribes abjured Islam, and stopped the payment of *zakat* [tithe], Abu Bakr said:

'By the name of Allah I will fight everybody who will differentiate between prayer and *zakat*. He also said, 'By the name of Allah if they refuse to hand over a camel-string they used to give to the messenger of Allah, I will fight them until they submit.' Moreover, Caliph Ali ibn Abi Talib fought the outlaws after the battle of Safein.

But those who mingle with the outlaws and the Moslem mutineers, and those who feel suspicious of the legitimacy of *Jihad* are the hypocrites and disbelievers of Islamic religion: they are renegades and they deserve chastisement by Hell therein they will abide. In His words to prove this, Allah said, 'Lo! The hypocrites (will be) in the lowest deep of the fire.' (4:145) He also said:

Bear unto the hypocrites the tidings that for them there is a painful doom. Those who choose disbelievers for their friends

Imam Adam Tutu Atrun examines his list of burned mosques. *Photo:
Alex de Waal.*

Burned church in Dabker. *Photo: Alex de Waal.*

instead of believers: Do they look for power at their hands? Lo, all power appertaineth to Allah. (4:138, 139)

Allah (*Subahna wa Ta'ala*) has told the truth.

The signatories are:

> Sheikh Musa Abdel Majid
> Sheikh Mushawar Juma Sahal
> Sheikh Mohamed Saleh Abdel Bagi
> Sheikh Qurashi Mohamed al Nur
> Sheikh al Nayer Ahmed al Habib
> Sheikh Ismail al Sayed Abdalla

The emphasised passage in the first paragraph represents the essence of absolutist, totalitarian government: the total and unequivocal condemnation of those who profess the same beliefs but infer from them a different, and more tolerant, political agenda. This passage, which exhorts the Sudanese people not only to kill Christians and traditional believers, but fellow Moslems as well, is central to an appreciation of the crime that is being perpetrated in the Nuba Mountains today.

Imams and Moslem scholars in the Nuba Mountains dispute the legitimacy of the *Fatwa* and the right of the Sudan Government to destroy or desecrate their places of worship. Ismail Suleiman al Nur studied in the Islamic school in Um Dowaban, Khartoum, for nine years, under Khalifa Yousif wad Badur, a famous teacher in Sudan. Now he is the Imam of Eri mosque, the teacher in Eri Koranic school, and hopes to build an Islamic Institute and Teaching Centre in the village. He told African Rights:[14]

> The enemy has no religion. They are burning our mosques and Korans, and even killing our Imams.
> We have heard the version of the Sudan Government—we are helping the *kufaar* [infidels] and therefore we too are *kufaar*. But for us we are fighting for our rights. They leave nothing for us—they burn our villages, take our animals, destroy our crops.

---

[14] Interviewed in Eri, 10 May 1995.

291

I have a message for Turabi. I would like to remind him of the *Sura* of the cow, where Allah says, he who kills another Moslem intentionally, will have everlasting Hell. We are not *kufaar*, we are Moslems. We want to defend our rights. This *Jihad* is for stealing and looting and killing innocents.

Imam Ismail was concerned that, despite his best efforts, villagers were getting confused about the message of Islam.

I am worried that people are becoming reluctant to go to Islam. Recently there was a call from the Sudan Government, that those Moslems in our area who want to pray faithfully must come to Mendi. Why? Is Allah in Mendi? Allah is everywhere. If you tell people that Allah is in one place, then you are making people doubt that their religion is correct. Islam is the religion of Allah, not just the religion of the Arabs.

We have a *khalwa* [Koranic school]. I teach the Koran to fifty children. We have a problem of mats. They are expensive, and the enemy often burns and loots them. So we have decided not to make or buy prayer mats, so we use the soil for prayers.

Imam Adam Tutu Atrun was equally angry. He disputed the Sudan Government's right to say that the mosques in the non-government areas were not "real mosques" and that the only "real mosques" where genuine prayers could be said existed in the army garrisons. The forty four mosques in his area all existed before the war, when the Sudan Government controlled the area, he pointed out. He wondered when and how they could have forfeited their status as mosques. The Moslems were all Moslems before the war, Imam Adam pointed out, "So how can the government say that there are no Moslems here?"[15]

Desecrating Mosques

Mosques and Islamic leaders in non-government held areas have been targets of the Government of Sudan, equally with churches, priests and church leaders. African Rights was unable to compile a

---

[15] Interviewed in Kauda, 11 May 1995.

comprehensive list of places of worship that have been destroyed, but some Nuba leaders believe that the Sudan Government has now destroyed more mosques than it has churches.

Imam Adam Tutu Atrun, leader of the Moslem delegation to the 1994 religious dialogue conference, has compiled a list of the mosques destroyed by the Government of Sudan in the Otoro and Tira el Akhdar area. He mentioned the following:

* Tombari: burned in 1987.
* Kalkada: desecrated in July 1989. The main mosque is a permanent building so it was not burned, but looted. Imam Omer Ali Juma was killed. The two mosques in Kalkada were also destroyed again in February 1994 (see page 178).
* Kumu: burned and looted in July 1994 (see page 209) and again in February 1995.
* Toror: a permanent building that could not be burned, but which was looted in February 1995. The Koran was torn up.
* Um Derdu: burned in February and again in March 1995.
* Tajura: burned in March 1995
* Kuchama: burned and looted on 17 March 1995.
* Kodi B: desecrated and burned on 20 March 1995. The army looted Korans, mats and prayer jugs
* Kauda: a well-built mosque so it could not be burned, but it was looted on 20 March 1995.

Imam Adam commented simply, "Islam does not allow Moslems to do this."[16]

The destruction of mosques is not confined to this area. The mosque in Karkaraya al Byeara was burned on 21 February 1995. Najib Musa Berdo, judge of the central court of Lagowa County, reported a similar widespread desecration of mosques in the western jebels.[17]

The Julud people are all Moslems. But they burned all the mosques in our area on the basis that they are the mosques of rebels.

---

[16] Interviewed in Kauda, 11 May 1995.
[17] Interviewed in Achiron, 7 May 1995.

Atrocities against Islamic places of worship by the Government of Sudan may have confused some Nuba people about the nature of Islam. But most Nuba Moslems are determined to remain true to their faith, despite the government onslaught. Ibrahim Katin Abdel Karim is the Imam of the mosque in Kuchama East in the Otoro hills.[18]

> We had just finished our prayers when the enemy attacked Kuchama East. It was on Friday 17 March 1995 at about 3:00 p.m. The enemy soldiers burned the village including the mosque. Twenty-five books of the Holy Koran, twenty books of el Hadith, two blackboards, five chairs and 33 prayers mat were burned. They looted three sacks of sorghum, two sacks of groundnuts, three tins of sesame, one mattress and one iron bed. All these items were *zakat* and the mosque's property. Other homes in the village were also looted and they took away all items they could carry with them to Heiban.
>
> I was not surprised that they looted and burned our mosque. For sometime I used to hear that the Government of Sudan thinks that we are pagans. They consider our stay in the rebel areas as betrayal to Islam and therefore we are apostates and deserve to be killed. The government thinks that we should have run away from South Kordofan to their so-called 'peace camps' and leave the areas controlled by the SPLA. What they cannot understand is that our problem is with the 'Islamic' government of al Bashir.

Though he did not profess surprise, Imam Ibrahim was deeply shocked by the outrage of the destruction of his mosque. But he was undaunted.

> It is the first time the Government has burned a mosque in Kuchama, both East and West. This will not discourage us to continue preaching Islam. Many of us had enough Islamic education. The government consider us rebel Imams and say we don't know Islam. They pretend to know Islam better than us because they are Arabs and Islam came to them first. However, I'm convinced that many of us know Islam better than most of their Imams in the North. I will continue preaching Islam here without

---

[18] Interviewed in Kujur el Sha'abiya, 13 May 1995.

the government assistance or help. Even if they ask me for an Imam training in government-controlled areas I will not accept it. I'm sure there is nothing new I can learn from their training except hypocrisy and lies. I studied Islam in the kind hands of *Mawlana Abbas Baballa* in Heiban for four years. I'm from the Gadiriya Sufi sect.

I call upon friends and the world to stop the Government of Sudan from looting our crops, killing innocent people, burning our villages. This policy of destruction and looting has gone on now for too many years. They should be stopped from burning churches and mosques. Any time they burn our mosques we will build them and our Islamic convictions are not affected whatsoever by their atrocities.

RELIGIOUS DIALOGUE UNDER THE SPLM AND THE SUDAN GOVERNMENT

Islamic extremism is all-pervasive in government-controlled areas of Sudan. But in the non-government controlled areas, the religious atmosphere is very different. In many respects, the Nuba tradition of religious tolerance lives on. But both Islam and Christianity are profoundly influenced by the extremist project of the government and the war. There has been a growth of Christianity, particularly the evangelical Sudan Church of Christ.[19]

There have been some religious tensions in the SPLA-controlled areas. These include some Christians and Moslems interfering in traditional believers' celebrations, in particular objecting to the consumption of alcohol. Some Imams and Church leaders have objected to intermarriage between Moslems and Christians, or to conversion from one religion to the other. The SPLA has also had friction with some religious leaders. For instance, the Sudan Church of Christ teaches a strictly pacifist doctrine, and thus its more devoted followers, such as the church youth, refuse to join the SPLA

---

[19] For a discussion of similar issues in Southern Sudan, see African Rights, "Great Expectations: The Civil Roles of the Church in Southern Sudan," Discussion Paper No. 6, April 1995.

for their "national service." While the SPLA has not closed any churches or banned any preachers, it has sought to restrict the numbers of church youth (suspecting that boys who want to avoid serving in the SPLA are using church work as a cover), and has tried to legislate against preaching pacifism (see below). As the civil administration has developed, administrators and judicial officers have also had to adjudicate in disputes between religious groups—forcing them to improvise.

Najib Musa Berdo, the judge of the central court in Lagowa, said that one shortcoming of the SPLM legal code is that it does not give adequate guidelines concerning religious disputes. The case he describes also illustrates the nature of many religious disputes and how they are resolved.[20]

> One of the difficulties is that the [SPLM] code seems not to be complete. There are some crimes with no relevant section in the Code.... Also lacking are some of the provisions for complete religious toleration. Some of the religious people, Christians and Moslems, try to disrupt the celebrations of the Kujurs [traditional priests], to attack them and disrupt what they are doing. When the Kujur complains, he finds nothing in the Code. What we normally do is arrest the aggressors, if they have destroyed something or poured out the *merissa* of these fellows, make them pay compensation and sign a compact to allow the celebrations to be completed.
>
> For example at Katla in 1993, someone died. Being a traditional believer, Kujurs and relatives were carrying him, following their tradition of dancing and singing around the dead person while he is being carried, and drinking *merissa* [sorghum beer]. Some Moslems went and poured out all their *merissa*, took the body of the dead person by force and buried him in the Islamic manner. This created a big fight where many people were wounded. If there had been no quick intervention [by the SPLA] many people might have been killed.
>
> I came and presented this case before the inter-religious conference. It was resolved that any sect that interferes with another religious sect has to be brought to court and sentenced. This

---

[20] Interviewed in Achiron, 7 May 1995.

includes up to the death sentence. From that time there have been no problems.

The conference was officially called the Religious Tolerance Conference and was convened in Tongole, Delami County, on 10 December 1994. Imam Adam Tutu Atrun led the Islamic delegation.[21]

I am a member of the Advisory Council and participated in the Tongole Religious Dialogue Conference as leader of the Moslem delegation. The idea of the conference came from our experience in the past. Most of the religions were coming to compete and divide the people, so we thought it was important to have dialogue. We have a resolution to establish an Islamic Institute. But we agreed that everyone should have freedom of religion, including Kujurs. We resolved that Christians should preach the right Christianity, and Moslems should preach the right Islam. When I say the 'right Islam' I mean what has come from the Koran and Sunna. Many try to make their own interpretations with the view of dividing and confusing people.

More than fifty Imams were invited to the conference. About forty came. Some could not come because of insecurity or distance or the work on the harvest.

The Kujurs did not participate as such. They were there in attendance and we talked to them. Some famous Kujurs from Delami were there, though the ones from this side [Heiban County] did not go. But the formal dialogue was between Christianity and Islam.

Ismail Suleiman al Nur, the Imam of Eri mosque, also attended the conference. He explained:[22]

We have an Islamic Council, set up in 1992. The head is Mohamed Juma Bahri, but he went to the South for the SPLM Convention and has not yet returned. In his place we made permanent the committee headed by Adam Tutu Atrun. This was in Debi.

---

[21] Interviewed in Kauda, 11 May 1995.
[22] Interviewed in Eri, 10 May 1995.

The Ansar el Sunna have a problem because the situation here does not allow them to have the women covered, as there are no clothes. And the culture of the people does not welcome these things [i.e completely covering women]. This was stressed in the religious conference.

The religious conference was convened by the Deputy Governor, Ismail Khamis Jellab, because there was some disharmony between the different religious groups. The Brothers of the Ansar el Sunna and Sufists had, for example, some differences of interpretations. Also there were disputes within the Christian sects. The Deputy Governor thought that people should come together, although the problems were not grave, and agree that Christians and Moslems should live together without problems.

The conference went smoothly beyond their expectations—many people thought beforehand that there would be religious disputes. We were about 47 Moslem Imams, from Delami, Heiban, Nagorban and Regifi. Those from Tullishi and Lagowa were not able to attend. A committee was set up within the conference, led by the Amir of the Moslems, Adam Tutu Atrun.

We have resolved to build an Islamic College and to teach culture while teaching religion. It will be here in Eri. But because of enemy attacks, we haven't yet been able to assemble the grass and bamboo for the construction.

The Conference was concerned not just with relations between the religious communities, but between them and the SPLM. The chairman was Alternate Commander Yousif Karra Haroun, and the interests of the SPLM were also well-represented: religious freedom was guaranteed but challenges to the SPLM on religious grounds were not endorsed. (Any Moslem who opposed the SPLM on such grounds would of course have left the SPLM-administered areas long ago. The position of the pacifistic Sudan Church of Christ is more ambiguous.) The Nuba journal *NAFIR* summarised the nineteen major resolutions of the Conference.[23]

---

[23] "A Report on the Religious Conference Held in Delami County on 10-15 December 1994 under the Auspices of the Advisory Council, South Kordofan." *NAFIR*, issue 2, July 1995. *NAFIR* is published by the Nuba Mountains Solidarity Abroad in London and the Nuba Relief, Rehabilitation and Development Society in the Nuba Mountains and Nairobi.

1. Harmony and co-operation and religions and the various sects of each religion are necessary. All should aim at planting the seeds of love and co-operation, and resolve issues that create hatred and disharmony.

2. Moslem and Christian preachers should be trained and supervised by their respective organisations. Their names should be recorded and registered.

3. The New Sudan Council of Churches should prepare a plan for establishing a Theological College.[24]

4. The Islamic Council should begin the establishment of an Islamic Institute and Teaching Centre (*Mahad*).

5. Any person who preaches contrary to the teachings of the Holy Books with the intention of creating religious disharmony or sectarianism shall be disciplined.

6. Any person who uses religion to direct people against the public interest or the will of the people, as represented by the governing authorities [i.e. SPLM], shall be disciplined.

7. Intermarriage between Moslems and Christians is permitted, and anyone who preaches or agitates to prohibit it shall be disciplined.

8. The observation, preservation and revival of good Nuba values, traditions and customs is emphasised to be necessary.

9. All people have the freedom to practise games and leisure, including dancing and the consumption of alcohol, without undermining community values.

10. Polygamy is acceptable to all whose beliefs permit it, and no religious leaders should exert ideological or psychological pressure against polygamists.

---

[24] *NAFIR* noted that the Sudan Church of Christ already has a Theological College in Um Dulu, but it does not serve the other denominations.

11. A broad-based committee should be formed to allocate and distribute any assistance or donations that are received, whether from religious or secular sources.

12. The numbers of Church Youth should be limited to those necessary for effective spiritual work. Service in the Church should not be abused as a pretext for avoiding National Service.

The conference resolutions have been well-received, though lack of paper and difficulties of travel have meant that they had still not been widely disseminated five months after the conference ended. The Moslem delegation in particular was happy, even with resolutions that appear to go contrary to some of the most widely-held Moslem conventions. Ibrahim Katin Abdel Karim, Imam of Kuchama East, explained:[25]

I was very happy with the intermarriage resolution between Moslems and Christians. I'm happy because there are many Moslem girls unmarried and no Moslems men to marry them. So it is advisable for these girls to marry their Christian brothers than to remain unmarried or even go to the government towns for prostitution or forced marriages by the enemy soldiers. Though our area of Kuchama didn't experience girls going to government towns for marriage it happened in other areas and may happen to us in the future so as elders we have to be careful.

One of the best resolutions of the conference was the establishment of the Islamic Institute and Teaching Centre, *Mahad*. I'm sure this Institute will graduate many Imams who will spread the true Islam in the Nuba Mountains. By true Islam I mean the Islam of tolerance and cooperation with other religious groups.

The Christian delegation was headed by the representative of the New Sudan Council of Churches, Barnaba Angelo. The Catholic and Anglican churches in the Nuba Mountains were also happy with the discussions and resolutions.

---

[25] Interviewed in Kujur el Sha'abiya, 13 May 1995.

As important as the resolutions, however, was the conduct of the conference itself. It lasted for six whole days, and was marked by vigorous debate, with all delegates able to speak and present their views. Though they did not officially participate (due to lack of an institutional structure to represent them) a number of senior traditional priests (kujurs) were in attendance, and their positions were presented to the conference.

The Tongole Conference is a remarkable contrast to the Religious Dialogue Conference held in Khartoum by the Government of Sudan on 8-10 October 1994, amid much publicity. More than one hundred delegates participated, including guests from 27 countries. A reader of the conference proceedings could be forgiven for believing that the Government of Sudan was a model of tolerance.

In the closing session, President Omer al Bashir said: "The Sudan embraces within the arms of its boundaries peoples of all races, cultures and religions. It is imperative that religious values be given their proper place and role in contemporary life...."[26] Dr Hassan al Turabi also presented a paper:

We, in Sudan, are reviving an old rule, by establishing an experiment of dialogue and religious co-existence. Within it every person is free to believe, to worship and refer to his religion in political and civil issues whenever he is in a state where the majority of the people believe in one religion. On the federal government level, religion does not deny the rights of the citizens or deprive them of their rights, we will not close the doors of free competition [for] public posts or political posts regardless of religious belief, because we know that this is the way that leads to social security in the country. We do know that peace between the religions is not a far-fetched thing, but that the challenge facing us is how to surpass religious fanaticism, and to do that, we should intensify dialogue and establish joint forums not to discuss theological issues, but to discuss what we could do altogether to

---

[26] Quoted in: "The Second International Conference on Interreligious Dialogue in Sudan," *Understanding*, 12, (Khartoum, 16 November 1994), p. 5.

spread religious values in the world, the world which is sliding into nasty paganism day after day.[27]

Like the whole conference, Turabi's address needs to be carefully decoded. The second sentence quoted clearly makes freedom of religion dependent upon living in a state with a majority of co-religionists. The final sentence alludes to Turabi's strong opposition to secularism, which he believes to be destroying all that is valuable in the world. The assault on the Nuba peoples who live under SPLM administration falls within Turabi's concept of a "common front", whose aim is "to reject any positivistic ideology which contradicts the divine message and to reject any anti-religious call that aims at destroying religious values."[28] "Reject" means "destroy by all means available."

Despite its name, the Khartoum conference was more in the way of an exchange of speeches on historical, theological and related issues than a true dialogue. There was little opportunity for any speakers other than those proposed by the government to speak. Many members of State Security were in the audience, and the atmosphere intimidated those on the floor who would have liked to present their experiences and opinions. When one Catholic teacher boldly spoke out and made proposals, the chairman of the conference refused to allow them to be debated. In fact, the final communiqué, which is in effect an enthusiastic endorsement of the Sudan Government's position, was not debated at all. The papers were simply handed to President Omer al Bashir at the close.

The "resolutions" of the conference were widely publicised in the government-controlled Sudanese media. But, despite the promises, nothing changed. The weeks following the conference were marked by continuing discrimination and harassment of non-Moslems and Moslems who are not government supporters in Khartoum—not to mention the abuses in the Nuba Mountains and elsewhere.

---

[27] "Inter-Religious Dialogue, Challenges and Horizons," paper presented by Dr Hassan al Turabi, reproduced in "The Second International Conference...", p. 25. His speech to the conference was rather different.
[28] *Op cit*, p. 24.

By contrast, the Tongole Conference received no publicity outside the SPLM-administered areas. Due to lack of pens and paper, the full proceedings could not even be recorded. It was solely designed as a genuine measure to address the local problems of religious dialogue, rather than a piece of propaganda. It indicates that the Nuba tradition of religious tolerance is alive.

CONCLUSION

The Sudan Government's assault on Islam in the Nuba Mountains is its most closely-guarded secret. It is not simply a matter of victimising Moslems. Islam itself, in the form of mosques, Holy Books, the *zakat*, and Imams themselves are among the targets of the Sudan Government, which has declared that true Islam cannot exist in the areas outside its control.

The assaults on the Christian church and traditional Nuba religion are equally crimes. But these attacks are well-known. In addressing its own citizens, the Sudan Government speaks of religious war. Any claim to religious sanction is revealed to be hollow by the widespread desecration of mosques and Korans, and the destruction or looting of the *zakat*. It is an assault on Islam itself.

V

THE SPLA RECORD

The SPLA in the Nuba Mountains has been consistently accused of serious human rights violations. The Sudan Government and its representatives, including government amirs, have of course put all the problems in the region at the door of the SPLA, taking a line that an untruth, repeated often and loudly enough, will eventually become accepted as the reality.

Reports by international organisations on the Nuba Mountains have also said that the SPLA is responsible for human rights abuses, though they have also mentioned the poor quality of the evidence available. In fact, virtually no evidence has been presented for such abuses—it is simply assumed that because the SPLA in the South (including the Nuba troops fighting there) have a record of violations of human rights, the same must be true in the Nuba Mountains. One or two known cases are assumed to represent a much wider pattern. It is also implicitly assumed that some of the accusations made by the Sudan Government and by government chiefs must have some basis in fact. However, as African Rights discovered, neither of these assumptions hold true. The record of the SPLA/SPLM in the Nuba Mountains must be investigated on its own account.

In the South, it is only in the last year that the SPLM—as a movement—has become a reality. Until the First SPLM Convention of April 1994, the SPLA had very few civil institutions worthy of the name. It was simply an army. But this was not the case in the Nuba Mountains. Civil institutions were set up almost from the outset, culminating in the formation of the Advisory Council in 1992. It was no accident that Cdr Yousif Kuwa was chosen to chair the First SPLM Convention.

The SPLA/SPLM record will be the subject of a forthcoming African Rights' report on the Nuba Mountains. A brief overview of the human rights record of the SPLA and the nature of the SPLM civil administration will be presented here.

HUMAN RIGHTS ABUSES BY THE SPLA

African Rights was able to investigate a number of specific allegations of human rights abuses by the SPLA. We discussed the human rights record in general with commanders and civilians, and investigated court records, where they exist.

Killing of Chiefs and Merchants

The SPLA was accused of the assassination of two Kawalib chiefs, Hussein Karbus el Ehemier and Ismail Ali Jiger, in a petition from twelve Delami leaders to the Commander of the 19th Division in Dilling, in July 1989. Other sources indicated that the two had "disappeared." The allegation was later publicised.[29]

African Rights met Mek Hussein Karbus in Um Dulu on 16 May 1995. The Mek was amused by the fact that his death had been prematurely reported and publicised. He explained that he was in fact one of the first supporters of the SPLA in his area, and had run away from threats on the government side. African Rights was unable to meet Mek Ismail Ali Jiger, because his village was about three days' walk away, but his daughter assured us that he too was alive and well.

The SPLA has been accused of the killing of the mek of Tira Limon, Abdel Salaam Musheri Chupa, in 1987. The SPLA does not deny this. Mek Musheri was captured in al Goz by the SPLA and brought to Achiron. The SPLA commander there, Mohamed Ali Tiya accused him of killing many people, arresting them and handing them over to the government. One of the people he was accused of having caused to be killed was Omda Idris Balad of Kerker. Musheri's successor as mek accused him of having led the government troops in attacks in which several villages were

---

[29] Africa Watch, "Sudan: Destroying Ethnic Identity: The Secret War Against the Nuba," *News from Africa Watch*, 10 December 1991.

burned.[30] Whatever the charges, however, there was no proper court held; the commander merely examined the accusations, consulted witnesses, and ordered that Musheri should be executed.

Another allegation, that was reported in the Sudanese press in early 1988, was that an "SPLA-affiliated" Nuba tribe (Shatt) had abducted and killed a trader and looted his property.[31]

African Rights' investigations revealed a more complex story. In December 1987, leading Fellata merchant in Shatt Damam sold the village's sugar ration in Kadugli rather than distributing it at the controlled price to the local residents. The people attacked and looted his property. At the time, the merchant was absent. The local Misiriya militia accused the people of conniving with the SPLA and abducting the merchant, and attacked the village, burned many houses and killed five villagers. Later, the Fellata merchant turned up unharmed—he had merely been travelling. The regional government proposed a conference for reconciliation, which the Shatt people rejected.

In June 1989, the SPLA in Delami launched attacks on mechanised farms and commercial traders. According to the Sudanese press, a tractor and trailer were seized and nine people abducted,[32] and in two separate incidents, five commercial lorries were looted and burned and six people killed.[33] African Rights was unable to confirm these incidents, but the SPLA readily accepted the general fact that such attacks had occurred. When African Rights passed by a burned-out commercial lorry in the Otoro hills, SPLA soldiers reported that it had been "ambushed" in the early days of the war.

---

[30] Mek Jibreel Alin Kabi, interviewed in Achiron, 8 May 1995.

[31] *Sudan Times*, 11 March 1988.

[32] *Sudan Times*, 19 June 1989.

[33] *Al Rayah*, 26 June 1989.

Treatment of Prisoners of War

The principal consistent human rights violation of the SPLA has been the killing of prisoners of war. At the time of African Rights' visit the SPLA held only one prisoner of war, a Ugandan who had been a volunteer Mujahid with the Sudan Government. Many captives are reportedly released, especially Nuba members of the PDF. African Rights was given the names of a number but it was not possible to locate any of them for interview. According to SPLA officers, most released captives return to the government side, having become accustomed to clothes, better rations and other "incentives" the government provides.

However, many captives are also killed. One SPLA officer explained to African Rights that there was no strictly-enforced policy on prisoners of war. Often, he said, "When taken prisoner by the SPLA, they [army soldiers] are not spared." But, he added, "Most PDF who are captured are just released." He elaborated:[34]

> With the army, the [SPLA] soldiers often kill them before they reach the base. If a prisoner of war reaches the base, then his life will be spared. If an SPLA soldier kills a captive, we don't discipline him. We only discipline him if he kills a captive after arriving at base and becoming a prisoner of war.
>
> One incident was last year, when we captured Captain Abdel Salaam, a security officer, in Buram. He was kept as a prisoner in the headquarters at Chanyaro. One of his guards shot him and he died at once. Later the guard was disciplined. He was transferred from his unit and required to be continuously in the front line.

This is a very mild punishment for a grave breach of the Geneva Conventions. It indicates that the SPLA does not place a high value on the life of a prisoner of war.

In 1992, SPLA forces in Tullishi captured two Iranian military advisors, but the soldiers at the front line executed them before they

---

[34] Interviewed in the Nuba Mountains, May 1995. His identity has been concealed, although he did not request anonymity.

could be brought to the commander. The SPLA not only committed a serious abuse of human rights, but lost an opportunity to prove the oft-alleged presence of Iranian soldiers in the ranks of the Sudanese armed forces. On this occasion its failure to establish a policy of respecting the rights of captives lost it a precious chance for making international political capital.

Detainees

The SPLA in South Kordofan holds one political detainee. He is Alternate Commander Telefon Kuku Abu Jelha, who was arrested in December 1993. He had been in contact with the Sudan Government and surrendered the town of Buram to government forces without a fight. At the time, he wrote a letter to Cdr Yousif Kuwa, who was in Southern Sudan, explaining his decision, which was based on his view that peace with the government was necessary at any price. A/Cdr Telefon was arrested on instructions from Cdr Yousif, and has been in detention ever since. Formal charges were laid only when Cdr Yousif returned in 1995. The reasons for the delay were that his letter to Cdr Yousif was an essential piece of documentary evidence, and that two senior officers are required to institute a court martial, and in the absence of Cdr Yousif, only one officer in the Nuba Mountains outranked A/Cdr Telefon. Within a week of Cdr Yousif's return, arrangements for a formal investigation and court martial had been established.

African Rights visited A/Cdr Telefon Kuku in his place of detention. He was not ill-treated, but complained of boredom—he only had a copy of the Koran to read. Visits from his family had been allowed at first but later restricted. African Rights is following his court martial closely.

Two other SPLA commanders died in Southern Sudan in 1993, after having been in SPLA detention. The circumstances of their deaths, along with other detainees, remain unclear. Cdr Yousif Kuwa gave the following account to African Rights:[35]

---

[35] Interviewed in Nairobi, 16 March 1995.

In early 1992 I ordered the arrest of the two alternate commanders Yunis Abu Sudur and Awad el Karim Kuku, for agitation and subversion. I arrested them in the Nuba Mountains, on the basis of intelligence reports reaching me. They were planning to create a split in the ranks of the SPLA in the Nuba Mountains. After preliminary investigation in the Mountains I decided that both required further investigation. They were escorted to the SPLA headquarters in Southern Sudan for more inquiries and for trial, if need be.

In detention they were together with those of Martin Majier Gai, Martin Kajburo, Martin Makur and others. In late 1993 I asked the leadership of the SPLA to pardon the two alternate commanders, Yunis and Awad. The leadership agreed and they were pardoned. Their release was subsequently ordered. Unfortunately, before their release was carried out, they were killed with the other prisoners. Apart from them, the three Martins were also killed in that incident. I was told that they tried to escape from detention. I'm not happy with what I have heard so far. I have asked for a more detailed explanation of the circumstances of their deaths. I'm waiting for more explanations.

The SPLA command has yet to reveal the full truth concerning this incident.

Civilians in the Nuba Mountains are regularly detained by the SPLA after they return from garrison towns and peace camps. Either they are restricted to an area near an SPLA base or actually kept in a prison. They go through a process of interrogation about the nature of the garrisons, the government forces present there, and other matters of military interest. This detention normally lasts a few days only but occasionally is longer. African Rights spoke to one escapee:[36]

> When we reached [the base], the SPLA arrested me and kept me for 45 days. There were four other women sent from the [army garrison] with me, they were also arrested too. The SPLA commander asked me, 'Why did you bring this letter from the government of Sudan?' The SPLA also interrogated me, 'How is the

---

[36] Interviewed in Tira Limon, May 1995. She did not request anonymity but her identity has been concealed.

government staying there, what type of weapons do they have, how do they treat civilians, where did they put you?' And so on.

I was kept in prison. We were given one cup of sorghum for two meals. There was one other woman in prison with me. We were not mistreated. We could go outside in the courtyard of the prison. The other women were released after seven days.

This woman said, "I don't know why I was kept for longer," but it can be surmised that it was because the letter was an invitation to the local SPLA commander to join the "Peace from Within;" this required a more senior SPLA officer to come to investigate.

Conscription

The SPLA has been widely accused of obtaining recruits by force. There is a basis of truth to this. As the New Kush Division first entered in 1989, a number of youths in the area of Lake Abyad were forcibly conscripted. There are also reports of forcible conscription from the western jebels from later in 1989. Such measures were quickly abandoned, partly because the SPLA discovered that involuntary recruits made poor soldiers—they often ran away. It has not resumed. One of the SPLA's main critics inside the areas that it controls, a schoolteacher called Jacob el Nur, was asked if he believed the was SPLA recruiting youths by force. He answered, "No, I don't think that. Maybe, but myself I don't think so."[37]

As the testimonies of SPLA recruits in Chapter I demonstrate, there was considerable social pressure on many youths to join the SPLA. Such pressure still exists and is encouraged by the Movement. However this is far from the forcible and violent conscription used by the Sudan Government for obtain soldiers for the PDF. Soldiering for the SPLA is commonly referred to as "national service" and described as a "duty" for youth, but in fact this is not enforced. One reason for this is that since 1991 at least, the major problem for the SPLA in the region has not been shortage of manpower, but lack of ammunition.

---

[37] Interviewed in Debi, 10 May 1995.

Because all travel is on foot, the SPLA requires porters to carry its ammunition, food and other supplies. Porters are routinely mobilised from the youth of villages: the SPLA commander requests the village sheikh or administrator for the number of porters he requires, who are then instructed to assist the troops. This is unpaid and involuntary labour, a form of levy. Most porters are required to carry the luggage only within their own Payam (sub-district) before handing over to porters from another village. Working as a porter is not popular and there are accounts of soldiers threatening and occasionally beating reluctant porters. There are also cases of requisitioning donkeys without consulting the owners.

Looting and Measures against Looting

Many SPLA soldiers are dressed in rags and have virtually no possessions. The temptation to use their weapons for self-enrichment—or simply for obtaining food—can be severe. Cdr Yousif Kuwa Mekki readily acknowledged this problem.[38]

> If you look at our soldiers, most of them are not educated and not politically conscious, so you should expect that if someone like this has a gun in his hand, he feels he is powerful and can do whatever he wants. And in fact specifically at the beginning of our entry in '89 a lot of soldiers started to rampage and to loot, and we started [to impose] very harsh punishments, even we [sent some to the] firing squad. We tried our best to stop that. Another time when we had hunger in '91-'92, some started to use their guns so they can acquire whatever [they need]. That is why we tried to politicise the soldiers. We try to tell them that it is not our purpose to come and loot our own people and harass them. Whoever does this will be punished. We gave them very harsh punishments.

Another problem highlighted by Cdr Yousif was the expense of marriage in Nuba society. Throughout Sudan, young men struggle to earn enough money pay the high level of brideprice necessary to marry. Nuba soldiers in the SPLA are no exception.

---

[38] Interviewed by the BBC in Um Dulu, 17 May 1995.

At the beginning, when the soldiers came, brideprice was very expensive. When a soldier wanted to marry he had to use his gun [to acquire cattle]. So I called the people, the village councils, and I put the problem to them: 'We have our soldiers, you know they have no salaries, there is nothing they can do to earn, to get money. If we are asking ten or twelve cows for a girl, the only way to marry is to loot. I think that if we solve this problem then we are reducing the looting.' So we agreed to reduce the brideprice to three cows and three goats. Later, in '92. we reduced it again, to two cows and two goats.

At the Religious Conference in December 1994, the monetary value of a cow was fixed at LS 6000 and a goat at LS 500, to prevent the inflation of brideprice should the girl's family insist on payment in cash.

SPLA soldiers still receive no salary, only rations. The SPLA has instituted a system of taxation in kind to obtain enough food for its troops (civilians employed in the administration receive neither salaries nor rations). It has also started farms, and requires that every soldier cultivate a farm to provide at least part of his ration. The commanders, including Yousif Kuwa himself, are also required to cultivate.

The problem of looting continues on a small scale. Some troops continue to steal from villagers. African Rights learned of cases of stealing clothes, fruit and water containers by soldiers.

Accountability

The leadership of the SPLA in South Kordofan insists that it imposes strict accountability on its forces. In a public speech, Cdr Yousif Kuwa asked civilians for their co-operation in this:[39]

We do not want the troops to impose upon [the people], to force anyone because they have guns. If you come to know that any of

---

[39] Speech at SPLA day, Um Dulu, 16 May 1995.

our forces are doing these things, let us know and we will know what measures to take against them.

The chief judicial officer for the Nuba Mountains (or "chief justice"), Romera Liwa Erum instructs all SPLA recruits on the law as part of their training:[40]

> I tell them to avoid raping, looting, threatening etc. Also I give them information about the judicial process and the courts. Some are quick to learn but others are illiterate and cannot understand.

African Rights investigated the central court martial records to evaluate the extent to which the SPLA had implemented measures against its soldiers who were guilty of transgressions. The papers dated back to May 1990, and therefore excluded the first period of the New Kush Division's entry into the Nuba Mountains, when serious problems of discipline had existed and the command had taken what it described as "harsh measures" including using the firing squad.

The papers did not include records of soldiers court martialled for looting, rape or killing civilians. The senior judicial officer, Romera Liwa Erum, said that this was because the first two categories of case were handled by lower courts martial, which did not keep records due to lack of paper, and the third category had not occurred.[41]

The most serious case in the papers was a General Court Martial held on 18 December 1992, of a lance corporal accused of planning to desert to the enemy, and three others who allegedly agreed to go with him. The ringleader was found guilty and sentenced to death. He was executed after written approval from Cdr Yousif Kuwa and the Commander-in-Chief John Garang. The second and third defendants were found guilty, fined fifteen cows (or five years in prison if they failed to pay) and dismissed from the SPLA. The final defendant was found not guilty of desertion but guilty of failing to report their plan; he was sentenced to two months' imprisonment

---

[40] Interviewed in Achiron, 7 May 1995.
[41] Interviewed in Achiron, 7 May 1995.

with labour. This was reported to be the only case in which a death sentence was imposed or carried out since 1990.

More worrying is the low level of concern of the SPLA commanders with minor abuses such as looting small quantities of food from villagers. A minority of SPLA soldiers routinely engages in such behaviour, and their commanders tend to dismiss complaints with the attitude, "What can one expect?" If the SPLA is to respect human rights, it is important that disciplines its troops for relatively small offences just as rigorously as it does for those guilty of major crimes.

THE SPLM ADMINISTRATION

Lack of basic material resources and problems stemming from isolation have a profound impact on all aspects of life in the SPLM-administered areas. Both mechanisms for respecting basic human rights and the capacity for creating civil structures are affected.

Facilities for prisoners are extremely basic—food is meagre and there is no reading material available. But that is no different from life for soldiers and citizens alike. Communication with SPLA headquarters in Southern Sudan is very limited—there is radio contact and occasionally people move by air or on foot. When the South Kordofan delegation went to the 1994 SPLM Convention, they took almost one hundred days to walk overland. Hence any decision that requires reference to a higher authority, such as the Chairman of the SPLM, or to Cdr Yousif Kuwa during his two-year absence, has taken an extremely long time. Within the Nuba Mountains, communication with most areas is possible only by walking. To summon a witness from the western jebels to Um Dulu in the Moro hills would have taken at least three weeks, as it is ten days' walk in either direction. This can make court proceedings slow and expensive.

Until African Rights' visit, there were no copies of any human rights instrument in the SPLA-controlled areas of South Kordofan. There was only a single copy of the SPLM Penal Code of 1984, parts of which had been hand-copied by judicial officers for their own use.

They were unable to copy the whole penal code because there is a dire shortage of paper. Most courts do not even have exercise books to record cases—only the most serious cases are written down, in summary form. There is not a single typewriter and until African Rights' second visit there was no carbon paper. The lack of written documentation makes it difficult to investigate many aspects of administration and the rule of law.

Civil Administration

Yousif Kuwa Mekki wears two hats: he is a military commander and a civilian governor. In contrast to every other senior commander in the SPLA, Cdr Yousif has placed the emphasis on political mobilisation and the establishment of a civil administration. He has put his experience at mobilising a peacetime electoral campaign to work in mobilising an insurgent movement. He told the BBC:[42]

> Since my presence in the Nuba Mountains in 1989, I did politics more than military work. Politically the people are a bit conscious. We didn't make the mistakes of the South. If you are aware of why you are suffering, you can bear it. In the South there is a lack of political activity.

As soon as the SPLA had consolidated areas of the Nuba Mountains, a civil administration began to be created. From the outset, the SPLM dealt with chiefs and village councils. Starting in 1991, elections were held for chieftancies throughout the SPLA-controlled areas. The electorate included all adult males and older women, and voters were asked to line up behind the candidate of their choice. Shortly afterwards, a civil administration began to be established, with heads of counties, payams and villages chosen by the SPLM. It is important to note that these steps were not taken because the world was watching—on the contrary, the world was *not* watching—but because the leadership recognised that they were necessary for the local situation.

---

[42] Interviewed by the BBC in Kapanguria, 1 May 1995.

A major step was taken in September 1992 with the formation of the South Kordofan Advisory Council. In its first meeting it debated the question of whether the war should be continued or abandoned. This inaugural meeting was held in Debi and chaired by Yousif Kuwa, in his capacity as Governor. There were two hundred delegates, most of them civilians, each representing a different area or institution. Yousif Kuwa insisted, "We chose the office not the person," when deciding the composition of the council. Those present in Debi on the final day of the meeting overwhelmingly voted to continue the war.

They also voted to keep the Advisory Council as a permanent institution. Given that the whole SPLM had never held a Convention at that time, the constitutional status of the council was unclear. But, by dint of the blessing of the Governor and the support of the people, its influence was secured. Since then the Advisory Council and its successors have discussed legal matters, and on occasion made changes in customary law (such as levels of bridewealth). But it is not empowered to change the penal code or legislate on matters to do with the military.

Yousif Kuwa left the Nuba Mountains in May 1993. During his two year absence, the council has continued to meet. It has passed and implemented important resolutions—an indication that it is functioning as an institution, rather than a showpiece.

A year later the council met again, in Buram, under the chairmanship of Acting Governor Ismail Khamis Jellab. At this meeting, the delegates renamed themselves the first General Assembly. They agreed that the General Assembly should meet annually, and that a smaller Consultative Council should be established, which should meet three times a year. The other two main items on the agenda were whether to continue the war (a shorter version of the previous year's debate, with the same conclusion) and the selection and briefing of the delegates to attend the First SPLM Convention, to be held in Chukudum in April 1994.

In October 1994, the General Assembly met in Tura. It discussed the improvement of civil administration and the separation of civil and military. It also discussed the strategy for relief, focusing on self reliance and increasing cultivation. Another issue it discussed was

316

the demobilisation of all teachers serving in the SPLA forces, so that they could return to teaching. This was later approved.

More widely, the Council and the civil administration have discussed the "modernisation" of Nuba culture. Certain traditional practices are widely labelled as harmful, such as bracelet fighting, very high bridewealth, and certain food taboos. There is an attempt to restrict or ban some of these practices, while retaining other aspects of traditional culture regarded as beneficial or harmless.

Provision of Services

Since the first entry of the SPLA in 1987, many rural areas of the Nuba Mountains have been without basic services. Since 1989, virtually no rural areas have had a functioning school or clinic or humanitarian assistance programme.

Health

Medical services in the SPLM-administered areas came virtually to a standstill as the war intensified in 1989. Rural clinics closed down as the war spread, and when the SPLA captured small towns such as Um Dorein and Kauda, it found the dispensaries empty of any drugs.

One of the first actions of Cdr Yousif Kuwa to provide services was to encourage a trained nurse, Adam Ali Kunda "Carter", to establish a network of clinics, including a nurses training college. This programme formally began on 1 January 1990, less than one month after the New Kush Division established its headquarters in Chanyaro. Adam "Carter" now bears the title of "Director of Nursing Services", and his training college in Debi is a modest but efficient institution. He was interviewed by the Nuba journal, *NAFIR*:[43]

A total of 456 graduates have completed our course. Our present course has 62 students.

---

[43] "Meeting the Challenge of Health: An Interview with Adam Ali Kunda 'Carter', Director of the Nursing College, Debi, Nuba Mountains," *NAFIR* 2, July 1995.

We have eight teachers. When they are not teaching they are sent on assignment to survey the needs. We have thirteen clinics in the liberated area, and two health centres.

Two of our teachers have the Sudan Nursing Certificate; we have a midwife with a Sudan Midwifery Certificate. The lowest-qualified are nurses who have intermediate school leaving certificate.

Our course lasts six months and covers six subjects: (1) environmental health and health awareness, (2) nursing, (3) surgery, (4) diseases of the stomach and intestines, (5) pharmacy and (6) gynaecology and obstetrics.

To date, virtually the only supply of medicine has been the black market. Small quantities of drugs are smuggled into the SPLA-controlled areas by circuitous routes. In May 1995, the prices of medicines on the black market were:

* One capsule Ampicyllin: LS 250 (approximately £0.30 or US$ 0.45).
* One aspirin: LS 150 (£0.18 or US$ 0.27).
* One chloroquine tablet: LS 300 (£0.35 or US$ 0.52).
* One penicillin injection: LS 3000 (£3.50 or US$ 5.20).

For people on the verge of destitution, as are the great majority of Nuba, these prices are far beyond their reach. Most people who are ill or injured receive traditional treatment only. For example, none of the wounded people seen by African Rights in Dabker had received any modern treatment.

One of the simplest but most crucial medical items is almost unavailable: soap. Some soap is available at extortionate prices on the black market, and in some places simple forms of soap are locally manufactured, but there are whole villages without a single bar of soap, and villagers may pass a year or more without using soap. This contributes to many skin infections and other diseases caused by poor hygiene.

Primary health care is an overwhelming priority for the people of the SPLM-administered areas. To date, there have only been expressions of concern from the international agencies whose mandate should oblige them to act, such as UNICEF and the World Health Organisation, and no action. The Sudan Government has blocked any initiatives, and no UN agencies have been ready to challenge its status as a sovereign government. Voluntary agencies have similarly been blocked.

On 28 March 1995, former US President Jimmy Carter negotiated a two-month ceasefire between the Sudan Government and the SPLA to enable UNICEF to launch a Guinea worm eradication programme. The problem of Guinea worm is acute in various parts of the Nuba Mountains, such as Buram district, where surveys in 1988 found rates of infection as high as 35% in some villages.[44] The agreement excluded the Nuba Mountains, and, as this report has made clear, government military actions continued unchecked during April. The organisation Nuba Mountains Solidarity Abroad drew President Carter's attention to this omission in a fax on 7 April. However, when the two-month ceasefire was extended, the Nuba Mountains was again excluded.

Education

The hunger for education was an important reason why many Nuba youths joined the SPLA. Years on, they have seen what education facilities existed before the war dwindle to nothing, and the opportunities for their own children all-but-vanish. Some school-age children are reportedly so desperate to learn that they are ready to go over to the government side in the hope of an education.

In 1993, the SPLM began a major initiative to encourage the setting-up of schools, supported by local communities. There has been an enthusiastic response, and numerous schools have been established. There are currently 29 schools in Nagorban County alone and a comparable number in Heiban County. Many children are enrolled: between two hundred and nine hundred for each school. There is a severe problem of shortage of teachers, and many people

---

[44] S. Cairncross and A. Tayeh, "Guinea Worm and Water Supply in Kordofan, Sudan," *Journal of the Institution of Water and Environmental Management*, 1988, 2.3, pp. 268-74.

who have completed some years of secondary education but have no formal teaching qualification have been drafted in to teach. Teachers and other educated people who were serving in the SPLA have been demobilised to enable them to teach. There are complaints, however, that some of the schools that were taken over by the SPLA as military bases still remain under military control, rather than being returned to educational use.

Different communities support their schools in different ways. Some schools and their teachers are supported by a system of school fees and others by contributions in kind. The school in Regifi, in the Moro hills, has seven teachers, and each of the students is required to pay LS 10 per month as a fee. There as elsewhere, teachers have to combine their jobs with growing their own food.

The headmaster of the three schools in Kauda area, Ismail Mundo Elno, outlined how the schools came to be established.[45]

There are three schools here, under my supervision, at Kauda, Kumu and Kodi A. They have been established two years. Before the war I worked in the forestry department, and then I returned to farming. But two years ago we met to discuss the situation of our children. We saw that the children were in a bad state, without schools. The SPLA was telling us that it is better for our small children to be educated. So we decided to make three schools, and appointed five teachers to each school.

The teachers are all students who completed grade nine of schooling, apart from one lady who completed grade ten. All the teaching is in Arabic except for in Kodi A where there are two teachers who can teach the English language. In Kauda the school has 257 children, in Kodi A it has 270, and in Kumu about three hundred.

We do not charge school fees here, and the teachers are not paid. Instead there is a Parents' Council that helps the teachers do some farm work. The school year starts in November and finishes on 1 June, so that the teachers can cultivate during the rains. The Parents' Council members then help the teachers with the harvesting and threshing.

---

[45] Interviewed in Kauda, 12 May 1995.

A Miri dancer. *Photo: Julie Flint.*

Otoro boys demonstrate all the stages of clothes production from locally-grown cotton. *Photo: Alex de Waal.*

We teach the children Arabic, mathematics, science, and religion. For religion, the children are divided into Christians and Moslems. And two teachers teach English.

The problems facing any headmaster are huge. Ismail outlined some of them:

There are a lot of problems facing us: clothes, school materials such as chalk and exercise books. There are no exercise books and pens. Every child has to bring his or her own things, if they have them. We have permanent blackboards painted on the wall, and one portable blackboard. For chalk we use either cassava sticks or dried white mud.

Our biggest problem at the moment is that villages are being burned. Children have all their clothes burned, and if they have paper, all their exercises are burned and their pens are destroyed. And as the parents have lost everything they cannot buy anything.

There is also a pressing need for adult education. The SPLA forces contain many men who interrupted their education to join the Movement, and are still anxious to study before it is too late. There is a near-total lack of reading material in any language: no books, no newspapers. Repeatedly, people complained that the intellectual starvation of such prolonged isolation was more debilitating than any physical hardships they had been compelled to undergo.

Relief

All the relief that is available for the poor and needy in the SPLM-administered areas has to be mobilised from within the community itself. The region has been absolutely, totally cut off from any international relief. The Nuba people endured the exceptionally severe man-made famine of 1991-3 without any international assistance whatsoever.

There is a strong spirit of communal solidarity in Nuba villagers. Those who have decided to remain in their villages know that their strength lies in their cohesion, and they support those who are suffering particularly. After the April 1995 attack on Seraf Jamous, the local omda organised a collection of sorghum from all the farmers in the area to provide food for the families who had been burned out. The farmers are all of course very poor and most could provide only one or two cups or sorghum, which is far from enough, but it helped sustain the most needy families for a critical few weeks.

Churches and mosques also organise some relief in a similar manner. Most mosques collect the *zakat* tax and then distribute it to the poor and needy. One of the harshest charges against the Sudan Government was that when it had destroyed mosques, it had burned or looted the grain collected as *zakat*—not just an offence against Islam, but also an attack on the charity provided for the very poor. Many churches also organise collections of food or clothes which are then donated to the poorest members of the congregation.

Following the October 1994 General Assembly meeting, villagers have been encouraged to create co-operative farms, whose produce can be used to feed those stricken by natural calamity or government atrocity. During African Rights' May visit, villagers could be seen preparing a number of these farms in anticipation of the rainy season. But all these measures have severe limits, and all depend on the harvest:[46]

> We suffered drought here last year, and the water has become less. So we are suffering from lack of food. Also some villages were burned. The non-burned areas do not have enough food to feed the burned areas. So people eat less, they sell cows and goats. Lira and Eri have plenty of sorghum. So people go and exchange animals for sorghum in those areas. People who don't have animals go and work on farms for food.
>
> Before, when harvests were good, we could supply the burned villages with enough food. Now we can't. Even the [SPLA] government has no resources. This year, some people will go hungry, especially if the rains are poor.

There is a similar story regarding clothing. Throughout the Nuba Mountains, clothes are in extremely short supply, which causes much distress to people. In some hills, villagers have begun to

---

[46] Sherab Lima Kodi, interviewed in Kujur el Sha'abiya, 13 May 1995.

overcome this problem by growing their own cotton, spinning it and weaving their own clothes. All the equipment and the dyes are locally manufactured; occasionally a brightly-coloured cloth purchased some years ago is unpicked and woven into the cloth to provide a more colourful pattern. In the Otoro hills, African Rights was shown every single part of the process of clothing production, on a self-reliant basis. Impressive though it is, such production can provide only a fraction of the clothing that is needed.

In April 1994, the Consultative Council voted to create the Nuba Relief, Rehabilitation and Development Society (NRRDS), to try to organise relief programmes inside the Nuba Mountains and attract support from abroad. A message was sent to Yousif Kuwa, who was in Nairobi at the time, and a secretariat was appointed in Nairobi. The first secretary-general of NRRDS was Mohamed Haroun Kafi, a former journalist and folklorist who had worked for Radio SPLA. Meanwhile, NRRDS committees were created for each county.

However, the record of the Nairobi secretariat in attracting international donations and funnelling them to the Nuba Mountains proved disappointing, and it was decided to set up the headquarters in the Nuba Mountains. The Consultative Council met with the county committees of the NRRDS on 12 April 1995, and substantially reorganised NRRDS in line with this thinking. Mohamed Haroun did not seek re-election and a new committee was formed.[47]

The NRRDS has made its priority the development of internal self reliance, though it has actively sought funds from international organisations. But it faces almost insurmountable problems of access and so far the relief that it has succeeded in delivering is very small in quantity.

Assistance to Widows and Orphans

The SPLM bears a particular responsibility to the widows and orphans of its soldiers who have died. As the Movement has very little money, it is clearly unable to provide a pension as a

---

[47] See: "NRRDS Re-organization," *NAFIR* 2, July 1995.

government would do. Some assistance is provided, but solely on an *ad hoc* basis—a fact that has made some widows angry. One of them is Jalila Hakim Tutu, a 25-year-old from Regifi in the Moro hills:[48]

> My husband Suleiman Margus joined the SPLA in 1986. He was killed in Ehamara battle in 1989. The news of his death was communicated to me by his brother Juma Margus. [Cdr] Ismail Jellab gave me some assistance. But what makes me angry with the SPLA is that I have to run after them for assistance. I beg for medicine and clothes for my two children Iserena and Anis. I know they [the SPLA] are in difficulties but they should follow up the fate of the widows. I now cultivate my farm and sometimes get three sacks of sorghum in a relatively good harvest. I can feed my children but I can't buy them clothes or medicine. I don't have money for that. The death of my husband caused me to face life alone. It is very difficult but what do I do?

Other widows tend to be more resigned to their poverty and lack of support from the SPLA. Susan al Janub went to the Koyi force headquarters to ask for help, "but in that place I saw that the soldiers themselves had nothing. So I did not ask."[49] The widows often have pathetically low hopes for what the future can bring for them and their children. African Rights spoke with Samira Suleiman el Kamin, a mother of two, whose husband Yousif Mamur was killed in March 1994. She did not expect any assistance as "I have only two children":[50]

> I cultivate sorghum in the farm and I miss husband's contribution very much as he helped me in the farm. He would have added more to the harvest. I now sell chickens to buy medicine when my children need medicine. It is sad life but we have no choice, it is our fate. I intend not to marry as the war goes on because the coming husband may also be killed. Even if he is not a soldier he could be killed as the enemy these days kills anyone they find.

---

[48] Interviewed in Um Dulu, 18 May 1995.
[49] Interviewed in Um Dulu, 17 May 1995.
[50] Interviewed in Um Dulu, 18 May 1995.

When our government of SPLA will be a position to provide assistance I only need a set of clothes for the children and myself. This is all that I want.

Another destitute widow is Amal Badi Angalo, who has to support seven children after her husband's death. Her account makes it clear how she has very different expectations of the responsibilities of the SPLA compared to the government.[51]

My husband was Andreas Shalal Kuku. Before the war he was a school watchman. He joined the SPLA in 1987, because he was treated badly by the administration of the school. He got angry and left to join the SPLA.

When Andreas left, I was cultivating according to my ability. But it was not like before, when he was earning money. Andreas went to Ethiopia and trained there. But he fell ill in the training centre and died there in 1988. I only heard about it in 1989, when the colleagues who were there with him returned to the mountains.

I did not receive anything from the SPLA. I have only received some assistance from the church, with one tin of sorghum. I never even thought of asking the Movement for assistance. I am not angry with the SPLA, because it is a Movement—people have joined it to liberate themselves. Even me, I may get killed, even though I am not a soldier. If someone dies, should you get angry with the SPLA or with the Government of Sudan?

If my husband had been killed during his duties at the school, I would get angry if they didn't pay me my pension. It is because they are a Government and they have money. But the SPLA is a Movement with no money, not even for salaries, certainly not for pensions for the widows.

Now I am having problems. There is not enough food for my children. My oldest son is in Khartoum and cannot help me. The second son has a mental disorder and cannot help. So there is no-one to help me. We have many problems. My children are completely naked; we cannot go to occasions like SPLA Day because we have no clothes, so we stay at home.

---

[51] Interviewed in Um Dulu, 17 May 1995.

The Rule of Law

The judiciary in the SPLM-administered areas is severely handicapped by lack of trained personnel and essential equipment such as legal texts, exercise books and the like. However, starting in 1990, the SPLM attempted to establish a judicial system. At first, it was based on military courts martial and traditional sheikh's courts. In 1992, this basic structure was expanded with the creation of central courts in each of the seven counties. The immediate challenge was to find the right people to staff the courts: they had to be trained.

Agostino al Nur Ibrahim Shamila was one of the first to go for training. He describes himself as "not a lawyer as such": he is a former catechist and holds the rank of first lieutenant in the SPLA. Agostino was summoned by Governor Yousif Kuwa on 4 March 1992, and then sent for a three month "crash course."[52]

> At that time we were facing a big problem: no people had any legal know-how. We felt that there was a need to establish a system. The leadership decided that to make things move on the side of the judiciary, it was necessary to give some people a crash programme in law.
>
> The programme was at Mirawi. Enoch Manyon trained us. He is a first lieutenant, a former major in the police force, from Bahr el Ghazal. He trained us in how to make a police investigation. We were taught using the Sudan Penal Code and the Criminal Procedure. We were not trained in the settlement of civil disputes—that was left to the local native courts. Matters of livestock, land, marriage cases, family law, it was told to us clearly, have to be settled by native courts accountable to tradition and customs. But pure criminal cases come to us immediately.
>
> There were two people on the course. A second batch was trained in 1993, of four or five people. The course lasted three months. We were not given any items: no pens, no books. But we took the initiative to try to buy exercise books and pens. The same happened for the second batch. There was no third batch.

---

52 Interviewed in Achiron, 7 May 1995.

The number of judges is currently seven: five are civilians and two are soldiers, including Agostino. The head of the judiciary, Romera Liwa Erum, is planning to train more judicial officers, but cannot presently do so because of lack of resources. Judicial officers are not paid. The two soldiers continue to receive their military rations, but the civilians are required to cultivate if they are to eat.

The basis of the law is the 1983 SPLM Penal Code, as amended in 1984. It was drafted by the late Martin Majier. Only one copy exists in the Nuba Mountains. It delegates many cases to the customary chief's courts, and follows customary law for many crimes. Thus the punishment for murder is the payment of *diya* (bloodmoney) plus a fine (or a prison term if the convicted fails to pay). The punishment for rape with an unmarried girl is the payment of bridewealth to the girl's family and compulsory marriage to the girl when she reaches marriageable age. For rape with a married woman, the punishment is a fine. The code has 74 sections and has been criticised by the judicial officers for its incompleteness. One judge, *Mawlana* Najib Musa Berdo, said:[53]

> One of the difficulties is that the [SPLM] code seems not to be complete. There are some crimes with no relevant section in the Code. For example, the Code talks about rape but not about adultery. This is a problem because we see many cases of adultery brought to us on appeal from lower courts.

There are four different levels of court: Sheikh's Court, Mek's Court or People's Court, Central (county) Court and the "High Court," which is the same as the military General Court Martial. The different courts are able to impose different levels of fine or imprisonment, and only the General Court Martial is empowered to impose the death penalty. Only once has the death penalty been imposed, in the defection case mentioned above.

Mawlana Najib listed some of the many problems he and his colleagues face in trying to provide justice. He started with the training: "What we have can't really be called training at all." He continued with a list:

---

[53] Interviewed in Achiron, 7 May 1995.

*   There is no stationery to keep the records.

*   There is a lack of clerks. In the central courts, judges act as clerks. In the lower courts, we tried to have clerks, but they are just volunteers, and we cannot always rely on them.

*   Lack of clothing: some people cannot appear in court as witnesses through lack of clothes.

*   There are no incentives for the judges, especially the civilians who do not receive rations. As a result there are often long delays in seeing cases because the judges have to cultivate their farms.

The problems of the Central Courts are compounded at the level of Mek's Court or People's Court. Sherab Lima Kodi, one of the meks of Otoro, explained:[54]

I am president of the People's Court here. It has four members, all elected. For all of us it is our first experience to work in a court. Our clerk is Farouk Idris, a farmer with grade nine schooling, so he can read and write. After we were elected, we were given some guidance in running the court, but no training. Agostino Nur from the SPLA judiciary came and advised us. The guidance concentrated on our powers—what we were authorised to do and not do. Our court sits every Tuesday in Kirindi central, in Luchulu. Sometimes the cases go on appeal to the central court in Kauda, where judge Ahmed Abella Kuku hears the cases.

Like everything else in the Nuba Mountains, the operation of the judiciary is subject to disruption caused by the attacks of the Sudan Government. Mek Jibreel Alin Kabi of Tira Limon, made a major effort to keep records, ultimately in vain:[55]

The court sits every Saturday. Most of the cases we see are on appeal. I have a clerk in my court, Ismail Lurti. He records all cases from start to finish. We used to have a register, filled up over five years, but it was burned or taken when the government attacked Seraf Jamous. Since then, we have been recording on any piece of paper.

---

[54] Interviewed in Kujur el Sha'abiya, 13 May 1995.
[55] Interviewed in Achiron, 8 May 1995.

328

The administration of justice in the SPLM-administered areas of the Nuba Mountains will be analysed in more detail in a future African Rights report.

CONCLUSION

In Southern Sudan, the human rights record of the SPLA and the civil administration of the SPLM have rightly come in for serious criticism. In the Nuba Mountains, the SPLA/SPLM has a different record. In the early years of the war, roughly from 1987-89, there were numerous abuses of the kind that have been characteristic of the war in the South. But almost at once there was a serious and protracted effort to discipline the troops and bring their abuses under control. This was not simply a matter of enforcing a code of conduct, but involved addressing fundamental social and economic issues such as the level of bridewealth and the supply of food to the SPLA forces. The problems of human rights abuses by SPLA soldiers have not been ended—in particular, serious abuses against prisoners of war remain common, and tolerance of minor infractions remains. However, serious abuses are now much fewer than before, and the command recognises that they still need to be reduced.

The SPLM in the Nuba Mountains was also well ahead of its counterparts in the South in the creation of the institutions of civil administration, notably the Advisory Council. Efforts to provide basic social services such as health began within a year of the SPLA securing areas, and were started without any outside assistance, nor any prospect of such assistance. The development of civil structures has been severely handicapped by lack of basic resources. But, among the ordinary people of the non-government held areas of the Nuba Mountains, there is a strong determination to ensure that the current momentum towards democratisation continues.

CONCLUSIONS

The policy of the Sudan Government, concealed under slogans such as "Popular Mobilisation", "Peace from Within" and "Peace Camps", amounts to despatching the Nuba to oblivion. The aim is to destroy the Nuba peoples as they have existed. This is not happening suddenly through rapid evacuation or massacre, but through a longer-term policy of attrition. There is wholesale destruction: the army would flatten the mountains too if they had the means. There is methodical rape, and there is the enforced acculturation of children. Should the government succeed, the Nuba—or those of them who remain—will no longer be an array of diverse peoples with their rich variety of languages and cultures; instead the "Nuba" will be a permanent underclass of deracinated people, condemned to second-class citizenship.

The Question of Genocide

There is no good word in the English language to describe this process of forcible dismemberment of a society: "ethnocide" is too technical and "ethnic cleansing" implies the physical removal of a population from its territory, which was only briefly the case in the Nuba Mountains, in 1992. "Genocide" is usually taken to imply the physical elimination of a people, as attempted by the Hutu extremists against the Tutsi minority in Rwanda. However, the legal definition of "genocide", as contained in the 1948 Convention, is broader.

> In the present Convention, genocide means any of the following acts committed with intent to destroy, in whole or in part, a national, ethnical, racial or religious group, as such;

330

(a) Killing members of the group;
(b) Causing serious bodily or mental harm to members of the group;
(c) Deliberately inflicting upon the group conditions of life calculated to bring about its physical destruction in whole or in part;
(d) Imposing measures intended to prevent births within the group;
(e) Forcibly transferring children of the group to another group.[56]

"Genocide" is an emotive word and is not to be used lightly. But the evidence presented in this report makes it abundantly clear that the policies of the Sudan Government meet the criteria as laid out in the Genocide Convention. The campaign against the Nuba can be called "genocide by attrition". It certainly warrants a tribunal to investigate crimes against humanity, and prosecute those responsible. Some of the men who have perpetrated this crime have been named in this report.

A key point to bear in mind is that "the Nuba" are not one group but many. The Sudan Government may argue that its policies will leave many Nuba people still alive and within the boundaries of the Nuba Mountains. But the survival of different Nuba groups—Otoro, Tira, Kawalib, Moro, Shatt, Korongo, Miri, Tullishi, Nyimang, Wali, Ghulfan, Abu Januq, Tima, etc.—is a different matter. Each of these groups—and many more who may number only a few thousand individuals—are entitled to protection against genocide.

International Responsibility

The war against the Nuba is a crime perpetrated by successive Governments of Sudan. The international role is one of omission—almost nothing has been done internationally either to expose the crime or prevent it from relentlessly progressing towards its completion.

---

[56] Convention on the Prevention and Punishment of the Crime of Genocide, 1948, Article II.

331

The most concrete international action occurred in 1992, at the height of the Tullishi offensive and the relocations. Several western embassies in Khartoum, led by the Netherlands, protested against the aerial bombardment of villages in the western jebels. The then-U.N. Under-Secretary General for Humanitarian Affairs, Jan Eliason, visited Khartoum in September and was forced by pressure from human rights organisations and journalists to put the Nuba on the agenda of his discussions with the government. In October, the U.S. Congress passed a resolution deploring human rights abuses in Sudan, and specifically mentioning the Nuba Mountains. But little happened: the Sudan Government appeased western governments, the U.N. and aid agencies by granting limited humanitarian access to the displaced camps, and fundamental human rights concerns were pushed aside.

The mandate of Operation Lifeline Sudan (OLS), launched in April 1989 with UNICEF as the lead agency, covers all the war zones of Sudan—the South and the so-called "transitional" areas in the North. It therefore encompasses the Nuba Mountains. But OLS operates under agreement with the Government of Sudan. The government has consistently prohibited any humanitarian access to all non-government held areas of the Nuba Mountains, and has severely restricted access to the garrison towns and peace camps. This has never been openly challenged by OLS, nor indeed by any other UN agency or bilateral agency. The reason is that senior staff in UNICEF believe that to challenge the Sudan Government on the Nuba Mountains would jeopardise their programmes elsewhere in Sudan, in both North and South. It is implicit blackmail, which raises profound questions about the concerns and ethics of humanitarian operations. But it is important to note that the failure of OLS to confront the Sudan Government over the Nuba Mountains also implies that the government would win such a confrontation—i.e. that the western donors would not be prepared to stand on principle, and would be ready to sacrifice the Nuba for their "humanitarian access" elsewhere.

The failure to work to assist or protect the Nuba is particularly reprehensible for agencies that have a special mandate for women and children. The extent of the violation of Nuba women's and children's rights need not be repeated here. Their rights are also violated in Khartoum, where the government's huge and abusive relocations programme, and its abduction of children for forcible acculturation, happens on the doorstep of the national offices of international agencies. But there is a deafening silence from the international children's agencies. Silence on the human rights of minority groups is the price to be paid for continuing to operate in government-held Sudan, and it is a price that, it seems, they are ready to pay.

Since the launch of "Popular Mobilisation" in mid-1993, the Sudan Government has tried to attract international agencies to the main towns and peace camps in the Nuba Mountains, to care for the "returnees" and start development programmes. In public statements, the government has expressed its gratitude to the World Food Programme, CARE and UNICEF for responding to the request, and bemoaned the fact that many other agencies have not yet responded. International agencies that consider the broader picture are right not to respond: the controlled supply of relief assistance to peace camps is an intrinsic part of the total strategy of political subjugation and social dismemberment.

The Sudan Government, having declared victory, is also eager to attract investment for further expansion of mechanised agriculture in the Nuba Mountains. Such an expansion, were it to occur, would be simultaneously a mechanism for dispossession of villagers, and rewarding merchants, army officers, and the opportunistic leaders of "Peace from Within." So far, international interest in financing such schemes is lacking. It should continue that way.

There is a growing suspicion that abandoning the Nuba is the price that the international community is ready to pay for peace in Sudan, or at least relatively smooth relations with the Sudan Government. In March 1995, when former U.S. President Jimmy Carter negotiated a ceasefire to facilitate UNICEF's Guinea worm eradication programme, it included the South but not the Nuba Mountains. When the Nuba Mountains Solidarity Abroad faxed President Carter on 7 April drawing his attention to the acute problem of Guinea worm in the Nuba Mountains, the reply was a polite request for more information. The Nuba Mountains were

333

omitted again when the ceasefire was extended in May. No doubt, introducing the Nuba question to the negotiations would have complicated matters and jeopardised the Southern ceasefire and the Guinea worm programme there. The trade off appears to be: UNICEF can eradicate Guinea worm, but only if the government can eradicate the Nuba.

The UN Special Rapporteur for Sudan, Gáspár Bíró, visited Kadugli in 1993, but was prevented by the Sudan Government from visiting the SPLA-controlled areas. That prohibition stands up to today, and indeed has been expanded so that Mr Bíró has been declared completely *persona non grata* by the Sudan Government. United Nations protocol means that even though Cdr Yousif Kuwa has invited Mr Bíró to the SPLA-held areas, he is unable to go. Western governments have not been energetic in pressing for the Sudan Government to allow Mr Bíró access, nor to bend the rules so that he can visit despite the government's opposition.

The same discomfort with the Nuba appears when the issue of self-determination is addressed. Many foreign governments increasingly believe that the separation of the South is the only viable way to end the civil war in Sudan. But what of the Nuba? Are they to be granted self-determination too, or is their eradication to be the acceptable price of a deal to end the war? Many politicians and diplomats would be relieved if the Nuba "problem" were to go away. If they delay long enough, the Sudan Government will oblige them by removing the Nuba altogether.

This implies an international conspiracy to abandon the Nuba. But, more than any conspiracy, there is a confusion: what is really happening in the Nuba Mountains, and what can be done? Western diplomats also fear that their suspicion that the government engaged in genocide may be correct—and that will entail an obligation to act. Their suspicion is correct. There is a moral imperative on all member states of the United Nations and those who profess to stand for basic human rights to prevent the crime of genocide, and punish those responsible. Foreign governments and international organisations have evaded this responsibility. Their main defence has been that they do not know what is going on. This excuse no longer holds—nobody can claim ignorance any longer.

334

The countries of the region, and especially the four members of the Inter-Governmental Authority on Drought and Desertification (IGADD), bear particular responsibilities towards the Nuba. The four IGADD members, Eritrea, Ethiopia, Kenya and Uganda, have jointly sponsored a series of peace talks between the Sudan Government and the SPLA in recent years. Unfortunately, the Nuba Mountains have remained off the IGADD agenda (in part because the SPLA has failed to raise the issue).

Three of the four IGADD governments (Eritrea, Ethiopia and Uganda) have emerged from brutal and protracted wars against highly abusive regimes. The leaders of these countries know from personal experience that a nation cannot be stable and peaceful while extreme abuses of human rights are perpetrated, and a significant minority has major grievances that remain unaddressed. Presidents Isseyas Afeworki, Meles Zenawi and Yoweri Museveni should be aware that the rights of the Nuba are ignored to the peril, not only of Sudan, but the whole region.

The Nuba Mountains should be on the agenda for IGADD. This should include a range of issues for discussion, including the recognition of the right of the Nuba peoples for representation in any negotiations on the political future of Sudan, the need to enforce respect for human rights in the Nuba Mountains, the need for material assistance to the SPLM-administered areas, and the imperative of halting the genocide.

A special responsibility falls upon the Organisation of the Islamic Conference and its member countries. The Sudan Government is committing its crimes in the name of Islam, and some of these crimes are against the Islamic religion itself. The OIC should condemn all crimes against humanity and the abuse of Islam, and should investigate the desecration of mosques and Holy Books. The Arab League and its members have a similar obligation.

The Nuba in Sudanese Politics

The Sudanese opposition has served the Nuba people little better than the current government of President Omer al Bashir.

335

When in government, the Umma Party was the leading force behind the militia policy and the campaign against the Nuba. It is Prime Minister Sadiq el Mahdi, Interior Minister Mubarak el Fadl, Kordofan Governor Abdel Rasoul el Nur and other leading Umma figures such as Fadallah Burma, who bear much of the responsibility for the current human rights disaster in the Nuba Mountains. Some Umma politicians, such as the former leader of the Parliamentary Group, Hireka Izz el Din, have since joined the military government and continued to participate in military campaigns.

Now they are in opposition, the words "democracy" and "human rights" roll off the tongues of Umma Party leaders with hollow predictability. But there is no indication that the Umma Party has changed its stand on the Nuba. It still sees the Baggara as one of its main political constituencies, and believes that supporting Baggara expansionism is a way to win back the Baggara leaders who are now with the government. The Umma Party has expressed no regrets, let alone made any apology, for its crimes in the Nuba Mountains. The Nuba remain deeply suspicious of Umma intentions, and the party has consistently opposed allowing self-determination for the Nuba.

A clear statement from the Umma Party acknowledging its past crimes in the Nuba Mountains and affirming a policy of respect for all the rights of the Nuba people is long overdue. Until such a firm commitment is made, the suspicions of the Nuba people that the Umma has the same policy as the current government will be quite justified.

The DUP does not have such a poor record in the Nuba Mountains, but it is still a party representing a narrow sectional interest, rather than a truly national party. With a broader vision for Sudan, the DUP could easily have capitalised on Nuba disenchantment with the Umma Party, and made a strategic alliance with the SNP or other Nuba groups in the 1980s. It failed to do so. Along with the Umma Party, the DUP is deeply divided over questions such as Islamic law and self-determination for the South, raising Nuba suspicions that it shares the current government's intention of imposing an Islamic state. The DUP has recently developed some interest in the marginalised peoples of Northern Sudan, but this has yet to translate into any policy commitments. The

Nuba people are waiting for a clear commitment to their fundamental rights from the DUP.

The Umma Party and the DUP dominate the opposition National Democratic Alliance (NDA), which presents itself as the alternative government to Omer al Bashir and Hassan al Turabi. However, the Nuba have good reason to suspect that an NDA government would not represent a fundamental change in northern policy towards the Nuba.

The SPLA has a huge debt to the Nuba. Not only has the Nuba Mountains been one of the major battlefronts in the war, but over three thousand Nuba troops have fought in the South, and have remained consistently loyal to Commander John Garang. The SPLA has also benefited from Cdr Yousif Kuwa, as a member of delegations to peace talks and on international tours. The SPLM relied heavily on Yousif Kuwa's skills as chairman of the 1994 Convention. But the SPLA commitment to the Nuba remains uncertain. Although the SPLA formally demands that the Nuba Mountains be granted self-determination, many suspect that this commitment may be abandoned for the sake of a wider compromise.

Deep Nuba fears were aroused by the signing of the "Chukudum Agreement" between the SPLA and the Umma Party on 12 December 1994. Clause 2 recognises "the right to self-determination as a basic human and peoples right." But Clause 4 contains a disagreement. Contradicting the SPLA position:

> 4.2 The Umma Party rejects the mention and inclusion of the Nuba Mountains, the Abyei Region and the Ingessena Hills in the Self-determination clause because it does not recognise the right to Self-determination for any group outside the Southern Sudan.

The Umma signatories were Dr Omer Nur el Dayem and Mubarak el Fadl.

The SPLA must elevate its commitment to the Nuba into an integral part of its negotiating position with northern political parties and with the government, whether through IGADD or any other intermediaries (such as President Carter). The SPLA should refuse to sign any agreement that does not give the Nuba people equal rights to Southerners.

The attitude towards the Nuba by the political parties and the SPLA command is indicative of a more widespread patronising attitude among the opposition leadership. They hold that solutions will be found by making deals among the leaders, not by popular mobilisation. This attitude has been disastrous for Sudan, and will continue to be so.

Self-Determination from Inside

Some Nuba people, and many of their foreign sympathisers, put their faith in an international rescue. Others hope that a deal between a government in Khartoum and the SPLA can resolve the crisis. But a focus on international responsibility and capacity for action should not obscure the fact that the central actors in this are the Nuba people themselves.

The Nuba faced the abyss of imminent collective annihilation in 1992. They are still facing genocide. But, facing this abyss totally alone, they have drawn upon a tremendous will for survival. They faced down the full might of the government *Jihad*. And then, at the very nadir of the war, the Nuba peoples began an exercise in democracy, in the form of convening the Advisory Council and debating the fundamental question: "should the war continue?" The democratic experiment has developed; at the outset it was sponsored by the SPLM, but it has gained a momentum of its own.

"Self-determination" has become a political slogan and a promise in contemporary Sudan. In the mouths of political leaders, it is an event (a referendum) and a decision (to separate or to combine into a unitary or federal state). But in the hands of villagers in the Nuba Mountains it is something far more profound: it is a process whereby ordinary people are able to discuss and debate, influence their civil and military leaders, and begin to take control of their collective political destiny. What the outcome of this process will be, nobody knows. There is a debate among Sudanese intellectuals and politicians as to whether the Nuba peoples warrant "self-determination". This debate is too late: the Nuba have already begun

338

to exercise self-determination. Should there be peace, the Nuba people will be the most organised, articulate and democratic in presenting their demands to the Sudan Government, the SPLA, the region and the world. It might be called "self-determination from within."

There is a danger that an international rescue would trample upon this essential process of self-determination. If international relief agencies were to rush into the SPLM-administered areas and establish big feeding camps, and remove the few remaining educated Nuba to staff their programmes (as routinely happens elsewhere), they would find themselves undermining the very spirit of resistance and self-reliance that has brought the Nuba through the fire up to now. Nuba leaders are fully aware of the disastrous consequences of "the poison of relief", as they call it, but it is unlikely that many Nuba farmers or educated people would resist its blandishments for long. By creating dependency and undermining the pride and self-determination of the Nuba people, the international agencies would, once again, find themselves doing the government's work. The Nuba people, who have achieved pride after so long and at such a high cost, must not be reduced to servility once again by their would-be saviours.

International relief agencies and human rights organisations must find a new way of working in the Nuba Mountains if they are not to trace the same path to doom that has been followed elsewhere in Africa. The essence of this approach must be solidarity: supporting the efforts of Nuba people to become masters of their own destiny. This is a political agenda; those who claim to be solely "humanitarians" have no place where a people are fighting for collective survival. "Neutrality" has no place between the forces of the genocidal oppressor and his would-be victims. Genocide is wrong, and only those who have the courage not only to say so, but to support the people's own resistance to genocide, are deserving of the privilege of working alongside a people whose experience of suffering and defiance has been as profound as any in history.

In a war which is waged directly against a civilian population, its economic base and its social fabric, basic material assistance in the form of medicine, seeds, clothes and educational materials are weapons against genocide. Loud and repeated condemnation of the Sudan Government for its crimes are also weapons. Most economic sanctions have already been invoked against the government, but moral condemnation can still hurt. Moslem people and the governments of Islamic countries should condemn Sudan for desecrating mosques and committing other crimes against Islam, while claiming to fight under the banner of Islam.

Cut off for so long, many Nuba tend to see themselves as a people who have much to learn from the outside world. They have less to learn than they might imagine. Isolation has advantages, though they may seem obscure at the time. It is important that the Nuba peoples recognise the validity of their history: their heroism, their extraordinary resilience, and the strength of their communal values. Mere survival is an achievement, which has helped to forge a new, stronger identity. Yagoub Osman Kaloka spoke for the Tira people:[57]

> The Tira have learned enough from this war. They have come through the serious hunger and suffering of 1990-92, they have become well built-up. They can resist. They know how to defend their culture.

If the Nuba peoples do succeed in resisting genocide, and surviving the onslaught against them, it will have been through their own efforts. But the odds are against them—the survival of the Nuba remains in the balance. We can only hope that, from now on, the Nuba people will not have to face their genocide alone.

---

[57] Interviewed in Tira Limon, 23 May 1995.

INDEX

Fama, 33, 63, 243, 256
Fariang, 92, 129, 198, 205
Farouk Orem, 199
Fayo, 45, 71
Fellata, 13, 77

Gardud, 60
Gardud al Basham, 43, 70, 89
General Union of the Nuba Mountains, 50, 55
Ghulfan, 11, 41, 120, 200
Gotang, 67

Habila, 40, 43, 89, 204
Hajar el Dabib, 63, 66
Hamad Abu Sudur, 44, 46, 201, 258
Hamed el Sheikh (Brig), 61
Hamar, 11, 64, 129
Hamdan Hassan Koury, 108
Haroun Abdel Rasoul Kafi, 99
Hassan al Turabi, 112, 303
Hawazma, 11, 65, 203
Hazim Yagoub Rahhal, 201
Heiban, 38, 68, 96, 135, 198, 209, 232, 251, 254, 256, 259, 271, 283
Hireka Izz el Din, 72, 203, 336
Humr—see Misiriya
Hussein Karbus el Ehemier, 46, 305
Husseini, Lt-Gen Sayed—see al Husseini

Ibrahim Nayel Idam (Brig.), 72
Idris Kaluwa, 199
Iranian military advisors, 116, 307
Islamic African Relief Agency, 211
Ismail Khamis Jellab (Cdr), 54, 64, 76, 116, 129, 316

Jebels Task Force, 65
Jellaba, 11, 40, 92, 100
Julud, 17, 21, 80, 115, 248, 295
Jurham Omer, 46

Kabshur Kuku Gimbil, 203
Kaduru, 41, 89
Kafi Tayara el Bedin, 33, 200, 202
Kalara, 70
Kalkada, 68, 86, 136, 236, 260, 268, 294
Kalogi, 92
Kamand, 89, 275, 309
Kamda, 24, 76, 118, 249
Kandermi, 67
Karandel, 49
Karkar, 67, 248
Karkaraya, 227, 285
Katcha, 83, 97, 201, 266
Katla, 117, 265, 298
Kauda, 36, 68, 198, 216, 232, 258, 262, 271, 282, 288, 294, 320, 328
Kawalib, 11, 21, 41, 62, 69, 136, 201, 274
Keiga, 39, 84, 85, 127, 133
Kernalu, 236, 329
Khalid Abdel Karim al Husseini, 109, 196
Khartoum, 51, 52, 58
Kodi, 230, 262, 269, 287, 294
Komolo, 56, 100
Korongo Abdalla, 27, 68, 80, 83, 103, 133, 200, 241, 265, 281
Korongo Angolo, 22, 82, 243
Kortala, 44, 89, 213
Kuchama, 90, 135, 136, 232, 251, 271, 273, 285, 294-5
Kujur, 21, 42, 297, 302

342

AFRICAN RIGHTS' PUBLICATIONS

Book

Rwanda: Death, Despair and Defiance, Second expanded edition August 1995, 1200 pages.

Reports

Somalia: Operation Restore Hope: A Preliminary Assessment, May 1993, 60 pages, price £4.95 or US$7.95.

Somalia: Human Rights Abuses by the United Nations Forces, July 1993, 35 pages, price £3.95 or US$6.95

The Nightmare Continues... Abuses Against Somali Refugees in Kenya, September 1993, 54 pages, price £4.95 or US$7.95.

Violent Deeds Live On: Landmines in Somalia and Somaliland, December 1993, 82 pages plus 12 photographs, price £5.95 or US$8.95, jointly published with Mines Advisory Group.

Sudan's Invisible Citizens, February 1995, 60 pages, (also available in Arabic) price £5.95 or US$8.95.

Rwanda: A Waste of Hope—The United Nations Human Rights Field Operation, April 1995, 69 pages, price £5.95 or US$8.95.

Discussion Papers

No 1: *Land Tenure, the creation of famine and prospects for peace in Somalia,* October 1993, price £2.00 or US$3.50.

No 2: *Components of a lasting peace in Sudan: First thoughts,* December 1993, 28 pages, price £2.00 or US$3.50.

No 3: *Rwanda, Who is killing; Who is dying; What is to be done,* May 1994, 49 pages, price £5.95 or US$8.95.

No 4: *Crimes Without Punishment: Sexual harassment and violence against female students in schools and universities in Africa,* July 1994, 25 pages, price £3.95 or US$6.95.

No 5: *Humanitarianism Unbound? Current dilemmas facing multi-mandate relief operations in Political Emergencies.* November 1994, 40 pages, price £4.95 or US$7.95.

No. 6: *Great Expectations: The Civil Roles of the Churches in Southern Sudan,* April 1995, 43 pages, price £4.95 or US$7.95